Early Midwestern Travel Narratives

An Annotated Bibliography

1634–1850

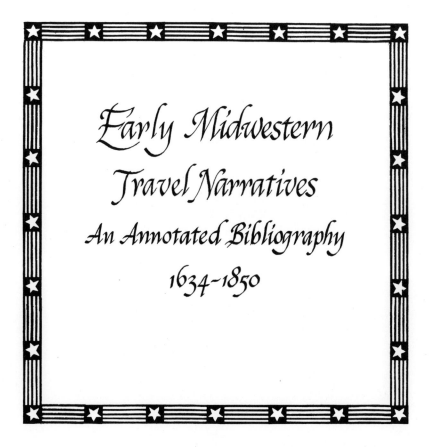

Early Midwestern Travel Narratives
An Annotated Bibliography
1634-1850

by
Robert R. Hubach

Associate Professor of English

Bowling Green State University

Bowling Green, Ohio

Detroit WAYNE STATE UNIVERSITY PRESS *1961*

Grateful Acknowledgment Is Made to the Ford Foundation
for Financial Assistance in Making Possible
the Publication of This Volume.

To

My Mother

and

the Memory of My Father

Preface

This book sprang from a three-fold interest—an interest in the American frontier, in literature in general, and in books of travel. Having made a study of Walt Whitman and the West and the importance of that region in his work, I began an analysis of the influence of the frontier upon the entire field of Midwestern and Western literature but soon realized that I would need to limit my efforts if I expected to produce anything of value. Even so, like most scholarly projects, this one has proved to be lengthier and more involved than I anticipated.

I have defined the Midwest as that section of America as far east as the western border of Pennsylvania and including all territory north of the Ohio River and north of the present states of Arkansas and Oklahoma to the Canadian border. I have mentioned travels in other regions if the narrators also visited the Midwest.

Except for certain works treated together in separate units, I have arranged the material in chronological order, the years the authors spent in the Midwest, rather than the first events described, if they took place outside this region, or the date of earliest known publication being the determining factor. Journals or diaries written over a longer period of time than one year are grouped at the end of the first year covered. If an author wrote two or more works, these sometimes are placed together, but if the nature of the contents differs or the years covered are extremely far apart, they are allocated to different chapters. I have made no attempt to list narratives beginning after 1849, although the terminal dates of the works commencing before 1849 are often much later than that year. I have excluded writings which are not travel narratives; thus, certain items which at first glance might seem to belong in the bibliography are omitted. Letters, unless decidedly narrative in tone, are not included, nor are materials in newspapers, unless later printed in periodicals or books, or brief narrative parts of longer works. Although I have made every effort to compile a complete list of both published and unpublished material, there are undoubtedly omissions because the titles of many printed works do not reveal their narrative characteristics or Midwestern setting, certain manuscripts remain undiscovered, and others are uncatalogued by the depositories where they are housed. Because of the interval of time between completion and publication of the manuscript, I have been unable to

guarantee inclusion of material printed after early 1959. Additions to the bibliography and suggestions will be welcome. I have omitted the facts of publication about reprints of books unless important modern editions have appeared or unless the material has later been printed in periodicals or as part of an anthology or series of reprint volumes. Names of publications of a biographical nature and relatively unimportant information about manuscripts have been relegated to the footnotes, most of which constitute a bibliography of books and articles about the narrators.

Previous studies of the travel tales have greatly facilitated the writing of this book. I am especially indebted to Professor Ralph L. Rusk's pioneering work in Midwestern literature and to Professor William Matthews' bibliography of American diaries. I believe, however, that a different and more complete list should be compiled and that, although I have not attempted to provide all information on every item, fuller interpretations of many of the works would add value to my study. My hope is that this book will fill a long existing need for a bibliography, summary, and interpretation of these early Midwestern travel narratives. The work is not a history text and should not be judged as such.

My indebtedness is great to the competent assistance of a number of staff members of historical societies and private, public, and college and university libraries. The staffs of the Cleveland Public Library, the Kansas City (Missouri) Public Library, and the Newberry Library of Chicago have cooperated in every possible way. Librarians in well over fifty depositories in the United States and Canada have written letters, without which information about certain unpublished narratives would have been unlisted. The Burton Historical Collection of the Detroit Public Library, the Chicago Historical Society, the Illinois Historical Library at Springfield, the Newberry Library, and the Indiana State Historical Society Library at Indianapolis have manuscript collections which I have used rather extensively. Outside the Midwest, the Library of Congress, the New York Public Library, Yale University Library, the Huntington Library at San Marino, California, and the University of Washington Library contain the largest number of catalogued unpublished manuscripts.

I wish to acknowledge the help of the late Harry E. Pratt, Miss Mildred Throne, and Dr. William C. Binkley, who edited brief previously published portions of the bibliography. Bowling Green State University contributed generous financial support to my research. Mrs. Paul Shepherd typed the manuscript and my mother, Mrs. Mary R. Hubach, checked certain parts of it. Without the encouragement of Professor R. C. Buley of Indiana University and my colleague, Dr. Howard O. Brogan, the manuscript might never have been published. Most important of all has been the help of Dr. Harold A. Basilius, Director, Professor Alexander Brede, Chief Editor, and the staff of the Wayne State University Press.

Bowling Green, Ohio, 1960   R. R. H.

Table of Contents

LIST OF PERIODICALS MOST OFTEN CITED AND ABBREVIATIONS USED

Jour. Ill. State Hist. Soc.	Journal of the Illinois State Historical Society
Jour. Sou. Hist.	Journal of Southern History
Kans. Hist. Quar.	Kansas Historical Quarterly
Kans. State Hist. Soc. Colls.	Kansas State Historical Society Collections
Kans. State Hist. Soc. Trans.	Kansas State Historical Society Transactions
Ky. Hist. Soc. Reg.	Kentucky Historical Society Register
La. Hist. Quar.	Louisiana Historical Quarterly
Lit. Dig.	Literary Digest
Mag. Amer. Hist. with Notes and Queries	Magazine of American History with Notes and Queries
Mag. Hist.	Magazine of History
Mag. Hist. with Notes and Queries	Magazine of History with Notes and Queries
Mag. of Amer. Hist.	Magazine of American History
Mag. West. Hist.	Magazine of Western History
Marietta Col. Hist. Colls.	Marietta College Historical Collections
Mass. Hist. Soc. Colls.	Massachusetts Historical Society Collections
Mass. Hist. Soc. Procs.	Massachusetts Historical Society Proceedings
Mich. Hist. Colls.	Michigan Historical (or Pioneer) Collections
Mich. Hist.	Michigan History (or Michigan History Magazine)
Mid-Amer.	Mid-America
Minn. Hist.	Minnesota History (or Minnesota History Bulletin)
Miss. Her.	Missionary Herald
Miss. Val. Hist. Assn. Procs.	Mississippi Valley Historical Association Proceedings
Miss. Val. Hist. Rev.	Mississippi Valley Historical Review
Mo. Hist. Rev.	Missouri Historical Review
Mo. Hist. Soc. Bull.	Missouri Historical Society Bulletin
Mo. Hist. Soc. Colls.	Missouri Historical Society Collections
Neb. Hist. Soc. Procs. Colls.	Nebraska Historical Society Proceedings and Collections
Neb. Hist. Soc. Pubs.	Nebraska Historical Society Publications
Neb. Hist. Soc. Trans. Reports	Nebraska Historical Society Transactions and Reports
Neb. Hist.	Nebraska History (or Nebraska History Magazine
New Eng. Hist. Geneal. Rec.	New England Historical and Genealogical Record
New Jer. Hist. Soc. Procs.	New Jersey Historical Society Proceedings
New Mex. Hist. Rev.	New Mexico Historical Review
New Mex. Hist. Soc. Pubs.	New Mexico Historical Society Publications
Nor. Amer. Rev.	North American Review
Nor. Dak. Hist. Quar.	North Dakota Historical Quarterly
Nor. Dak. Hist. Soc. Colls.	North Dakota Historical Society Collections
Nor. Dak. Hist.	North Dakota History
Northw. Ohio Quar.	Northwest Ohio Quarterly
Ohio Arch. Hist. Quar.	Ohio Archaeological and Historical Quarterly
Ohio Hist. Quar.	Ohio Historical Quarterly (Before 1953, Ohio Arch. Hist. Quar.)
Old Northw. Geneal. Quar.	Old Northwest Genealogical Quarterly
Oreg. Hist. Soc. Pubs.	Oregon Historical Society Publications
Oreg. Hist. Soc. Quar.	Oregon Historical Society Quarterly
Oreg. Pion. Assn. Trans.	Oregon Pioneer Association Transactions
Pac. Hist. Rev.	Pacific Historical Review
Pac. Northw. Quar.	Pacific Northwest Quarterly
Penna. Arch.	Pennsylvania Archives
Penna. Col. Recs.	Pennsylvania Colonial Records
Penna. Hist. Soc. Colls.	Pennsylvania Historical Society Collections
Penna. Mag. Hist. Biog.	Pennsylvania Magazine of History and Biography
Pop. Sci.	Popular Science Monthly
Procs. Amer. Phil. Soc.	Proceedings of the American Philosophical Society
P. M. L. A.	Publications of the Modern Language Association of America
Quar. Rev.	Quarterly Review
Sou. Dak. Hist. Colls.	South Dakota Historical Collections
Sou. Dak. Hist. Rev.	South Dakota Historical Review
Southw. Hist. Rev.	Southwestern Historical Review
Tenn. Hist. Mag.	Tennessee Historical Magazine
Utah Geneal. Hist. Mag.	Utah Genealogical and Historical Magazine
Utah Hist. Quar.	Utah Historical Quarterly
Va. Mag. Hist. Biog.	Virginia Magazine of History and Biography
Wash. Hist. Quar.	Washington Historical Quarterly
West. Penn. Hist. Mag.	Western Pennsylvania Historical Magazine
West. Res. Hist. Soc. Pubs.	Western Reserve Historical Society Publications
West. Res. Hist. Soc. Tracts	Western Reserve Historical Society Tracts
Wis. Hist. Soc. Colls.	Wisconsin Historical Society Collections
Wis. Hist. Soc. Procs.	Wisconsin Historical Society Proceedings
Wis. Mag. Hist.	Wisconsin Magazine of History
Wm. Mary Coll. Hist. Mag.	William and Mary College Historical Magazine

Chapter 1

Introduction: Travelers and Tales;

General Bibliography

Once the Midwest was a wilderness, far different from the populous agricultural and industrial region of today. Although the early days were not without great hardships and brutality, the virtues of the pioneers and the romance and beauty of the past era are often either forgotten or scorned.

This earlier age is not entirely lost because a vast number of accounts written by travelers in the frontier Midwest still exists. In those times, the keeping of journals and diaries was a common pastime and people taking trips recorded their impressions as a matter of course. Hundreds of narratives, composed by individuals of various nationalities, dispositions, and types, describing all sections of the Midwest, have been preserved from as early as the year 1634.

The people who wrote these early tales had various motives for entering the wilderness. Leaving the sheltered life of Europe or the Eastern seaboard required great courage; yet many men risked their lives and fortunes in the new region. In spite of the dangers involved, including capture and torture by the Indians, the wilderness lured hosts of people to strange destinies. Some were explorers, commissioned to claim territory in the names of their governments; others were trappers and fur traders, bent on profit. Christian missionaries sacrificed personal comfort in order to win souls for God. A few of the early narrators were surveyors; some were soldiers sent to the Midwest to fight Indians or foreign troops. Scientists, merchants, lawyers, teachers and reformers ventured into the new domains, seeing in the West opportunities for study, trade, or the pursuit of a profession.[1] Primeval forests, open prairies and mighty lakes and rivers cast their spells upon settlers and emigrants. From the beginning, the frontier captured the imaginations of countless travelers, and this power of the West has been a formative influence in American history.

Travel narratives in English date back as far as Othere and Wulfstan of Anglo-Saxon times. In nearly all countries this form is one of the earliest types to develop, and in America it was no exception.[2] Long before professional authors appeared, people recorded their travels so that friends, relatives, sovereigns, or future generations could share their experiences. Men only slightly educated often scribbled hasty travel memoranda which made interesting and sought-after reading. Many of the narratives were well written, but even those that were not so reflected a desire upon the part of the authors to leave a tangible record.

Since the travel narrative is not difficult to write and since it is an excellent vehicle for the recording of unusual events,[3] it became a popular form for the amateur writer. At the time these tales were written, inhabitants of eastern North America and Europe who were thinking of emigrating, were eager to learn about conditions on the frontier. Later readers were attracted to the narratives for their historical value or for their romantic atmosphere. Since the travel tales are stimulating to the imagination, they verge upon poetic art, owing part of their effect, like poetry, to the wonder produced.[4] When one recalls the travel elements in such favorites as *The Arabian Nights, Robinson Crusoe,* or the popular legend of Davy Crockett, he will realize how appealing the tales of the frontier can be.

An analysis of the travel narrative form will help in understanding the merits and limitations of the writers of Midwestern travel tales. Since it is seldom fiction, the travel narrative usually lacks plot and the other necessary components of a short story or novel. Characterization, one of the most important elements of a work of fiction, is either omitted or is included only in brief descriptions of people in the tale or in indirect insights into the personalities of the authors. It compares more favorably with other types of non-fiction. The better narratives, which have been generally underestimated, are often longer, more interesting, and display greater craftsmanship than the essay, article, or news story. Because first impressions are stimulating, the travelers in many cases depicted the region more vividly than did residents. The tales, which are often biographical or autobiographical in nature, are usually historical in content. Although whatever accounts can be called fictitious obviously lack most of the technical requirements of the established forms of fiction, they are no less imaginative.

Travel narratives can be sub-divided according to form into diaries, journals, or accounts. Diaries and journals contain dated day-to-day entries, the former written for personal reasons, the latter usually as part of a job. The dividing line between them is often slim, because journals are seldom entirely impersonal.[5] The account is the most literary of the three forms, sometimes being written with chapter divisions like a novel. The most usual of these three types is probably the journal.[6] Occasionally notes or letters were collected and loosely arranged as narratives. Anecdotes and brief incidents were at times included as parts of the tales.

Important and interesting as the travel narratives are, they have many deficiencies. Written largely by amateurs, they seldom display technical skill, often containing serious mistakes in mechanics, are sometimes too long and too full of unimportant and dull material, and are almost totally lacking in humor and subtlety. The satire present is sometimes malicious and the information included is occasionally erroneous or exaggerated. Swift, in commenting upon *Gulliver's Travels*, noted that travelers were often suspected of enlarging upon facts.[7] Many of the details of pioneer life, such as crime and sex, are purposely omitted by most of the Midwestern travel writers, but the main purpose of a few of the tales, particularly those of Indian captivity, was to shock the reader, while others were written to propagandize and influence political opinion. Like most of the literature produced by a young nation, the narratives are often too utilitarian to rank as belles-lettres;[8] but, in spite of their defects, they represent the actual thoughts of the common man better than do most books by professional authors.

A preliminary survey of important Midwestern travel narrators will familiarize the reader with the major names at the outset. The most celebrated traveler to the Midwest before 1850 was Charles Dickens, whose critical *American Notes* was the result of a trip to the United States in 1842. Almost equally well known are the books of two authoresses, also British, Mrs. Frances Trollope who visited America between 1828 and 1830, and Harriet Martineau, who toured the Midwest in 1835–1836. The most famous exploring expedition was that of Lewis and Clark in 1804–1806. The best known American authors to write accounts of their visits to the Midwest before 1850 were William Cullen Bryant and Washington Irving, both in 1832, and Walt Whitman, in 1848. Although not the first Frenchmen to write narratives of Midwestern exploration, Marquette, Joliet, Tonti, Hennepin, LaSalle, and LaVèrendrye are the most familiar names. The earliest Americans to

compose significant accounts were Major Robert Rogers, Colonel George Croghan, Alexander Henry, Jonathan Carver, and George Washington. John G. Heckewelder was the first Englishman to write a major narrative. The most important nineteenth-century authors of Midwestern travel books will be discussed in later chapters.

The travel narratives have greatly influenced other works of literature. The English novel is indebted to the picaresque novel of Spain, which had as its hero a roguish person who traveled extensively and underwent many adventures. It was not a great step from the travel tale to this kind of fiction with its incidental plot and characterization.

The Romantic Movement of the eighteenth and nineteenth centuries owes part of its origin to these narratives. Readers, who were stimulated by the accounts of far-away and primitive places developed a taste for literature which reflected this material.[9] The idea of "the noble savage" seems to have come from the travelers rather than from Rousseau, who derived his conception of the "natural" man from reading about the North American Indian. An opposite idea, that of the cruel savage, was derived from some of the same books.[10] The caustic spirit reflected in Baron LaHonton's *Voyages* . . . , wherein he discussed the philosophy of primitive life, helped shape the outlook of Addison, Steele, and Swift, and he was a source for LeSage, Montesquieu, and Chateaubriand.[11] The last three exerted an influence, in turn, upon later writers.[12] The American novelists William Bartram and James Fenimore Cooper are among those most obviously influenced by the romanticism of Rousseau. John G. Heckewelder was evidently a second source for Cooper's idealized Indians.[13] Edmund Burke's "On Conciliation with America" shows acquaintance with some of the narratives, and Schiller, Chateaubriand, and Bryant betray familiarity with a specific tale, Carver's well-known *Travels Through the Interior Parts of North America*. Wordsworth also seems to have read Carver, as well as Thomas Ashe and Bartram;[14] and Lord Byron and Robert Southey were acquainted with American travel literature. Longfellow derived his myth of Hiawatha from Schoolcraft and may have used Charles Sealsfield's *Life in the New World* and John C. Frémont's *Report of the Exploring Expedition to the Rocky Mountains* for his poem *Evangeline*.[15] Mrs. Kirkland's *A New Home—Who'll Follow?*, a realistic interpretation of the Michigan frontier, was a forerunner of other such treatments of the Midwest. Bryant, Irving, Mrs. Trollope, Dickens, and Walt Whitman were influenced in later works by their earlier travels. Such relatively recent poets as Joaquin Miller and Vachel Lindsay show knowledge of travel tale material.

Since many of the early Midwestern journals, diaries, and narratives reflect life of this period more realistically than most other forms of literature, the history recorded by the narrators is of great value and in many cases unduplicated. In fact, a large number of the narrators are better known as historical figures than as writers. An insight into social and economic conditions of the times can be gained from these works. The organization of exploring expeditions and military units; missions, churches, and schools on the frontier; social experiments, backwoods family and village life, and relationships between whites and Indians are described. Several of the narrators were scientists who interpreted what they saw in terms of their training and professional interests. The way many of the authors used charged words to gain effects or influence opinions would be a study for a semanticist. A history of religion on the frontier could be written from the numerous diaries highly tinged with various religious sentiments. Literature as a reflection of life is obvious from a study of the travel tales; life as a reflection of literature is evident from the effect the narratives had upon those who read them and became emigrants and settlers and upon others who read and stayed at home.

Hundreds of the Midwestern narratives of travel have been printed in both book and periodical form and numerous reprints have been issued. English translations, sometimes inadequate, of most of the journals in foreign languages have been made. There remains, however, a large number of unpublished manuscripts, housed mainly by historical societies and in private, public, and university libraries.

Before any scholarly books on the travel tales appeared, a number of anthologies, such as Joseph Pritt's *Incidents of Border Life . . .* (1839), containing reprints of the most popular or exciting narratives, were printed. The earliest volume giving a significant discussion of the subject was William H. Venable's *Beginnings of Literary Culture in the Ohio Valley* (1891). The most complete work up to the present is Ralph L. Rusk's *The Literature of the Middle Western Frontier* (1925), which contains a valuable discussion of narratives published in book form and has a bibliography of books which omits most narratives originally published in periodicals, all material printed after 1925, and unpublished manuscripts. Much more numerous than these are volumes on special aspects of Midwestern travel tales and separate bibliographies. B. Grinnell's *Trails of the Pathfinder* (1911) is perhaps the most complete collective account of some of the most important narrators.

Bibliographies of the early Midwestern travel narratives are greater in number than are books of comment about the tales. There are compilations of many specialized bibliographies. There are catalogs of manuscripts in the historical collections of the states of Illinois, Iowa, Michigan, Minnesota, Missouri, Ohio, and Wisconsin, as well as lists of material in the Library of Congress, in the William R. Coe Collection at Yale University, and in certain other libraries. Many additional books contain less extensive bibliographies than any of these.

And periodicals have much bibliographical material not found in books. Although many of the tales have been printed and much has been written about them, there is a need to assemble all of the important information in a volume devoted exclusively to early Middle Western travel narratives.

BIBLIOGRAPHY

Many present-day printings of manuscripts and reprintings of original editions of the travel tales show the interest of a large number of modern readers. Every Midwestern state has one or more historical quarterlies, and almost every year an early journal is printed or reprinted as a whole or in part in at least one of them. The following bibliography, divided because of its length into sections, lists books, articles, bibliographies, important encyclopedias, theses, specialized dictionaries, and certain anthologies which contain significant background material or general discussions of early Midwestern travel narratives, journals, and diaries. It does not include works of history or literary interpretation unless they discuss the tales, and it omits anthologies of narratives of Indian captivities (listed in Chapter 3) and books which mention only one journal or tale.

1. LITERARY STUDIES

Atkeson, Mary M. *A Study of the Local Literature of the Upper Ohio Valley, with Especial Reference to the Early Pioneer and Indian Tales, 1820–1840.* Ohio State University Bulletin, Contributions in English, No. 2, XXVII, No. 3. Columbus, Ohio State University, 1921.

The Cambridge History of American Literature. William P. Trent, John Erskine, Stuart P. Sherman, and Carl Van Doren, eds. 4 vols., New York and London, G. P. Putnam's Sons, 1917–21.

The Cambridge History of English Literature. A. W. Ward and A. R. Waller, eds. 15 vols., New York, G. P. Putnam's Sons; Cambridge, Eng., Cambridge University Press, 1907–1933.

Chinard, Gilbert. *L'Amérique et le Rêve Exotique dans la Litterature Française au XVIIe et au XVIIIe Siècle.* Paris, Librairie Hachette et Cie, 1913.

DeMenil, Alexander N. "A Century of Missouri Literature." *Mo. Hist. Rev.,* XV (1920), 74–125.

———— *The Literature of the Louisiana Territory.* St. Louis, St. Louis News Co., 1904.

Dickinson, Thomas H. *The Making of American Literature . . . With Some Considerations of the Way Men and Women Lived, their Vocations, Opinions, and Amusements.* New York, Century Co., 1932.

Dondore, Dorothy. "Points of Contact Between History and Literature in the Mississippi Valley." *Miss. Val. Hist. Rev.,* XI (1924), 227–36.

Esarey, Logan. "The Literary Spirit Among the Early Ohio Valley Settlers." *Miss. Val. Hist. Rev.,* V (1918), 143–57.

Hazard, Lucy Lockwood. *The Frontier in American Literature.* New York, Thomas Y. Crowell, 1927.

Hubach, Robert R. "Illinois, Host to Well-Known Nineteenth-Century Authors." *Jour. Ill. State Hist. Soc.*, XXXVIII (1945), 446–67.

———— "Literary Visitors to the Hoosier State: A Chapter in American Cultural History." *Ind. Mag. Hist.*, XLV (1949), 39–50.

———— "St. Louis, Host of Celebrated Nineteenth Century British and American Authors." *Mo. Hist. Rev.*, XXXVIII (1944), 275–87.

Jamison, Isabel. "Literature and Literary People of Early Illinois." *Ill. State Hist. Soc. Trans.*, XIII (1909), 123–39.

Keiser, Albert. *The Indian in American Literature.* New York, Oxford University Press, 1933.

Kunitz, Stanley J. and Howard Haycraft. *American Authors, 1600–1900.* New York, The H. W. Wilson Co., 1938.

Leisy, Ernest E. *American Literature: an Interpretative Survey.* New York, Thomas Y. Crowell Co., 1929.

Mott, Frank Luther. *Literature of Pioneer Life in Iowa.* Iowa City, State Historical Society of Iowa, 1923.

Murray, Agnes M. "Early Literary Developments in Indiana." *Ind. Mag. of Hist.*, XXXVI (1940), 327–33.

Parrington, Vernon Louis. *Main Currents in American Thought.* 3 vols., New York, Harcourt, Brace and Co., 1927–1930.

Quinn, Arthur Hobson *et al. The Literature of the American People, an Historical and Critical Survey.* New York, Appleton-Century-Crofts, 1951.

Rusk, Ralph Leslie. *The Literature of the Middle Western Frontier.* 2 vols., New York, Columbia University Press, 1925.

Spiller, Robert E., Willard Thorp, Thomas H. Johnson, and Henry Seidel Canby. *Literary History of the United States.* New York, Macmillan Co., 1948. Supplement. New York, Macmillan Co., 1959.

Venable, William Henry. *Beginnings of Literary Culture in the Ohio Valley; Historical and Biographical Sketches.* New York, P. Smith, 1891.

Walker, Hugh. *The Literature of the Victorian Era.* Cambridge, Eng., Cambridge University Press, 1910.

Williams, Mentor. "Men with Hammers." *Michigan Alumnus,* LII (Spring, 1946), 238–54.

2. WORKS PRIMARILY DEVOTED TO HISTORY

Albach, James R. *Annals of the West: Embracing a Concise Account of Principal Events which Have Occurred in the Western States and Territories.* Pittsburgh, W. S. Haven, 1857.

Blakeley, Russell. "History of the Discovery of the Mississippi River and the Advent of Commerce in Minnesota." *Colls. Minn. Hist. Soc.*, VIII (1898), 303–418.

Branch, E. Douglas. *Westward, the Romance of the American Frontier.* New York and London, D. Appleton and Co., 1930.

Brebner, John Barlett. *The Explorers of North America, 1492–1806.* London, A. and C. Black, 1933.

Buley, R. Carlyle. "Glimpses of Pioneer Mid-West Social and Cultural History." *Miss. Val. Hist. Rev.*, XXIII (1937), 481–510.

———— *The Old Northwest. Pioneer Period, 1815–1840.* 2 vols., Indianapolis, Indiana Historical Society, 1950.

Campbell, T. J. *Pioneer Laymen of North America.* 2 vols., New York, The America Press, 1915.

———— *Pioneer Priests of North America, 1642–1710.* 3 vols., New York, Fordham University Press, 1908–1919.

Chittenden, Hiram Martin. *The American Fur Trade of the Far West.* 2 vols., Stanford, Cal., Academic Reprints, 1954.

DeVoto, Bernard. *Across the Wide Missouri.* Boston, Houghton Miffllin Co., 1947.

Deprez, Eugene. "Les Grands Voyages et les Grandes Découvertes Jusqu'à la Fin du XVIIIe Siècle: Origines, Développement, Conséquences." *Bulletin du Comité International des Sciences Historiques*, No. 9 (1930), 555–614.

Dondore, Dorothy. *The Prairie and the Making of Middle America.* Cedar Rapids, Ia., Torch Press, 1926.

Faris, J. T. *On the Trail of the Pioneers, Romance, Tragedy and Triumph of the Path of Empire.* New York, George H. Doran Co., 1920.

Finley, John H. *The French in the Heart of America.* New York, C. Scribner's Sons, 1915.

Flower, George. *History of the English Settlement in Edwards County, Illinois. Chicago Hist. Soc. Colls.,* I. Chicago, Fergus Printing Co., 1882.

Fowler, Otto. *Sault Ste. Marie and its Great Waterway.* New York and London, G. P. Putnam's Sons, 1925.

Goodwin, Cardinal L. "Early Explorations and Settlements of Missouri and Arkansas, 1803–1822. *Mo. Hist. Rev.*, XIV (1920), 385–424.

———— *The Trans-Mississippi West (1803–1853).* New York and London, D. Appleton and Co., 1922.

Greely, Adolphus W. *Explorers and Travellers.* New York, C. Scribner's Sons, 1902.

Grinnell, George Bird. *Trails of the Pathfinders.* New York, C. Scribner's Sons, 1911.

Hale, John Peter. *Trans-Alleghany Pioneers; Historical Sketches of the First White Settlers West of the Alleghenies 1748 and After. Wonderful Experiences of Hardship and Heroism of Those Who First Braved the Dangers of the Inhospitable Wilderness, and the Savage Tribes that Inhabited It . . . ,* Cincinnati, The Graphic Press . . . , 1886.

Havighurst, Walter. *Wilderness for Sale, the Story of the First Western Land Rush.* New York, Hastings House, 1956.

Hirsch, Arthur H. "Historical Values in Mid-Century Literature of the Middle West." *Ill. State Hist. Soc. Trans.*, XXXVI (1929), 117–25; *Jour. Ill. State Hist. Soc.*, XXII (1929), 375–87.

Inglehart, John E. "The Coming of the English to Indiana in 1817 and Their Hoosier Neighbors." *Ind. Mag. Hist.*, XV (1919), 89–178.

Jones, Dallas L. "Chicago in 1833. Impressions of Three Britishers." *Jour. Ill. State Hist. Soc.*, XLVII (1954), 167–75.

Keyes, Charles R. "Earliest Explorations of Iowa-land." *Ann. of Ia.*, 3rd Series, X (1912), 265–72.

Lass, William E. "Tourists' Impressions of St. Louis, 1766–1859." *Mo. Hist. Rev.*, LII (1958), 325–38; LIII (1958), 10–21.

Ludewig, Herman E. *The Literature of American Local History; A Bibliographical Essay.* New York, R. Craighead, 1846.

Mirsky, Jeannette, *The Westward Crossings; Balboa, Mackenzie, Lewis and Clark.* New York, A. A. Knopf, 1940.

Monaghan, Jay. *The Overland Trail.* Indianapolis and New York, Bobbs-Merrill Co., 1947.

Nasatir, A. P., ed. *Before Lewis and Clark. Documents Illustrating the History of the Missouri, 1785–1804.* 2 vols., St. Louis, St. Louis Historical Documents Foundation, 1952.

Nute, Grace Lee. *The Voyageur.* St. Paul, Minnesota Historical Society, 1931.

Quaife, Milo. M. *Chicago and the Old Northwest 1673–1835. . . .* Chicago, University of Chicago Press, 1913.

Rodman, Jane. "The English Settlement in Southern Illinois." *Ind. Mag. Hist.*, XLIII (1947), 329–62.

Speck, Gordon. *Northwest Exploration.* L. K. Phillips, ed. Portland, Ore., Binfords and Mort, 1954.

Thwaites, Reuben Gold. *France in America, 1497–1763.* New York and London, Harper and Brothers, 1905.

Webb, Walter P. *The Great Plains*. New York, Ginn and Co., 1931.

Winsor, Justin, ed. *Narrative and Critical History of America*. 8 vols., Boston and New York, Houghton Mifflin Co., 1884–1889.

3. WORKS PRIMARILY ABOUT TRAVEL

Adams, William Henry Davenport. *Celebrated Women Travellers of the Nineteenth Century*. London, W. S. Sonnenschein and Co., 1906.

Appleton's Hand-Book of American Travel. New York, D. Appleton and Co., 1872.

Berger, Max. *The British Traveller in America, 1836–1860*. New York, Columbia University Press, 1943.

Carson, W. Wallace. "Transportation and Traffic on the Ohio and the Mississippi before the Steamboat." *Miss. Val. Hist. Rev.*, VII (1920), 26–38.

Drew, H. L. "Literary Visitors to the Rock River Valley, 1832–1882." *Ill. Lib.*, XVIII (1936), 42–52.

Dunbar, Seymour. *A History of Travel in America, Showing the Development of Travel and Transportation from the Crude Methods of the Canal and the Dog Sled to the Highly Organized Railway Systems of the Present, Together with a Narrative of the Human Experiences and Changing Social Conditions that Accompanied this Economic Conquest of the Continent*. 4 vols., Indianapolis, Bobbs-Merrill Co., 1915.

Firestone, Clark B. *The Coasts of Illusion, a Study of Travel Tales*. New York and London, Harper and Bros., 1924.

Henshaw, Leslie S. "Early Steamboat Travel on the Ohio River." *Ohio Arch. Hist. Quar.*, XX (1911), 378–402.

Hulbert, Archer Butler. *Historic Highways of America*. 16 vols., Cleveland, Arthur H. Clark Co., 1902.

———— *Pioneer Roads and Experiences of Travelers* . . . Cleveland, Arthur H. Clark Co., 1904.

Jones, Dallas L. "Illinois in the 1830's. Impressions of British Travelers and Immigrants." *Jour. Ill. State Hist. Soc.*, XLVII (1954), 252–63.

Lindley, Harlow, ed. "Indiana as Seen by Early Travelers." *Ind. Hist. Colls.*, IV (1916), 3–596.

———— "Western Travel, 1800–1820." *Miss. Val. Hist. Rev.*, VI (1919), 167–91.

McDermott, John F. "Gallipolis [Ohio] as Travelers Saw It, 1792–1811." *Ohio Arch. Hist. Quar.*, XLVIII (1939), 283–303.

Mesick, Jane L. *The English Traveller in America*. New York, Columbia University Press, 1922.

Nevins, Allan. *American Social History as Recorded by British Travellers*. New York, Henry Holt and Co., 1923.

Parish, John C. "Through European Eyes." *The Palimpsest*, I (1920), 144–68.

Pelzer, Louis. *Marches of the Dragoons in the Mississippi Valley; an Account of Marches and Activities of the First Regiment United States Dragoons in the Mississippi Valley Between the Years 1833 and 1850*. Iowa City, State Historical Society of Iowa, 1917.

Peterson, William J. "The Mississippi River Through Many Eyes." *Ia. Jour. Hist.*, XLVI (1948), 339–77.

Rodman, Jane. "The English Settlement in Southern Illinois as Viewed by English Travelers, 1815–1825." *Ind. Mag. Hist.*, XLIV (1948), 37–68.

Snelling, William Joseph, ed. *Tales of Travels West of the Mississippi*. Boston, Gray and Bowen, 1830.

Tuckerman, Henry Theodore. *America and her Commentators, With a Critical Sketch of Travel in the United States*. New York, C. Scribner, 1864.

Venable, William Henry. "Some Early Travelers and Annalists of the Ohio Valley." *Ohio Arch. Hist. Quar.*, I (1888), 227–39.

Williams, Mentor. "They Wrote Home About It." *Michigan Alumnus*, LI (1945), 339–51.

4. ANTHOLOGIES

Banta, Richard Elwell, ed. *Hoosier Caravan. A Treasury of Indiana Life and Lore*. Bloomington, Ind., Indiana University Press, 1951.

Bingley, William, ed. *Travels in North America, from Modern Writers. With Remarks and Observations . . .* , London, Harvey and Darton, 1821.

Cox, Isaac Joslin, ed. *The Journeys of René Robert Cavelier, Sieur de LaSalle, as Related by his Faithful Lieutenant, Henri de Tonty; his Missionary Colleagues, Father Zenobius Membré, Louis Hennepin, and Anastasius Douay; his Early Biographer, Father Christian LeClercq; his Trusted Subordinate, Henri Joutel; and his Brother, Jean Cavelier; . . .* New York, A. S. Barnes and Co., 1905.

Flanagan, John T., ed. *America Is West. An Anthology of Middlewestern Life and Literature*. Minneapolis, University of Minnesota Press, 1941.

Kellogg, Louise Phelps, ed. *Early Narratives of the Old Northwest, 1634–1699*. New York, Charles Scribner's Sons, 1917.

McFarling, Lloyd., ed. *Exploring the Northern Plains, 1804–1874*. Caldwell, Idaho, Caxton Printers, 1955.

Margry, Pierre, ed. *Découvertes et Établissements des Français dans le Sud de l'Amérique Septentrionale (1615–1754). Mémoires et Documents Origineaux Recueillé et Pub. Par. P. Margry*. 6 vols., Paris, Maissonneuve et Cie, 1879–1888.

Mereness, Newton D., ed. *Travels in the American Colonies*. New York, The Macmillan Co., 1916.

Neider, Charles, ed. *The Great West*. New York, Coward-McCann, 1958.

Quaife, Milo M., ed. *Pictures of Illinois One Hundred Years Ago*. Chicago, R. R. Donnelley and Sons Co., 1918.

Reminiscences of Early Chicago. Chicago, R. R. Donnelley and Sons Co., 1912.

Shea, John D. G., ed. *Discovery and Exploration of the Mississippi Valley*. . . . New York, Redfield, 1852.

Thwaites, Reuben Gold, ed. *Early Western Travels (1748–1846). A Series of Annotated Reprints*. 32 vols., Cleveland, Arthur H. Clark Co., 1904–1907.

———— ed. *The Jesuit Relations and Allied Documents; Travels and Explorations of the Jesuit Missionaries in New France, 1610–1791; the Original French, Latin, and Italian Texts, with English Translations and Notes*. . . . 73 vols., Cleveland, The Burrows Brothers Co., 1896–1901.

5. ENCYCLOPEDIAS AND SPECIALIZED DICTIONARIES

Allibone, Samuel A. *A Critical Dictionary of English Literature and British and American Authors, Living and Deceased, from the Earliest Accounts to the Latter Half of the Nineteenth Century*. Philadelphia, J. B. Lippincott, 1908.

Appleton's Cyclopedia of American Biography. James Grant Wilson and John Fiske, eds. New York, D. Appleton and Co., 1899–1900.

Dictionary of American Biography. Allan Johnson, ed. 21 vols. New York, Charles Scribner's Sons, 1928.

Dictionary of National Biography. Leslie Stephens and Sidney Lee, eds. 22 vols., New York, Macmillan and Co.; London, Smith Elder and Co., 1908–1909.

The Encyclopedia Americana. Lavinia P. Dudley, *et al.*, eds. 30 vols., New York, Chicago, Washington, 1959.

Encyclopedia Britannica. Walter Yust, *et al.*, eds. 24 vols., Chicago, London (Eng.), Toronto, Encyclopedia Britannica, 1958.

Hart, James D. *The Oxford Companion to American Literature.* New York, Oxford University Press, 1956.

Sabin, Joseph, ed. *A Dictionary of Books Relating to America from Its Discovery to the Present Time.* 29 vols., New York, Joseph Sabin, 1868–1936.

6. GUIDE BOOKS AND CATALOGUES OF COLLECTIONS

[Anderson Galleries.] *. . . Western Americana; an Extraordinary Collection Dealing with the Local History and March of Events in the Regions Lying Within the Ohio and Mississippi Valleys and Westward to the Pacific Ocean . . .* New York, Anderson Galleries, 1923.

Biggert, Elizabeth C., comp. *Guide to the Manuscript Collections in the Library of the Ohio State Archaeological and Historical Society.* Columbus, Ohio State Archaeological and Historical Society, 1953.

Bleyden, Paul, comp., and Bernard S. Levin, ed. *Guide to the Manuscript Collections in the Historical Society of Pennsylvania.* Philadelphia, Historical Society of Pennsylvania, 1949.

The British Museum Catalogue of Printed Books, 1881–1900. 58 vols., Ann Arbor, Mich., J. W. Edwards, 1946.

Butler, Ruth Lapham, comp. *A Check List of Manuscripts in the Edward E. Ayer Collection.* Chicago, The Newberry Library, 1937.

A Catalog of Books Represented by Library of Congress Printed Cards. Issued to July 31, 1942. 167 vols., *Supplement. Cards Issued August 1, 1942–December 31, 1947.* 42 vols., Ann Arbor, Mich., Edwards Bros., 1942 and 1948.

Catalog of a Collection of Books and Manuscripts on the War of 1812, and Other Americana Made by the Late Mr. John W. Loreve, Exhibited by the Caxton Club in . . . the Art Institute of Chicago . . . Chicago, Caxton Club (?), 1917.

Forbes, (Mrs.) Harriette (Merrifield), comp. *New England Diaries, 1602–1800, a Descriptive Catalogue of Diaries, Orderly Books and Sea Journals.* Topsfield, Mass., Privately printed, 1923.

Guide to the Depositories of Manuscript Collections in Illinois. Chicago, Historical Records Survey, 1940.

Guide to Depositories of Manuscript Collections in the United States. Columbus, Ohio, Historical Records Survey, 1938.

Guide to Manuscript Collections in Iowa. Vol. I. Des Moines, Iowa, Historical Records Survey Project, 1940.

Guide to Manuscript Collections in Michigan. Vol. I. Michigan Historical Collections, University of Michigan. Detroit, Historical Records Survey Project, 1941.

Guide to the Manuscript Collections in the Toronto Public Libraries. Toronto, Toronto Public Libraries, 1954.

Guide to the Manuscript Collections of the Oregon Historical Society. Portland, Oregon Historical Records Survey, 1940.

Guide to Manuscript Materials of American Origin in the Illinois Historical Survey. Urbana, Illinois Historical Survey, Publication No. 3, 1951.

Guide to the Western Historical Manuscripts Collection. Western Historical Manuscripts Collection Bulletin No. 6. Columbia, University of Missouri, 1952.

Kane, Lucile M., and Kathryn A. Johnson, comps. *Manuscript Collections of the Minnesota Historical Society. Guide Number 2.* St. Paul, Minnesota Historical Society, 1955.

Nute, Grace Lee, and Gertrude W. Ackerman, comps. *Guide to the Personal Papers in Manuscript Collections of the Minnesota Historical Society.* St. Paul, Minnesota Historical Society, 1935.

Smith, Alice E., comp. *Guide to the Manuscripts of the Wisconsin Historical Society.* Madison, State Historical Society of Wisconsin, 1944.

Withington, Mary C., comp. *A Catalogue of Manuscripts in the Collection of Western Americana Founded by William Robertson Coe, Yale University Library.* New Haven, Conn., Yale University Press, 1952.

7. GENERAL AND SPECIALIZED BIBLIOGRAPHIES

Beers, Henry P. *The French in North America.* Baton Rouge, Louisiana State University Press, 1957.

Brooks, James G. *As Others See Us: A Study of the Progress in the United States.* New York, Macmillan and Co., 1908.

Buck, Solon Justus. "Travel and Description, 1765–1865." *Ill. Hist. Colls.,* IX (1914), 3–252.

Burpee, Lawrence J. "Working Bibliography of the Western Canadian Fur Trade." In "A Chapter in the Literature of the Fur Trade." *Bibliographical Society of America Papers,* V (1910), 58–60.

The Cambridge Bibliography of English Literature. F. W. Bateson, ed. 4 vols. New York and London, Macmillan Co. and Cambridge, Eng., Cambridge University Press, 1941.

Cox, Edward Godfrey, comp. *A Reference Guide to the Literature of Travel.* Vol. II. Seattle, University of Washington, 1938. (*University of Washington Publications in Language and Literature,* Vol. X.)

Durrie, Daniel Steele. "A Bibliography of the State of Wisconsin." *The Historical Magazine,* 2nd Series, VI (1869), 29–41.

Evans, Charles. *American Bibliography. A Chronological Dictionary of All Books, Pamphlets, and Periodical Publications Printed in the United States of America from the Genesis of Printing in 1639 down to and Including the Year 1800. With Bibliographical and Biographical Notes.* Chicago, the Author, 1903–1934.

Griffin, Appleton, P. C. *Discovery of the Mississippi, A Bibliographical Account.* New York, A. S. Barnes and Co., 1883. Also in *Mag. Amer. Hist. with Notes and Queries,* IX (1883), 190–99.

Howes, Wright, comp. *U. S-iana (1700–1950). A Descriptive Check-List of 11,450 Printed Sources Relating to Those Parts of Continental North America Now Comprising the United States.* New York, R. R. Bowker Co., 1954.

Hubach, Robert R., comp. "They Saw the Early Midwest. A Bibliography of Travel Narratives, 1673–1850." *Jour. Ill. State Hist. Soc.,* XLVII (1954), 385–97.

——— "They Saw the Early Midwest. A Bibliography of Travel Narratives, 1722–1850." *Jour. Ill. State Hist. Soc.,* XLVI (1953), 283–89.

——— "They Saw the Early Midwest. A Bibliography of Travel Narratives, 1727–1850." *Ia. Jour. Hist.,* LII (1954), 223–34.

——— "Unpublished Travel Narratives of the Early Midwest, 1720–1850: A Preliminary Bibliography." *Miss. Val. Hist. Rev.,* XLII (1955), 525–48.

Larned, J. S. *Literature of American History. A Bibliographical Guide.* Boston, Houghton Mifflin Co., 1902.

A List of Books Indispensable to a Knowledge of Kansas History and Literature; Issued as an Aid to Libraries and Students. Topeka, Kansas State Printing Plant, 1916.

MacPike, E. F. "American and Canadian Diaries, Journals, and Notebooks." *Bulletin of Bibliography,* XVIII (1944), 91–92; (1944), 107–15; (1945), 133–35; (1945), 156–58.

Martin, Chester. "Bibliographical Note." In *Lord Selkirk's Work in Canada. Oxford Historical and Literary Studies,* VII, 8–13. Oxford, Clarendon Press, 1916.

Matthews, William, comp. *American Diaries: an Annotated Bibliography of American Diaries Written Prior to the Year 1861.* Berkeley, University of California Press, 1945.

Monaghan, Frank, comp. *French Travellers in the United States —1765–1932. A Bibliography.* New York, New York Public Library, 1933.

Narratives of Captivity among the Indians of North America. A List of Books and Manuscripts on this Subject in the Edward E. Ayer Collection of the Newberry Library. Chicago, University of Chicago Press, 1912. *Supplement I.* Clara A. Smith, comp. Chicago, University of Chicago Press, 1928.

Rich, Obadiah, comp. *Bibliotheca Americana Nova. A Catalogue of Books Relating to America. . . .* 2 vols., London, Rich and Sons, 1846.

Roorbach, O. A., comp. *Bibliotheca Americana. Catalogue of American Publications, Including Reprints and Original Works, from 1820 to 1852, Inclusive.* New York, Peter Smith, 1939.

Sampson, F. A. "Bibliography of Books of Travel in Missouri." *Mo. Hist. Rev.,* VI (1911), 64–81.

Streeter, Floyd B., comp. *Michigan Bibliography. A Partial Catalogue of Books. . . .* 2 vols., Lansing, Michigan Historical Commission, 1921.

Thomson, Peter G., comp. *A Bibliography of the State of Ohio, Being a Catalogue of the Books and Pamphlets Relating to the History of the State.* Cincinnati, the Author, 1880.

Turner, Frederick Jackson and Frederick Merck, comps. *List of References on the History of the West.* Cambridge, Harvard University Press, 1922.

"United States. Description and Travel." *Annual Report of the American Historical Association for the Year 1904.* Supplement. *Writings on American History, 1924.* (Washington, Government Printing Office, 1928), pp. 33–34.

Wagner, Henry Raup, comp. *The Plains and the Rockies; a Bibliography of Original Narratives of Travel and Adventure, 1800–1865.* San Francisco, J. Howell, 1921. Revised and extended by Charles L. Camp. San Francisco, Grabhorn Press, 1937. 3rd ed. Columbus, O., Long's College Book Co., 1953.

Williams, J. F. "Bibliography of Minnesota." *Colls. Minn. Hist. Soc.,* III (1880), 13–75.

8. UNPUBLISHED THESES AND DISSERTATIONS

Carson, James W. *British Travelers in Southern Ohio, 1803–1860.* M. A. Thesis, Miami University, 1951.

Greer, Ann L. *Early Development in America, 1825–1850, of Travel Books as Literature.* Ph.D. Dissertation, University of Southern California, 1955.

Grove, W. Alan. *Reports Concerning America Prevalent in England During the Latter Half of the Eighteenth Century.* M. A. Thesis, Miami University, 1935.

Hamline, Ruth. *Travel Literature of Colonists in America, 1754–1783.* Ph.D. Dissertation, Northwestern University, 1947.

Hildreth, William Henry. "Travel Literature of the Ohio River Valley (1794–1832)." *Abstracts of Doctoral Dissertations,* No. 47. Columbus, Ohio State University Press, 1945.

Jones, Joseph. *British Literary Men's Opinion about America, 1750–1832.* Ph.D. Dissertation, Stanford University, 1934.

Nisbet, Ada. *Bibliography of English Travel Literature in Nineteenth-Century America.* Ph.D. Dissertation, University of California at Los Angeles. n. d.

Todd, Edgeley W. *Literary Interest in the Fur Trade and Fur Trapper of the Trans-Mississippi West.* Ph.D. Dissertation, Northwestern University, 1952.

Utz, Cornelius. *Life in Missouri, 1800–1840, as Pictured in Travellers' Accounts, Letters, and Journals.* M.A. Thesis, University of Missouri, 1933.

9. MISCELLANEOUS

Brooks, James G. *As Others See Us; A Study of Progress in the United States.* New York, Macmillan and Co., 1908.

Clark, Thomas D. "Manners and Humors of the American Frontier." *Mo. Hist. Rev.,* XXXV (1940), 3–24.

Rutland, Robert. "The American Indian through English Spectacles, 1608–1791." *Chrons. of Okla.,* XXIX (1951), 169–72.

Chapter 2

The Earliest Midwestern Travel Narrators,

The French

Although Spaniards had explored Florida and the region immediately west, they did not journey into the Middle West during their early explorations. Long before the English or Americans colonized the central part of the continent, the French established a vast domain, which they called New France, extending from eastern Canada to the southernmost part of the Mississippi Valley. The purpose of the present chapter is not to present the story of the rise and fall of the French in the New World, which has been fully told by the distinguished historian, Francis Parkman,[1] but to emphasize the travel narratives and diaries of the explorers, fur traders, priests, and missionaries in New France. For more than a century, Frenchmen and French Canadians wrote virtually the only narratives of Midwestern travel and exploration. This period of their dominance of the frontier has been largely disregarded by students of literature. The following account of the many fascinating and well-written French narratives indicates the necessity of considering the travel literature of this era in any estimation of the literary and cultural achievements of the New World during the seventeenth and eighteenth centuries.

Vimont, Father Barthelemy. *Relation de ce que s'est Passé en la Nouvelle France en . . . , 1642* (Paris, 1643). Extract in Pierre Margry, ed., *Découvertes et Établissements des Français dans l'Ouest et dans le Sud de l'Amérique Septentrionale (1614–1754). Mémoires et Documents Originaux Recueillé et Pub. par P. Margry* (Paris, Maissonneuve et Cie., 1879–1888), I, 47–59. English translation in *Relation of 1642 [concerning Jean Nicolet]* in Reuben Gold Thwaites, ed., *The Jesuit Relations and Allied Documents . . .* (Cleveland, The Burrows Co., 1896–1901), XXIII, 275–79, and in Louise Phelps Kellogg, ed., *Early Narratives of the Old Northwest, 1634–1699* (New York, Charles Scribner's Sons, 1917), pp. 15–16. Extracts in "Jean Nicolet's Visit to Wisconsin," *Wis. Hist. Soc. Colls.*, XVI (1902), 1–3.[2]

Jacques Cartier opened the St. Lawrence Valley in 1535. Samuel de Champlain laid the foundations of the colony of Quebec in 1608 and traveled as far west as Lake Huron in 1615.[3] It was not until 1634, however, that one of his explorers made a trip that was to be described in a travel narrative. Father Barthélemy Vimont, a personal friend of Jean Nicolet, wrote an account in 1642 of the latter's voyage into the Huron country

and mentioned the hardships he suffered. Nicolet, a *coureur de bois* (woods runner or illegal fur trader), left Quebec for the west on July 2, 1634. When he reached what is now Wisconsin and heard that the men he would meet were without hair upon their faces and hands, he supposed that he was near the Orient. He donned a robe of Chinese damask and walked out on the prairie, a pistol in each hand, to be received as a god by the savages. In 1634–1635 he explored a wide region west of Lake Michigan, eventually reaching the Mississippi,[4] and in 1636 discovered the Straits of Mackinac. He is important because he was probably the first white man to see the Middle West.

Since Vimont's narrative and most of the others mentioned in this chapter are written in French, a complete evaluation of their literary merits is beyond the scope of the present study. Additional information about Vimont and other authors is contained in the footnotes.

Lalemant [Lallemant], Father Jerome. *Rélation de ce qui s'est Passé . . . en la Mission aux Hurons . . . 1640–1642* (Paris, S. Cramoley, 1641). English translation in "The Journey of [Charles] Raymbault and [Isaac] Jogues to the Sault . . . 1641." In Thwaites, XXIII, pp. 223–27, and Kellogg, pp. 23–25.

The first Jesuits to have their trips to the Midwest chronicled were Father Charles Raymbault and Father Isaac Jogues. The author of the *Rélation*, Father Jerome Lalemant, probably used the original manuscripts of these two friends in writing his brief tale, which describes their crossing Lake Huron and reaching Sault Ste. Marie. Here they were received by the Indians to whom they offered their services. Lalemant held the positions of superior of the missions to the Hurons from 1636 to 1645 and superior of all the missions in New France from 1645 to 1650 and from 1659 to 1665. He was later murdered by Indians.

Voyages of Peter Esprit Radisson, Being an Account of his Travels and Experiences among the North American Indians, from 1652 to 1684. Transcribed from Original Manuscripts in the Bodleian Library and the British Museum (London, Gideon D. Scull; Boston, The Prince Society, 1885). Extracts in Kellogg, pp. 34–65, and in "The Voyages of Groseilliers and Radisson," Robert F. Kerr, ed., *Sou. Dak. Hist. Colls.*, I (1902), 163–78.[5]

Pierre Esprit Radisson came to Canada about 1651. With his brother-in-law, Médard Chouart, known as Sieur des Groseilliers, he may have made a first trip to the west in 1655. More important was a journey the two men took in 1659 because at that time they may have reached the upper Mississippi, the first Europeans to penetrate that far. The manuscripts of this voyageur and fur trader are composed of six personal narratives, covering a period of thirty-two years. Five are written in English and one in French, and include the period of Radisson's affiliation with the English and the Hudson's Bay Co.

Allouez, Jean Claude. *Journal.* In Margry, ed., I, 249–311; in John D. G. Shea, trans., *Discovery and Exploration of the Mississippi Valley* (New York, Historical Collections of Louisiana, 1852), pp. 67–77; and in Thwaites, L, 249–311; LI, 21–69; LIV, 197–214. Extracts in Kellogg, ed., pp. 98–137, 142–60, and in Charles W. Mann, ed., *Manners and Customs of the Western Indians* (Chicago, Boston, Atkinson, Mentzer and Grover, 1906) [*The Old Northwest Leaflets* . . . , Vol. I, No. 2].[6]

The name of Jean Claude Allouez will be remembered because of his important missionary work in the northern Great Lakes region and in Canada. He reached the Sault in 1665 after many hardships, and founded a mission there in 1668. He returned to Quebec but made a second trip westward in 1669 to attend the famous Sault Ste. Marie Pageant of 1671 and deliver a speech to the Indians gathered there. His *Journal* shows keen observation and at times his language is vivid.

Perrot, Nicolas. *Mémoire sur les Moeurs, Coustumes et Réligion des Sauvages de l'Amérique Septentrionale.* R. P. J. Tailhan, ed. (Leipzig and Paris, A. Franck, 1864). English translation in Emma Helen Blair, ed., *The Indian Tribes of the Upper Mississippi Valley and Region of the Great Lakes as Described by Nicholas Perrot, French Commandant in the Northwest* . . . (Cleveland, Arthur H. Clark Co., 1911), and in part in Kellogg, pp. 73–92.[7]

As a youth Nicolas Perrot emigrated to New France and, after serving with the Jesuit missionaries, became a fur trader. He may have been one of the Frenchmen who in 1663 went to Lake Superior with the Ottawa trading caravan. In 1668 he reached Green Bay, and in 1670, mainly because of his knowledge of Indian languages, he was appointed by Governor Frontenac as interpreter for an expedition to the west. He again visited Green Bay in 1671 to obtain delegates to the Sault Ste. Marie Pageant, held in June of the same year. He built Fort St. Nicolas at the mouth of the Wisconsin River and Fort St. Antoine on Lake Pepin. He took possession of the upper Mississippi region in the name of France in 1689 and for several more years served France by preserving the friendship of the western Indian tribes. He spent the last years of his life writing his experiences.

Galinée, René Bréhan de. *Voyage de MM. Dollier de Casson et de Galinée* . . . (Montreal, Historical Society of Montreal, 1875) and in Margry, I, 113–66. Extracts in "The Most Noteworthy Incidents in the Journey of Messieurs Dollier and Galinée (1669–1670)," James H. Coyne, trans. and ed., *Ontario Historical Society Papers and Records*, IV (1903), 3–75; in Kellogg, pp. 167–209; and in Berthold Fernow, *The Ohio Valley in Colonial Days* (Albany, Joel Munsell's Sons, 1890), pp. 217–19.

In 1669–1670 another Jesuit, René de Galinée, accompanied by Dollier de Casson, journeyed by water from Montreal via the lower to the upper Great Lakes, with a stop at the mission at the Sault. His is perhaps the most readable and interesting of the early narratives.

Dablon, Father Claudius. *Relation de ce qui s'est passé de plus remarquable aux Missions des Pères de la Compagnie de Jésus, en la Nouvelle France les années 1670 & 1671* . . . (Paris, Sebastian Mabre-Cramoisy, 1673). In Shea, pp. 1–52. Extracts in "Of the First Voyage Made by Father Marquette toward New Mexico, and How the Design Was Conceived," *Ill. Hist. Colls.*, I (1903), 8–40; in "Account of the Second

Voyage of Father Marquette," *Cath. Hist. Rev.*, VII (1925), 291–301; and in "Father Marquette at Chicago, from Marquette's Narrative and Dablon's Relation," *Old South Leaflets*, No. 46 (Boston, Directors of the Old South Work, 1897).[8]

Father Claudius Dablon, one of the ablest, most energetic, and conscientious missionaries of New France, was sent to Canada in 1655 and to the northwest in 1669 as superior of the Ottawa mission. From his headquarters at the Sault, he sent Father Allouez to explore the region around Green Bay and to establish missions. The following year he himself accompanied Allouez to central Wisconsin. His descriptions of the wilderness are enthusiastic and his accounts of the Lake Superior copper mines and of the Sault Ste. Marie Pageant detailed. Returning to Quebec permanently in 1671, he appointed Marquette to accompany Joliet on the voyage of discovery on the Mississippi River. He later edited Marquette's narratives.

Joliet, Louis. *Journal* (Paris, Thévenot, 1681). Reprinted in Margry, I, 259–70. Translated by Benjamin F. French in Shea and translated in part in Jared Sparks, *Life of Father Marquette* (Boston, Hillard Gray and Co.; London, R. J. Kennett, 1844).[9]

Marquette, Jacques. *Voyage et Découverte du P. Marquette et Sr. Jolliet dans l'Amérique Septentrionale.* In *Recueil de Voyage* . . . (Paris, Thévenot, 1681). Translated in Shea; in Thwaites, LIX; in part in Shea, "Journal of Marquette's First Visit to the Mississippi," *Mich. Hist. Colls.*, XXI (1894), 467–88; and in Kellogg, pp. 228–57. See also "Marquette's Last Journal," *ibid.*, pp. 262–80 and *Mich. Hist. Colls.*, XXI (1894), 488–94; the *Relation* by Dablon; and "Father Marquette at Chicago . . . ," *Old South Leaflets*, No. 46.[10]

The names of Jacques Marquette and Louis Joliet are so closely associated that it is almost impossible to treat their works separately. Since the journal attributed to Marquette has survived whereas Joliet's original narrative has been lost, Marquette's literary fame is the greater of the two. Joliet, the earliest French-Canadian to win renown as an explorer, first met Marquette, a missionary from France, at the Sault in 1669. The following year Joliet again went west and in 1671 attended the ceremony at which the western country was annexed to New France. The next year he was selected by Governor Frontenac to find the great river somewhere beyond Lake Michigan, and Marquette was delegated chaplain of the expedition. Joliet and Marquette began their famous voyage on May 17, 1673. They crossed from the Wisconsin River to the Mississippi and traveled as far south at latitude 30°. Turning back there, they navigated up the Illinois River. Joliet, who probably spent the winter exploring Lake Michigan, returned to Canada in 1674 to report the discoveries but lost his maps and journal when his canoe was overturned near Montreal. Marquette, after trying to found a mission among the Illinois Indians, died on the way to Michilimackinac in 1675. Joliet lived twenty-five years longer and passed most of his later life at Quebec. The surviving brief journal of Joliet was probably recalled from memory or possibly written in collaboration with the publisher. Marquette's much longer narrative is dignified and rich in expression.

Tonty [Tonti], Henry de. *Mémoire Envoyé en 1693 sur la Découverte du Mississippi et des Nations Voisines, par le Sieur de La Salle, en 1678, et Depuis sa Mort.* . . . English translation as "Memoir Sent in 1693 on the Discovery of the Mississippi and the Neighboring Nations by M. de LaSalle, from the Year 1678 to the Time of his Death, and by the Sieur de Tonty to the Year 1691" in Thomas Falconer, *On the Discovery of the Mississippi* (London, S. Clarke, 1844). Reprinted in *French's*

Historical Collections of Louisiana . . . (New York, 1846–1853), I (1846), 52–78; Isaac J. Cox, ed., *The Journeys of René Robert Sieur de LaSalle, as Related by his Faithful Lieutenant, Henri de Tonty; his Missionary Colleagues, Father Zenobius Membré, Louis Hennepin, and Anastasius Douay; his Early Biographer, Father Christian LeClereq; his Trusted Subordinate, Henri Joutel; and his Brother, Jean Cavalier . . .* (New York, A. S. Barnes & Co., 1905), I, 31–65; *Ill. Hist. Colls.*, I (1903), 128–64; and Kellogg, 286–322. French text in Margry, *Relations et Mémoires Inédits* (Paris, 1867), pp. 5–36.

"Relation de Henri de Tonty, Entreprises de M. de LaSalle, de 1678 à 1683." In Margry, I, 573–616. French and English in *Relation of Henry de Tonti . . .*, Melville B. Anderson, trans. (Chicago, Caxton Club, 1898).

An Account of Monsieur de la Salle's Last Expedition and Discoveries in North America Presented to the French King, and Published by the Chevalier Tonti, Governour of Fort St. Louis, in the Province of the Islinois (London, J. Tomson, etc., 1698), and *Dernières Découvertes dans l'Amérique Septentrionale de Monsieur de la Salle, par Chevalier de Tonti* (Paris, J. Guignard, 1697).[11]

The story of LaSalle's important exploration of the Midwest has been told in four narratives as well as in the writings of LaSalle himself. The events and tragic conclusion of the great explorer's life are too familiar to deserve detailed treatment. Facts about his associates and their writings, however, are less well known.

Henry Tonty, an Italian, was first introduced to LaSalle in 1678 when the latter was seeking assistance in France for his explorations in North America. Tonty immediately enlisted in LaSalle's service and was sent to the Niagara River to superintend the building of LaSalle's ship, the *Griffon*. Traveling through the Great Lakes to Michilimackinac and into Lake Michigan, LaSalle's party advanced into Illinois and built Fort Crèvecoeur on Lake Peoria in 1679–1680. When LaSalle returned to Quebec in the spring of the latter year, Tonty was left in command in the Illinois country. Wounded by Indians and deserted by his men, he escaped to Green Bay and met LaSalle at Michilimackinac in 1681. They went back to Illinois, built Fort St. Louis, and in the spring of 1682 explored the Mississippi to its mouth. Although not hearing of LaSalle's assassination until 1689, Tonty remained in Illinois a decade after he received the news of LaSalle's assassination. In 1700, he joined Iberville's new colony near the mouth of the Mississippi and died near Mobile in 1704.

Hennepin, Louis. *Description de la Louisiane, Nouvellement Découverte au Sud'oüest de la Nouvelle France, par Ordre du Roy. Avec la Carte du Pays; les Moeurs, & la Manière de Vivre des Sauvages . . .* (Paris, Sebastian Huré, 1683). English translation with additions entitled *A New Discovery of a Vast Country in America . . . between New-France and New Mexico . . . with a Continuation, Giving an Account of the Attempts of the Sieur de la Salle upon the Mines of St.-Barbe* (London, 1698). Part of the first book in Shea, *Discovery and Exploration . . .*, pp. 107–45; in "Hennepin's Narrative, from his 'La Louisiana' of 1683," *Ill. Hist. Colls.*, I (1903), 46–105, and in Cox, I, 66–87. See also *Amer. Ant. Soc. Trans. Colls.*, I (1820), 61–104.[12]

Louis Hennepin, a native of Belgium, accompanied LaSalle and Tonty as a missionary on their 1678–1682 expedition. He wrote an account of the trip which is based in part upon a narrative by Father Membré but is full of falsehoods. As far as

general interest and minuteness of description go, Hennepin's is the most prominent of all the narratives of early American exploration.[13] He thus has a greater claim to the status of author than any of the preceding writers. His book was translated from the original into several languages and went through a number of editions. A second work by Hennepin included his later experiences in the Midwest.

Membré, Zenobius. *Prémier Établissements de la Foy dans la Nouvelle France*. Chrétien le Clereq, comp. (Paris, 1691). English translation of part in Shea, pp. 147–63 and in Cox, I, 131–59.[14]

Zenobius Membré, a Recollect missionary, was sent from France to Canada in 1675. He began his ministry to the men of the LaSalle expedition at Niagara in 1678. Suffering great hardships after an Indian attack in Illinois, he reached the mission at De Père. He met LaSalle at Mackinac in 1681 and accompanied him to the mouth of the Mississippi, but perished with the settlement after LaSalle left it in 1687. Membré's voluminous journals of the LàSalle explorations are written in a simple although occasionally obscure style.

Joutel, Henri. *Journal Historique du Dernier Voyage que feu M. de la Salle Fit dans le Golfe de Mexique . . . Rédigé et Mis en Ordre par Monsieur de Michel* (Paris, E. Robinot, 1713). English translation as *A Journal of the Last Voyage Perform'd by Monsr de la Salle . . .* (London, A. Bell, etc., 1714). Reprinted in French in Margry, II, 91–534, and in English in *French's Historical Collections of Louisiana*, Vol. I; translated by Melville B. Anderson (Chicago, The Caxton Club, 1896).[15]

The journal of Henri Joutel is much like Tonty's account except that it is concerned only with LaSalle's second voyage. Joutel met LaSalle in France in 1684 and sailed with him for the mouth of the Mississippi. His narrative relates events in his journey to Fort St. Louis on the Illinois after the death of LaSalle, his winter there in 1687–1688, and his trip via the Great Lakes to Canada. When he returned to France, he assembled his notes into a narrative, which he complained was later changed from the original by the Paris publisher. The journal is simple in style but it is the most detailed and exact description of LaSalle's last expedition.

LaSalle, René-Robert Cavelier, Sieur de. *Relation of the Discoveries and Voyages of Cavelier de La Salle, from 1679 to 1681, the Official Narrative. . . .* Melville B. Anderson, trans. (Chicago, Caxton Club, 1901). "LaSalle on the Illinois Country," in Margry, I, 102–11, 435–555, and II, 93–102. Extracts in *Ill. Hist. Colls.*, XXIII (1934), 1–16; "Memoir of the Sieur de LaSalle. Reporting to Monseigneur [sic] de Seignelay the Discoveries Made by Him under the Order of his Majesty," *ibid.*, I (1903), 115–25; and in French, pp. 1-27. See also Hiram Williams Beckwith, ed., *Documents . . . Relating to the Northwest and the State of Illinois* (Springfield, Ill., H. W. Hokker, 1903).[16]

Although LaSalle himself wrote no book-length journal of his exploits, some of his letters, patents, and documents contain sections which are narrative in nature and should not be excluded from the present study. His accomplishments lie in the realm of discovery and exploration rather than in that of literature. It is doubtful, however, as contended, that he navigated the Ohio River. His domineering character is perhaps too often emphasized and his questing spirit and contribution to humanity are too often forgotten. The narratives of the LaSalle expedition are among the most fascinating of the Midwestern travel tales—full of action and excellent description.[17]

*The Western Country in the 17th Century. The Memoirs of La-
mothe Cadillac and Pierre Liette.* W. F. Giese, trans. of Liette
memoir. Milo M. Quaife, ed. (Chicago, R. R. Donnelley and
Sons Co., 1947).

Lahontan, Louis-Armand de Lom d'Ares, Baron de. *Nouveaux
Voyages de Mr. le Baron de Lahontan, dans l'Amérique Septentrionale . . .* (2 vols., The Hague, 1703). English Edition entitled *New Voyages to North-America. Containing an Account
of the Several Nations of that Vast Continent; their Customs,
Commerce, and Way of Navigation upon the Lakes and Rivers
. . .* (2 vols., London, H. Bonwicke, T. Goodwin, M. Wotton,
B. Tooke, and S. Manship, 1703).[18]

The only other known Midwestern narratives of the 1680's and
1690's were written by two men who made contact with LaSalle's
party. Pierre Liette had obtained permission from Tonty to accompany the Illinois Indians on a buffalo hunt in 1688, and
Tonty left him in charge of the Indians in 1691. Liette's descriptive account covers his Midwestern experiences during 1687–
1702. Although Cadillac's name appears with Liette's in the
title of the English translation, Cadillac's account is not a Midwestern travel narrative.

Baron Louis-Armand de Lahontan embarked with his regiment for New France in 1683 to engage in an unsuccessful campaign against the Iroquois. He returned to France but was later
again sent west with Tonty. He abandoned his post as commandant at Fort St. Joseph on the St. Clair River above Detroit
to go to Mackinac and later traveled farther west. According to
his book he encountered some of LaSalle's men whom he suspected of concealing their commander's death. He claimed to
have ascended the upper Mississippi and to have discovered the
River Long before he returned to France in 1692. In 1703 he
published his famous *Nouveaux Voyages . . .*, which ran through
several editions and greatly influenced other writers.[19] In the
first English edition of his work he included a series of "Dia-
logues" with the Huron Indians, wherein he discussed the philosophy of primitive life; his style is literary and his attitude
cynical.

Journal of Paul du Ru (*February 1 to May 8, 1700*), *Missionary
Priest to Louisiana; Translated, with Introduction and Notes,
from a Manuscript in the Newberry Library.* Ruth Lapham
Butler, trans. (Chicago, The Caxton Club, 1934).[20]

Des Ursins, Marc Antoine de la Loire. "Detail of the Journey to
the Mines of the Illinois." F. G. Holweck, trans. In "Earliest
History of Mine la Motte," *Mo. Hist. Rev.,* XX (1925–1926),
205–7.[21]

LePage du Pratz, Antoine Simon. *Histoire de la Louisiane.
Contenant la Découverte de ce Vaste Pays . . .* (3 vols., Paris,
DeBure, l'aîné, etc., 1758). English translation entitled *The
History of Louisiana, or of the Western Parts of Virginia and
Carolina: Containing a Description of the Countries that Lye
on Both Sides of the River Missisipi: with an Account of the
Settlements, Inhabitants, Soil, Climate and Products . . .* (2
vols., London, T. Becket and F. A. DeHondt, 1763).

Fourcade, Sieur. "Relation of a Voyage from LaRochelle, France,
to Louisiana in 1720–1723 by Fourcade, a Surgeon." 21 pp.
MS. Chicago Historical Society.

Paul du Ru, Marc Antoine Des Ursins, Antoine LePage du
Pratz and the Sieur Fourcade were the next French travelers to
write known accounts of visits to the Middle West. Du Ru, a
Jesuit missionary with the explorer Iberville in Louisiana, com-
posed a journal of his voyage up the Mississippi in 1700. Des
Ursins, French intendant of the Illinois country, in 1719 wrote
an official report and description of the region between Kaskaskia,
Illinois, and the lead mines at Mine la Motte, in what is now

Madison County, Missouri. LePage de Pratz, who was of Dutch
ancestry, published his book about his travels in the Mississippi
Valley between 1718–1739, including trips on the Arkansas, Red,
Missouri, Ohio, and Miami rivers. It contains interesting comments on such topics as hunting and the dangers of wolves.
Fourcade's brief manuscript, describing the French settlements
in the Louisiana and Illinois country in the early 1720's, is the
earliest known unpublished Midwestern travel narrative. The
dearth of journals during the first two decades of the eighteenth
century indicates that a decline in frontier exploration and travel
occurred at this time.

Charlevoix, Pierre François Xavier de. *Histoire et Description
Generale de la Nouvelle France, avec le Journal Historique
d'un Voyage Fait par Ordre du Roi dans l'Amérique Septen-
trionnele* (3 vols., Paris, Nyon Fils, 1744). English translation in *Journal of a Voyage to North America . . . In a Series
of Letters . . .* (2 vols., London, 1761). Reprint edited by L. P.
Kellogg (2 vols., Chicago, The Caxton Club, 1923).[22]

One of the most learned of French Jesuits, Pierre François
Xavier de Charlevoix, voyaged to Canada in 1705 to become
professor of rhetoric in the college at Quebec, but returned to
France to teach. He was later commissioned by the French government to go back to Canada to determine the boundaries of
Acadia and to find a new route to the West. In 1721 he proceeded
by canoe up the St. Lawrence, through the Great Lakes to Detroit, Mackinac, Green Bay, and the Illinois River. He then
traveled down the Mississippi, reaching Biloxi early the following year. His journal, mainly about Canada, is composed of a
series of narrative letters and is valuable for the unemotional
and accurate observation of the country and the Indians.

La Harpe, Bénard. *Journal historique de l'établissement des
Français à la Louisiane* [Extracts] (Nouvelle Orleans, A. L.
Boimare, etc., 1831). In Margry, VI, Part 2, 357–82.

Delisle, Legardeur. "A Search for Copper on the Illinois River:
the Journal of Legardeur Delisle, 1722." Stanley Faye, ed.,
Jour. Ill. State Hist. Soc., XXXVIII (1945), 38–57.

D'Artaguiette, Diron. Travel Journal, Sept., 1722–Sept., 1723.
In Newton D. Mereness, ed., *Travels in the American Colonies*
(New York, Macmillan Co., 1916), pp. 17–92.[23]

Bourgmont, Sieur de. Account of the Trip of the Sieur de Bourgmont. In Margry, VI, Part 2, 398–452. English translation in
*Discoveries and Establishments of the French within the West
and within the South of North America (1614–1754).* Beatrice
Paddock, trans. (Wichita, Kans., Wichita City Library, 1936).

Anonymous. "Green Bay in 1726." *Wis. Hist. Soc. Colls.,* I
(1854), 21–23, and 1903 reprint.

Guignas, Michel. "The Expedition Arrives Among the Sioux:
Fort Beauharnois Built." *Wis. Hist. Soc. Colls.,* XVII (1906),
22–28. Reprinted as "With LaPerrière to Minnesota in 1727,"
Minn. Hist., VI (1925), 362–69.

Bénard La Harpe wrote some journals in diary form of the
trip he made from Louisiana up the Arkansas River in 1721–
1722 on Bienville's instructions. Legardeur Delisle, a French
superintendent of mines searching for precious metals, traveled
up the Illinois during 1722 and wrote a poorly worded journal
descriptive of the mines and terrain. A journal of 1722–1723 by
Diron D'Artaguiette about a trip from New Orleans up the Mississippi to the Illinois country is much more interesting, including remarks about personal affairs, complaints, and reports on
conditions. The Sieur de Bourgmont, a cavalier of the military
order of Saint-Louis and commander of the Missouri River, composed a diary of a journey in 1724 by a military detachment
through a part of the present state of Kansas to the source of

the Arkansas River, which included interesting observations on Indians and their customs. An unidentified French traveler wrote an account in 1726 of Green Bay, Wisconsin, and a treaty with the Fox Indians. In a narrative letter of 1728, Father Michel Guignas related to the Marquis de Beauharnois, governor of New France, events in the trip of René LaPerrière and his party from Mackinac to Green Bay and descriptions of the customs of the Fox and Sioux Indians.[24] All of these accounts have been translated into English.

LaVèrendrye, Pierre Gaultier de Varennes, Sieur de. *Mémoire du Sieur de la Vèrendrye au Sujet des Établissements pour Parvenu à la Découverte de la Mer de l'Ouest.* In Margry, VI, Part 2, 585–611. English translation in *Journals and Letters of Pierre Gaultier de la Vèrendrye and his Sons.* Lawrence J. Burpee, ed., *Publications of the Champlain Society,* Vol. XVI (Toronto, 1927).

Exploration du Nord-ouest. "Journal de Lavèrendrye . . ."; "Journal of LaVèrendrye, 1738–39." [French and English texts.] *Report on Canadian Archives* (Ottawa, Brown Chamberlin, 1890). English translation in C. S. Stevenson, trans., *Sou. Dak. Hist. Colls.,* VII (1914), 323–48, and in Henry E. Haxo, trans., *Nor. Dak. Hist. Quar.,* VIII (1941), 229–71.

"Journal of the Voyage Made by Chevalier de la Vèrendrye, with One of his Brothers, in Search of the Western Sea [1742–1743], Addressed to Marquis de Beauharnois." C. S. Stevenson, trans., *Sou. Dak. Hist. Colls.,* VII (1914), 349–58; Anne H. Blegen, trans., *Oreg. Hist. Soc. Quar.,* XXVI (1925), 51–64, 116–29. See also *Oreg. Hist. Soc. Quar.,* XXVI (1925), 85–115.[25]

An imagination fired by optimistic reports of the Indians led a French Canadian, Pierre Gaultier LaVèrendrye, to formulate a plan for seeking the Pacific by way of the Great Lakes. His report that the ocean lay only five hundred leagues beyond Lake Superior gained strong support and he was granted a monopoly of the fur trade north and west of this lake. In 1731 he started west with his three eldest sons and nephew, reaching Rainy Lake. The next year he erected Fort St. Charles at the Lake of the Woods. In spite of the death of his nephew and the murder of one of his sons by the Indians in 1736, he made his way overland to the Mandan villages on the upper Missouri. He returned to Montreal in 1744, but two of his sons continued exploring as far as the Black Hills or the Rocky Mountains. He was the discoverer of part of Canada, of western Minnesota, and of the Dakotas. He and his sons were the first white men to see the upper Missouri. His western journals, covering the years 1731–1743, show keen observation and narrative skill. They have been published several times and much has been written about him.

Folmer, Henri. *Voyage des Frères Mallet . . . Extrait du Journal.* In Margry, VI, Part 2, 465–92. English translation in "The Mallet Expedition of 1739 Through Nebraska, Kansas and Colorado to Santa Fe." *Colorado Magazine,* XVI (1939), 161–73.

"Selections from the Diary and Gazette of Father Pierre Potier, S. J. (1708–1781)." E. R. Ott, trans. and ed., *Mid-Amer.,* XVIII (1936), 199–202.

Grignon, Augustin. "Seventy-two Years' Recollections of Wisconsin. *Wis. Hist. Soc. Colls.,* III (1857), 195–295.

Brief mention should be made of Henri Folmer's journal of the attempt by the Mallet brothers to reach New Mexico by ascending the Missouri River in 1739; they were the first Frenchmen to reach New Mexico by land. They returned east the following year by way of the Arkansas River. Pierre Potier, a Jesuit at Assumption Mission on Bois Blanc Island in the river below De-

troit, wrote a brief diary consisting of entries in fragmentary form of his experiences during 1743–1747. A much longer and more important work is an autobiography by Augustin Grignon covering the years 1744–1818. It relates the adventures in what is now Wisconsin, of his grandfather, Charles DeLanglade,[26] and his father. It describes encounters with the Menomonees and Winnebagoes, and shows the influence of the French and Indian War upon the history of that state. All of these journals have been translated into English.

Chaussegros de Léry, Joseph-Gaspard. "Journal de Joseph-Gaspard Chaussegros de Léry Lieutenant des Troupes, 1745–1755 (Visite des Postes d'en Haut Jusqu'à Détroit Inclusivement)." In *Rapport de l'Archiviste de la Province de Québec pour 1927–1928,* pp. 355–429. English translation in *Journal,* Sylvester K. Stevens and Donald H. Kent, eds. Prepared by Frontier Forest and Trails Survey, Federal Works Agency, Works Projects Administration (Harrisburg, Pennsylvania Historical Commission, 1940).

——— "Journal de la Campagne que Sr de Léry, Officier dans les Troupes Détachées de la Marine Entretenues en Canada, a Faite au Détroit en l'Année 1749, par Ordre de M. le Marquis de la Galissonnière, Gouverneur Géneral dans Laquelle il a Fait des Observations Astronomiques et Autres, Conformément à ses Ordres et Instructions en Date du 26 Mai 1749." In *Rapport de l'Archiviste de la Province de Québec pour 1926–1927,* pp. 334–48.

——— "Les Journaux de Campagne: Juin 6–Sept. 25, 1749; Mars 7, 1754–Août 5, 1755." L. Oughtred Waltz, trans., 164 pp. MS., Burton Historical Collection, Detroit.

——— "Journal de la Campagne d'Hiver, du 13 Février au Neuf Avril 1756, que Gaspard-Joseph Chaussegros de Léry, Lieutenant dans les Troupes Détachées de la Marine et à Présent Capt. et Chvi. de St-Louis, a Faite en Conséquence des Ordres de Pierre de Rigaud . . ." In *Rapport de l'Archiviste de la Province de Québec pour 1926–1927,* pp. 372–94. English translation by L. O. Waltz, 39 pp. MS., Burton Historical Collection, Detroit.[27]

Joseph-Gaspard Chaussegros de Léry was a French lieutenant who wrote lengthy journals of his visit to a military post above Detroit as early as 1745 and of frontier military campaigns in 1749, 1755, and 1756, including travel in the Ohio country.

Bonnecamps, Father Joseph Pierre de. "Account of the Voyage on the Beauiful River Made in 1749, Under the Direction of Monsieur de Céloron." *Ohio Arch. Hist. Quar.,* XXIX (1920), 397–423.

Céloron de Blainville [Bienville], Pierre Joseph de. *Journal de le Compagne, que moy Céloron, Chevalier de l'Ordre Royal Militaire de Saint-Louis, Capitaine, Commandant un Détachement Envoyé dans la Belle Rivière, Ai Faite Par les Ordres de M. la Marquis de LaGalissonnière, Commandant Géneral de Toute le Nouvelle-France et Pays de la Louisiane.* In Margry, VI, Part 2, 666–726. English translation in "Céloron's Expedition down the Ohio," *Wis. Hist. Soc. Colls.,* XVIII (1908), 36–58, and A. A. Lambing, trans., "Céloron's Journal," *Ohio Arch. Hist. Quar.,* XXIX (1920), 335–96.[28]

Father Joseph Bonnecamps ventured from Quebec via Niagara into the Ohio country with Captain Céloron de Blainville in 1749. In his diary he mentions several encounters with Indians and tells how he reached the fort of the Miamis and the Miami River and then traveled to Lake Erie and Detroit and back to Quebec by way of the Great Lakes. The French greatly feared that the English would occupy the entire Ohio River region and consequently La Galissonière, governor of New France, in 1749 sent a company of men headed by Céloron to take possession of the region. Céloron, a French-Canadian, had been commandant of the post of Michilimackinac and as early as 1739 had become familiar with the Ohio River country. He kept a daily record of the events involved in his taking possession of the country in the name of Louis XV, beginning with his departure from LaChine, Quebec, on June 15. His contact with the English at several places and his attempts to persuade the Indians to return to French alliance are well told, while his description of the Ohio River, where he reached it, shows an appreciation of nature. What makes the trip extremely interesting is the fact that at the mouth of every important branch of the Ohio he deposited metal plates bearing French inscriptions declaring the sovereignty of France. He did not succeed in weaning the Indians away from the English, however, and returned to Canada, ending his journal on September 27. He assumed command at Detroit in 1750.

"Journal of Jacques Repentigny Legardeur St. Pierre of his Expedition for the Discovery of the Western Sea, 1750 to 1752." *Report on Canadian Archives, 1886* (Ottawa, Maclean Roger and Co., 1887). (Both original and English translation given.)

Bossu, Jean Bernard. *Nouveaux Voyages dans l'Amérique Septentrionale* . . . (Amsterdam and Paris, la Veuve Duchesne, 1778). English translation in *Travels Through that Part of North America formerly Called Louisiana.* John Reinhold Forster, trans. (2 vols., London, T. Davies, 1771).

——— *Nouveaux Voyages aux Indes Occidentales, Contenant une Relation des differens peuples qui habitent les environs du grands fleuve Saint-Louis, appellé vulgairement les Mississippi, leur Religion, leur Gouvernement; leurs Guerres, leur Commerce* (Paris, LeJay, 1768).

La Chapelle, Baron Passerat de. "La Chapelle's Remarkable Retreat through the Missssippi Valley, 1760–61." Louise P. Kellogg, trans. and ed. *Miss. Val. Hist. Rev.,* XXII (1935), 63–78.

[Navarre, Robert.] *Journal of Pontiac's Conspiracy, 1763* (Detroit, Speaker-Hines Printing Co., 1912). Extracts in "Diary of the Siege of Detroit," *Mich. Hist.,* XII (1928), 437–42.

Jacques LeGardeur de Saint-Pierre in 1750–1752 followed a route similar to that taken by LaVèrendrye, traveling from Montreal through Mackinac, Rainy Lake, into Canada, and returning to Montreal. Jean Bernard Bossu, "Captain in the French Marine," wrote an entertaining travel book in the form of narrative letters, *Nouveaux Voyages dans l'Amérique Septentrionale,* covering his first two visits to the New World during the years 1751–1762. He loved dramatic incidents and picturesque scenes, and his work was considered of great enough worth by Carlyle for recommendation to Emerson. Although Bossu's three visits to America were mainly spent in the South, he visited the Mississippi Valley Region and saw several Indian tribes. Like some of the other travelers of this period, he displayed some scientific interest, for he conjectured that some large bones discovered in the neighborhood of the Ohio were the remains of seven elephants which had perished in the swamps after making their way from Asia. He therefore believed that Asia was probably joined to Louisiana. A third visit during 1771–1772 is chronicled in an untranslated volume.[29]

In 1760–1761 Baron Passerat de La Chapelle and his troops marched from Detroit to Lake Michigan, the Illinois River, and Fort St. Louis. His historically important diary shows that he feared an attack from the English and retreated to New Orleans.[30] A journal of Pontiac's Conspiracy, covering the siege of Detroit and the period between May and July 31, 1763, probably by Robert Navarre, is the last of the French early Midwestern travel tales. The original manuscript was found by Francis Parkman who believed it to be the work of a French priest.

Chapter 3

The Narratives of Midwestern Indian Captivity

The most stirring and exciting of all the Midwestern travel tales are the narratives of Indian captivity. Readers have delighted in these stories from their beginnings. Numerous anthologies and reprints of the narratives appeared in the eighteenth and nineteenth centuries, and revived interest in the tales is evident in the publication of several fictionalized renditions and a book which retells some of them.[1] Curiosity over conditions on the frontier, belief or disbelief in "the noble savage," and concern over what some people thought were popish French intrigues with the Indians prompted many of the colonists to read the accounts. Some of the narratives were written as part of an anti-Indian, anti-French propaganda campaign. After 1790, however, with the Indian menace receding, the main attraction was the story itself, with the usual accompanying violence and horror.

Not all of the tales of Indian captivity include travels, but those which do so contain certain characteristics which distinguish them from other travel narratives. They are, first of all, a product of the Western Hemisphere only, an American contribution to literature. They are devised to capture the sympathy of the reader for the narrator and arouse antipathy for the Indian. Even though the author is not the captive, they are nearly always written in the first person. The tales are usually lengthy and often contain details which detract from the main events in the story. The best of the narratives follows a series of increasingly important incidents leading to a climax and a brief dénouement. The poorer ones pile event upon event—sometimes horror upon horror—until the reader becomes lost in the accumulation. Their tone is almost invariably serious and often extremely sentimental. Descriptions of localities such as forest trails and Indian camps are often vivid. Although not great works, they deserve more attention than twentieth century historians and students of literature have given them.

The narratives included in this chapter describe captivities which took place from 1720 to about 1835, a time span of over a century. More captivities occurred in the eastern part of the Midwest than in the trans-Mississippi region, and a large percentage of the captives were women. Three of the tales were written by women. The stories vary in length from very brief pamphlets to entire volumes, and in literary merit their differences are almost as great. Although they are less numerous than many other types of travel narratives, the number of times they were reprinted and included in anthologies is proof of their popularity.

Since writings about the narratives of Indian captivity are relatively few, the most important works of a general nature on the subject are the numerous anthologies of captivity tales published in the nineteenth century. Henry D. Northrop's *Indian Horrors; or, Massacres by the Red Man . . .* (1891) is a rather sensationalized summary of numerous captivities and tortures, including those of Boone, Henry, and Colonel James Smith. Professor R. L. Rusk has a brief bibliography of narratives of frontier Indian captivities in *The Literature of the Middle Western Frontier* (1925), II, 96–100, as does R. W. G. Vail in *The Voice of the Old Frontier* (1949). The most complete bibliography up to the present is found in two publications of the Newberry Library of Chicago, *Narratives of Captivity Among the Indians of North America* (1912) and *Supplement I* (1928), which list almost five hundred books and manuscripts on the subject in that library. For comments of a general nature on the narratives the following works, in addition to some of the introductions in the anthologies, are to be noted: Albert Keiser, *The Indian in American Literature* (1933), pp. 19–20, 32; Howard H. Peckham, *Captured by Indians* (1954), pp. vii–xii; and Robert Rutland, "The American Indian Through English Spectacles," *Chronicles of Oklahoma*, XXIX (1951), 169–72. The following list of abbreviated titles of anthologies, from which information about reprints of the anthologies has been excluded, should prove helpful. In the bibliographical information about individual narratives following this, names of authors of anthologies will show in which collections the tales appear.

The Affecting History of Dreadful Distresses of Frederick Manheim's Family . . . (n.p., printed for Chapman Whitcomb, 1792–1793).

The Book of American Indians . . . (Dayton, O., B. F. Ellis, 1854).

Butterfield, Consul Willshire. *An Historical Account of the Expedition Against Sandusky* . . . (Cincinnati, Robert Clarke and Co., 1873).

De Hass, Wills. *History of the Early Settlement and Indian Wars of Western Virginia* . . . (Philadelphia, H. Hoblitzell, 1851).

Doddridge, Joseph. *Notes, on the Settlement and Indian Wars* . . . (Wellsburgh, Va., the Author, 1824).

Drake, Samuel Gardner. *Indian Captivities* . . . (Boston, Antiquarian Bookstore and Institute, 1839).

———— *Tragedies of the Wilderness* . . . (Boston, Antiquarian Bookstore and Institute, 1841). [The same as *Indian Captivities*.]

Dunn, Jacob Piatt, *True Indian Stories* . . . (Indianapolis, Sentinel Printing Co., 1908).

Hale, John Peter. *Trans-Allegheny Pioneers* . . . (Cincinnati, Graphic Press, 1886).

Heckewelder, Johann Gottlieb Ernestus. *A Narrative of the Mission of the United Brethren* . . . (Cleveland, The Burrows Brothers Co., 1907).

Hildreth Samuel Prescott. *Pioneer History* . . . (New York, A. S. Barnes and Co., 1848).

Kephart, Horace. *Captives Among the Indians* . . . No. 3 (New York, Outing Publishing Co., 1915).

Loudon, Archibald. *A Selection, of Some of the Most Interesting Narratives, of Outrages, Committed by the Indians* . . . (Carlisle, Pa., A. Loudon, 1808 [–1811]).

McClung, John Alexander. *Sketches of Western Adventure* . . . (Maysville, Ky., L. Collins, 1832).

McKnight, Charles. *Our Western Border* . . . (Philadelphia, Cincinnati, Chicago, and St. Louis, J. C. McCurdy & Co., 1875).

McMechen, James H. *Legends of the Ohio Valley* . . . (Wheeling, Lewis Baker and Co., 1881).

Metcalfe, Samuel L. *A Collection of Some of the Most Interesting Narratives of Indian Warfare in the West* . . . (Lexington, Ky., William G. Hunt, 1821).

The Olden Time . . . (2 vols., Cincinnati, Robert Clarke and Co., 1876).

Peck, George. *Wyoming; Its History, Stirring Incidents, and Romantic Adventures* (New York, Harper and Brothers, 1858).

Pritts, Joseph. *Incidents of Border Life* . . . (Chambersburg, Pa., J. Pritts, 1839).

Sargent, Epes. *American Adventure by Land and Sea* . . . (New York, Harper and Brothers, 1842).

Schoolcraft, Henry Rowe. *The American Indians* . . . (Buffalo, George H. Derby and Co., 1851).

———— *Western Scenes and Reminiscences* . . . (Auburn, Derby and Miller; Buffalo, Derby, Orton and Mulligan, 1853). (The same as *The American Indian*.)

Sipe, Chester Hale. *The Indian Chiefs of Pennsylvania* . . . (Butler, Pa., Ziegler Printing Co., 1927).

Spooner, Walter W. *The Back-woodsmen or Tales of the Borders* . . . (Cincinnati, W. E. Dibble and Co., 1883).

Thatcher, Benjamin Bussey. *Tales of the Indians* . . . (Boston, Waitt and Dow, 1831).

Wimer, James. *Events on Indian History* . . . (Lancaster, Pa., G. Hills and Co., 1843).

Withers, Alexander Scott. *Chronicles of Border Warfare* . . . (Clarksburg, Va., Joseph Israel, 1831).

Since the following list of Midwestern captivities is rather long and since some of the narratives are not important, descriptions of the content and style of the accounts have been minimized, but author, title, facts of publication, and information about appearance in anthologies have been included.[2] In nearly all items the first edition, rather than later ones, is cited.

Boucher, Pierre, Sieur de Boucherville. "Relation des Aventures de Mr de Boucherville à son retour des Sioux en 1728 et 1729." Copy in *la Saberdache* (rouge), I, 41–113, at the Archives of the Quebec Seminary, Quebec.

———— "Narrative." English translation in *La Bibliotheque Canadienne*. Michel Bibaud, ed. (Montreal, 1826), III, 11ff. Extracts in "Captivity of a Party of Frenchmen among Indians in the Iowa Country, 1728–1729." *Ia. Jour. Hist.*, XIV, (1916), 96–118.

Aside from incidental episodes in the journals of trappers, explorers, and Jesuits such as Nicolas Perrot, the first known tale of Middle Western Indian captivity was written by Pierre Boucher, Sieur de Boucherville, who describes an interesting captivity among the Kickapoos during the years 1728–1729. The Indians treated him well and eventually allowed him to visit the Illinois nation to arrange a peace treaty, after which he was released.

Stuart, Charles. "The Captivity of Charles Stuart, 1755–57." Beverley W. Bond, Jr., ed., *Miss. Val. Hist. Rev.*, XIII (1926), 58–81.

A period of twenty-six years elapsed before the next Indian captivity described in a known tale took place. Charles Stuart was captured in a Pennsylvania border raid on October 29, 1755, and was led over Indian trails to Detroit. He was finally sent to England and returned to New York. Although he had no sense of literary style, Stuart was an accurate observer and told of some gruesome torture methods.

Smith, James. *An Account of the Remarkable Occurrences in the Life and Travels of Col. James Smith, Now a Citizen of Bourbon County, Kentucky, during his Captivity with the Indians in the Years 1755, '56, '57, '58, & 59 in Which the Customs, Manners, Traditions, Theological Sentiments, Mode of Warfare, Military Tactics, Discipline and Encampments, Treatment of Prisoners, &c. Are Better Explained, and More Minutely Related, than Has Been Heretofore Done by Any Author on that Subject. Together with a Description of the Soil, Timber and Waters, Where He Traveled with the Indians During his Captivity* . . . (Lexington, John Bradford, 1799). Reprinted in anthologies by the following: Drake, Kephart, Loudon, McClung, McKnight, the author of *The Olden Time*, Pritts, Sargent, and Wimer. Retold in *Human Interest Events of Old Middle West History*, C. S. Van Tassel, ed. (Bowling Green, O., Historical Research Bureau, n. d.).[3]

Seaver, James E. *A Narrative of the Life of Mrs. Mary Jemison, Who Was Taken by the Indians, in the Year 1755 [sic], When Only about Twelve Years of Age, and Has Continued to Reside Amongst Them to the Present Time. Containing an Account of the Murder of her Father and his Family; her Sufferings; her Marriage to Two Indians; her Troubles with her Children; Barbarities of the Indians in the French and Revolutionary Wars; the Life of her Last Husband, &c.; and Many Historical Parts Never Before Published. Carefully Taken from her own Words, Nov. 29th, 1823* . . . (Canandaigua, N. Y., J. D. Bemis and Co., 1824). (Later editions extended the narrative to include the last years of her life.) Reprinted in Harriet S. (Clark) Caswell, *Our life among the Iroquois Indians* (Boston and Chicago, Congregational Sunday-school and Publishing Society, 1892); Anna C. (Johnson) Miller, *The Iro-*

quois . . . (New York, D. Appleton and Co., 1855); and in Sipe. Retold in Howard H. Peckham, *Captured by Indians*, pp. 62–78.[4]

The two most popular early narratives of Midwestern Indian captivity were those about the adventures of Colonel James Smith and Mrs. Mary Jemison. Smith was eventually taken by the savages to an Indian town on the Muskingum River in Ohio. Later he went to Lake Erie with an Indian who had adopted him as his brother. He finally reached Detroit, traveled to near Montreal, and arrived home in 1760. His story is told in the first person with good dialog but contains too many events to be well constructed. It went through so many editions, however, that a separate bibliography of his writings has been published.[5]

In 1758, twelve-year-old Mary Jemison was seized by Indians who raided her parents' home in western Pennsylvania. She was taken to an Indian village near the present Steubenville, Ohio, was adopted by the savages, married twice among them, had several children, and lived until ninety without returning to civilization. James E. Seaver, a physician, interviewed her when she was an old woman, and related her life-story in the first person. Mary grew to be a legend because of this account.

"Thomas Gist's Indian Captivity, 1758–1759." Howard H. Peckham, ed., *Penna. Mag. Hist. Biog.*, LXXX (1956), 287–311.

Brown, Thomas. *A Plain Narrative of the Uncommon Sufferings, and Remarkable Deliverance of Thomas Brown, of Charlestown, in New-England; Who Returned to his Father's House the Beginning of Jan. 1760, After Having Been Absent Three Years and About Eight Months: Containing an Account of the Engagement between a Party of English, Commanded by Maj. Rogers, and a Party of French and Indians, in Jan. 1757; in Which Capt. Spikeman Was Kill'd; and the Author of This Narrative Having Received Three Wounds (One of Which Thro' his Body) He Was Left for Dead on the Field of Battle:—How He Was Taken Captive by the Indians, and Carried to Canada, and from Thence to the Mississippi, Where He Lived About a Year, and Was Again Sent to Canada . . .* (2nd ed., Boston, Fowle and Draper, 1760). Reprinted in *Mag. Hist. with Notes and Queries*, Extra No. 4 (1908).[6]

Most of the early narratives of Midwestern Indian captivity were written against the background of the French and Indian War. Thomas Gist was captured with his companions by Hurons near Fort Pitt and carried to a town opposite Fort Pontchartrain (Detroit), in October 1758. He was adopted by an Indian family and well treated until he broke away in September of 1759. His journal, written after these events, shows him to be a courageous and likeable young man. Thomas Brown was left for dead after a clash in New England between the forces of Major Robert Rogers and the French and Indians in 1757. He was taken captive and transported down the Ohio River to the Mississippi, and finally back to Canada, whence he returned to New England. His account is brief but interesting.

Henry, Alexander. *Travels and Adventures in Canada and the Indian Territories, Between the Years 1760 and 1776. In Two Parts* (New York, I. Riley, 1809). Reprinted in Drake; Schoolcraft, *The American Indian . . .* and *Western Scenes and Reminiscences . . .*; and Thatcher. Edited by Milo M. Quaife (Chicago, R. R. Donnelley and Sons Co., 1921). Retold by Peckham, *Captured by Indians*, pp. 80–87. Summarized in "The Adventures of Alexander Henry." Stanley Newton, ed., *Mich. Hist.*, VI (1922), 558–64.

Rutherford, John. "A Prisoner of the Indians." William Thorp, ed., *Mag. Hist.*, (1905), 154–60.

Alexander Henry, a fur trader and the first English traveler of the upper Great Lakes, came to Michilimackinac in 1761 and was captured by Chippewas at Fort Mackinac in 1763. He was released in 1764 from a second captivity but returned to the Northwest a few weeks later, where he remained for many years. His book has been reprinted four times but is not widely known. Although it is not completely reliable since it was written long after the events took place, Schoolcraft praised it highly, saying in *Narrative Journal of Travels . . .* that it abounded in sensible reflections and was written in a clear and simple style. Henry's later journal will be discussed in Chapter 6.

Another narrative of a captivity during the same period was one by John Rutherford, who was attacked by Indians at a bend of the Huron River near Detroit in 1763, but who escaped with the help of a Frenchman.

Morris, Thomas. *Miscellanies in Prose and Verse* (London, James Ridgway, 1791). Reprinted in R. G. Thwaites, *Early Western Travels, 1748–1846* (32 vols., Cleveland, Arthur H. Clark Co., 1904), Vol. I, and in "Journal of Experience among the Miami Indians," *Mag. Hist.*, XIX, Extra Number (1921), 5–29.

Thomas Morris, an Englishman, was captured by the Miami Indians when he set out from Cedar Point on Lake Erie during Pontiac's War in 1764. A young chief freed him as he was about to be tortured and, after a flight through the woods, Morris reached Detroit. He described the savages realistically at a time when they were viewed romantically in Europe. His work is interesting and has literary merit.

Jeffries, Ewel. *A Short Biography of John Leeth, Giving a Brief Account of his Travels and Sufferings among the Indians for Eighteen Years . . . from his Own Relation* (Lancaster, O., Printed at the Gazette Office, 1831). Reprinted with introduction by Thwaites (Cleveland, Burrows Bros. Co., 1904).

In 1831 Ewel Jeffries wrote a matter-of-fact account based on information obtained from John Leeth [Leith], who had been taken prisoner in 1774 by the Delaware Indians in Ohio. Leeth was again captured in 1776 but was sold and granted liberty on the promise not to leave his buyer. After being employed as a trader at Detroit, he rejoined the Delawares in 1778 and lived with them for several years. The biography is written in the first person in a simple style, with a large part devoted to an account of the author's religious experiences.

Filson, John. *Life and Adventures of Colonel Daniel Boon, the First White Settler of the State of Kentucky.—Comprising—an Account of his First Excursion to Kentucky in 1769. Then a Wild Wilderness Inhabited by no Other Human Beings but Savages—His Remove There with his Family in 1773—and of his Various Encounters with the Indians, from the Year 1769 to 1782* (Brooklyn, C. Wilder, 1823). Reprinted in Imlay (1793 ed.), McClung, McKnight, Metcalfe, Pritts, and Withers. Retold in Peckham, pp. 98–115.[7]

One of the most famous frontiersmen, Daniel Boone, was captured by Shawnees in 1778 when he and a party of men crossed the Ohio River from Boonesborough, Kentucky, to replenish their supply of salt at the salt springs of the Blue Licks, near the Licking River. When he learned that the Indians were planning to attack Boonesborough, he offered to surrender his men, feigned friendship with the chief, who adopted him, and eventually escaped.[8] John Filson's is one of the most interesting of the captivity narratives, its popularity being indicated by the large number of reprints. Gilbert Imlay borrowed the story for *A Topographical Description of the Western Territory of North America*, which in turn was probably the source for Lord Byron's lines devoted to Boone in *Don Juan*. Filson's narratives of his own travels will be discussed in Chapter 5.

Dodge, John. "A Narrative of the Capture and Treatment of John Dodge, by the English at Detroit." In *The Remembrancer; or, Impartial Repository of Public Events for the Year 1779* (London, J. Almon, 1779), pp. 73–81.

McDonald, Philip and Alexander McLeod. *A Surprising Account of the Captivity and Escape of Philip McDonald & Alexander McLeod of Virginia, from the Chickkemogga Indians. And of their Great Discoveries in the Western World, from June 1779 to January 1786 . . .* (Keene, N. H., Henry Blake and Co., 1794).[9]

A brief narrative by John Dodge describes how in 1779 he was captured first by the British and then by the Indians. He rescued another captive from the stake but was himself held prisoner for many months. The short and largely fictitious account by Philip McDonald and Alexander McLeod tells of a journey through the Ohio country from 1779 through 1786, a captivity, and an escape.

Stone, William Leete. *The Poetry and History of Wyoming: Containing Campbell's Gertrude, with a Biographical Sketch of the Author, by Washington Irving, and the History of Wyoming from its Discovery to the Beginning of the Present Century* (New York and London, Wiley and Putnam, 1841).

Todd, John. *The Lost Sister of Wyoming* (Northampton, Mass., J. H. Butler, 1842).

Meginness, John Franklin. *Biography of Frances Slocum, the Lost Sister of Wyoming. A Complete Narrative of her Captivity and Wanderings among the Indians* (Williamsport, Pa., Heller Bros.' Printing House, 1891).

Slocum, James. *Frances Slocum, the Indian Captive* (Brownsville, Pa., 1876).

Slocum, Charles Elihu. *History of Frances Slocum the Captive . . .* (Defiance, Ohio, the Author, 1908).

Reprints of the various stories in Dunn, McKnight, Lewis H. Miner, *The Valley of Wyoming . . .* (New York, Robert H. Johnston and Co., 1860), Peck, Pritts, and Sipe. Retold by Peckham, pp. 116–32.[10]

In 1779, little Frances Slocum was carried away from her parents' home in the Wyoming Valley of Pennsylvania by Delawares. No information about her was obtained until 1837, when it was then learned that she had been adopted by an Indian couple. She had married twice and had had several children. When George W. Ewing stopped at an Indian cabin, he discovered that the woman there was the long lost Frances Slocum, who had been so happy with the savages that she would not return to her relatives. Her story is told in detail by William L. Stone and by the Reverend John Todd; the most complete narrative is by John P. Meginness. The many retellings of her tale indicate its popularity.

Stuart, Isaac. "Captain Isaac Stuart's Journey to the Westward." G. Hulbert Smith, ed. *Miss. Val. Hist. Rev.*, XXIII (1937), 555–59. Also in *The Affecting History of Dreadful Distresses . . .* and in Loudon.

The captivities of the 1780's were productive of more narratives than those of any other decade. Captured about fifty miles west of Fort Pitt in 1780, Captain Isaac Stuart was carried to the Wabash River and after about two years was hired from the Indians by a Spaniard, with whom he traveled west to the Mississippi and southwest from there. He dictated the brief account to J. C. Esquire.

Knight, Dr. John and John Slover [and Hugh H. Brackenridge]. *Narrative of a Late Expedition Against the Indians: with an Account of the Barbarous Execution of Col. William Crawford: and the Wonderful Escape of Dr. Knight and John Slover from Captivity* [Pamphlet] (Philadelphia, Printed by Francis Bailey, 1783).

———— *Indian Atrocities. Narratives of the Perils and Sufferings of Dr. John Knight and John Slover, among the Indians, during the Revolutionary War . . .* (Nashville, W. F. Bang and Co., 1843). Reprinted in Butterfield, DeHass, Doddridge, Heckewelder, Loudon, McClung, McKnight, McMechen, Metcalfe, *The Olden Time*, Pritts, Sargent, Spooner, Withers, and John Blair Linn, "The Sandusky Expedition," *Penna. Arch.*, 2nd Series, XIV (1892), 704–44. Retold by Peckham, pp. 133–46.

Serving in Colonel William Crawford's ill-fated expedition against the Hurons on the Sandusky River in 1782, Dr. John Knight was captured, along with Crawford and others, by Delaware Indians during the retreat. After the murder. of all the others, Knight escaped from a guard who was leading him to the Shawnee town of Wapatomica and walked to Fort McIntosh (Beaver, Pennsylvania). He reported the defeat to Fort Pitt the following day. Hugh Henry Brackenridge, father of Henry M. Brackenridge, persuaded Dr. Knight to write up an account of the captivity. Brackenridge also interviewed John Slover, a survivor of the battle, transcribed Slover's narrative, and submitted the two tales to a Philadelphia printer in 1782.[11] They went through several editions and were reprinted in many anthologies.

Rosenthal, Baron. "Journal of a Volunteer Expedition to Sandusky, from May 24 to June 13, 1782." *Penna. Mag. Hist. Biog.*, XVIII (1894), 129–57, 293–328.[12]

"Journal of Michael Walters, a Member of the Expedition against Sandusky in the Year 1782." J. P. MacLean, ed. *West. Res. Hist. Soc. Pubs.*, IV (1899), 177–88.

Details of the Crawford expedition of 1782 have been preserved in accounts other than the Knight and Slover narratives. One, written in diary form by Baron Rosenthal ("John Rose") of St. Petersburg, Russia, contains a description of the march made by the troops, a resumé of the tragedy, a criticism of the campaign, and an estimate of the value of the officers in the expedition. A journal by Michael Walters, who enlisted in Crawford's expedition as a youth, describes how he was captured by the Indians and finally arrived home in Pennsylvania by way of Canada. Poorly written; part is missing.

Janney, Abel. "Narrative of the Capture of Abel Janney by the Indians in 1782." *Ohio Arch. Hist. Quar.*, VIII (1900), 465–73.

On March 12, 1782, Abel Janney and two companions were attacked by four Indians and a white man, who killed his companions. The Indians tied a string around Janney's neck and made him carry provisions to an Indian camp. After several months he escaped and was led to Detroit by another tribe who turned him over to the whites. His diary of these events is carelessly written.

Biggs, William. *Narrative of the Captivity of William Biggs While He Was a Prisoner with the Kickapoo Indians, Then Living Opposite the Old Weawes Town on the West Bank of the Wabash River . . .* (Printed for the Author, 1826). Reprinted in *Ill. State Hist. Soc. Trans. for the Year 1902*, VII (1902), 202–15, and in "Heartman's Historical Series," No. 37 (New York, C. F. Heartman, 1922).

Ridout, Thomas. "An account of my Capture by the Shawanese Indians, dwelling on the River Ohio in North America, and of my Residence among them during the Spring and Part of the Summer of the year 1788." *Blackwood's Magazine,* CCXXIII (1928), 289–314.

William Biggs, a member of the George Rogers Clark Expedition against the British in 1788, was captured while marching with a young friend from Bellefontain, on the Mississippi, to nearby Cahokia, Illinois. The Kickapoos, who shot his companion and roped Biggs, eventually granted him great liberty and finally sold him to one of his friends at a nearby trading town. Some of the wording in the narrative is poor, but it contains many interesting episodes. Thomas Ridout, an Englishman, was captured in the same year by Shawnees on the Ohio River and endured many hardships during a march to Detroit, where he was released. He wrote a good account of his experiences.

Memoirs of Charles Dennis Rouso [Rusoe] *d'Eres, a Native of Canada: Who Was with the Scanyawtauragahrooote* [sic] *Indians Eleven Years, with a Particular Account of his Sufferings, &c. During his Tarry with Them, and his Safe Return to his family Connections in Canada* . . . (Exeter, Henry Ranlet, 1800).[13]

Largely unbelievable is Charles D. Rouso d'Eres' story of his long captivity from c.1788 to c.1799 among the "Scanyawtauragahrooote" Indians. He said that he was carried from Quebec to Michilimackinac and down the Red River, upon which he continued for forty days, and that during his captivity he saw Tartarrae in New Spain, discovered monkeys, and enjoyed many strange adventures before a safe return to Detroit, whose inhabitants took him for an Indian.

Tanner, John. *A Narrative of the Captivity and Adventures of John Tanner* (U. S. Interpreter at the Saut de Ste. Marie.) *During Thirty Years Residence among the Indians in the Interior of North America. Prepared for the Press by Edwin James* . . . (New York, G. and C. and H. Carvill, 1830). Popularized account in *Grey Hawk; Life and Adventures among the Red Indians* (Philadelphia, J. B. Lippincott and Co., 1883). A short account of the captivity in *A Collection of Indian Anecdotes* (Concord, N. H., William White, 1837).[14]

The captivity of John Tanner among the Ottawa and Ojibway Indians as recorded by Edwin James, a travel narrator to be discussed in Chapter 8, is only a small part of a lengthy work which covers many interesting adventures in a thirty-year residence, from 1789 to 1822, in many parts of the Midwest. During this time Tanner became extremely well acquainted with the Indian and his lore. In Michigan he met Governor Cass and was appointed Indian interpreter at the Sault. His exciting book was reprinted several times and translated into French (1835) and German (1840). An account of his captivity was included in William H. Keating's *Narrative of an Expedition* . . . (2 vols., 1823).[15]

Johnston, Charles. *A Narrative of the Incidents Attending the Capture, Detention, and Ransom of Charles Johnston, of Botetourt County, Virginia, Who Was Made Prisoner by the Indians, on the River Ohio, in the Year 1790; Together with an Interesting Account of the Fate of his Companions, Five in Number, One of Whom Suffered at the Stake* . . . (New York, J. and J. Harper, 1827). Reprinted in McKnight; edited by Edwin E. Spanks (Cleveland, Burrows Brothers Co., 1905).[16]

Spenser, Oliver M. *Indian Captivity; a True Narrative of the Capture of the Rev. O. M. Spencer by the Indians, in the Neighbourhood of Cincinnati. Written by Himself* (Cincinnati, Western Christian Advocate, 1834). First book-form publication at New York (B. Waugh and T. Mason, for the Sunday School Union of the Methodist Episcopal Church, 1835) and at Washington, Penna. (O. W. Brice, 1835). Reprinted in Spooner; edited by Milo M. Quaife (Chicago, R. R. Donnelley and Sons Co., 1917).[17]

Charles Johnston, a Virginian in the services of John May, was seized by Indians on the Ohio River in 1790. He was eventually bought by a white man and travelled down Lake Erie to the East. He stated that his book contained events which Rochefoucauld had inaccurately reported in his volume on America. It was reprinted in several anthologies.

O. M. Spencer's narrative was written forty years after the events described in it took place and hence lacks the value of a contemporary journal. Starting west in 1790, Spencer was captured by Indians on the Ohio River. He was purchased by the British, went to Detroit, and returned home by way of Niagara. He later became a minister and the account, which went through many editions, has an old-fashioned, religious flavor.

"Captivity of Israel Donaldson." *The American Pioneer,* I (1842), 425–33.

Johonnot, Jackson. *The Remarkable Adventures of Jackson Johonnot, of Massachusetts: Who Served as a Soldier in the Western Army, in the Massachusetts Line, in the Expedition under General Harmar, and the Unfortunate General St. Clair. Containing an Account of his Captivity, Sufferings, and Escape from the Kickapoo Indians* . . . (Lexington, 1791; Boston, Samuel Hall, 1793). Reprinted in *The Affecting History of Dreadful Distresses* . . . , Loudon, McClung (2nd ed.), McKnight, Mereness, Metcalfe, and Pritts.

Bunn, Matthew. *A Journal of the Adventures of Matthew Bunn, a Native of Brookfield, Massachusetts, Who Enlisted with Ensign John Tillinghast, of Providence, in the Year 1791, on an Espedition into the Western Country;—Was Taken by the Savages and Made his Escape into Detroit the 30th of April, 1792* . . . (Providence, R. I.; Litchfield, [Reprinted by Thomas Collier], 1796). Reprinted as "The Life and Adventures of Matthew Bunn," *Buffalo Hist. Soc. Pubs.,* VII (1904), 377–436.[18]

Laning, Paul F. "The Captivities and Escapes of John Miller and Daniel Convers, 1791–1794." *Inland Seas,* XII (1956), 86–94.

"Narrative of John Brickell's Captivity Among the Delaware Indians." *The American Pioneer,* I (1842), 43–56.

The well-written narrative of Israel Donaldson tells of his capture near Hamilton, Northwest Territory, in 1791, of being led to a Shawnee camp, and of his escape. Jackson Johonnot, an Englishman, wrote a short but rather sensational story of his capture by Kickapoos on the banks of the Wabash, and his escape to Fort Jefferson from the upper Miami River, all in 1791. The journal of Matthew Bunn, published several times, tells how the author was captured near the Big Miami River in the same year, was led north, and after much ill-treatment escaped to Detroit in 1792. Here he was accused of treason by the British and was sent to Niagara. He had many later adventures, all entertaining and historically valuable. Included in S. P. Hildreth's *Pioneer History* . . . (New York, 1848) are interesting stories of the captivities of John Miller, an Indian who lived with the whites but was captured by Indians in the Ohio region, and of Daniel Convers, who in 1791 was captured when still a boy and was not saved until years later. John Brickell was taken captive in western Pennsylvania in 1791, led to Sandusky and the Anglaise River, and liberated in 1795. These and later events, including his settlement in what is now Columbus, Ohio, in 1797, make good reading.

Hunter, John Dunn. *Manners and Customs of Several Indian Tribes Located West of the Mississippi; Including Some Account of the Soil, Climate, and Vegetable Productions, and the Indian Materia Medica; to Which Is Prefixed the History of the Author's Life During a Residence of Several Years among Them* (Philadelphia, J. Maxwell, 1823). Reprinted in *The Book of American Indians . . .* (Dayton, O., B. F. Ellis, 1854).

Written with pleasing simplicity is John D. Hunter's exceptionally interesting but largely fictitious account. He said he was captured as a child (about 1796) and spent many years with the Indians, migrating with them from the Illinois country to the Rockies, back to the convergence of the Kaw and the Missouri rivers, and then west again. His untrue stories of hearing Tecumseh and meeting Daniel Boone provoked a number of attacks,[19] but the book went through several editions, and a German translation was issued in 1824.[20]

Cutler, Jervis. *A Topographical Description of the State of Ohio, Indian Territory, and Louisiana; . . . to Which Is Added an Interesting Journal of Mr. Chas. LeRaye, While a Captive with the Sioux Nation, on the Waters of the Missouri River; by a Late Officer in the U. S. Army* (Boston, Charles Williams, 1812). LeRaye's captivity reprinted in "The Journal of Charles LeRaye," *Sou. Dak. Hist. Colls.,* IV (1908), 150–80.[21]

Only one known captivity journal, that by Charles LeRaye, was written about events which took place during the first decade of the nineteenth century. LeRaye left Canada in 1801 to trade on the Missouri River, where he was captured by Sioux Indians. There are some very readable descriptions of the Missouri, the Kaw, the Rocky Mountain regions and Indian customs.

Hutson, Austin. "Killed by the Indians." *Jour. Ill. State Hist. Soc.,* V (1912), 96–103.

Isaac Hutson and his family moved from Ohio to Crawford County, Illinois, in 1810. While he was away from home, Indians captured his wife and family inside the cabin and burned the dwelling with its living occupants. The story, though brief, is exceptionally well told.

"Extracts from a Diary Kept by Charles Askin." *Canadian Archives Publications,* No. 7 (1912), 235–48. Edited by Milo M. Quaife in *Miss. Val. Hist. Rev.,* I (1914–1915), 561–65; printed as "Charles Askin's Journal of the Detroit Campaign, July 24–September 12, 1812," in *Burton Hist. Recs.,* II (1931), 711–29.

Charles Askin's brief military diary is an eye-witness's account of the horrible treatment which the survivors of the Fort Dearborn massacre of 1812 received from the Indians on the road to Detroit.

Matson, Nehemiah. *Pioneers of Illinois Containing a Series of Sketches Relating to Events that Occurred Previous to 1813; Also Narratives of Many Thrilling Incidents Connected with the Early Settlement of the West, Drawn from History, Tradition and Personal Reminiscences* (Chicago, Knight and Leonard, 1882). Practically the same account of Mary Lee printed in Matson's *French and Indians of Illinois River* (Princeton, Ill., Republican Job Printing Establishment, 1874).

Pioneers of Illinois . . . , contains a story about two women, Mrs. Lee and Mary Lee (afterwards Mrs. Besson), who were made prisoners after the Chicago Massacre. The former was asked to marry a Waupekee who already had three wives, but

she was rescued by a trader who bought her from the Indians. In 1813, savages surrounded the house of a Mr. Wolsley near Cahokia, killed his wife and three children, burned the dwelling, and carried the child Amanda off into the Indian country. She escaped from an Indian village, was recaptured, but later was freed by the terms of a peace treaty. Both tales are short but interesting.

Kinzie, Juliette Augusta (Magill, Mrs. John R. Kinzie). *Waubun, the "Early Day" in the North-West . . .* (New York, Derby and Jackson; Cincinnati, H. W. Derby and Co., 1856). Reprint edited by Milo M. Quaife (Chicago, R. R. Donnelley and Sons Co., 1932).

Wau-bun contains some of the same events described in Matson's narratives. Mrs. Juliette A. Kinzie has included a story of the captivities of those taken in the Chicago massacre of 1812.[22] Most of the work, devoted to later events and travels, including sidelights on the Black Hawk War, is discussed in Chapter 10.

Darnell, Elias. *A Journal Containing an Accurate and Interesting Account of the Hardships, Sufferings, Battles, Defeat, and Captivity of Those Heroic Kentucky Volunteers and Regulars, Commanded by General Winchester, in the Years 1812–13. Also, Two Narratives, by Men that Were Wounded in the Battles on the River Raisin, and Taken Captive, by the Indians* (Paris, Ky., Printed by Joel R. Lyle, 1813). Reprinted by William Abbatt in *Mag. Hist. with Notes and Queries,* Extra Number VIII (1914), 183–253.[23]

Elias Darnell, in a military diary of the War of 1812, includes similar brief simple narratives by Timothy Mallary and John Davenport, who were wounded and captured in battle on the River Raisin in 1813. They were well treated and later escaped to Detroit.

H., G. "G. H. Escapes from Five Pottawattomie Indians in 1814." *Mich. Hist. Colls.,* XII (1888), 436–55.

G. H. has not been identified. An exciting and very readable account of his capture near the Mississippi River in 1814.

Lewis, Mrs. Hannah (Mrs. Jane Lewis). *Narrative of the Captivity and Sufferings of Mrs. Hannah Lewis, and her Three Children, Who Were Taken Prisoners by the Indians, near St. Louis, on the 25th May, 1815, and among Whom They Experienced All the Cruel Treatment Which Savage Brutality Could Inflict—Mrs. Lewis, and her Eldest Son Fortunately Made Their Escape . . . Leaving her Two Youngest Children in the Hands of the Unmerciful Barbarians* (Boston, Henry Trumbull, 1817).[24]

Swan, Mrs. Eliza. *An Affecting Account of the Tragical Death of Major Swan, and of the Captivity of Mrs. Swan and Infant Child by the Savages, in April Last—(1815). This Unfortunate Lady and her Little Son Were Taken Prisoners by the Indians, at a Small Village Near St. Louis, and Conveyed near 700 Miles Through an Uncivilized Wilderness, Where They Were Fortunately Redeemed by a Spanish Trader, in July Last* (Boston, H. Trumbull, 1815).[25]

A garbled reprint (1833) of Mrs. Lewis' brief but interesting book is probably the work of the person who compiled or wrote *Narrative of the Capture . . . of Misses Frances and Almira Hall.* Similar to Mrs. Lewis' book is the brief one by Mrs. Eliza Swan.

Narrative of the Capture and Providential Escape of Misses Frances and Almira Hall. Two Respectable Young Women (Sisters) of the Ages of 16 and 18—Who Were Taken Prison-

ers by the Savages at a Frontier Settlement, near Indian Creek, in May Last, When Fifteen of the Inhabitants Fell Victims to the Bloody Tomahawk and Scalping Knife; among Whom Were the Parents of the Unfortunate Females . . . (New York, William P. Edwards, 1832).

The sensationalized and inaccurate account of the captivity of the Hall girls was probably printed to arouse animosity toward the Fox and Sac Indian tribes, the remaining Indians who opposed the advance of Western migration.[26] Sylvia and Rachel Hall, who in the story are called Frances and Almira,[27] were actually captured, but the pamphlet about them was written from hearsay and is somewhat inaccurate. In 1832, after witnessing the murder of their parents, the girls were carried off and given as wives to two young chiefs. On the tenth day of their captivity they were ransomed by a band of Winnebagoes sent out by friends.

A Narrative of the Horrid Massacre by the Indians, of the Wife and Children of the Christian Hermit, a Resident of Missouri, with a Full Account of his Life and Sufferings, Never Before Published (St. Louis, Leander W. Whiting and Co., 1840).

Another anonymous narrative, also probably part of the anti-Indian propaganda of the period, is the story of "the Christian hermit." Settled in Missouri, he was captured in 1834. His property was confiscated and his wife, two sons and daughter were murdered, but he escaped with the help of an Indian friend. The pamphlet has a religious tone and was apparently based upon *The Narrative of the Massacre by the Savages of the Wife and Children of Thomas Baldwin . . .* (New York, 1835). The name of the hermit is said to be James B. Taylor.

Filley, William. *Life and Adventures of William Filley, Who Was Stolen from his Home in Jackson, Mich., by the Indians August 3d, 1837, and his Safe Return from Captivity, October 19, 1866, After an Absence of 29 Years* (Chicago, Filley and Ballard, 1867). Extract in *Harper's Mag.*, XXXV (1867), 631–33.
Filley's account is fraudulent but makes interesting reading.

Chapter 4

Earliest English-Language Travel Tales

on the Midwest, 1742–1775

The British settlers and their descendants who colonized the Atlantic Seaboard might have been satisfied to live comfortable existences where they were. Instead, many of them chose to forsake their homes and seek the western wilderness. One of the most important of the many reasons for the surge of immigration into the Midwest was the desire for material gain. Fur trading with the Indians was the first economic activity of the early frontiersmen. Homesteaders, eager to acquire cheap land, followed the traders. The youth of many of the colonists and the restlessness and dissatisfaction that often accompany youth also played a part in the desire to leave old ways of life and seek fame or new opportunities elsewhere. Sometimes it was poverty, a proprietor's foreclosure, a government's confiscation, or a criminal offense that made a man forsake the past.[1] The authors of the earliest journals listed below had such purposes as exploring, negotiating with or converting the Indians, surveying, or engaging in military campaigns.

The earliest English language travel journal was not composed until 1742, one hundred years after Father Barthelemy Vimont's account of Jean Nicolet's voyage into the Huron territory. The years from 1742 to 1775 are covered by thirty-eight accounts of Midwestern travel by the English. Although not great literature, they have preserved, as have no other documents, an interesting and romantic period. Such figures as Washington, Rogers, Carver, and Heckewelder were among the first to write in English about the frontier. From these beginnings has sprung an indigenous American literature.

All of the early Midwestern travel narratives were primarily utilitarian in purpose. Even those that were published during the lives of the authors could scarcely be classified as belles-lettres. Most of them were called journals and were written in diary form, with day-to-day entries. In content, nevertheless, they are generally interesting and of greater historical value than the majority of later tales.

Salley, John Peter. "Journal" in W. M. Darlington, ed. *Christopher Gist's Journals* (Pittsburgh, J. R. Weldin and Co., 1893); in Harrison Fairfax, "The Virginians on the Ohio and the Mississippi in 1742." *Va. Mag. Hist. Biog.*, XXX (1922), 211–22, and "A Brief Account of the Travels of John Peter Salley, a German Who Lives in the County of Augusta in Virginia," *La. Hist. Quar.*, V (1922), 323–32.[2]

The man who became a folk hero to people of the Blue Ridge Mountains, John Salley,[3] began his trip westward in 1742 at the invitation of a Mr. John Howard. Howard had been commissioned to go west and had obtained an Order of Council for ten thousand acres of land. With three other men, Salley and Howard journeyed down the Ohio and Mississippi rivers but were captured by the French at New Orleans. Salley made friends with a French prisoner who helped him escape. Except for Radisson's crude journals, Salley's account is the first known Middle Western travel narrative originally written in English. It is composed in simple language, partly in diary and partly in narrative form, and shows his appreciation of the spacious country along the Ohio River.

"The Journal of Conrad Weiser, Esqr., Indian Interpreter, to the Ohio." *Penna. Col. Recs.*, V, 348–58. Reprinted in *Early History of Western Pennsylvania* (Pittsburgh and Harrisburg, 1846), Appendix, pp. 13–23 and in R. G. Thwaites, ed., *Early Western Travels, 1748–1846* (32 vols., Cleveland, Arthur H. Clark Co., 1904), I, 15–44. Another reprinting, preserved among the family papers, was edited by Heister M. Muhlenberg in *Penna. Hist. Soc. Colls.*, I (1853), 23–33.[4]

Born in Germany, Conrad Weiser emigrated to the colonies, learned several Indian tongues, and became Indian interpreter for the first official embassy to the Indians beyond the Alleghenies. Some of the Indians had revolted, and his journal contains his speech to them as well as an account of the satisfactory settlement which he and George Croghan negotiated in 1748. Though many entries in the diary are mere jottings, certain parts of it show the author's literary skill.

Gist, Christopher. "A Journal of Christopher Gist's Journey, Begun . . . October 31, 1750, Continued down the Ohio, Within 15 Miles of the Falls Thereof. . . ." In *A Topographical Description of . . . North America* (London, Thomas Pownall, 1776). Reprinted in J. S. Johnston, ed. *First Explorations of Kentucky* (Louisville, John P. Morton and Co., 1898) and in Lois Mulkearu, *A Topographical Description . . .* (Pittsburgh, University of Pittsburgh Press, 1949). Extracts in Charles A. Hanna, *The Wilderness Trail . . .* (2 vols., New York and London, G. P. Putnam's Sons, 1911), II, 143–52.

———— Exploration Journal, July, 1751–March, 1752. [Exploration for the Ohio Company down the Ohio River to Big Kanawka.]

———— "Journal of Mr. Christopher Gist, Who Accompanied George Washington in his First Visit to the French Commander of the Troops on the Ohio, 1753." In *Mass. Hist. Soc. Colls.*, 3rd Series, V (1836), 101–08. This and the preceding journal by Gist in W. M. Darlington, ed. *Christopher Gist's Journals*.[5]

In 1750, Christopher Gist, a surveyor, began exploring for the Ohio Company, a rich corporation of landowners. He crossed the Ohio at the fork of the Muskingum River and by January, 1751, was at Shawneetown, on the Scioto. Warned that Indians favorable to the French would kill him if he continued westward, he turned back. Later the Ohio Company sent him out again, and Washington chose him as his guide when he went west in 1753. The first white American to make a careful exploration of the Ohio River lands in southern Ohio, Gist recognized the importance of the West and tried to win the Indians away from the French. His journals are written in diary form in simple prose.

Croghan, George. "Journal of 1751." In *Penna. Col. Recs.*, V, 530–36, and in part in N. B. Craig, *The Olden Time* (Pittsburgh, Dumars and Co., 1846; reprinted Cincinnati, 1876), I, 135–36. Reprinted in Israel D. Rupp, *Early History of Western Pennsylvania* (Pittsburgh, D. W. Kauffman; Harrisburg, W. O. Hickok, 1846), Appendix, pp. 75–98.

———— "Journal of 1754." *Penna. Col. Recs.*, V, 731–35, and Rupp, Appendix, pp. 50–53.

———— "George Croghan's Journal, 1759–1763." Nicholas B. Wainwright, ed., *Penna. Mag. Hist. Biog.*, LXXI (1947), 303–444.

———— "Journal of 1760–61." [Expedition under Major Robert Rogers to secure possession of Detroit and other Western posts.] *Mass. Hist. Soc. Colls.*, 4th Series, IX (1871), 362–79.

———— "Journal of 1765." In George W. Featherstonhaugh, *Monthly Journal of American Geology*, I (1831), 257–72; in a pamphlet published at Burlington, N. J., 1857; in Mann Butler, *History of the Commonwealth of Kentucky* (2nd ed., Cincinnati and Louisville, 1836), Appendix; and in *Ill. Hist. Colls.*, XI (1916), 1–64. Another version of the journals is published in E. B. O'Callaghan, *New York Colonial Documents*, VII (1856), 779–88, and a variant of this in Samuel P. Hildreth, *Pioneer History of the Ohio Valley* . . . (Cincinnati, H. W. Derby and Co.; New York, A. S. Barnes and Co., 1848), pp. 68–85, reprinted in *The New Regime, 1765–1767* (Springfield, Ill., Illinois State Historical Library, 1916). Thwaites used both versions in "A Selection of George Croghan's Letters and Journals Relating to Tours into the Western Country —November 1750–November, 1765," in *Early Western Travels*, I, 53–166, but he excluded the 1759–1763 journal.[6]

———— *George Croghan's Journal of His Trip to Detroit in 1767*. . . . Howard H. Peckham, ed. (Ann Arbor, University of Michigan Press, 1939).

George Croghan, an emigrant from Ireland, learned Indian languages and customs and traded with tribes on the frontier, but when the French opened hostilities against the English in 1752, his business was ruined. After assisting Washington and Braddock against the French, he was sent to open the Illinois country to English occupation. Captured by Indians near Shawneetown on the Ohio River, he was later released, met Pontiac, agreed upon a peace, and went to Detroit. There are two versions of his journals. One is "personal," detailed, and largely topographical; the other is the official report emphasizing Indian affairs. Although the writing itself is in diary form and is unpolished, addresses to the Indians and accounts of events of historical significance make interesting reading.

Journal of Captain William Trent from Logstown to Pickawillany, A.D. 1752 . . . Alfred E. Goodman, ed. (Cincinnati, R. Clarke and Co., 1871). Reprinted in C. A. Hanna, *The Wilderness Trail*, II, 291–98.[7]

Captain William Trent, an Indian trader who played an important part in a British attempt to build a fort where the French were constructing Fort Duquesne, also wrote a narrative of a trip from Wastown to Pickawillany which contained a good account of the Miami Indians in Ohio and reports of several speeches.

"Journal of Peter Pond." *Connecticut Magazine*, X (1906), 239–59. Reprinted in *Wis. Hist. Soc. Colls.*, XVIII (1908), 314–54, and in Charles M. Gates, ed. *Five Fur-Traders of the Northwest* . . . (Minneapolis, University of Minnesota Press, 1933), pp. 11–59. Extracts from Pond's journals in *Jour. Amer. Hist.*, I (1907), 89–93, 357–65.[8]

Famous for his exploration of northern Canada, Peter Pond spent the years from 1756 to 1775 in what is now the state of Wisconsin and in other parts of the Old Northwest. His autobiography contains an insight into himself and his period, as well as an account of the fur trade, of travel, and of contact with Indians. His spelling and vocabulary are interesting.

"Two Journals of Western Tours, by Charles [*sic*] Frederick Post: One, to the Neighborhood of Fort Duquesne (July–September, 1758); the Other, to the Ohio (October, 1758–January, 1759)." First journal in Charles Thomson, *An Enquiry into the Causes of the Alienation of the Delaware and Shawanese Indians from the British Interests* (London, 1759; Philadelphia, 1867), pp. 130–71. Reprinted in Robert Proud, *The History of Pennsylvania* . . . (Philadelphia, Zachariah Poutson, Jr., 1798), II, Appendix, 65–95; Israel D. Rupp, II, Appendix, 75–98; Craig, I, 99–125; *Penna. Arch.*, 1st Series, III (1853), 520–44; and R. G. Thwaites, I, 185–233.

———— *The Second Journal* . . . (London, J. Wilkie, 1759). Reprinted in Proud, II, Appendix, 96–132; Rupp, II, Appendix, pp. 99–126; and Craig, I, 145–77.[9]

Christian Frederick Post, a German-born Moravian, was the first English-speaking missionary to the Indians to write journals of Midwestern trips. His two journals describe journeys to Ohio, the first in 1758 and the second in 1758–1759. They emphasize the hazards of frontier travel, Indian hostilities, and the desolate condition of the country. The language of the printed journals has been modernized from German-English.

"Lieut. [Diederick] Brehm's Report to his Excellency General Amherst of a Scout Going from Montreal by LaGalette—round part of the North Shore of Lake Ontario to Niagara, from thence round the South Shore of Lake Erie to Detroit, up Lake St. Claire and part of Lake Huron, returning by land to Fort Pitt." *New Eng. Hist. Geneal. Rec.*, XXXVII (1883), 22–26.

"Thompson Maxwell's Narrative—1760–1763." *Wis. Hist. Soc. Colls.* XI (1888), 213–17. In Benjamin Gleason, *Narrative of the Military Life of Major Thompson Maxwell, of Massachusetts, 1757–1820* (Boston, D. Clapp and Sons, 1891).

Brief journals written by Lieutenant Diederick Brehm and Major Thompson Maxwell, who accompanied Major Robert Rogers on his expedition against Detroit. The former details the trip in 1760–1761 up the St. Lawrence River and through Lakes Ontario and Erie to Detroit and thence up Lake St. Clair and part of Lake Huron and the return by land to Fort Pitt. Written in the first person, it describes the lakes and shores, the soil at Detroit, and swamps near Sandusky. Maxwell proceeded farther west, visiting Mackinac, crossing Lake Superior in 1762, and reached the site of present Chicago in 1763. His readable narrative gives an account of Pontiac's attack upon Fort Mackinac and tells of his stay at Detroit.

Rogers, Robert. *Diary of the Siege of Detroit in the War with Pontiac*. Franklin B. Hough, ed. (Albany, 1860).

—— *Journals of Major Robert Rogers; Containing an Account of the Several Excursions He Made Under the Generals Who Commanded upon the Continent of North America . . .* (London, Printed for the Author, 1765). Expanded edition, Franklin B. Hough, ed. (Albany, J. Munsell's Sons, 1883).

—— "Journal of Robert Rogers . . . on his Expedition for Receiving the Capitulation of Western French Forts." *Bulletin of the New York Public Library*, XXXVII (1933), 265–76. [Corrects errors in previous editions.]

—— "Journal Sept. 1766–July, 1767." *Amer. Ant. Soc. Procs.*, New Series, XXVIII (1918), 224–73.[10]

Perhaps none of the travel narrators led a more exciting life than the American-born Major Robert Rogers, a man of strange moral contrasts. After spectacular exploits as captain of an independent company of rangers, he was sent by the British to receive the surrender of the French at Detroit in 1760. In 1766 he gained the command of Fort Mackinac, where he lived for two years. His influence upon Jonathan Carver's work was great and he commissioned him to undertake an exploratory journey into the present state of Minnesota. The latter part of Roger's life was a tragedy: he was accused of treason and fled to England, where he died in obscurity. His Western journals, though awkward in style, give a vivid picture of the Great Lakes region and of Indian trade.

"Lieut. James Gorrell's Journal." *Wis. Hist. Soc. Colls.*, I (1854; 1903 reprint), 25–48.

James Gorrell's factual but readable military diary begins at Detroit in 1761 and ends at Montreal in 1763. It describes several councils held with Indians and shows the corruption of the Indians by the French Canadians and the means used to incite them against the English.

Hutchins, Thomas. "Travel Journal [1762]." In Charles A. Hanna, *The Wilderness Trail*, II, 362–67.

—— *A Topographical Description of Virginia, Pennsylvania, Maryland, and North Carolina, Comprehending the Rivers Ohio, Kenhawa, Sioto, Cherokee, Wabash, Illinois, Mississippi, &c. . . . And an Appendix, Containing Mr. Patrick Kennedy's Journal up the Illinois River, and a Correct List of the Different Nations and Tribes of Indians, . . .* (London, Printed and Sold by J. Almon, 1778). Extracts in "Journal from Fort Pitt to the Mouth of the Ohio in the Year 1768." *Ind. Hist. Soc. Pubs.*, II (1895), 417–21.[11]

Thomas Hutchins, a captain in the British army, was sent by George Croghan to posts on the Western lakes and to the Wabash and Scioto to hold councils with Indians as early as 1762. His book, *A Topographical Description*, which recounts his experiences in the Midwest in 1766 and in 1768–1770, is one of the most valuable sources for events in the Illinois country during the British period. Patrick Kennedy's journal of an expedition up the Illinois River in 1773, will be discussed later in this chapter.

Porteous, John. Diary from Niagara to Detroit, June 26–30, 1762. In the John Porteous Papers. MS. Burton Historical Collection, Detroit Public Library.

—— Diary on trip from Schenectady to New York, Schenectady, Detroit, Mackinac, L'Arbre Croche, St. Marys, Channel Islands, St. Ignace, Mackinac, Mar. 15, 1765–May 23, 1766. Burton Historical Collection. Published in part in "Schenectady to Michilimackinac, 1765 & 1766," *Ontario Historical Society Papers and Records*, XXXIII (1939), 75–98.

—— Diary from Mackinac to Detroit, Sept. 17–27, 1766. MS. Burton Historical Collection.

—— Journal from Detroit to Schenectady, Oct. 23–Dec. 2, 1766. MS. Burton Historical Collection.

—— Diary from Schenectady to Mackinac, with Alexander Ellice, April 20–June 6, 1767. Burton Historical Collection. Printed in *Historical Bulletin, No. 2, Algonquin Club of Detroit* (Mar., 1938). Reprinted in "From Fort Niagara to Mackinac in 1767." F. Clever Bald, ed. *Inland Seas*, II (1946), 86–97.

—— Diary from Mackinac to St. Marys and Detroit, July 17–Aug. 4, 1771. MS. Burton Historical Collection.

The manuscripts of the American travel diaries of John Porteous consist of eight volumes of notes, papers, and letters. Porteous, a Scotchman, traveled extensively in the Great Lakes region while he was engaged in the fur trade. The descriptions of the weather, geography, and business associates are detailed and are of historical value, but only parts of them have been published.

Hay, Lieut. Jehu. *Diary of the Siege of Detroit*. F. B. Hough, ed. (Albany, 1860).

The story of Pontiac's siege of Detroit in 1763 is preserved in two known diaries. Lieutenant Jehu Hay wrote a military journal which is valuable for fullness of detail. The other work, in French, probably by Robert Navarre, has been discussed in Chapter 2.

"An Historical Account of Colonel Bouquet's Expedition Against the Ohio Indians in the Year 1764" and "Notes of the Settlement of the Country along the Monongahela, Alleghany, and Upper Ohio River and their Tributaries." In Craig, I, 217–21, 241–60. Reprinted as *Historical Account of Bouquet's Expedition . . .* with an introduction by Francis Parkman (Cincinnati, Robert Clarke and Co., 1868), pp. 45–88.[12]

The unsatisfactory relations existing between the Indians and British after the Conspiracy of Pontiac are reflected in a journal by Colonel Henry Bouquet and in an account of his expedition in 1764 against the Ohio Indians. The diary tells how he crossed the Muskingum River, rebuked the Indians, and secured the return of prisoners. It is evident that Bouquet treated the Indians firmly but justly.

Fraser, Lieut. Alexander. Letter from Fraser to General Thomas Gage dated Illinois, 27 April 1765. 30 pp. MS. in the Gage Papers. William L. Clements Library, University of Michigan, Ann Arbor.

Pittman, Philip. *The Present State of the European Settlements on the Mississippi; with a Geographical Description of that River . . .* (London, J. Nourse, 1770).

In an unpublished thirty-page letter to General Thomas Gage in April, 1765, Lieutenant Alexander Fraser, a British army officer, describes a trip from Fort Pitt to Fort Chartres which he undertook to promote friendly relations with the Indians.

Pittman's *The Present State of the European Settlements on the Mississippi* contains descriptions of the Illinois and Missouri country. Pittman was an engineer with the British troops and made surveys and investigations in the Midwest during the last part of 1765. The work is valuable but not entirely reliable.

[Barthe, Charles André?] Diary of a Journey into the Indian Country, 1765–1766. MS. Burton Historical Collection.[13]

One of the earliest unpublished manuscripts of Midwestern travel is a diary, probably by a man named Charles Andre Barthe, of a trip into the Miami, Wabash, and White River regions and then to Detroit in 1765–1766.

Beatty, Rev. Charles. *The Journey of a Two-Months' Tour; with a View of Promoting Religion among the Frontier Inhabitants of Pennsylvania and of Introducing Christianity among the Indians to the Westward of the Alegheny Mountains. To Which Are Added Remarks on the Language and Customs of Some Particular Tribes among the Indians . . .* (London, William Davehill and George Pearch, 1766).[14]

Charles Beatty, a Presbyterian clergyman, undertook a trip in 1766 to the Muskingum, then far beyond the frontier, in an attempt to convert the Indians to Christianity. His account is written in diary form and makes interesting reading. A Swedish translation was published at Stockholm in 1772.

"Journal of Captain Harry Gordon's Journey from Pittsburg down the Ohio and Mississippi to New Orleans, Mobile, and Pensacola, 1766." In Thomas Pownall, *Topographical Description of . . . North America . . .* (London, 1776); reprinted at Pittsburgh (University of Pittsburgh Press, 1949). Extracts in *Jour. Ill. State Hist. Soc.*, II (1909), 55–64, and in *Mo. Hist. Soc. Colls.*, III (1911), 437–43; reprinted in full at London (1911), partly in Charles Hanna, *The Wilderness Trail*, II, 40–55, and in Newton D. Mereness, ed. *Travels in the American Colonies* (New York, Macmillan Co., 1916).[15]

Captain Harry Gordon's Journal, "Being an Account of an expedition made by him down the Ohio River and up the Mississippi to St. Louis in 1776, with some account of St. Louis by J. Stoddard Johnson." 14 pp., transcript. Durrett Collection, University of Chicago Library.

Several of the journals of the period after Pontiac's Conspiracy show an interest in conciliating the Indians and winning their friendship. Captain Harry Gordon, a Scotchman by birth and Chief Engineer in the Western Department in British North America, was sent down the Ohio and Mississippi in 1766, accompanied by George Croghan, to look over the defense system and to propose means of securing the Indian trade for the English in the territory from which the French had been expelled. His diary contains an accurate description of the rivers and adjacent lands. The brief journal of the journey down the Ohio and up the Mississippi remains unpublished.

Clarkson, Matthew. "Diary West of the Alleghanies, in 1766." In Henry R. Schoolcraft, *Information Respecting the History, Conditions, and Prospects of the Indian Tribes of the United States* (Philadelphia, J. P. Lippincott, 1851–1857), IV 265–78.[16]

Morgan, George. "Voyage Down the Mississippi, November 21, 1766–December 18, 1766." In C. W. Alvord and C. E. Carter, *The New Regime, 1765–1767, Ill. Hist. Colls.*, XI (1916), 438–47.

———— "Morgan's Journal, September 30, 1767–November 1, 1767." In C. W. Alvord and C. E. Carter, *Trade and Politics, 1767–1769, Ill. Hist. Colls.*, XVI (1921), 67–71.[17]

Matthew Clarkson, an agent for Indian traders, wrote brief notes during the 1766–1767 period describing Indian customs and social and trade conditions in the Middle West. He traveled from Fort Pitt to Fort Chartres and Kaskaskia. George Morgan, another Indian agent and a land speculator, undertook a venture into the Illinois country in the interests of the firm by which he was employed. His 1766 journal tells of a trip down the Mississippi from Kaskaskia, and the 1767 diary describes a journey from Philadelphia to Mingo Town, on the Ohio River. Morgan became known as a leader in the movement for the establishment of a civil government in the Illinois country.

Carver, Jonathan. *Travels through the Interior Parts of North-America, in the Years 1766, 1767, and 1768* (London, Printed for the Author, 1778).[18]

One of the most popular of all travel books was Jonathan Carver's *Travels*, which rapidly ran through twenty-three editions. Carver, the first English-speaking traveler to explore west of the Mississippi, was born in Weymouth, Massachusetts, served in the war with France, and explored as far west as the present state of Minnesota in 1767. In 1769 he went to England to publish his journal but failed to secure expected assistance from the government and was forced to earn his living as a hack-writer. The journal remained unpublished until 1778, two years before Carver's death. In spite of its borrowings and occasionally incredible stories, it shows imagination, and the descriptions received the praise of the poet, Coleridge.

"John Jennings 'Journal from Fort Pitt to Fort Chartres in the Illinois Country,' March–April, 1766." *Penna. Mag. Hist. Biog.*, XXXI (1907), 145–56. Reprinted in C. W. Alvord and C. E. Carter, *The New Regime, 1765–1767, Ill. Hist. Colls.*, XI (1916), 167–77.

"John Jennings Journal at Fort Chartres and Trip to New Orleans, 1768." *Penna. Mag. Hist. Biog.*, XXXI (1907), 304–10. Extract in C. W. Alvord and C. E. Carter, *Trade and Politics, 1767–1769, Ill. Hist. Colls.*, XVI (1921), 336–39.[19]

John Jennings was a soldier in the Revolution and a prominent figure in the Pennamite War in Pennsylvania. His first journal is an account of a trading expedition down the Ohio River and up the Mississippi in 1766 and includes descriptions of French villages. The 1768 journal is similar, telling of experiences in the Illinois country, followed by a trip down the Mississippi.

Lees, John. *Journey of J. L., of Quebec, Merchant* (Detroit, Society of Colonial Wars of the State of Michigan, Speaker-Hines Press, 1911).[20]

Taylor, G. *A Voyage to North America Perform'd by G. Taylor, of Sheffield, in the Years 1768, and 1769; . . . up the River Mississippi, to the Illinois, and down from Fort Chartres, over the Ohio River . . .* (Nottingham, S. Cresswell for the Author, 1771).[21]

John Lees, living at Quebec as early as 1764, took a trip up Lake Erie to Detroit and back from April to October, 1768. In his journal he describes Indian tribes and hunting and weather conditions. Although disjointed and weak, his writing is interesting, partly because it mentions such people as Robert Rogers. G. Taylor's *A Voyage to North America* devotes little space to the frontier but includes an account of a trip up the Mississippi and Ohio rivers. It is important because it was one of the first works to recommend the Middle West for British colonization.

Washington, George. "Remarks & Occurs in October" and "Where & how—my time is—Spent." Printed as *Tour of the Ohio*. In the *Virginia Almanack*. Reprinted in Worthington Chauncey Ford, ed. *The Writings of George Washington* (New York and London, G. P. Putnam's Sons, 1889), II, 285–

316; in John C. Fitzpatrick, ed. *The Diaries of George Washington, 1748–1799* (Boston and New York, Houghton Mifflin Co., 1925), I, 412–42, *passim;* and in Archer B. Hulbert, "Washington's 'Tour of the Ohio' and Articles of 'The Mississippi Company,'" *Ohio Arch. Hist. Quar.*, XVII (1908), 431–88.

George Washington and the West; Being George Washington's Diary of September, 1784, Kept During his Journey into the Ohio Basin in the Interest of a Commercial Union Between the Great Lakes and the Potomac River, and Commentary upon the Same by Archer Butler Hulbert . . . (New York, The Century Co., 1905).[22]

Washington's interest in the West had its origin in actual trips to the frontier. The printed version of hastily written notes of a trip with Christopher Gist in 1753–1754 shows that young Washington had penetrated as far west as western Pennsylvania and the Ohio River.[23] A diary of a trip up the Ohio River and a brief stay at Mingo Town is said to have been written in 1760. More significant is his description of a tour of the Ohio country in 1770 for the purpose of acquiring Western land by personal purchase. He journeyed from Mount Vernon to Great Meadows, Pennsylvania, and as far west as thirty-two miles from the mouth of the Muskingum River. Records of this trip have survived in two journals, one written in crude fragments and the other in greater detail. Since he did not intend to publish these diaries, Washington made no attempt to write in a literary style. His notes are, however, the most detailed early descriptions in English of the Ohio region. In 1784 he wrote a diary of his journey into the Ohio basin for the purpose of finding a way of uniting the Great Lakes and the Potomac River. This interest in the commercial potentialities of the West undoubtedly helped form his faith in his country's destiny.

Jones, Rev. David. *A Journal of Two Visits Made to Some Nations of Indians on the West Side of the River Ohio in the Years 1772 and 1773* (Burlington, N. J., Isaac Collins, 1774). Reprinted in *Sabin's Reprints* No. 11 (New York, 1865).[24]

The Reverend David Jones, a native of the state of Delaware, studied many years for the ministry before being ordained and before making unsuccessful attempts to convert the Indians of the Ohio country. With George Rogers Clark and Thomas Hutchins, he traveled on the Ohio River and preached to the Shawnees at Chillicothe and to the Delawares on the Muskingum from May, 1772 to April, 1773. Although he possessed a keen intellect and had versatile abilities, his book lacks literary merit because of a careless style and a pervasive religious tone. His pictures of Indian life are interesting, however. He speaks, for instance, of polygamy and cruelty among the Shawnees. His partially published journal of 1796 will be described in Chapter 5.

Hite, Isaac. "Journal of Isaac Hite, 1773." Virginia C. Hall, ed. *Hist. Phil. Soc. of Ohio Bull.*, XII (1954), 263–81.

Kennedy, Patrick. *Journal of an Expedition Undertaken by Himself and Several Coureurs de Bois in the Year 1773, from Kaskaskia Village, in the Illinois Country, to the Head Waters of the Illinois River.* In Thomas Hutchins, *A Topographical Description . . .* (1778).[25]

Lacey, John. "Journal of a Mission to the Indians in Ohio by Friends from Pennsylvania—July–September, 1773." *Historical Magazine*, Second Series, VII (1870), 103–7.[26]

Macelner, David. "An Abstract of the Journal of a Mission to the Delaware Indians, West of the Ohio." In Eleazar Wheelock, *A Continuation of the Narrative of the Indian Charity-school, Begun in Lebanon, in Connecticut . . .* (New Hampshire, 1773), pp. 44–68.[27]

"Extracts from the Journal of John Parrish, 1773." *Penna. Mag. Hist. Biog.*, XVI (1892), 443–48.[28]

One journal by a member of a surveying party, one narrative of exploration, and three missionary journals contain accounts of Middle Western travel experiences during 1773. Isaac Hite described surveying activities in the Ohio Valley region. Patrick Kennedy told of a search for copper mines he and several other scouts made, starting from Kaskaskia and proceeding to the headwaters of the Illinois River. He included observations on the country and lists of Indian tribes. John Lacey, a Quaker, wrote a brief diary of a missionary journey from Pennsylvania to the Indians of Ohio. Similar are David Macelner's account of a missionary journey to the Muskingum Valley and Quaker John Parrish's travel journal of a missionary trip from Lancaster, Pennsylvania, down the Ohio and back. Parrish's unpublished journal of 1795 will be discussed in Chapter 6.

Heckewelder, John Gottlieb. *A Narrative of the Mission of the United Brethren among the Delaware and Mohegan Indians, from its Commencement, in the Year 1740, to the Close of the Year 1808 . . .* (Philadelphia, McCarty and Davis, 1820).

———— "A Canoe Journey from the Big Beaver to the Tuscarawes in 1773; A Travel Diary of John Heckewaelder." August C. Mahr, trans. and ed. *Ohio Arch. Hist. Quar.*, LXI (1952), 283–98.

———— *Reise von Bethlehem in Pennsilvania bis zum Wabashfluss im Nordwestlichen Gebiet der Vereinigten Staaten von Nordamerika . . .* (Halle, Renger, 1797). In M. C. Sprengel, *Auswahl der Besten Ausländischen und Statistischen Nachrichten zur Aufklärung der Volker- und Landerkunde*, VII, 1–94. Extracts in *Penna. Mag. Hist. Biog.*, XI (1887), 466–75; XII (1888), 34–54, 165–84.

———— "Map and Description of Northeastern Ohio . . . in 1796." Charles C. Baldwin, ed. *Mag. West. Hist.*, I (1884), 109–14. Reprinted in *Western Reserve and Northern Ohio Historical Society Tract* No. 64 (Cleveland, O., W. W. Williams, 1884).

"Notes of Travel of William Henry, John Heckewelder, John Rothrock, and Christian Clewell, to Gnadenhuetten on the Muskingum, in the Early Summer of 1797." *Penna. Mag. Hist. Biog.*, X (1886), 125–57.[29]

Among the important early missionary diaries of the Midwest are those of Johann Gottlieb Heckewelder, son of a Moravian exile from England. Heckewelder became a missionary in 1771 at the age of twenty-eight and two years later was captured by the Indians and British and taken to Sandusky and finally to Detroit. After a temporary residence at Cuyahoga, he went back to Pennsylvania in 1786 but later returned to Ohio, where he resided as a missionary until 1810. It has been said that his writings were to Ohio what those of the Jesuits were to the farther west. His book is history first hand. His romantic faith in the natural goodness of the Indians was unrealistic and aroused the unfavorable criticism of such people as Lewis Cass,[30] although it undoubtedly influenced the attitude of the novelist, James Fenimore Cooper.

Fleming, Col. William. Journal of the Point Pleasant Campaign, 1774, including Journal of Travel in Kentucky, 1779–1780 and 1783. MS., 112 pp., partially published. Durrett Collection, University of Chicago Library. The Kentucky journal in N. D. Mereness, ed. *Travels in the American Colonies* (New York, Macmillan Co., 1916), pp. 615–74.

Whittlesey, Charles. "Lord Dunmore's Expedition to the Scioto Towns, 1774" (Cleveland, Sandford and Co., 1842). Reprinted in *Fugitive Essays . . . Relating to the Early History of Ohio . . .* (Hudson, O., Sawyer, Ingersoll and Co., 1852), pp. 126–54.

Memoirs and Adventures of Captain Matthew Phelps, . . . Particularly in Two Voyages, from Connecticut to the River Mississippi, from December 1773 to October 1780 . . . Compiled from the Original Journal and Minutes Kept by Mr. Phelps . . . by Anthony Haswell (Bennington, Vt., Anthony Haswell, 1802).

The Journal of Nicholas Cresswell, 1774–1777 (New York, 1924). Selections in Mark Van Doren, *An Autobiography in America* (New York, A. and C. Boni, 1929), 108–21. Summary in *National Review* (London), XC (1927), 122–32.[31]

Colonel William Fleming wrote of his activities in the Point Pleasant Campaign of 1774, a battle near the upper Ohio between whites and Indians in which he was wounded three times. Years later, Charles Whittlesey wrote the story of the British Lord Dunmore's march to the Ohio and a battle near Point Pleasant. Intent on destroying Indian towns on the Scioto River, Dunmore advanced into the Ohio country, reached an agreement making the Ohio River the Indians' eastern boundary, and returned to Virginia. The *Memoirs and Adventures of Captain Matthew Phelps,* which are devoted mainly to sea journeys, show that Phelps was not in the Midwest until 1774. A journal expressing antagonism to the cause of the American Revolutionaries and the propaganda of the period is that written during the years 1774–1777 by a young Englishman, Nicholas Cresswell, who, after visiting some of the Eastern states, made an unsuccessful trading trip along the Ohio River. It contains good observations on people and places.

Chapter 5

Midwestern Travel Narratives of the Revolutionary

War Period to the First Presidential Election,

1775–1789

With the advent of the American Revolution, a sudden decrease in the number of Middle Western travel tales becomes evident. Attention shifted to the east coast, where most of the war took place, and travel into the interior was largely forgotten.[1] A new era had begun. The figure who dominates the history of the Western frontier during this period is George Rogers Clark; and, fortunately, his journal, those of some of his associates, and that of Colonel Hamilton, who was British governor of the Northwest during the Revolution, have been preserved. After the war, since incentives for settlement of the Northwest Territory were great, the number of travel accounts again increased.

Long, John. *Voyages and Travels of an Indian Interpreter and Trader, Describing the Manners and Customs of the North American Indians; with an Account of the Posts Situated on the River Saint Laurence, Lake Ontario, &c. . . .* (London, Printed for the Author, 1791). Reprinted in R. G. Thwaites, ed. *Early Western Travels . . .* (32 vols., Cleveland, Arthur H. Clark Co., 1904), Vol. II; edited by Milo M. Quaife (Chicago, R. R. Donnelley and Sons Co., 1922).

After serving briefly in the Revolution, John Long, a British subject, set out to engage in the Northwest fur trade, going to Mackinac by way of Lake Erie and Lake Huron in the spring of 1777 and traveling as far as Lake Superior and Canada. He learned the Chippewa vocabulary before returning to join the combined British and Indian expedition to Prairie du Chien in the spring of 1780, after which we went to Montreal. Simple and direct in style, his book gives one of the few pictures of the frontier during the first half of the Revolution.

Journal of [Lieut. Gov.] *Henry Hamilton.* John D. Barnhart, ed. (Crawfordsville, Ind., R. E. Banta, 1951). Extracts in A. B. Hulbert, *Historical Highways of America* (16 vols., Cleveland, A. H. Clark Co., 1902–1905), VII, 170–75.[2]

Colonel Henry Hamilton, stationed at Detroit, is an important figure in the history of the Revolution because in late 1778 he captured Fort Vincennes, a key station previously won from the British by George Rogers Clark. It was retaken by Clark in February 1779, however, and Hamilton himself was sent to Virginia as a prisoner of war. This part of the frontier, except for Detroit, which remained in British hands, was organized as Illinois

County, Virginia.[3] Hamilton's diary describes his journey during October and November 1778, along the Wabash route to Vincennes.

Clark, Col. George Rogers. "George Rogers Clark Papers, 1771–1781." James A. James, ed. *Ill. Hist. Colls.*, VIII (1912), 114–54, 164–74, 208–302. The 1779 journal in *Amer. Hist. Rev.*, I (1895), 90–96. The Clark journals are reprinted as *The Conquest of the Illinois* (Chicago, R. R. Donnelley and Sons Co., 1920).[4]

"Journal of Joseph Bowman." *Ill. Hist. Colls.*, VIII (1912), 155–64.[5]

Because of his successful campaigns against the British, Clark has become an American hero. From Governor Patrick Henry of Virginia he obtained a commission to lead an expedition against the British ports north of the Ohio River. With a force of fewer than two hundred men, he set out in May 1778 from Wheeling, went down the Ohio, and marched to and captured Kaskaskia and Cahokia, towns on the Mississippi. In February 1779, he took Vincennes, Governor Hamilton himself, as noted above, being among the prisoners. Clark was unable to proceed against Detroit, however, because of his inadequate force. Part of his journal, written in a simple and unliterary style, tells of his march to Kaskaskia and later activities in the Illinois country.

The only known journal written by one of Clark's men is that by Major Joseph Bowman, a young Virginian. It is a brief diary covering the period from January to March 1779, and tells of Clark's march on Fort Vincennes and his capture of the post.

"Personal Narrative of William Lytle." *Hist. Phil. Soc. of Ohio Quar. Pubs.*, I (1906), 3–30.[6]

After leaving Pennsylvania for Virginia in 1779 with his father, William Lytle descended the Ohio and settled near Beargrass at the Falls of the Ohio. Among other incidents in his interesting narrative he describes a search for buffalo, an encounter with a bear, and a meeting with Indians. Lytle was the great-grandfather of William Harris Lytle, the poet.

"John Filson's Narrative of his Defeat on the Wabash, 1780." Leonard C. Helderman, ed. *Filson Club History Quarterly*, XII (1938), 187–99.[7]

John Filson, prominent early Kentucky settler and narrator of the Daniel Boone Indian captivity tale, tells an interesting story about a trip in 1780 from Post St. Vincent to relieve inhabitants of the Wabash River region who were besieged by Indians. His party was forced to retreat and escaped by means of a raft, which, however, split in the water. Only after a painful seven-day journey did they reach the Falls of the Ohio. The tale holds the reader's attention and is well written.

Harrow, Capt. Alexander. "Visits to the Shipyard." *Burton Hist. Coll. Leaflets*, II (1924), 26–29.[8]

Anderson, Lieut. Isaac. "Journal." In James McBride, *Pioneer Biography. Sketches of the Lives of Some of the Early Settlers of Butler County, Ohio* (2 vols., Cincinnati, R. Clarke and Co., 1869), I, 278–85. Reprinted in *Loughery's Defeat and Pigeon Root Massacre, with Introductory Sketch.* Charles Martindale, ed. (Indianapolis, Bowen-Merrill Co., 1888). Extracts in *Penna. Arch.*, 2nd Series, XIV, 685–90 and in *Ohio Arch. Hist. Society Publications*, VI (1898), 389–92.[9]

Diary of David Zeisberger. E. F. Bliss, ed. (2 vols., Cincinnati, 1885). Extracts in *Ontario Historical Society Papers and Records*, XII (1914), 176–98.[10]

Alexander Harrow, a captain in the British navy, wrote a log-book recording his visits to the king's shipyard at Detroit from August to November 1781. Extracts from it have been printed. Lieutenant Isaac Anderson's journal of 1781–1782 is mainly an account of Loughery's expedition into Ohio, giving only bare details of an Indian ambush and captivity. David Zeisburger arrived on the Muskingum in May 1772, where he eventually became the patriarch of the Christian colony there. He described his life and missionary work in various Ohio and Michigan towns during the years 1781–1798 in a lengthy journal, which is similar to other Moravian diaries. John Heckewelder supplemented this account by mentioning Zeisburger's activities in the West until 1776 in *A Narrative of the Mission of the United Brethren among the Delaware and Mohegan Indians . . .* (Philadelphia, 1820).

"A Jornal [*sic*] Kept by Wm. Kelso" of a Trip down the Ohio and Mississippi Rivers with a Cargo of Flour, 1782. 12 pp. MS. Listed in Elizabeth Biggert, comp. *Guide to the Manuscript Collections in the Library of the Ohio State Archaeological and Historical Society* (Columbus, 1953), No. 585.

William Kelso ventured down the Ohio and Mississippi rivers in 1782 for the purpose of transporting a cargo of flour. His brief journal describing the trip is the only known unpublished Midwestern travel narrative of the Revolutionary War period.

McCully, George. "The Itinerary of [Ephraim] Douglass's Journey to Detroit." *Mag. Hist.*, Extra Numbers, III (1910), 39–49.[11]

The purpose of Ephraim Douglass' journey from the East across Ohio to Detroit in June and July 1783 was to notify the Indians at Detroit of the terms of peace after the Revolutionary War. The printed part of George McCully's diary describes his crossing the Scioto River and meeting Indian tribes.

Perrault, Jean B. "Narrative of the Travels and Adventures of a Merchant Voyageur in the Savage Territories of Northern America Leaving Montreal the 28th of May 1783 (to 1820)." John S. Fox, ed. *Mich. Hist. Colls.*, XXXVII (1909–1910), 508–619. Extracts in Henry Rowe Schoolcraft, *History of the Indian Tribes . . .* (Philadelphia, Lippincott, Grambo, and Co., 1857).[12]

Jean B. Perrault, a French-Canadian, wrote a journal in French briefly describing a fur trading expedition from Mackinac to St. Louis and Cahokia during the winter of 1783–1784 and his return in the spring. Later he engaged in trade on the Chippewa and Upper Mississippi and for twelve years after 1793 he was employed by the Northwest Company. At Mackinaw during 1811–1812, becoming despondent because his employers turned against him, he engaged himself to the Hudson's Bay Company. He later moved to the Sault, where he remained until his death in 1844. The narrative, probably written from diaries, is long and detailed.

Smyth, John F. D. *A Tour in the United States of America; Containing an Account of the Present Situation of that Country; the Population, Agriculture, Commerce, Customs, and Manners of the Inhabitants . . . with a Description of the Indian Nations . . .* (2 vols., London, G. Robinson, J. Robson, J. Sewell, 1784).[13]

In about 1783 an Englishman, John F. D. Smyth, toured the United States and wrote a book which included an account of a trip down the Ohio River from Kentucky and down the Mississippi, with descriptions of these rivers. Although making favorable comments about the better qualities of frontiersmen, he warned the British against immigration and prophesied the rapid decline of America. His is the first of a number of books after the Revolution by Englishmen who were pessimistic about the future of the United States.

Robertson, Capt. Daniel. "Trip from Michilimackinac to Lake Superior." *Mich. Hist. Colls.*, IX (1886), 643–46.[14]

Captain Daniel Robertson's journal includes a letter in diary form describing a boat trip from Mackinac to Lake Superior in 1784. It mentions heavy fogs and the difficulty of navigation but is unimportant except for an expressed appreciation of nature and the detailing of natural resources.

Imlay, Gilbert. *A Topographical Description of the Western Territory of North America . . . In a Series of Letters to a Friend in England* (London, J. Debrett, 1792).[15]

A native American, Gilbert Imlay, after serving in the Revolution, bought land in Kentucky as early as 1783 and arrived in that region by April 1784. There he became a deputy surveyor and unsuccessful land speculator. Although his book includes frontier events as late as the year 1791, it is almost certain that he was not in Kentucky after 1785 and that much of his work was based upon what he had read after he had left the West. The book was originally written as a series of letters, Letters III and IV of which describe the Ohio River country and other parts of the eastern Midwest. All but the first edition included Filson's *Discovery, Settlement and Present State of Kentucke* and *The Adventures of Col. Daniel Boon.* Imlay's romantic enthusiasm impressed many European readers. As early as 1793 he engaged in a scheme to seize Louisiana. His liaison wih Mary Wollstonecraft relates him to the history of the English Romantic Movement.

[Filson, John.] "Two Westward Journeys of John Filson, 1785." Beverly W. Bond, ed. *Miss. Val. Hist. Rev.*, IX (1923), 320–30.[16]

Montgomery, Samuel. "A Journey through the Indian Country beyond the Ohio, 1785." *Miss. Val. Hist. Rev.*, II (1915), 261–73.[17]

John Filson, mentioned earlier, is probably the author of an unsigned journal of a trip from Pittsburgh down the Ohio and up the Wabash to Post St. Vincent in the spring of 1785. The writing shows his keen observation. Particularly interesting are his comments on the vice and profanity at the post. Samuel Montgomery wrote a brief but polished and clearly worded account of a trip in the same year to arrange a treaty between the United States and the Indians on the Ohio just west of present-day Cincinnati.

Buell, Sergt. Joseph. Military Journal [Fragments]. In Samuel Prescott Hildreth, *Pioneer History; Being an Account of the First Examination of the Ohio Valley, and the Early Settlement of the Northwest Territory. Chiefly from Original Manuscripts; Containing . . . the Diaries of Joseph Buell and John Mathews; the Records of the Ohio Company, &c., &c., &c.* (Cincinnati, H. W. Derby and Co.; New York, A. S. Barnes and Co., 1848), pp. 140–64.

Smith, James. "Tours into Kentucky and the Northwest Territory . . . 1783 [?]–1795–1797." Josiah Morrow, ed. *Ohio Arch. Hist. Quar.*, XVI (1907), 348–401.[18]

Buell describes troop movements and events in the frontier region from Fort McIntosh to Post St. Vincent from December 1785 to September 1787. Only part of the diary has been published. Three journals of tours into Kentucky and the Northwest Territory were written by the Reverend James Smith of Virginia. The first trip was probably taken in 1785; the others, in 1795 and 1797. The latter two contain important information on such towns as Gallipolis and Cincinnati, on the Indian mounds, the Ohio River, and the dangers encountered in the wilderness.

Sargent, Winthrop. Diary, 1786. MS. Massachusetts Historical Society. Listed in Harriette Forbes, comp. *New England Diaries, 1602–1800* (Privately printed, 1923), p. 254.[19]

After serving in the Continental Army, Sargent traveled in 1786 from Boston to survey the Seven Ranges in Ohio. His diary contains long descriptions of the places he passed through. Sargent later took part in the activities of the Ohio Company and the settlement of Marietta, Ohio. His later diaries will be discussed in Chapter 6.

"Diary of Major Erkuries Beatty." *Mag. of Amer. Hist.*, I (1877), 175–79, 235–43, 309–15, 380–86, 432–38.[20]

Decalves, Don Alonzo. *New Travels to the Westward; or, Unknown Parts of America, Being a Tour of almost Fourteen Months. Containing an Account of the Country, upwards of Two-Thousand Miles West of the Christian Parts of North-America; with an Account of White Indians, their Manners, Habits, and Many Other Particulars . . . Confirmed by Three Other Persons* (Boston, J. W. Folson [1788]).[21]

Matthews, John. "A Journal &c." July 10, 1786–Apr. 28, 1787. *Marietta Col. Hist. Colls.*, III (1918), 187–214.[22]

Major Beatty, paymaster of the Western army, described in detail several trips by both water and land between Pittsburgh and the Falls of the Ohio during 1786–1787. He comments on the country, inhabitants, local customs, Indian depredations, and meetings with Boone and others. Don Alonso Decalves is a pseudonym. His book is about a 1786–87 voyage, probably fictitious, up the Mississippi to what was then called the Far West and back. Its popularity is shown by the publication of several editions of the work within a short period. Like Winthrop Sargent, Matthews was a surveyor for the Ohio Company. In his journal he described a trip from Massachusetts to the Ohio which included visits to Indian camps.

A Journal by Thos. Hughes for His Amusement . . . (1778–1789). R. W. David, ed. (Cambridge, Eng., University Press, 1947).

Sharan, James. *The Adventures of James Sharan; Compiled from his Journal, Written During his Voyages and Travels in the Four Quarters of the Globe* (Baltimore, James Sharan, 1808).

Realistic observation of frontier life during 1786–88 and of Indians who traded at Detroit is preserved in *A Journal by Thomas Hughes,* a member of the British Regiment assigned to duty in Canada. Hughes traveled down Lake Erie to Detroit,

which he described as a small town of about two hundred inhabitants, fortified with an old stockade and blockhouse. He found nothing romantic in the American concept of equality and said that the inhabitants of Detroit were a motley set of English and French who lived much beyond their means. His allusions to Indian tribes beyond the Mississippi indicate that he had discussed them with Indians near the Lakes. He wrote the journal "for his amusement & designed [it] only for his perusal by the time he attains the age of 50, if he lives so long."

Among James Sharan's several trips to America, one was made to the Middle West in 1787. Sharan was a widely traveled Britisher, who ascended the Mississippi River to its juncture with the Missouri, then went back to the mouth of the Ohio and east to Niagara Falls. The brief narrative of the trips consists largely of description.

[Mathews, Maj. Robert.] Diary of a Journey from Quebec to Detroit, May 12–June 9, 1787, and a Short Description of Administrative Duties there. 54 pp. MS. Copy from the original in Public Archives of Canada. Listed in *Guide to the Manuscript Collection in the Toronto Public Libraries* (Toronto, Toronto Public Libraries, 1954), p. 55.

"Mrs. Mary Dewees's Journal from Philadelphia to Kentucky, 1787–1788." *Penna. Mag. Hist. Biog.*, XXVIII (1904), 182–98.[23]

"Extracts from Capt. McKay's Journal." Milo M. Quaife, ed. *Wis. Hist. Soc. Procs. . . . 1915* (1916) [63rd Annual Meeting], pp. 186–210. [Includes extracts from journals by McKay's lieutenant, John Evans, written in 1796, and John Hay, of Cahokia.] Extracts in *Before Lewis and Clark, Documents Illustrating the History of the Missouri, 1785–1804.* A. P. Nasatir, ed. (St. Louis, St. Louis Historical Documents Foundation, 1952), II, 490–95, and in *Medical Repository*, Second Hexade, III (1806), 27–36.[24] Extract from Evans' journal in *Before Lewis and Clark*, II, 495–99.

The diary by Major Mathews, aide-de-camp to Lord Dorchester, describes a trip from Quebec to Detroit and his administrative duties at the latter post in 1787. One of the first women to venture into the frontier and write about her experiences was Mary Dewees, who, after crossing the mountains of Pennsylvania, descended the Ohio to Kentucky by flatboat in 1787–1788. Her journal is in diary form and contains lively descriptions and an appreciation of nature.

The partially published journal of Captain James McKay covers a longer period, 1787–96, and a different section of the Middle West. McKay, born in Scotland, was employed by the British to explore the Great Lakes region and the Missouri River territory. He gave the geography of these and said that in 1787 he went to the Mandan tribes on the upper Missouri. He also told of Jean Baptiste Truteau's journey in 1795.

Angell, Col. Israel. Diary, 1788. MS. Listed in Hariette Forbes, *New England Diaries, 1602–1800*, p. 10.[25]

Parsons, Enoch. Diary, 1788. Cited and quoted in *New Eng. Hist. Geneal. Reg.*, I (1847), 160.

After serving through most of the Revolution, Col. Angell became a farmer and cooper at Johnston, Rhode Island, in 1781. In 1788 he took a trip to the Ohio Valley, which he recorded in a diary. At the age of nineteen, Parsons, of Lynn, Conecticut, made a tour of the Northwest country with his father in the spring and summer of 1788. His diary of the journey, likewise, is unpublished except for brief extracts.

"Journal of Rev. Manasseh Cutler of a Journey from Ipswich, Massachusetts, to the Muskingum, in 1788." In William P.

and Julia P. Cutler, *The Life, Journals, and Correspondence of Manasseh Cutler, LL.D.* (2 vols., Cincinnati, R. Clarke and Co., 1888). Extracts in *New Eng. Hist. Geneal. Reg.*, XIV (1860), 105–06, 234–36, 364–66, and in *New Jer. Hist. Soc. Procs.*, 2nd Series, III (1872–1874), 75–96.[26]

Having successfully studied law, medicine, botany, and theology, Manasseh Cutler was chosen representative of a number of old Revolutionary War soldiers to contract with Congress for 1,500,000 acres of public lands northwest of the Ohio. On the Muskingum he materially assisted a group of Connecticut farmers who, under the leadership of Rufus Putnam, founded Marietta, Ohio, the first organized settlement in the Northwest Territory. Returning to Massachusetts soon afterwards, he eventually became a member of Congress. His description of what is now eastern Ohio, printed in 1787, was apparently not based upon actual observation.[27] His son, Ephraim Cutler, wrote a later journal, discussed in Chapter 6.

Hildreth, Samuel Prescott. "Early Emigration Or, the Journal of some Emigrant Families . . . from New England to Muskingum, in 1788." *The American Pioneer*, II (1843), 112–35.

Saugrain de Vigni, Antoine François. "Dr. Saugrain's Note-books, 1788; Stay Opposite Louisville; Observations upon Post Vincennes, Diary of Journey from Louisville to Philadelphia by Eugene F. Bliss . . ." *Amer. Ant. Soc. Procs.*, New Series, XIX (1908–1909), 222–38. Reprinted at Worcester, Mass. (Davis Press, 1909).

"Dr. Saugrain's Relation of his Voyage down the Ohio River in 1788." *Amer. Ant. Soc. Procs.*, New Series, XI (1898), 369–80.[28]

A narrative by S. P. Hildreth, an author mentioned in Chapters 3 and 7, describes the trips of the families of John Rouse and Captain Jonathan Devoll from New England to Ohio in 1788. Antoine Saugrain de Vigni, the French naturalist, scientist, physician, and philosopher, traveled west in the spring of 1788 to find a suitable place for a French settlement. He was attacked by Indians opposite the Big Miami, wounded, and taken captive, but he escaped to Louisville after having lost part of one foot through frostbite. His notebooks show a realistic attitude towards the frontier.

Drowne, Dr. Solomon. Travel Journal. [No title given.] *Mag. of Amer. Hist.*, IX (1883), 285–86.[29]

Journal and Letters of Col. John May, of Boston, Relative to Two Journeys to the Ohio Country in 1788 and '89 . . . W. M. Darlington, ed. (Cincinnati, R. Clarke and Co., Printed for the Historical and Philosophical Society of Ohio, 1873). Extracts in *New Eng. Hist. Geneal. Reg.*, XXX (1876), 43–49.

"Journal of Col. John May, of Boston, Relative to a Journey to the Ohio Country, 1789." *Penna. Mag. Hist. Biog.*, XLV (1921), 101–79.[30]

In addition to Cutler, other early settlers of Marietta, Ohio, kept travel diaries during 1788–1789. One by Dr. Solomon Drowne, dated from November 1788 to June 1789, includes a description of ceremonies during the treaty with Indian tribes at Fort Harmar, Ohio. Drowne also wrote diaries of Midwestern travel mentioned in Chapter 6. John May's journals are spirited accounts of two journeys, one in 1788 and another in 1789, from Boston to Ohio. On the first trip, May took a flatboat from Pittsburgh to Marietta, where he had land, and returned to the East the same year. There are notes on hunting and insights into lives of the settlers.

"The Private Journal of James Backus." In William W. Backus, *A Genealogical Memoir of the Backus Family . . .* (Norwich, Conn., Press of the Bulletin Co., 1889), pp. 16–102.[31]

Putnam, Rufus. Journal. Extracts in Mary Cone, *Life of Rufus Putnam* (Cleveland, William W. Williams, 1886).[32]

Backus was an early settler at Marietta and wrote a journal during 1788–1791 covering his journey to that settlement and his subsequent life in Ohio. The diary contains good pictures of early travel, pioneer community life, and Indians and describes his work as an agent for the Ohio Company. Rufus Putnam, brother of Israel, was the leader of the group that founded Marietta. His journal covers a much longer period than that by Backus. He served in the French and Indian War and the Revolution and was a member of the Massachusetts legislature before he helped organize a group of Revolutionary War soldiers to form a settlement in the Ohio country. In 1787, along with Cutler and Backus, he secured a tract of land from Congress between the Ohio and the Muskingum rivers at 66⅔ cents an acre and laid out the settlement of Marietta. He visited Post Vincennes with John G. Heckewelder, undertook successful negotiations with Indians, became a member of the Ohio constitutional convention in 1802, and organized the first Bible society west of the Alleghanies. The printed portion of his journal is factual and historically important.

Finley, Rev. James Bradley. *Autobiography . . . or Pioneer Life in the West.* W. P. Strickland, ed. (Cincinnati, Methodist Book Concern, 1854).[33]

A long narrative of life in the Old Northwest by a pioneer Methodist, the Midwestern years of which extend from 1788 through 1853. As a seven-year-old boy he descended the Ohio River to Kentucky with his parents. He began preaching in the Scioto circuit in 1809 and extended his ministry to various towns in the nearby territory, receiving a charge at Detroit and preaching as far west as Pontiac by 1819. His final charge was in Cincinnati in 1851. Although the book contains accounts of interesting encounters with Indians, the emphasis upon religion throughout lessens the narrative appeal. His *Life among the Indians* . . . , covering a later period, will be described in Chapter 9.

Chapter 6

Midwestern Travel Tales Written During the

Washington Administration and to the End of the

Eighteenth Century, 1789–1801

After a decline in the number of travel tales written during the Revolution, an increase became apparent during the first years of the expanding new nation. Although the population on the eastern seaboard grew rapidly during the first years of national existence, the dangers of the West prevented all but the bravest people from venturing into the new territories. Several small towns sprang up on the Ohio River and its tributaries but further migration was checked temporarily by hostile tribes of Indians. Many of the travel narratives of this period were written by army men or missionaries, whose professions took them of necessity into the Middle West. During the last decade of the century, the population in the Ohio area began to grow, and with its expansion came a great increase in the number of travel tales. In fact, a larger number of Midwestern travel narratives was written during these ten years than in any previous period of equal length. The attitude toward settling the new region, in spite of hardships of travel, was favorable, although a shadow of skepticism had already begun to appear. The most important narrators during this era, Bishop Asbury, Henry M. Brackenridge, Jean Baptiste Trudeau, André Michaux, Alexander Henry, and Dr. Daniel Drake, lacked the literary stature and personal prominence, however, of several men preceding them and many coming afterwards. Although travel literature does not ordinarily reflect literary tastes as accurately as poetry or fiction, in some respects the tales of the period revealed eighteenth-century characteristics, such as didacticism and skepticism, while others showed tendencies of the Romantic Movement that had already begun and was to continue in the succeeding century, such as emphasis upon emotion, delight in far-away places, and interest in primitive nature.

Anonymous. "Journal of a Survey of the South Shore of Lake Erie Made in 1789." *Buffalo Hist. Soc. Pubs.*, VII (1904), 364–76. Extracts in Buffalo *Express*, Mar. 30, 1890.

"Journal of Miss [Ann] Powell of a Tour from Montreal to Detroit, 1789." Eliza S. Quincy, ed. *Mag. of Amer. Hist.*, V (1880), 37–47. Reprinted in W. R. Reddell, *The Life of William Dummer Powell* (Lansing, 1924), 60–73.[1] Extracts in C. M. Dow, *Anthology and Bibliography of Niagara Falls* (Albany, 1921), I, 89–91.

Forman, Samuel S. *Narrative of a Journey down the Ohio and Mississippi in 1789–90* (Cincinnati, R. Clarke and Co., 1888).

Hay, Henry. "A Narrative of Life on the Old Frontier." Milo M. Quaife, ed. *Wis. Hist. Soc. Procs., 1914* (1915), 208–61. Reprinted as "Fort Wayne in 1790," *Ind. Hist. Soc. Pubs.*, VII (1921), 295–361.[2]

Sargent, Winthrop. Diary, Sept. 1, 1789–May 13, 1790. MS. Massachusetts Historical Society. Listed in Harriette Forbes, comp. *New England Diaries, 1602–1800* (Privately printed, 1923), p. 254.[3]

Whatcoat, Rev. Richard. Diary, 1789–1791. MS., partially published. Garrett Biblical Institute, Evanston, Illinois. Portions quoted in W. W. Sweet, ed., *Religion on the American Frontier* (Chicago, University of Chicago Press, 1946), IV, 73–122.[4]

Mackenzie, Sir Alexander. *Voyages from Montreal on the River St. Lawrence through the Continent of North America, to the Frozen and Pacific Oceans, in the Years 1789 and 1793* . . . (London, T. Cadell, Jr., and W. Davies, etc., 1801).[5]

The "Journal" by an unidentified author dealing mainly with topography, weather, and distances chronicles a survey of the south shore of Lake Erie during June 28–August 1, 1789. A young native of Montreal, Ann Powell, wrote a journal—a fluent account—of a difficult trip up the Great Lakes which contains an appreciative description of Lake Erie. Samuel Forman's is a brief story. An excellent picture of the fur trade, Indian life, and customs among the French settlers during the same years is contained in a narrative by Henry Hay, who recorded a journey from Detroit to the Miami and a winter at Fort Wayne. Another unpublished diary by Winthrop Sargent, mentioned in Chapters 5 and 6, has accounts of various trips on the Mississippi. Richard Whatcoat was the prominent frontier Methodist bishop. His diary includes a record of his travels over large areas of colonial territory. The great British explorer of Canada, Sir Alexander Mackenzie, evidently touched northern Michigan during his trips from Montreal in 1789 and 1793.

Anonymous. "Notes of a Journey from Philadelphia to New Madrid, Tennessee, 1790." *Penna. Mag. Hist. Biog.*, XXXVI (1912), 209–16.

Brown, William. Travel Diary. In T. Speed, *The Wilderness Road, Filson Club Publications,* II (1886), 56–63.[6]

Heward, Hugh. "Journal from Detroit to the Illinois." In *The John Askin Papers.* Milo M. Quaife, ed. (Detroit, Detroit Library Commission, 1928), I, 339–60.[7]

St. Clair, Arthur. "Report of Official Proceedings in the Illinois Country from March 5th to June 11th, 1790." In the *St. Clair Papers . . .* William Henry Smith, ed. (Cincinnati, R. Clarke and Co., 1882), II, 164–80.[8]

"Journal of Thomas Walcutt." *Mass. Hist. Soc. Colls.,* 1st Series, XVII (1879–1880), 174–206. Reprinted at Cambridge, Mass. (1889), with notes and in A. B. Hulbert, *Historic Highways of America* (16 vols., Cleveland, A. H. Clark Co., 1902–1905), XII, 43–63.[9]

Five accounts exist of trips into the Midwest during the year 1790. One of these, by an unidentified person, shows the prevailing fear of the wilderness traveler of encountering hostile Indians. It describes a river journey down the Ohio and part of the Mississippi. William Brown's diary tells of a similar trip along the Ohio River route to Kentucky. Hugh Heward, a fur trader, wrote a diary, probably an amplified report prepared at a later date than the original trip, of an overland trek from Detroit to the Illinois. The "Report" by the British Governor Arthur St. Clair of a trip to the Illinois country for the purpose of establishing a new government is a travel narrative and is of historical interest in view of St. Clair's important assignment and his later defeat by the Indians. Several French villages are described at length. One diarist, Thomas Walcutt, of Boston, walked from Baltimore to Marietta, Ohio. His journal includes an account of the return trip to Philadelphia. The entries are substantial and contain details of public and social affairs and comments on taverns, food, and travel.

Pope, Col. John. *A Tour through the Southern and Western Territories of the United States of North-America . . .* (Richmond, J. Dixon, 1792).[10]

"Diary of Major William Stanley." *Hist. Phil. Soc. of Ohio Quar. Pubs.,* XIV (1919), 17–32.[11]

The Journal of the Rev. Francis Asbury, Bishop of the Methodist Episcopal Church, from August 7, 1771, to December 7, 1815 (3 vols., New York, N. Bangs and T. Mason, for the Methodist Episcopal Church, 1821).[12]

Van Cleve, Benjamin. "An Unpublished Autobiography." Mary D. Steele, ed. *Mag. West. Hist.,* XI (1890), 303–407. Extracts in *The American Pioneer,* II (1843), 148–53, 219–24, 293–96.

"Memoirs of Benjamin Van Cleve." Beverley W. Bond, Jr., ed. *Hist. Phil. Soc. of Ohio Quar. Pubs.,* XVII (1922), 1–71. Extracts in *Ill. State. Soc. Trans.* 1903, VIII (1904), 62–64.[13]

Colonel Pope's *Tour* is a diary of a trip through the Mississippi and Ohio valleys during 1790–1791. He wrote in a rather effective literary style and described Indians, scenery, towns, and social customs. Major Stanley's diary of 1790–1810 describes an Ohio River trip from Wheeling to Cincinnati, where he clerked in a store, and a journey in 1792 to Louisville, New Madrid on the Mississippi, and eventually to New Orleans. He came back to Kentucky in 1793, made several other trips, and returned to Cincinnati in 1810. Although the work shows signs of hurried composition, it gives a good picture of frontier trade. Stanley became one of the principal merchants of Cincinnati.

Perhaps the most important narrative by a clergyman of the early Middle West is Bishop Asbury's *Journal.* Born in England, Asbury was sent by John Wesley as a missionary to America in 1770 when he was only twenty-five years of age. He was later

appointed superintendent of Methodist work in America. In spite of poor health, he traveled on horseback between five and six thousand miles every year. His many visits to Kentucky and Ohio from 1790 to 1815 make his *Journal* an indispensable source for frontier social history.

An autobiography by Benjamin Van Cleve, beginning in 1790 and continuing to 1820, gives another interesting picture of the Northwest Territory. Van Cleve was a member of the first party of pioneers to land at Dayton in 1790. He visited Fort Massac in 1794. His memoirs and diary describe life at Cincinnati, Dayton, and Greenville, Ohio, and reveal interest in politics, farming, surveying, and religion.

François Auguste Chateaubriand, the celebrated French Romanticist and author of *Atale,* a novel set in the American wilderness, took part in a scheme for the discovery of the Northwest Passage and claimed to have descended the Ohio and Mississippi rivers in 1791. Probably, he never saw the Middle West.[14] It is said that his ecstasy over primitive nature was so great than when he reached the Canadian shore of Lake Erie, he ran into the forest and began hugging the trees. A loud roar drove him back to the boat, where he discovered that the noise was made by the waves. In spite of such discrepancies, his American trip undoubtedly provided him with serious ideas for his writings. He is important as an author who led many readers, especially Europeans, to view the frontier in a romantic light. Mrs. Caroline Kirkland, an author discussed in Chapter 12, is one of those who gained much of their early concept of this region from Chateaubriand.

"A Picture of the First United States Army: the Journal of Captain Samuel Newman." Milo M. Quaife, ed. *Wis. Mag. Hist.,* II (1918), 40–73.[15]

Journal of Captain Bradley; an Epic of the Ohio Frontier. Frazer E. Wilson, ed. (Greenville, O., F. H. Jobes and Son, 1935).[16]

An interesting journal of St. Clair's disastrous campaign against the Northwest Indians in 1791 was written by Samuel Newman, who was slain two days after making the last entry in the diary. It includes an account of the march from Philadelphia to Cincinnati and northward. After describing the army's choicest troops, he confirms the judgment of a contemporary that men who can be purchased at two dollars a month from prisons or brothels scarcely make good Indian fighters. A highly personal journal it gives a good picture of army life. Captain Daniel Bradley was another participant in the St. Clair Campaign. Although his journal is less important than Newman's diary, it covers a longer period, 1791–1795, and has some notes on the countryside and on garrison life.

Drowne, Dr. Solomon. Diaries, May 10–June 9, 1792, and June 1–14, 1795. MSS. owned by Henry Russell Drowne of New York. Listed in Forbes, *New England Diaries,* p. 86.

Vial, Pedro. *Diary,* 1792–1794. 47 leaves, folio, MS. including letters. New York Public Library.

In addition to the printed journal of 1788–1789, described in Chapter 5, Dr. Solomon Drowne wrote two frontier diaries. The 1792 diary recounts a journey with his family from Providence to Alexandria and to Belpré, Ohio. The 1795 one is an account of a trip from Providence by way of Philadelphia as far west as the present state of Kansas. The first known Midwestern travel tale by a Mexican, Pedro Vial, covers a trip from Santa Fé to St. Louis on the Illinois and back over the route which later became the Santa Fé Trail. Entirely in Spanish, it is an official document of an expedition ordered by De la Concha, a Mexican governor.

Lincoln, Gen. Benjamin. "Journal of a Treaty Held in 1793 with the Indian Tribes North-West of the Ohio, by Commissioner of the United States." *Mass. Hist. Soc. Colls.*, 3rd Series, V (1836), 109–76.[17]

"Jacob Lindley's Account." *Friends' Miscellany*, II (1832), 49–156. Reprinted in *Mich. Hist. Colls.*, XVII (1890), 565–632.

Lindley, Jacob, Joseph Moore, and Oliver Paxson. "Expedition to Detroit, 1793." *Mich. Hist. Colls.*, XVII (1890), 565–671.[18]

General Benjamin Lincoln, a Revolutionary War soldier and United States commissioner, is the author of a rather important journal covering a trip in 1793 with John Heckewelder from Philadelphia via Niagara to Detroit and subsequent treaty negotiations with Indians northwest of the Ohio River. The journal includes many pleasant travel notes and comments on social affairs. Jacob Lindley, Joseph Moore, and Oliver Paxson, Quakers appointed to settle differences between the United States and Indians at Sandusky, Ohio, composed well-written accounts of their 1793 trips from Philadelphia by way of Lake Erie to Sandusky and their travels around Detroit. Lindley's narrative is the longest and most interesting of the three. Moore's diary supplements Lindley's but is less complete.

Anonymous. "Two Journals of the Kentucky Volunteers, 1793 and 1794." Richard C. Knopf, ed. *Filson Club History Quarterly*, XXVIII (1953), 247–81.

Sargent, Winthrop. "Extracts from Winthrop Sargent's Journal, 1793–1795." *Ohio Arch. Hist. Quar.*, XXXIII (1924), 273–82.

——— Diary, July 17–Aug. 11, 1798. MS. Massachusetts Historical Society. Listed in Forbes, *New England Diaries*, p. 255.[19]

Two diaries by unidentified members of General Anthony Wayne's army which fought against the Indians under the command of Major General Charles Scott, record trips from Kentucky into the Ohio, Wabash, and Maumee river regions. Both journals, evidently hastily written, contain observations on weather, landscape, and supply difficulties, and one has an interesting description of the Ohio River.

Only part of another of Winthrop Sargent's journals, one written in 1793-1795, has been published. It mentions Indian difficulties at Cincinnati, horticultural experiments in the new country, social affairs, and the weather. His diary of 1798 tells of a summer trip on the Mississippi River.

Brackenridge, Henry Marie. *Recollections of Persons and Places in the West* (Philadelphia, James Kay, Jun. and Brother, etc., n. d. [1834]). Extract in Lloyd McFarling, *Exploring the Northern Plains* . . . (Caldwell, Ida., 1955), pp. 29–37.[20]

Brackenridge's *Recollections* is one of the most important books of the Middle Western frontier. The son of the author Hugh Henry Brackenridge, he was sent as a five-year-old boy from Fort Pitt to Ste. Genevieve, on the Mississippi, to learn the French language. Several years later, he made another voyage down the Ohio and then in the early 1800's visited St. Louis. He traveled up the Missouri in 1811 and was in the Midwest as late as 1821. His accurate and entertaining autobiography is fair to both Eastern and Western points of view and presents one of the best pictures of a pioneer boyhood. His *Views of Louisiana* . . . , a journal of his 1811 trip, will be described in Chapter 7.

"Narrative of Andrew J. Vieau, Sr." *Wis. Hist. Colls.*, XI (1888), 218–46.

Beginning with his father's trip to Mackinac in 1793 and life at Green Bay, Andrew Vieau continues his narrative with an account of his own life at Green Bay from 1818 and later resi-

dences in Milwaukee and Chicago, a return to Green Bay and Milwaukee, and events in various Wisconsin towns until 1858.

Anonymous. "From Greene Ville to Fallen Timbers. A Journal of the Wayne Campaign." Dwight L. Smith, ed. *Ind. Hist. Soc. Pubs.*, XVI (1952), 237–333.[21]

"William Clark's Journal of General Wayne's Campaign." *Miss. Val. Hist. Rev.*, I (1914–1915), 418–44.[22]

Todd, Robert. Diary, July 15–Oct. 21, 1794. MS., 51 pp., small notebook. Indiana State Historical Society, Indianapolis.

Witherell, B. F. H. "Reminiscences of the North-West." *Wis. Hist. Soc. Colls.*, III (1857), 297–377.[23]

Several soldiers' accounts of the march to Fallen Timbers and General Anthony Wayne's victory over the Shawnee Indians there have been preserved. A military journal by an unidentified officer of Wayne's army records events beginning at Greenville, in the present state of Ohio, on July 28 and continuing to September 4, 1794. It is the most complete record of the Wayne Campaign yet to be discovered. The author, interestingly enough, held Wayne in contempt. Lieutenant William Clark, later to become famous as the partner of Meriwether Lewis in Jefferson's exploratory expedition of 1804–1806, wrote a diary beginning at Greenville on July 28 and continuing to October 26. While marching to join Wayne's army, Clark was attacked by Indians. He defeated them and was able to join Wayne. This historically important account, written before his other journals, will be discussed in Chapter 7. An unpublished diary by Robert Todd, a Kentuckian and a brigadier general in the War of 1812, describes events from July 15 to October 21, 1794, including twenty-eight pages devoted to the battle at Fallen Timbers. B. F. H. Witherell's objectively written tale also mentions the same battle and covers events in Michigan as late as 1828.

"The Journal of Needham Parry–1794." *Ky. Hist. Soc. Reg.*, XXXIV (1936), 379–91, and "John D. Shane's Copy of Needham Parry's Diary of Trip Westward in 1794." *Filson Club Historical Quarterly*, XXII (1948), 229–47.[24]

Putnam, Israel. "A Journey to Marietta in 1794." *New England Magazine*, New Series, XIII (1895–1896), 642–51.[25]

"Journal of Jean Baptiste Trudeau [Truteau, a corrupt spelling adopted by his children] on the Upper Missouri, 'Première Partie,' June 7, 1794–March 26, 1795." *Amer. Hist. Rev.*, XIX (1914), 299–333, and *Sou. Dak. Hist. Colls.*, VII (1914), 403–74.

"Journal of Jean Baptiste Trudeau among the Arikara Indians in 1795." [Part II of the Journal.] Mrs. H. T. Beauregard, trans. *Mo. Hist. Soc. Colls.*, IV (1912), 9–48. Reprint of entire English translation in "Journal of Truteau on the Missouri River, 1794–1795." In A. P. Nasatir, ed. *Before Lewis and Clark* . . . (St. Louis, St. Louis Historical Documents Foundation, 1952), I, 259–311.

Le Journal du voyage fait par Jean-Baptiste Trudeau sur le Haut-Missouri en 1795. MS. Quebec Seminary Archives, Quebec. [To be edited by Fernand Grenier and Fernand Ouellet and probably printed 1960 in *Publications des Archives du Séminaire de Québec*.][26]

General Wayne's victory motivated a great migration into the Ohio Valley. The story of a boat trip in 1794 from Pennsylvania to Ohio, Indiana, and Kentucky, a return to the East, and eventual settlement in Adams County, Ohio, is contained in the diary of Needham Parry. Parts of one of the manuscripts, which consist mainly of colloquial notes on persons and places, have been lost. Israel Putnam and a cousin journeyed to Marietta in 1794, six years after Israel's brother, Rufus, mentioned in Chapter 5, founded the town. After visiting Belpré, Ohio, Israel returned to Connecticut but came back to Ohio the following year. The printed extracts from the diary are valuable for their picture of General Rufus Putnam and life at Marietta.

Jean Baptiste Truteau's epic journey to the Northwest deserves a rather detailed treatment. Born in Montreal in 1748, Truteau became the first schoolmaster of St. Louis and taught at interrupted intervals for over forty years. In 1794 he was engaged by the *Companie de descubridores del Misuri* (Missouri Exploring Co.) to head an exploratory expedition to exploit the fur trade of the Upper Missouri and to reach the source of the Missouri River and beyond to the Pacific. Since the governor of St. Louis instructed him to keep a record of the trip, Truteau began his journal on June 7, 1794, the day of his departure, and continued it into 1795. The work was a valuable contribution to the existing knowledge of the Upper Missouri and the Indian tribes there, but the expedition was unprofitable because of desertions, jealousies, and lack of confidence in Jacques Clamorgan, one of the organizers. Truteau's interesting journal came to the attention of Thomas Jefferson who realized its importance and in 1804 sent an entire translation of it to Captain Meriwether Lewis.[27]

Condict, Lewis. "Journal of a Trip to Kentucky in 1795." *New Jer. Hist. Soc. Procs.*, New Series, IV (1919), 103–27.[28]

Parrish, John. Record of a trip to Lower Sandusky, 1795. MS. Listed in *Guide to the Manuscript Collections of the Historical Society of Pennsylvania*, 2nd ed. (Historical Society of Pennsylvania, Philadelphia, 1949), No. 468.

Wade, John. "Notes on the Wabash River in 1795." Dwight L. Smith, ed. *Ind. Mag. Hist.*, L (1954), 277–90.

Condict's journal reveals a medical doctor's difficult trip from New Jersey via Pittsburgh down the Ohio River and on land by horseback to visit his mother in Kentucky. It includes an account of the return trip. His comments on the manners and morals of the people of Cincinnati are interesting. John Parrish, whose 1773 journal has been described, wrote of a trip in 1795 from Pennsylvania to Lower Sandusky to conclude a treaty with Indians. John Wade, one of Wayne's officers, wrote some unimportant travel notes covering a journey from Fort Knox to Fort Wayne in 1795, including meetings with various Indians.

Portions of the Journal of André Michaux, Botanist, Written during his Travels in the United States and Canada, 1785 to 1796 . . . C. S. Sargent, ed. *American Philosophical Society Proceedings*, XXVI (1889), 1–145. Extracts translated into English in R. G. Thwaites, ed. *Early Western Travels* . . . (32 vols., Cleveland, Arthur H. Clark Co., 1904), III, 27–104.[29]

Weid, Isaac. *Travels through the States of North America, and the Provinces of Upper and Lower Canada, during the Years 1795, 1796 and 1797* (2 vols., London, J. Stockdale, 1807).

Thomas Jefferson, as vice-president of the American Philosophical Society, solicited subscriptions to enable André Michaux to make discoveries in the Western country, but because of foreign complications the project did not materialize. Michaux entered the United States in 1795 and began an expedition into the Midwest in August, 1795, reached Terre Haute and Kaskaskia and spent some time in the French villages, upon whose plight he made realistic comments. His journal was published in French in 1889 and parts of it were printed in English in 1889 and 1904. Michaux's son, François André, later wrote a more important book on Midwestern travels made in 1802, which is summarized in Chapter 7.

Isaac Weid's travels in America and Canada took him to the present state of Michigan. His book was popular and was translated into German and French.

"Extract from the Journal of General Moses Cleaveland." In *Early History of Cleveland.* Charles Whittlesey, ed. (Cleveland, O., Fairbanks, Benedict and Co., 1867), pp. 181–84.[30]

"Extracts from the Diary of Amzi Atwater, 1796." In *Early History of Cleveland*, pp. 228–29.

Holley, John Milton. "Holley's Journal—Conneaut to the South East Corner of the Reserve." In *Early History of Cleveland*, pp. 192–202, 206–07.

———— "Survey of the Parallels, and some of the Townships." In *Early History of Cleveland*, pp. 215–23, 242–49.

"Journal of Seth Pease to and from New Connecticut, 1796–98." In *Early History of Cleveland*, pp. 178–81, 277–87. Reprinted in *West. Res. Hist. Soc. Tract No. 94* (1914), 27–132.[31]

The person after whom Cleveland, Ohio, was named, Moses Cleaveland, who had been a general in Washington's army, was one of thirty-six men who formed the Connecticut Land Company, sent to survey and settle that part of the Western Reserve at the mouth of the Cuyahoga River on Lake Erie. Cleaveland's partly published journal of 1796 contains notes on surveying and conferences with the Indians. Diaries by three other men in the expedition have been preserved. Amzi Atwater wrote a brief record of his experiences at the village of Cleveland and near the Cuyahoga River in 1796. Also in this year John M. Holley wrote a journal similar to Cleaveland's, containing notes on camping experiences and the topography and natural history of the same region. Seth Pease's journal (four diaries) about trips from Connecticut to Cleveland and back during 1796–1798 contains surveying notes and interesting observations on places and people.

"Journal of Peter Audrain." *Mich. Hist. Colls.*, VIII (1886), 444–47.[32]

Farmer, Silas. "Detroit During Revolutionary Days." *Mag. West. Hist.*, III (1886), 250–57. Reprinted as "Revolutionary Days, or Detroit in 1796," *Mich. Hist. Colls.*, XXIX (1901), 190–200.[33]

Jones, Rev. David. "Extracts from a Manuscript Journal." *Mich. Hist. Colls.*, VIII (1886), 392–95.[34]

There are three accounts of trips to Michigan in 1796. Peter Audrain's brief journal describes adventures in western Ohio and in Michigan. Silas Farmer wrote a very lively and entertaining narrative about the trip of Colonel Richard England, the commander of Detroit, from Fort Niagara via Lake Erie to Michigan. An account of reactions of the soldiers' wives aboard the boat toward the trip and toward Detroit and a description of a canoe race between an Indian and a French girl make good reading. Reverend David Jones, whose Indian missionary journal has been discussed in Chapter 4, wrote a diary (partially published) about his journey from Pittsburgh through Ohio to Detroit as chaplain of Wayne's army, July 3 to November 3, 1796.

Collot, Georges Henri. *Voyages dans l'Amérique Septentrionale, ou, Description des Pays Arroses par le Mississippi, l'Ohio, le Missouri, et Autres Rivières Affluentes* . . . (Paris, A. Bertrand, 1826). Translated into English as *A Journey in North America* . . . (2 vols., Paris, Arthur Bertrand, 1826). Extracts in English in "A Journey in North America," *Ill. State Hist. Soc. Trans., 1906*, XIII (1909), 269–98; "Descriptions of St. Louis," *Glimpses of the Past*, I (1934), 20–22; and "Gen. Collot's Voyage down the Ohio River in 1796," *Hist. Phil. Soc. of Ohio Bull.*, III (1945), 7–12.[35]

View of the Climate and Soil of the United States of America: to which are Annexed Some Accounts of Florida, the French Colony on the Scioto, Certain Canadian Colonies, and the Savages or Natives: Translated from the French of C. F. Volney . . . (London, J. Johnson, 1804).[36]

At the request of the French minister to the United States, Georges Collot, who had served during the American Revolution, went West in 1796 and in his book described his trip down the Ohio and Mississippi rivers, treating the appearance of the territory and recording his arrest at Fort Massac, on the lower Ohio. He was suspicious of America's political motives and believed that the frontier would eventually become a separate political unit. Constantin François Volney, disgusted with Europe, came to America in 1795, but was disillusioned when he could find no ideal democracy; and when in 1796 he saw the meanness of wilderness life and encountered a large amount of anti-French sentiment, he renounced his intention of becoming an American settler and returned to Europe. These unfavorable reactions, which should be compared with the similar ones of Smyth and de Vigni, were in both cases influenced by the enmity that existed between France and America at the time.

Austin, Moses. "A Memorandum of M. Austin's Journey from the Lead Mines in the County of Wythe in the State of Virginia to the Lead Mines in the Province of Louisiana West of the Mississippi, 1796–1797." George P. Garrison, ed. *Amer. Hist. Rev.*, V (1900), 518–42.[37]

Baily, Francis. *Journal of a Tour in Unsettled Parts of North America, in 1796 & 1797* . . . *With a Memoir by the Author* (London, Baily Brothers, 1856). Extracts in A. B. Hulbert, *Historic Highways of America* (Cleveland, 1904), XI, 106–50.[38]

The Journal of Andrew Ellicott, Late Commissioner on Behalf of the United States . . . *for Determining the Boundary between the United States and the Possessions of His Catholic Majesty in America, Containing Occasional Remarks on the Situation, Soil, Rivers, Natural Productions, and Diseases of the Different Countries on the Ohio, Mississippi, and Gulf of Mexico* . . . (Philadelphia, Budd and Bartram, for T. Dobson, 1803).[39]

Chambers, Charlotte. Diary. In Lewis H. Garrard, *Memoir of Charlotte Chambers* (Philadelphia, Printed for the Author, 1856), *passim.*[40]

An entertaining and valuable tale of being lost in the wilderness and later visiting all the villages of the Illinois country is related in Moses Austin's diary of 1796–1797, with which his diary of 1801, discussed in Chapter 7, should be compared. Francis Baily, an Englishman who later became a well-known astronomer, describes a voyage in an open boat down the Ohio and Mississippi from Pittsburgh and the return to New York. Although the journal of Andrew Ellicott, Pennsylvanian commissioned to survey the boundary between the United States and Florida, deals mainly with the lower Mississippi Valley, the first two chapters contain a detailed account of his trip down the Ohio and Mississippi. The diary of Charlotte Chambers, who lived at Ludlow Station, Ohio, and Cincinnati, gives a fairly good record of social life and religious work for the Bible Society of Ohio.

Worthington, Thomas. Unpublished diaries, manuscripts, and journals, June 24, 1796–Mar. 16, 1827. 29 vols. Originals and photostats. Manuscripts Division, Library of Congress, Washington.[41]

After studying surveying, Thomas Worthington made a journey to Chillicothe, Ohio, and finally moved there two years later.

Prosperous and pious, he spent much of his time in the management of his farm and his mills. In 1803 he became a member of the First General Assembly of Ohio and later was elected United States senator and governor of Ohio.

Burnet, Jacob. *Notes on the Early Settlement of the Northwestern Territory* (Cincinnati, Derby, Bradley and Co., 1847).[42]

An important source for the early history of Cincinnati is Jacob Burnet's *Notes*, an autobiographical book describing his trip from the East to Cincinnati in 1796 and his life in Ohio until 1847. He rode the circuit with the territorial judges and held many political offices. Depending too much upon his memory in relating events, he weakened the value of his work.

Anonymous. Journal, August 20–October 9, 1797. 7½ pp., MS., unbound. Indiana Historical Society Library, Indianapolis.

A brief tale which describes a trip in 1797 from Clarksville, Indiana, near the Falls of the Ohio, to St. Louis and back. The author is as yet unidentified but may be William Clark.

Swan, Maj. Caleb. "The Northwestern Country in 1797." *Mag. of Amer. Hist.*, XIX (1888), 74–77.[43]

Major Caleb Swan, paymaster to the Western army, describes a trip from Detroit through the northwestern country and back in 1797. He includes brief notes on Indians and the countryside.

Sample, George. "Sketch of Western Settlements." *The American Pioneer*, I (1842), 157–60.
David Thompson's Narrative. J. B. Tyrrell, ed. *Publications of the Champlain Society*, Vol. XII (Toronto, Champlain Society, 1915).[44]

George Sample's "Sketch" is a brief account of a trip from Somerset, Pennsylvania, to Cincinnati in 1797 and of a trip to New Orleans in 1806. David Thompson, the British explorer, well known for his later exploration of the Pacific Northwest, tells in his *Narrative* of reaching the Mandan villages on the Missouri River in 1797, describes weather, buffalo, and Indians, and recounts incidents in a journey by water during the same winter from the source of the Mississippi to the north shore of Lake Superior. Washington Irving is said to have offered to buy the narrative, but Thompson, then an old man, refused to sell, thereby probably denying the world a sequel to *Astoria*.

Hastings, Sally. *Poems on Different Subjects. To which Is Added a Descriptive Account of a Family Tour to the West, in the Year 1800, in a Letter to a Lady* (Lancaster, Pa., William Dickson, 1808).
Tracy, Uriah. Journal of a Tour, June 16–Sept. 4, 1800. MS., copy in an unidentified hand. Yale University Library, New Haven, Conn.[45]

Included in Sally Hastings' letter are notes on the upper Ohio River region. Uriah Tracy was a prominent lawyer and at one time United States senator. His journal covers a tour from Litchfield, Connecticut, into the Middle West.

Kluge, John Peter. "Diary of the Journey of Br. and Sr. Kluge and Br. Luckenbach from Bethlehem to Goshen on the Muskingum, October 15 to November 18, 1800." Lawrence H. Gipson, ed. *Ind. Hist. Colls.*, XXIII (1938), 39–52.
——— "Diary . . . from Goshen on the Muskingum to White River, March 24 to May 25, 1801. *Ind. Hist. Colls.*, XXIII (1938), 67–101.
——— "Extracts from the Diary . . . from the White River to Bethlehem from September 16, to November 12, 1806." *Ind. Hist. Colls.*, XXIII (1938), 455–65.[46]

A diary by Moravian John Peter Kluge describes the journey of Kluge, his wife and a Mr. Luckenbach from Bethlehem, Pennsylvania, to Goshen. A second section tells of the trip from there to the White River in Indiana. The group traveled by land, stopping at inns and farms along the way. A partially published diary by Kluge records the hardships of travel and fear of hostile Indians during the return to Bethlehem in 1806.

Johnson, William. "A Young Man's Journal of 1800–1813." *New Jer. Hist. Soc. Procs.*, New Series, VII (1922), 49–59, 122–34.[47]

Roberts, Zophar. *A Journal of a Tour from Lake-George to the North-West Territory, Made in the Fall of the Year 1800, and the Winter and Spring of 1801; with a Description of the Soil, Productions, Rivers, Natural Curiosities, &c. of that Eden of America. To which is Added, a Concise Account of the Present State of Kentucky* (Albany, N. Y., Printed for the Author, 1801).[48]

Extracts have been published from this journal by William Johnson, a merchant in New York and New Jersey, who chronicled a trip from New Jersey to New Orleans by way of the Ohio and Mississippi rivers in 1800 and 1801. An accompanying editorial narrative supplements the actual journal. Zophar Roberts, a traveler from the Eastern states, disliked the slavery system he found in Kentucky, but he called the country north of the Ohio "that Eden of America." Although brief and unimportant, the book contains a description of the topography and appearance of the Northwest Territory.

A Memoir of Rev. Joseph Badger (Hudson, O., Sawyer, Ingersoll and Co., 1851).[49]

Harmon, Daniel Williams. *A Journal of Voyages and Travels in the Interior of North America, between the 47th and 58th Degrees of North Latitude, Extending from Montreal Nearly to the Pacific, a Distance of about 5,000 Miles; Including an Account of the Principal Occurrences During a Residence of Nineteen Years in Different Parts of the Country* (Andover, Mass., Flagg and Gould, 1820).[50]

Joseph Badger, founder of the first church in the Western Reserve, came to the Ohio country as a Presbyterian missionary to the Indians in 1801. His missionary work took him to Youngstown and Detroit in the same year, and with his family he moved by wagon to Ohio in 1802. His diary records visits made as late as 1807 to Cleveland, Ashtabula, Sandusky, Marion, and other towns in Ohio, as well as to towns in Pennsylvania and Virginia. The book is concerned mainly with religious activities, often described in very readable prose. Harmon, who spent nineteen years of his life in the service of the Northwest Fur Company, began a long trek west and north in 1800, touching Lake Huron, St. Joseph Island, Sault Ste. Marie, and traveling up Lake Superior before continuing on into Canada. Most of his journal deals with the Far West. A diary written in plain language, it is an interesting narrative of the life of a trader.

Henry, Alexander. *New Light on the Early History of the Great Northwest.* Elliott Coues, ed. (3 vols., New York, F. P. Harper, 1897). Extracts in *Nor. Dak. Hist. Soc. Colls.*, III (1910), 360–68.[51]

———— "The Winter of 1807–1808 at Pembina, North Dakota." Howard E. Simpson, ed. *Nor. Dak. Hist. Quar.*, V (1931), 239–47.[52]

Reynolds, John. *My Own Times, Embracing Also the History of My Life* (Belleville, Ill., Parryman and Davison, 1855).[53]

Alexander Henry, author of the Indian captivity tale summarized in Chapter 3, wrote several journals beginning in July, 1800, covering his exploration of the Northwest. Placed in charge of the business of the Northwest Company, he traveled from Lake Superior to the Lake of the Woods, Winnipeg River, Red River, and the mouth of the Park River. He described the building of a trading post, Indian life, business, personal affairs, and several trips made while he was in North Dakota and Canada before being sent to Saskatchewan in 1808. The journal, which is rather formal in style, is valuable and interesting. John Reynolds, who later became governor of Illinois, journeyed to the same region with his parents in 1800. His book deals with social, economic, and political conditions in the pioneer period as late as the Black Hawk War in 1832 but discusses few specific dates or events.

Pioneer Life in Kentucky. A Series of Reminiscential Letters from Daniel Drake, M.D., of Cincinnati, to his Children. Edited, with Notes and a Biographical Sketch, by his Son, Charles D. Drake (Cincinnati, Robert Clark and Co., 1870).[54]

One of the most important figures in the early cultural history of the Middle West was Dr. Daniel Drake. His simply written reminiscences tell of his trip to Cincinnati in 1800, where he became a medical student. After two trips to Philadelphia, where he received his medical degree from the University of Pennsylvania, he traveled to Lexington, Kentucky, to become professor of medicine at Transylvania University. In 1819 he founded the Ohio Medical College at Cincinnati but returned to Transylvania in 1823. His book describes events in Cincinnati as late as 1848. He understood the frontier, encouraged pioneer enterprise, and had great faith in the future of Western literature. He wrote several other books about Cincinnati, the West, and frontier cultural beginnings: *Notices concerning Cincinnati* (1810), *Natural and Statistical View, or Picture of Cincinnati and the Miami Country* (1815), and *Discourses on the History, Character, and Prospect of the West* (1834).

"Personal Narrative of Capt. Thomas G. Anderson." *Wis. Hist. Soc. Colls.*, IX (1909, reprint of 1882 vol.), 137–206.

"Capt T. G. Anderson's Journal." *Wis. Hist. Soc. Colls.*, IX (1909), pp. 207–61.[55]

Zumwalt, Solomon. "Biography of Adam Zumwalt. Part I." Mrs. James and Vivian McCarty, eds. *Mo. Hist. Rev.*, XLVIII (1954), 252–63.

———— "Three Generations in the Span of a Continent." *Mo. Hist. Rev.*, XLVIII (1954), 341–51.[56]

Captain Thomas Gummersall Anderson, an Indian agent of Lower Canada, wrote a long but readable narrative of a journey from the East in 1800 for the purpose of trading with Indians and of travel on the Mississippi, trading in Wisconsin, and events as late as 1828. A shorter diary describes military activities at Fort McKay, Prairie du Chien, Wisconsin, in 1814, including an account of the British capture of Prairie du Chien. Solomon Zumwalt recounts the life of his father, Adam, a very religious man, who went down the Ohio in 1800, settled in St. Charles County, Missouri, and had numerous dealings with Indians. He includes Adam's memories of the War of 1812 and some autobiographical material: his own birth in 1807, his marriage, and his trip to Oregon by way of the Platte River in 1846.

Chapter 7

Narratives from the Beginning of the Nineteenth

Century to the War of 1812

From the few straggling settlements along the rivers and Great Lakes in the 1790's, the Middle West developed into a vital unit of the nation during the first half of the nineteenth century. A large number of important travel books about the region were written between 1801 and 1812. Works of literary merit by such well-known figures as Thaddeus Mason Harris, Lorenzo Dow, Patrick Gass, Meriwether Lewis and William Clark, Zebulon M. Pike, Henry Ker, John Bradbury, Henry M. Brackenridge, and John Melish deal with the Midwest during these years. The westward trend of exploration and settlement is indicated by the increase in the number of tales about travel in the trans-Mississippi portion of the country. The Northwest Territory was a region of Indians, forts, and a few struggling river and lake settlements. The region west of the Mississippi was a wilderness of roving animal herds and savages, barely touched by the white man. Although some of the explorers, settlers, and preachers behaved in a way that would shock their twentieth-century descendants, many of them were men of vision, willing to sacrifice their lives to attain their goals. Some of the most interesting travel books were written during these years. The prose style of the best of them reflects the characteristics of the age, and the contents of most of them reveal a great deal about frontier life.

Austin, Moses. "Journal of Voyage Down the Mississippi." In *The Austin Papers*, I, 69–74. In *Amer. Hist. Assn. Ann. Rep.* (Washington, Government Printing Office, 1919).[1]
"Diary of Captain Philip Buckner." William B. McGroarty, ed. *Wm. Mary Coll. Hist. Mag.*, 2nd Series, VI (1926), 173–207.[2]
Johnson, William. "A Young Man's Journal of 1800–1813." *New Jer. Hist. Soc. Procs.*, New Series, VII (1922), 49–59.[3]
[Walker, James.] Journal, 1801. 17 pp. typescript. Original privately owned. Historical and Philosophical Society of Ohio, Cincinnati.
Walker, James and Sarah. Journals of trips from Cincinnati, Ohio, to the East and back, 1801–1844. MS. In Family Papers of the Walkers of Conway, N. H., and Butler County, Ohio. Listed in Elizabeth Biggert, comp., *Guide to the Manuscript Collections in the Library of the Ohio State Archaeological and Historical Society* (Columbus, 1953), No. 1064.

Hover, Ezekial. Diary, 1801–1802. 14 pp. MS. Listed in Biggert, *Guide*, No. 537.

Moses Austin, mentioned in Chapter 6, in a brief diary of a trip in 1801 from Ste. Genevieve down the Mississippi described traffic on the Mississippi and Ohio rivers. Captain Philip Buckner's partially published 1801 diary chronicles a journey from his home in Kentucky down part of the Ohio en route to Natchez, and includes a stop at Cincinnati. A similar trip down the Ohio from Pittsburgh to Louisiana, begun in 1800, was made by young William Johnson, a boy whose diary shows his interest in literature and in writing poetry. A journal, probably by James Walker, who became an early resident of Cincinnati, tells the story of the journey of the Walker family from New Hampshire to Cincinnati in 1801. He and Sarah Walker wrote other accounts of trips from Cincinnati to the East and back dating as late as 1844. Ezekial Hover wrote a brief diary of a trip from Pennsylvania through Michigan and Ohio in 1801 and 1802. He and his family eventually settled in Trumbull and Allen counties, Ohio.

Bacon, David. "An Unsuccessful Mission to the Shawanese, 1802." *Connecticut Missionary Magazine*, III. Reprinted in *Northw. Ohio Quar.*, XVI (1944), 22–40.[4]
Berquin-Duvallon. *Vue de la Colonie Espagnole du Mississippi, ou des Provinces de Louisiane et Floride Occidentale; en l'Année 1802, par un Observateur Résident sur les Lieux . . .* (Paris, Imprimerie Expéditive, 1803).
"Memoir of David Hoover," *Ind. Mag. Hist.*, II (1906), 17–27.
Little, Nathaniel. "Journal of Nathaniel W. Little." *Old Northw. Geneal. Quar.*, X (1907), 237–45.[5]

David Bacon made several trips to the Midwest to convert the Indians. In a long letter printed as a narrative he described his canoe trip to the Shawanese near the Maumee River in 1802 and the unwillingness of the Indians to follow the ways of the whites. Berquin-Duvallon's French work, of which the English title is *Travels in Louisiana and the Floridas, in the Year, 1802 . . .* (New York, 1806), contains only incidental information on the Midwest.

At the age of twenty-two David Hoover traveled with his father and family from North Carolina to Ohio in 1802. In his narrative, much of which is devoted to his opinions, he describes Cincinnati as a village and tells about Indians on the White River. Nathaniel Little's diary of the same year recounts events in a trip from Massachusetts to central Ohio and back in the interests of the Scioto Company. His comment on the Ohio River settlement is revealing: "The inhabitants of the small towns appear rather indolent and tavern keepers appear to be doing the best of any of them." (p. 242)

Michaux, François André. *Voyage à l'ouest des Monts Alléghanys, dans les États de l'Ohio, et du Kentucky, et du Tennessee, et retour à Charleston par le Hautes–Carolines . . .* (Paris, Levrault, Schoell et Cie., 1804). English translation, *Travels to the Westward . . .* , by B. Lambert (from the French edition of 1802), (London, B. Crosby and Co., 1805). Reprinted in R. G. Thwaites, ed. *Early Western Travels, 1748–1846* (32 vols., Cleveland, Arthur H. Clark Co., 1904), III, 117–306.[6]

The book of a trip in 1802 containing the lengthiest description of the Ohio Valley is *Travels to the Westward . . .* by F. A. Michaux, the French scientist, son of André Michaux, who was discussed in Chapter 6. It tells of a journey down the Ohio and into Kentucky and the South and exhibits an awareness of the Western forests and of people in such towns as Marietta and Gallipolis. A German translation was published at Weimer in 1805.

Perrin du Lac, François Marie. *Voyage dans les Deux Louisianes, et chez les Nations Sauvages du Missouri, par les États-Unis, l'Ohio et les Provinces qui le Bordent, en 1801, 1802, et 1803; avec un Aperçu des Moeurs, des Usages, du Caractère . . . et des Peuples de ces Diverses Contrées* (Paris, Capelle et Renand, etc., 1805). Translated into English as *Travels through the Two Louisianas, and among the Savage Nations of the Missouri . . .* (London, R. Phillips for J. G. Barnard, 1807). Extracts in A. P. Nasatir, ed. *Before Lewis and Clark . . .* (St. Louis, St. Louis Historical Documents Foundation, 1952), II, 708–12.[7]

Dickson, Col. Joseph. "Personal Narrative." *Wis. Hist. Soc. Colls.*, V (1868), 315–17.

François Marie Perrin du Lac, a Frenchman, wrote an account of his voyage in 1802 down the Ohio, up the Mississippi to St. Louis, and up the Missouri to the White River in the present state of South Dakota. His book deals with the fur trade and the Indians of Upper Louisiana and gives only a sketchy account of the Ohio Valley. Part of it may have been taken from Truteau's *Journal*. Colonel Joseph Dickson's brief narrative describes life in Illinois from 1802 past 1832, including experiences in the Black Hawk War, in which he was wounded.

Harris, Rev. Thaddeus Mason. *Journal of a Tour into the Territory Northwest of the Alleghany Mountains; Made in the Spring of the Year 1803* (Boston, Manning and Loring, 1805). Reprinted in Thwaites, *Early Western Travels*, III, 309–82.[8]

Reverend Thaddeus M. Harris, a native of Boston, was accompanied into the Ohio settlements and backwoods in 1803 by two friends. His book is an arrangement of notes he wrote describing his travels. Although slightly ill-humored, it is at the same time appreciative of the natural beauty of the wilderness.

"The Journals of Captain Meriwether Lewis and Sergeant John Ordway Kept on the Expedition of Western Exploration, 1803–1806." Milo M. Quaife, ed. *Wis. Hist. Soc. Colls.*, XXII (1916), 31–402.[9]

Lewis, Capt. Meriwether and Lieut. William Clark. MS., 1803–1804, partially published. Minnesota Historical Society, St. Paul.

Several months before the Lewis and Clark expedition crossed the continent, Captain Meriwether Lewis, nicknamed "The Sublime Dandy," wrote a journal consisting largely of topographical notes of a trip down the Ohio and up the Mississippi from August to December, 1803. This was printed with the journal of John Ordway, a sergeant in Captain Bissell's Company of the first infantry at Kaskaskia, to which Lewis came to enlist recruits for his expedition. An unpublished portion of the Lewis and

Clark journals begins on December 13, 1803, seven weeks before the earliest notation in the Thwaites edition of the journals.

Swearingen, Lieut. James Strode. Journal, "Remarks on the Road from Detroit to Chicago," July–August, 1802. In *Chicago and the Old Northwest*, Milo M. Quaife, ed. (Chicago, University of Chicago Press, 1913), pp. 373–77.[10]

Hopkins, Gerard T. Journal, 1803–1804. MS. Listed in *Guide to the Manuscript Collections in the Historical Society of Pennsylvania* (Philadelphia, 1949), No. 291.

Lieutenant James S. Swearingen wrote of an 1802 march from Detroit to Chicago. The journal consists largely of brief notes on such subjects as topography and the weather. As commander of a post he had numerous dealings with the Indians. The journal by Gerard T. Hopkins, a member of a Quaker deputation to the Western Indians for the purpose of interesting them in agriculture and other useful knowledge, describes a trip from Baltimore to Fort Wayne during 1803 and 1804. Includes interesting comments on topography, agriculture, economic conditions, and Indian life and customs.

Curot, Michel. "A Wisconsin Fur-Trader's Journal, 1803–04." *Wis. Hist. Soc. Colls.*, XX (1911), 396–471.[11]

Tabeau's Narrative of Loisel's Expedition to the Upper Missouri. Annie H. Abel, ed., Rose Abel Wright, trans. (Norman, University of Oklahoma Press, 1939).[12]

Verchères de Boucherville, René Thomas. *Journal.* [Extracts] In *Canadian Antiquarian and Numismatic Journal*, 3rd Series, Vol. III (1901). English translation in *Niagara Historical Society Publications*, No. 20 (1911), 43–55; reprinted in *War on the Detroit . . .* Milo M. Quaife, ed. (Chicago, R. R. Donnelley and Sons Co., 1940), pp. 3–179.

A French-Canadian fur trader, Michael Curot, wrote a factual diary in French of his experiences in Wisconsin during 1803 and 1804. Pierre Antoine Tabeau's narrative, also translated from the French, traces Loisel's expedition to the Upper Missouri in 1803 and 1805 and describes the Indians and topography of the region. After serving with Mackenzie in Canada, Thomas Verchères de Boucherville journeyed in 1803, when he was only eighteen, to Lake Nipissing, to Sault Ste. Marie and the Winnipeg, and to trade with the Indians. Returning by way of Mackinac, he volunteered in 1812 when war began in the Detroit River region and served with the British in this area until as late as 1816. His journal has been only partially published, both in French and in English.

James, Gen. Thomas. *Three Years among the Indians and Mexicans* (Waterloo, Ill., Office of the "War Eagle," 1846). Reprinted at St. Louis (Missouri Historical Society, 1916); edited by Milo M. Quaife (Chicago, R. R. Donnelley and Sons Co., 1953).[13]

General Thomas James' narrative, told in the first person but probably written by Nathaniel Niles, a local teacher-lawyer, begins with the journey of his family to Illinois in 1803 and continues with their removal to Missouri in 1807. Includes accounts of his trip in 1809 for the Missouri Fur Company from St. Louis up the Missouri and back in 1810, keelboat navigation of the Ohio and Mississippi between Pittsburgh and St. Louis in 1813, a descent of the Mississippi to the mouth of the Arkansas River in 1821 as part of an expedition to Santa Fé, a return in 1824, and experiences in the Black Hawk War of 1832.

Anonymous. Diary of a Trip to Ohio from Philadelphia, 1804. MS. Clifford Papers. Listed in *Guide to the Manuscript Collections . . . of Pennsylvania*, No. 136.

Couch, Jesup N. Journal. From Reading in Connecticut to Chillicothe, Ohio, 1804. 73 pp. MS. Listed in Biggert, *Guide*, No. 298.

Gibbons, James. Journals, 1804. MS. Listed in *Guide to the Manuscript Collections . . . of Pennsylvania*, No. 235.

Straghan, John. "Journal by Rivers Sea & Land," July–August, 1804. MS. Listed in Biggert, *Guide*, No. 982.

Jesup N. Couch, who became an Ohio state legislator and judge of the Ohio Supreme Court, describes a journey from Connecticut to Chillicothe. James Gibbon's journals of 1804 contain information about topography, settlements, Quaker families, and immigration, all of which he obtained during a tour through part of Pennsylvania and Ohio. John Straghan's "Journal" covers his travel in 1804 from "Free poart," Pennsylvania, down the Monongahela, Ohio, and Mississippi Rivers to New Orleans.

Foord, James. "To the West on Business in 1804." *Penna. Mag. Hist. Biog.*, LXIV (1940), 1–21.[14]

Scott, George. Missionary Journal. *Western Missionary Magazine* (1803), 1–13.[15]

Stoddard, Maj. Amos. *Sketches, Historical and Descriptive, of Louisiana* (Philadelphia, Mathew Carey, 1812).[16]

On a trip to Kentucky in 1804 to investigate titles, James Foord crossed the Ohio River into the Ohio Country. His journal, consisting of brief entries, is statistical rather than descriptive. George Scott's journal briefly recounts a mission to Sandusky, Brownstown, and vicinity in the same year. On March 9, 1804, Major Amos Stoddard received Upper Louisiana from Spain in the name of France and on the next day assumed the government in the name of the United States. He kept the peace and helped destroy prejudice against the Indians. This information and other material he incorporated in his *Sketches*, containing comments on history, topography, Indians, and settlements.

Dow, Lorenzo. *Perambulations of a Cosmopolite . . .* (Rochester, Printed for the publisher, 1842). Published under different titles, e.g.: *The Dealings of God, Man, and the Devil . . .* (New York, W. Faulkner, 1854).[17]

"The Diary of Hugh Faries." In *Five Fur-Traders of the Northwest*. Charles M. Gates, ed. (Minneapolis, University of Minnesota Press, 1933), pp. 189–241.[18]

Malhiot, François Victor. "A Wisconsin Fur-Trader's Journal, 1804–05. *Wis. Hist. Soc. Colls.*, XIX (1910), 163–215.[19]

One of the most eccentric figures of the frontier was Lorenzo Dow, a Methodist circuit rider who left his wife the day after his wedding, September 3, 1804, and began a preaching tour from Westerville, New York, to the Mississippi Territory, returning in 1805. His book, first published in 1814 and reprinted many times, contains diary entries telling of preaching in Steubenville, Zanesville, New Lancaster, Chillicothe, Springfield, and places farther west. Although Dow lacked literary skill and any great intellect, his lengthy book is a lively and valuable record of the life of a religious zealot.

Two fur traders who wrote journals of events in 1804 and 1805 were Hugh Faries and François Malhiot. The former, an employee of the Northwest Company in charge of fur trading around Rainy Lake post during the absence of the supervisor, wrote interesting notes on the weather, Indians, and the social life of the voyageurs. The latter, a French-Canadian supervising the Fond du Lac Department south of Lake Superior, wrote a spirited journal in French of the repair and rebuilding of the post and of his life and experiences with the Indians.

"Diary of William Joseph Clark." *Key. Hist. Soc. Reg.*, XXV (1927), 193–206.

Not to be confused with Lieutenant William Clark, William Joseph Clark, born in 1776, kept a diary which describes a trip in 1804 from Clark County, Kentucky, to St. Louis to take the deposition of Daniel Boone for the Widow Swinney. He returned to Kentucky in 1806. The work contains a few amusing incidents.

Gass, Sgt. Patrick. *A Journal of the Voyages and Travels of a Corps of Discovery, under the Command of Capt. Lewis and Capt. Clarke . . . from the Mouth of the River Missouri, through the Interior Parts of North America to the Pacific Ocean, During the Years 1804, 1805, and 1806 . . .* (Pittsburgh, David McKeehen, 1807).[20]

"The New Found Journal of Charles Floyd, a Sergeant under Captains Lewis and Clark." *Amer. Ant. Soc. Procs.*, New Series, IX (1893–1894), 238–52. Reprinted in R. G. Thwaites, ed. *Original Journals of the Lewis and Clark Expedition* (New York, 1905), VII, 3–26.[21]

Whitehouse, Pvt. Joseph. *Journal*. In Thwaites, *Original Journals*, VII, 29–190.[22]

Dunbar, William. *Discoveries Made in Exploring the Missouri, Red River, and Washita, by Captains Lewis and Clark, Doctors Sibley and William Dunbar . . .* (Natchez, Andrus, Marshall, and Co., 1806). Extracts in the "Political Cabinet" as Appendix to the *Monthly Anthology* (Boston, 1802) and later collected under the title of *American State Papers* (Boston, 1808), pp. 39–92.

———— *The Travels of Capts. Lewis & Clarke, from St. Louis, by Way of the Missouri and Columbia Rivers, to the Pacific Ocean; Performed in the Years 1804, 1805, & 1806, by Order of the Government of the United States. Containing Delineations of the Manners, Customs, Religion, &c. of the Indians . . .* (London, Longman, Hurst, Rees and Orme, 1809).

Lewis, Capt. Meriwether and Lieut. William Clark. *History of the Expedition of Captains Lewis and Clark, to the Sources of the Missouri, Thence across the Rocky Mountains and down the River Columbia to the Pacific Ocean . . .* (2 vols., Philadelphia, Bradford and Inskeep; New York, Abraham H. Inskeep, J. Maxwell, Printer, 1814). Reprinted in Thwaites *Original Journals . . .*, I–V (1904–1905). Reprint edited by John B. McMaster (3 vols., London, D. Nutt, 1905). Extracts in "Lewis and Clark Description of Pawnee Nation," *Neb. Hist.*, X (1927), 195–200; "Lewis and Clark in North Dakota," *Nor. Dak. Hist.*, XIV (1947), 5–45, 73–145, 173–241, 287–391; XV (1948), 15–74; "Lewis and Clark in South Dakota," *Sou. Dak. Hist. Colls.*, IX (1918), 514–96; Lloyd McFarling, *Exploring the Northern Plains . . .* (Caldwell, Ida., 1955), pp. 2–12, 15–26; and in Charles Neider, *The Great West* (New York, Coward-McCann, 1958). Condensed by Bernard DeVoto into a one-volume edition (Boston, Houghton Mifflin Co., 1945).[23]

Clark, William. Original records and Journal, 1803–1806. MS. At present in custody of Mr. Louis Starr of New York.

The story of Lewis and Clark's epic expedition to the Pacific in 1804–1806 has been told so often and so well that a detailed account of it is unnecessary here. After the purchase of the Louisiana Territory in 1803, President Jefferson instructed the two men to explore the Missouri River and find the most direct route to the Pacific. The explorers left Pittsburgh on August 31, 1803, and in the spring of 1804 began their slow journey up the Missouri River. After reaching the Pacific, they started their return trip in March, 1806, arriving at St. Louis in September. Although the diaries are often tedious, they have a great deal of human interest, and no summary can capture their original scope or flavor.

Sergeant Patrick Gass's journal of the expedition was first to be published. Although popular, frequently reprinted, and translated into French and German, it is merely a lengthy factual diary. Since Sergeant Charles Floyd died on the trip, his brief journal does not extend beyond August, 1804. The journal of Private Joseph Whitehouse, May, 1804 to November, 1805, supplements the better known accounts, is detailed, and interestingly worded. Lewis's own journal, dated January, 1804 to September, 1806, is likewise detailed and has many notes on such things as distances and topography. After Lewis's death in 1809, Clark edited the journal with the aid of Nicholas Biddle, and Paul Allen supervised the printing. William Dunbar was the first non-member of the expedition to tell the story in a book, printed in 1806. His later book, *The Travels of Capts. Lewis & Clark* . . . has some anecdotes not in any other edition. An unpublished portion of the Lewis and Clark journals has been discussed earlier in the present chapter. Clark's recently discovered journal of the 1803–1806 expedition gives a day-by-day account of the trip. His other narratives were written in 1794, 1797, and 1808.

"Henry Bartlett's Diary to Ohio and Kentucky, 1805." *Va. Mag. Hist. Biog.*, I (1911), 68–86.[24]

Breathitt, John. "Commencement of a Journal from Kentucky to the State of Pennsylvania–&c. March 28th 1805." *Ky. Hist. Soc. Reg.*, LII (1954), 5–24.

Espy, Josiah. "Memorandums of a Tour Made by Josiah Espy in the State of Ohio and Kentucky and Indiana Territory in 1805." *Ohio Valley Historical Society Miscellanies* (Cincinnati, Robert Clarke and Co., 1870), No. 1.[25]

Henry Bartlett's carelessly written diary tells of a trip from Virginia to Chillicothe and Scioto, Ohio, and then to Kentucky in 1805. A good narrative of a backwoods preacher is appended. John Breathitt described in the lengthy passages of a diary of the same year, his trip through Chillicothe, New Lancaster, Springfield, and Morristown, Ohio, en route from Kentucky to Pennsylvania. He called the first-named town "the Metropolis of the State of Ohio." Josiah Espy's memoranda tell of a journey from Massachusetts to the Little Miami River, Yellow Springs, Dayton, and Cincinnati, Ohio, and into Indiana and Kentucky and his return home. Religious in tone, the diary shows the author's power of observation and acuteness of judgment.

[King, Nicholas?] *An Account of a Voyage up the Mississippi River from St. Louis to its Sources; Made under the Order of the War Department by Lieut. Pike, of the United States Army, in the Years 1805 and 1806. Compiled from Mr. Pike's Journal* (Washington, 1807?). Extracts in *Colls. Minn. Hist. Soc.*, I (1902 reprint), 302–42.

Pike, Zebulon Montgomery. *An Account of Expeditions to the Source of the Mississippi, and through the Western Parts of Louisiana, to the Sources of the Arkansaw, Kans, LaPlatte, and Pierre Jaun Rivers; Performed by Order of the Government of the United States during the Years 1805, 1806, and 1807. And a Tour through the Interior Parts of New Spain, when Conducted through those Provinces, by Order of the Captain-General, in the Year 1807* (Philadelphia, C. and A. Conrad and Co.; Petersburgh, Somervell and Conrad . . . ; Baltimore, John Binns, 1810). The standard edition is Elliott Coues, ed. *The Expedition of Zebulon Montgomery Pike, to Head Waters of the Mississippi River, through Louisiana Territory, and in New Spain, during the Years 1805–6–7* (3 vols., New York, F. P. Harper, 1895). *Southwestern Expedition* reprint edited by Milo M. Quaife (Chicago, R. R. Donnelley and Sons Co., 1925). Extract in Charles Neider, *The Great West*.[26]

Zebulon Montgomery Pike, the explorer and discoverer of the peak that bears his name, began a military expedition in 1805, by order of the government, to trace the Mississippi River to its source and locate places for fortified posts. His journal of the 1805–1806 trip gives a detailed report on the hardships endured, hunting and surveying, life among various Indian tribes, French trading interests, and topography. He journeyed as far north as Leech Lake and notified British and Indian occupants of the region that they were under American control. In 1806 he went from St. Louis to the Rocky Mountains by way of northern Mexico and Texas. He wrote the account of his expeditions immediately after his return and gained well-deserved fame upon its publication in 1810. A paraphrase of his journal was written in the third person, possibly by Nicholas King, and likely published in 1807.

Anonymous. Journal of a trip from Champaign County, Ohio, down the Mississippi River to New Orleans . . . ; Return by Way of Philadelphia, November 25, 1805–July 28, 1806. 141 pp. MS. Illinois State Historical Library, Springfield.

Adams, Samuel. Diaries, 1805–1814. MS. notebook owned by Frank Williams, Beech Grove, Ind.; transcript, Indiana Historical Society.

Shaker Papers. MS. journals and diaries in the Shaker Papers, 1805–1874. 15 vols. Library of Congress.[27]

The anonymous journal describes a trip from Ohio down the Mississippi River with a cargo of flour and the return by way of Philadelphia. Samuel Adams' diaries cover trips from Pennsylvania to and from Knox County, Indiana, in 1805, 1806, 1809, and 1814. In the Shaker Papers (1805–1874), there are fifteen unpublished journals of individuals who grew up in Union Village, Ohio, or who migrated there and remained members of the Shaker Society.

"Baltimore to Waynesville in 1805: Extracts from the Memoirs of Rebecca Wright Hill." *Bull. Fr. Hist. Soc.*, XL (1951), 24–33.

Hunt, Anne L. *Early Recollections*. (n. p., n. d.) Extracts in *Glimpses of the Past*, I (1934), 41–51.

Memoranda and Correspondence of Mildred Ratcliff (Philadelphia, 1890). Extracts, pp. 38–172 passim.[28]

Young, Jacob. *Autobiography of a Pioneer* (Cincinnati, Cranston and Crofts; New York, Hunt and Eaton, 1857).

In 1805, at the age of twelve, Rebecca W. Hill traveled by wagon from Baltimore to below Wheeling and eventually settled in the Miami country. Her memoirs, covering events in the Midwest as late as 1819, describe pioneer hardships interestingly. Mrs. Anne L. Hunt's *Recollections* contain a detailed narrative of a trip down the Ohio from Pittsburgh in 1805 and describe Shawneetown, Ste. Genevieve, and St. Louis. Mrs. Mildred Ratcliff wrote a journal of her travels and religious work in the South and in Ohio during 1805–1833. Jacob Young's lengthy *Autobiography* describes his ministerial experiences and travels in the Midwest beginning in 1805, when he was appointed to the Marietta circuit of the Methodist church. He attended the Chillicothe conference in 1807 and was again in Ohio most of the time from 1809 through 1855. His book, decidedly religious in tone, contains facts about circuits, appointments, and stays in various towns and has interesting passages. He was associated with Alfred Brunson and Reverend James B. Finley, who also wrote travel narratives, mentioned in Chapters 5 and 8.

Ashe, Thomas. *Travels in America, Performed in 1806, For the Purpose of Exploring the Rivers Allegheny, Monongahela, Ohio, and Mississippi, and Ascertaining the Produce and Con-*

dition of their *Banks and Vicinity* (3 vols., London, Richard Phillips, 1808).[29]

Thomas Ashe, a British visitor to the United States in 1806, wrote a series of letters about his trip, which he collected in a book. He traveled down various rivers, including the Ohio and the Mississippi, and made adverse comments about most of what he saw. The Falls of the Ohio were to him an awful scene; the population of Kentucky, he thought, would soon decline. Yet he was perhaps the first person to write a book about the United States that was abusive but financially profitable to the author. Even the *Edinburgh Review* adversely criticized this sort of attitude, which aroused so much bitterness that Americans began to resent all British travelers and to look with suspicion upon any Englishman's travel narrative that was not wholeheartedly favorable. Although his volume might seem insignificant when placed beside the many other travel tales of the period, it played an important part in keeping alive the enmity that had existed since the American Revolution. Christian Schultz's book, discussed later in this chapter, was a direct reply to Ashe.

Anonymous. Journal of a Voyage up the Mississippi and Red Rivers, 1806. MS. Library of Congress.
Atkins, Quintius F. "Missionary Journal." *West. Res. Hist. Soc. Tracts,* L (1879), 110–13.[30]
"Rev. Paul Henkel's Journal." F. E. Cooper, trans. *Ohio Arch. Hist. Quar.,* XXIII (1914), 162–218.[31]
Stuart, John C. "A Journal Remarks or Observations in a Voyage down the Kentucky, Ohio, Mississippi Rivers &c." *Ky. Hist. Soc. Reg.,* L (1952), 5–25.

The voyage in the anonymous journal originates in New Orleans. The diary of Quintius Atkins, a historically useful work, is mainly a summary of his missionary journey to the Wyandot Indians on the Sandusky River in 1806. Another missionary journal of the same year is by Reverend Paul Henkel, a German Lutheran, who wrote pleasant religious notes about a seventy-two-day journey to Point Pleasant, Ohio. John C. Stuart's diary of 1806, evidently hastily written, relates events in a trip down the Kentucky, Ohio, and Mississippi Rivers in a flatboat.

Hildreth, Samuel Prescott. Autobiographical Sketch. *New Eng. Hist. Geneal. Reg.,* April, 1849. Extracts in *Boston Medical and Surgical Journal,* October 24, 1849.[32]
Life and Times of Ephraim Cutler, Prepared from his Journals and Correspondence by his Daughter [Julia Perkins Cutler] ... (Cincinnati, R. Clarke and Co., 1890). Excerpts in Emanuel Spencer, ed. "Glimpses of Log-Cabin Life in Early Ohio," *Mag. of Amer. Hist.,* XXIV (1890), 101–11.[33]
"Personal Narrative of Col. John Shaw of Marquette County, Wisconsin." *Wis. Hist. Soc. Colls.,* II (1855), 197–232.

The autobiographical sketch by Samuel P. Hildreth, the author of tales of Indian captivity, mentioned in Chapter 3, describes a journey on horseback from the East to Marietta, Ohio, in September, 1806, the beginning of his medical practice at Belpré, and his return to Marietta in 1808, where he continued to practice until 1861. The journals of Ephraim Cutler, son of Manasseh Cutler, cover travels in Ohio during a period of thirty-three years beginning in 1806 and describe his journey to Ohio, visits to various towns in that state, religious activities, and life at Warren, Ohio. Julia P. Cutler's biography is based upon these journals, and includes a diverting account of a cattle drive from the Ohio River to Baltimore. Colonel John Shaw's narrative describes a trip down the Ohio and up the Mississippi to St. Louis beginning in 1806 and relates happenings in the Midwest as late as 1855, including several military events during the War of

1812 and trading expeditions from St. Louis to Prairie du Chien. He describes such interesting events as an earthquake at New Madrid and trade as well as fights with Indians.

Adams, William L. Journal of the Barge, *Lovely Nan,* Lewis West, Master, New Orleans to Louisville, commencing at Natchez, July 9, 1807. MS. Listed in Biggert, *Guide,* No. 118.
Bedford, Dr. John R. "A Tour in 1807 down the Cumberland, Ohio, and Mississippi Rivers from Nashville to New Orleans." *Tenn. Hist. Mag.,* V (1919), 40–68, 105–22.[34]
Heriot, George. *Travels through the Canadas, Containing a Description of the Picturesque Scenery on Some of the Rivers and Lakes; with an Account of Productions, Commerce, and Inhabitants of Those Provinces* ... (London, Richard Phillips, 1807).
Schultz, Christian. *Travels on an Inland Voyage through the States of New-York, Pennsylvania, Ohio, Virginia, Kentucky and Tennessee, and through the Territories of Indiana, Louisiana, Mississippi, and New-Orleans; Performed in the Years 1807 and 1808* ... (2 vols., New York, Isaac Riley, 1810).[35]

A voyage by barge from Natchez to Louisville in 1807 is recounted in the journal of William Adams. Dr. John R. Bedford wrote a hastily composed diary of a trip from Nashville down the Cumberland, Ohio, and Mississippi rivers in the same year. It contains weather observations, character sketches, and descriptions. George Heriot, a Canadian, described the upper Great Lakes region, including Detroit and Michilimackinac.

Christian Schultz was a native American who traveled through part of Ohio and the Illinois country, visiting Shawneetown, Fort de Chartres, Cahokia, and other places in the fall of 1807, part of the territory Thomas Ashe had covered. Schultz's book, which was published from a series of letters, was the direct result of his having read Ashe's *Travels in America.* Schultz felt that Ashe should be answered by someone who could defend his country against Ashe's verbal attack. It is a long work and important to any student of Anglo-American literary relations.

Cuming, Fortescue. *Sketches of a Tour to the Western Country, through the States of Ohio and Kentucky; a Voyage down the Ohio and Mississippi Rivers, and a Trip through the Mississippi Territory, and Part of West Florida. Commenced at Philadelphia in the Winter of 1807, and Concluded in 1809* (Pittsburgh, Cramer, Spear and Eichbaum, 1810). Reprinted in Thwaites, *Early Western Travels,* Vol. IV. Extracts in "Maysville to Chillicothe in Four Days." Clyde W. Park, ed. *Hist. Phil. Soc. of Ohio Bull.,* XII (1954), 159–62.[36]
Journal of the Life, Travels, and Gospel Labours of William Williams (Cincinnati, Lodge, L'Hommedieu, and Hammond, 1828).[37]

Fortescue Cuming was an Irishman who bought land in Ohio in 1806 and, in order to see his purchase, made a trip to America in 1807 to 1809, travelling down the Ohio and Mississippi rivers. His *Sketches* is a detailed and accurate record of frontier social and political conditions. William Williams, a Quaker, wrote a diary covering events in Ohio and the Indiana Territory during 1807 and 1814–1816. Long entries describe Quaker meetings.

Westward with Dragoons; the Journal of William Clark on his Expedition to Establish Fort Osage, August 25 to September 22, 1808. ... Kate L. Gregg, ed. (Fulton, Mo., Ovid Bell Press, 1937).[38]

After the successful expedition of 1804–1806, William Clark was sent from St. Louis in 1808 to establish Fort Osage. He wrote a journal descriptive of the trip, the weather and topography, the wilderness, the building of the fort, treaty-making with the Osage Indians, and his return to St. Louis. The entries are somewhat monotonous, however.

Boyd, Col. John P. Military Diary, 1808–1812. 277 pp. MS. Indiana Historical Society, Indianapolis. There is a similar orderly book in Burton Historical Collection, Detroit.[39]

The character of Colonel John P. Boyd was described by a fellow officer in the War of 1812 as "a compound of ignorance, vanity, and petulance." His unpublished orders and letters of 1808–1812 are well written, however, and constitute a sort of military diary of activities and movements of troops from Vincennes to the scene of the Battle of Tippecanoe and back, and include a description of the building of Fort Harrison.

Anonymous. "A Personal Narrative." *Mich. Hist. Colls.*, VIII (1886), 662–69.
Ker, Henry. *Travels through the Western Interior of the United States, from the Year 1808 up to the Year 1816 . . .* (Elizabethtown, N. J., the Author, 1816).[40]
Robbins, Frank. "The Personal Reminiscences of General Chauncey Eggleston." *Ohio Arch. Hist. Quar.*, XLI (1932), 284–320.
Williams, Ephraim S. "Personal Reminiscences." *Mich. Hist. Colls.*, VIII (1886), 233–59.
———"Incidents of Early Days in Michigan." *Mich. Hist. Colls.*, IX (1886), 166–72.
——— "Remembrances of Early Days." *Mich. Hist. Colls.*, X (1888), 137–42.
——— "A Trip on April Fool's Day." *Mich. Hist. Colls.*, XIV (1890), 539–41.
——— "Remembrances of Early Days in Saginaw in 1833." *Mich. Hist. Colls.*, X (1888), 142–47.
"Narrative of Alexis Clermont." *Wis. Hist. Soc. Colls.*, XV (1900), 452–57.
"Narrative of Spoon Decorah." *Wis. Hist. Soc. Colls.*, XIII (1895), 448–62.

The anonymous "Personal Narrative" extends from 1808 to 1812 and describes the establishment of a trading post for Indians at Fort Madison, Iowa, and an attack on the fort. Henry Ker, a native American who spent most of his youth in London, wrote a book covering his travels during 1808–1815. Although concerned largely with the region southwest of the Middle West, it contains an account of a trip down the Ohio and Mississippi in 1808. Ker, who apologized for his occasionally poor style, often wrote effectively: "When we arrived near the mouth [of the Ohio], we found the current diminishing, and our boat on the point of stopping, the cause then unknown to me; when all of a sudden, I beheld the Mississippi flowing down with pomp and grandeur." (p. 24)

Frank Robbins, in "Reminiscences of General Chauncey Eggleston," tells of the latter's trip from Massachusetts to Ohio in 1808 and his life and business ventures in Aurora, Ohio, for several years afterwards. He includes description of a phase of the War of 1812.

Ephraim S. Williams' five narratives together constitute a valuable record of pioneer life in Michigan. They begin in 1808 and include interesting descriptions of the War of 1812, of early Detroit, loghouse building at Pontiac, Indian characteristics and fishing customs, and events as late as 1849. A brief tale beginning about 1820 tells of a search for pine wood and relates incidents of logging when the author was merely a boy. His "Remembrances of Early Days" (1823–1834) discusses Indians and an Indian trail and describes a journey from Pontiac to Grand Blanc and the Saginaw. A trip, perhaps in 1829, by pony and cutter and later by wagon to Detroit and return across a dangerous river is the subject of another narrative. A final tale tells of fur trading with Indians at Saginaw and of searching for copper in the same region during 1833 to 1838.

Two narratives written by an editor of the *Wisconsin Historical Society Collections* are Alexis Clermont's brief account of the Black Hawk War and other events during 1808–1850 and the story of Spoon Decorah, an Indian who lived in various parts of the Midwest from about 1808 to 1887. The Indian, an old man at the time the editor interviewed him, recalled the Black Hawk War and made a plea for better treatment of the Indian by the whites.

Bond, Edward. Diary, 1809. 10 pp. MS. Original owned by William Perry Marshall, Richmond, Ind.; transcript, Indiana Historical Society.

After a trip from North Carolina to Pennsylvania and Virginia in 1793, Edward Bond journeyed to Ohio and the Indiana Territory in 1809. His diary covers the latter trip and is an interesting revelation of a conscientious Quaker's thoughts and feelings.

Lee, D. and J. H. Frost. *Ten Years in Oregon* (New York, The Authors, 1844).
Bradbury, John. *Travels in the Interior of America, in the Years 1809, 1810, and 1811; Including a Description of Upper Louisiana, together with the States of Ohio, Kentucky, Indiana, and Tennessee, with the Illinois and Western Territories, and Containing Remarks and Observations Useful to Persons Emigrating to those Countries* (Liverpool, Smith and Galway; London, Sherwood, Nealy, and Jones, 1817). Reprinted with additions (London, 1819); reprint of 1819 edition in Thwaites, *Early Western Travels*, V, 25–320. Extract in Lloyd McFarling, ed. *Exploring the Northern Plains . . .* (Caldwell, Ida., 1955), pp. 39–45.[41]
Colby, John. *The Life, Experience, and Travels of John Colby, Preacher of the Gospel* (3rd ed., Cornish, Me., S. W. and C. C. Cole, 1829).[42]
"Autobiographical Sketch of William Henry Rector." *Oreg. Hist. Soc. Quar.*, XXIX (1928), 323–36; XXX (1929), 63–69.

A religious narrative by D. Lee and J. H. Frost tells of a trip from Canada to Mackinac, St. Louis, and up the Missouri to Oregon in 1809–1810. Included is an account of Wilson P. Hunt's Astoria expedition. John Bradbury, an English botanist, wrote an unbiased and informative book of travel in Ohio, Indiana, and Illinois and from St. Louis up the Missouri River during 1809–1811. He made part of the western journey with members of the Hunt expedition and with Henry M. Brackenridge. Gives notes on places, Indians, and botany. According to Thwaites, some of the material for the book was not gathered until a journey at the close of the War of 1812.

Reverend John P. Colby, a Baptist minister of more zeal than writing ability or preparation for his calling, describes religious conditions of 1810 in the Ohio Valley in a monotonous, unfinished book covering travels during 1809–1817. A brief sketch by William H. Rector recounts his father's settling in Ohio in 1809 and describes various trips in the Midwest until the family immigrated in 1845 to Oregon by way of Independence and Fort Laramie.

Audubon, John James. "Audubon's 'Journey up the Mississippi.'" John F. McDermott, ed. *Jour. Ill. State Hist. Soc.*, XXXV (1942), 148–73.
——— *Journal of John James Audubon Made During his Trip to New Orleans in 1820–1821.* Howard Corning, ed. (Boston, Club of Odd Volumes, 1929).

———— *Ornithological Biography, or an Account of the Habits of the Birds of the United States of America; . . . Interspersed with Delineations of American Scenery and Manners* (5 vols., Edinburgh, Adam Black, etc. [Vol. I] and Adam and Charles Black, etc. [Vols. II–V], 1831–1839).

Journal of John James Audubon . . . Made While Obtaining Subscriptions to his "Birds of America" 1840–1843. Howard Corning, ed. (Boston, Club of Odd Volumes, 1929). Extracts in "John J. Audubon and his Visit to Iowa," David C. Mott, ed. *Ann. of Ia.*, 3rd Series, XVI (1928), 403–19, and general extracts in Marie R. Audubon, *Audubon and His Journals* (2 vols., New York, C. Scribner's Sons, 1897) and in McFarling, *Exploring the Northern Plains*, pp. 190–200.[43]

By the end of the first decade of the nineteenth century the Midwest had begun to attract travelers with scientific interests. The journal of the 1810 trip up the Mississippi by John James Audubon, well-known ornithologist, has been lost, but an account of it, based upon *Winter's Wreath* (published in 1829) and containing a detailed description of the Mississippi country, has been preserved. His journal of a trip from Cincinnati to New Orleans with John Mason in 1820–1821 lacks literary merit. The *Ornithological Biography* (1831–1839) shows the influence of several travel narrators whose adventures Audubon scattered through the first three volumes. His journal of a trip up the Missouri River in 1843 with Edward Harris should be compared with Harris's account of the same trip, which is mentioned in Chapter 13.

Day, Mills. Journal of Travels from Washington, D. C., to Conneaut, Ohio, May–July, 1810. 2 vols. MS. Yale University Library, New Haven, Conn.

Hale, Jonathan. Diary, 1810. 6 pp., typescript, copied from his MS. book. Rutherford B. Hayes Library, Fremont, O.

A Journey to Ohio in 1810 as Recorded in the Journal of Margaret Van Horn Dwight. Max Farrand, ed. (New Haven, Yale University Press, 1914).[44]

Miller, Robert. "Early Days in Indiana." *Mag. Hist.*, XXIII (1916), 22–26.

Mills Day's "Journal" is a lengthy unpublished diary. Jonathan Hale is the author of a good, brief diary of events in 1810 during his first journey from Connecticut to Ohio. Published narratives of the same year include Mrs. Margaret Van Horn (Bell) Dwight's long, rather lively diary of a trip by horse-drawn conveyance from Milford, Connecticut, across Pennsylvania, along the Ohio River to Youngstown, and by horse from there to Warren, Ohio. Robert Miller's interesting account describes a trip to Indiana and pioneer life there, including a bear hunt and a pursuit of a woman by a panther.

Bernard, John. *Retrospections of America, 1797–1811.* Mrs. Bayle Bernard, ed. (New York, Harper and Bros., 1887).[45]

Kit Carson's Own Story of His Life. Blanche C. Grant, ed. (Taos, N. M., 1926). Reprint edited by Milo M. Quaife (Chicago, R. R. Donnelley and Sons Co., 1935). Extract in Charles Neider, *The Great West*.[46]

Forster, John Harris. "Some Incidents of Pioneer Life in the Upper Peninsula of Michigan." *Mich. Hist. Colls.*, XVII (1892), 332–45.

Berryman, Rev. Jerome C. "A Circuit Rider's Frontier Experiences." *Kans. State Hist. Soc. Colls.*, XVI (1923–1925), 177–226.

Narrative of Albert Cavalier in the 1810's; dated September 6, 1878. 12 pp. MS. in the Rutherford B. Hayes Papers. Rutherford B. Hayes Library, Fremont, O.

John Bernard was a well-known British actor-manager who kept a journal of his tour in the eastern Midwest in 1810–1811. He liked the Americans and showed no condescension towards them. The famed scout, Kit (Christopher) Carson, in relating events of his boyhood in his autobiography, stated that his parents moved to Missouri in 1810 when he was a year old, that he lived in Howard County, Missouri, for fifteen years, was apprenticed for two years to learn the saddler's trade, but decided to join the first party he could find leaving for the Rockies and started for Santa Fé in August, 1826. His narrative, covering Midwestern experiences as late as 1842, makes good reading. John Harris Forster's tale of activities during 1810–1847 contains information on three men, Edouard Sansavaine, John Reid, and C. C. Douglas, and their experiences in the wilds of upper Michigan. It is divided into topics and discusses such interesting subjects as snowshoeing and mine speculation. Reverend Jerome C. Berryman's narrative, covering the years from 1810–1866, tells of varied experiences on the frontier including teaching Indian children. Religiously didactic, he disapproved of the emancipation of the slaves. A good narrative by Albert Cavalier recounts an Ohio journey.

Brackenridge, Henry Marie. *Views of Louisiana; together with a Journal of a Voyage up the Missouri River, in 1811* (Pittsburgh, Cramer, Spear and Eichbaum, 1814). Second (expanded) ed. called *Journal of a Voyage up the River Missouri in 1811 . . .* (Baltimore, Coale, etc., 1816). Reprint of 2nd ed. in Thwaites, *Early Western Travels*, VI, 19–166. A German translation was published at Weimar in 1818.[47]

Melish, John. *Travels in the United States of America, in the Years 1806 & 1807, and 1809, 1810, & 1811 . . .* (2 vols., Philadelphia, Printed for the Author, 1812).[48]

Henry Marie Brackenridge, the author of *Recollections of Persons and Places in the West*, mentioned in Chapter 6, took a trip in 1811 similar to John Bradbury's. He went up the Missouri River from St. Charles, in the Missouri Territory, to Manuel Lisa's fort near Mandan village and back. He made the journey with Lisa, of the Missouri Fur Company, and on the way met Bradbury and Wilson Hunt. The journal is generally more interesting than Bradbury's and contains some rather poetic descriptions. He details the difficulty of starting the voyage because of the reluctance of the men to stop drinking and frolicking with their friends at the taverns and describes, for example, a meal of mush and hominy along the way, and buffalo carcasses on the river bank. He portrays vividly the complaints of the men about the rigorous work necessary to keep their craft moving, the sickness from pleurisy, fever, and coughs, the fears of attacks from hostile Sioux, and the great Western plains during the summertime, with vast herds of wild animals adding a touch of life to the lonely scene. These and other incidents give the book unusual charm. Rusk says that the work "is written, not only in an entertaining style, but with an evident regard for accuracy, and deserves to be ranked as a classic of its kind." (*The Literature of the Middle Western Frontier*, New York, 1925, I, 124.)

John Melish, an Englishman, wrote a book, only a part of which is devoted to the Midwest. In 1811 he descended the Ohio from Pittsburgh, passing through Marietta, Gallipolis, Cincinnati, Jeffersonville, and Indiana and the Illinois Territory en route to the Mississippi. On returning, he traveled via Chillicothe, Springfield, Zanesville, Canton, and Cleveland. He prepared for this trip by reading all the books of American travel he could find, but he realized that many of them were inaccurate and spiteful. He tried to be as unbiased as possible and succeeded in producing a remarkably accurate work. The information for his brief later book, *A Description of the Roads in the United States* (Philadelphia, 1814), was evidently obtained during this tour.

Anonymous. "To Illinois in 1811." *Jour. Ill. State Hist. Soc.*, XXXVI (June, 1943), 208–10.

"Extracts from the Diary of Major Sibley." *Chrons. of Okla.*, V (1927), 196–218.[49]

Taylor, Rowse. "A Journey by Carriage from Newport, Rhode Island, to Smithfield, Ohio, 1811." *Bull. Fr. Hist. Soc.*, VIII (1918), 90–100; IX (1919), 18–26.[50]

"John Tipton's Tippecanoe Journal." *Ind. Mag. Hist.*, II (1906), 170–84. Reprinted from the *Indianapolis News*, May 5, 1879.[51]

The anonymous account is a brief, carelessly written narrative relating incidents in a trip from Pennsylvania to Illinois. Major George Chapman Sibley's partly published diary in the form of a long letter tells of a visit in 1811 to the lodge of an Osage Indian chief and describes the Kansas and Platte rivers and the Pawnee Indians. Rowse Taylor, a Quaker, wrote a rambling and detailed account of his family's journey by carriage from Rhode Island to Ohio. John Tipton's journal about the march and encampment of the riflemen of Harrison County, Indiana, and the Tippecanoe campaign of 1811 is probably the only circumstantial account left of the event. Poorly written.

Biography of Mrs. Lydia B. Bacon. Written for the Massachusetts Sabbath School Society, and Approved by the Committee of Publication (Boston, Massachusetts Sabbath School Society, 1856). Reprinted in "Mrs. Lydia B. Bacon's Journal, 1811–1812." Mary M. Crawford, ed. *Ind. Mag. Hist.*, XL (1944), 367–86; XLI (1945), 59–79.[52]

"Journey of Mr. [Wilson Price] Hunt and his Companions from Saint Louis to the Mouth of the Columbia by a New Route across the Rocky Mountains." Translation from *Nouvelles Annales des Voyages* (Paris, 1821). In *The Discovery of the Oregon Trail*, Philip A. Rollins, ed. (New York, London, C. Scribner's Sons, 1935), Appendix A, pp. 281–308.[53]

Walker, Adam. *A Journal of Two Campaigns* (Keene, N. H., the Author, 1816). Reprinted in *Ind. Hist. Colls.*, VII (1922), 693–710, and in *American State Papers, Military Affairs*, I, 268–95.[54]

Dort, Titus. "A Personal Reminiscence." *Mich. Hist. Colls.*, I (1878), 507–9.

"Mrs. Nancy Howard, of Port Huron, and her Interesting Recollections." *Mich. Hist. Colls.*, XIV (1890), 531–35. Reprinted from the *Detroit Free Press*, Aug. 29, 1889.

Mrs. Lydia Bacon's readable diary tells about her trip with her husband, Lieutenant Josiah Bacon, a quartermaster in the 4th Regiment, United States Infantry, from Boston Harbor down the Ohio River to Vincennes in 1811, her wait at Vincennes while her husband took part in a campaign against hostile Indians along the Wabash in 1811 and 1812, and her return east by way of Detroit in 1812. Mr. Hunt's own account of his journey in 1811–1812 is a historically valuable narrative. Hunt was Lisa's rival in navigating the Missouri, and both Bradbury and Brackenridge were with him during part of their trips up the Missouri. The journal of Adam Walker, who was a member of Bacon's regiment, is written up from notes and covers two campaigns in Michigan and Indiana during the same years. Titus Dort's reminiscence extends over the years 1811–1860. It is a brief, simple narrative discussing his life in Ohio and Detroit and his election to the state legislature. The interesting Midwestern experiences which Mrs. Nancy Howard described in her narrative (1811–1887) include her trip from Ohio to Detroit, her move to Grosse Pointe, the plundering of her house by Indians, her return to Detroit in 1834, and her removal to Port Huron.

Chapter 8

Midwestern Travel Narratives of the War of 1812

and of Events to 1820

Because of the many battles on the frontier during the War of 1812, a much larger number of Midwestern travel narratives was written during this conflict than during the American Revolution. The war was described by military personnel and civilians. General Hull's march to Detroit and his defeat there, General Hopkins' unsuccessful expedition against the Indians, and the massacre of Captain Heald's party were among the more popular of the events related.

Although no travel narrators as great as Lewis and Clark made appearances during 1812–1819, a large number of important figures such as James Flint, Morris Birkbeck, Stephen Long, H. R. Schoolcraft, and Edwin James visited the Midwest during the period. The region, though still a vast frontier, attracted more and more visitors, particularly Englishmen interested in observing conditions and considering the land as a place for future settlement.

"Journal of William K. Beall, July–August, 1812." *Amer. Hist. Rev.*, XVII (1912), 782–808.[1]

"The Robert Lucas Journal." J. C. Parish, ed. *Ia. Jour. Hist.*, IV (1906), 343–437.[2]

Merritt, Capt. William Hamilton. "Journal of Events Principally on the Detroit and Niagara Frontier." *Publications of the Champlain Society* (Toronto), XVII (1928), 543–648.[3]

[Reynolds, James.] *Journal of an American Prisoner at Fort Malden and Quebec in the War of 1812.* G. M. Fairchild, Jr., ed. (Quebec, F. Carrel, 1909).[4]

Diary of John Robison, Captain of Ohio Militia Company, during March from Middleton to Detroit, where he was on Duty until Hull's Surrender, and Return to Cleveland, April 27–Sept. 3, 1812. MS., typed copy. Burton Historical Collection, Detroit.

"Journal of Ensign William Schillinger, a Soldier of the War of 1812." James A. Green, ed. *Ohio Arch. Hist. Quar.*, XLI (1932), 52–85.

William K. Beall, an assistant quarter-master-general under General James Taylor, was captured by the British during Hull's campaign, and was taken aboard the schooner *Thames* near Detroit. While on board he wrote an imaginative, personal journal. Later he was transferred to another boat which saw service on Lake Erie. Captain Robert Lucas, later governor of Iowa, who helped organize a battalion of volunteers and served as a detached officer during the war, wrote a lengthy diary of events

of the war in Ohio. The journal of Captain W. H. Merritt, an Englishman, mentions that in 1812 all of Michigan Territory fell to General Isaac Brock, the British commander. James Reynolds, a surgeon's mate, is the supposed author of *The Journal of an American Prisoner.* . . . He was in charge of the sick on two vessels which were dispatched from Maumee to Detroit and which the British captured. John Robison's diary of 1812 describes a march from Ohio to Detroit and return to Cleveland. He was on duty in Detroit until Hull's surrender. The diary of William Schillinger is concerned mainly with weather, sickness in camp, and his journey to Fort Amanda.

"John Kinzie's Narrative of the Fort Dearborn Massacre." Mentor L. Williams, ed. *Jour. Ill. State Hist. Soc.*, XLVI (1953), 343–62. Reprinted from *Chicago Tribune*, Aug. 15, 1953.[5]

"Nathan Heald's Journal." In *Chicago and the Old Northwest.* Milo M. Quaife, ed. (Chicago, University of Chicago Press, 1913), pp. 402–05.[6]

Charles Askins' diary of the frightful events at Fort Dearborn, Nehemiah Matson's narrative, and Mrs. Juliette Kinzie's *Waubun* have been treated as captivity tales in Chapter 3. An account by Mrs. Kinzie's husband, John Kinzie, is a travel tale only in that it describes troop movements in the Chicago area. Captain Nathan Heald, who commanded the detachment at Fort Dearborn, described in a very brief journal the massacre near the fort, the march from Chicago to Detroit, and his later life in Louisville and the Missouri Territory.

Brown, Ashley. "The Expedition of Colonel John B. Campbell of the 19th U. S. Infantry in Nov. 1812 from Franklintown to the Mississinewa Indian Villages." *Northw. Ohio Quar.*, VIII (1936),

Anonymous. Reminiscences of a campaign against the British and Indians, 1812–13, by a veteran of the "Pittsburgh Blues." Ca. 1860. 8 pp. typescript. In the John W. Lowe Collection of Books and Manuscripts on the War of 1812. Cited in *Catalogue of a Collection of Books and Manuscripts . . . Made by the Late Mr. John W. Lowe . . .* (1917), No. 199.

Ashley Brown's article is a rather poorly written but interesting narrative. Includes an account of the attack on Campbell's camp by the Indians. The anonymous "Reminiscences" briefly describes the principal events in the campaign in Ohio, Indiana, and the Northwest, including the first and second sieges of Fort Meigs.

The Travels and Adventures of David C. Bunnell, During Twenty-three Years of a Sea-faring Life; Containing an Accurate Account of the Battle of Lake Erie, under the Command of Com. Oliver H. Perry; Together with Ten Years' Service in the

Navy of the United States, etc. (Palmyra, N. Y., J. H. Bortles, 1831).

Larwill, Joseph H. Diary, Apr. 5, 1812–Sept. 17, 1813. MS. Burton Historical Collection, Detroit.

Luttig, John C. *Journal of a Fur Trading Expedition.* Stella M. Drumm, ed. (St. Louis, Missouri, Historical Society, 1920).[7]

Newsom, Nathan. "A Short Summary of a Journey, Taken by Volunteers from Gallia County [Ohio]; for the Purpose of Destroying Indians & the Invasion of Canada, August 9, 1812–February 31 [*sic*], 1813." 22 pp. Typed comments, map, and annotations by R. E. Banta. MS. Listed in Elizabeth Biggert, comp. *Guide to the Manuscript Collections in the Library of the Ohio State Archaeological and Historical Society* (Columbus, 1953), No. 756.

Schermerhorn, John F. and Samuel J. Mills. *A Correct View of that Part of the United States which Lies West of the Allegany Mountains, with Regard to Religion and Morals* (Hartford, Conn., Peter B. Gleason and Co., 1814).[8]

The Discovery of the Oregon Trail. Robert Stuart's Narrative. Philip Ashton Rollins, ed. (New York and London, Charles Scribner's Sons, 1935). Diary reprinted as *On the Oregon Trail . . .* (Norman, University of Oklahoma Press, 1953). Summarized in Washington Irving's *Astoria* (1836) and in H. M. Chittenden, *The American Fur Trade of the Far West* (2 vols., rev. ed., New York, Press of the Pioneers, 1935).[9]

Williams, Samuel. *Two Western Campaigns in the War of 1812–13* (Cincinnati, R. Clarke and Co., 1870). Reprinted in *Ohio Valley Historical Series*, No. 7, Miscellanies, [Pt.] 2 (Cincinnati, 1871).

In addition to Elias Darnell's diary and the tales by Mallary and Davenport, treated as captivity narratives in Chapter 3, several other travelers wrote accounts of the events of 1812 and 1813. David C. Bunnell's book presents the Battle of Lake Erie from the viewpoint of a sailor under the command of Commodore Perry. Lieutenant Joseph H. Larwill's diary, perhaps the most complete account of the Battle of Mississinewa, contains a summary of experiences at the River Raisin, Fort Meigs, Fort Stephenson, and on Lake Erie at the time of Perry's victory. John C. Luttig, a clerk of the Missouri Fur Company of St. Louis, gives a good picture of the life of traders and Indians in his journal of a fur trader's expedition to the upper Missouri in 1812–1813. Nathan Newsom's title sufficiently explains the contents of his MS.

Under the auspices of the Connecticut and Massachusetts Home Missionary societies, John F. Schermerhorn and Samuel J. Mills preached to Indians from Cincinnati to New Orleans. They recorded their tour in *A Correct View*, which describes the dangers of Indian attacks, flooded rivers, and even starvation. Robert Stuart's diary is mainly about the Far West but contains the story of a dangerous trip sponsored by John Jacob Astor's Pacific Fur Company from Astoria to the Oto Village and from there to St. Louis over some country which had never before been seen by white men. This journey was made famous by Irving's *Astoria*. Samuel Williams' book is a brief description of two Western campaigns.

Voyages, Travels and Discoveries of Tilly Buttrick, Jr. (Boston, John Putnam, 1831). Reprinted in R. G. Thwaites, ed. *Early Western Travels . . .* (32 vols., Cleveland, Arthur H. Clark Co., 1904), VIII, 15–89.[10]

Hubbard, Bela. "Memoir of Luther Harvey." *Mich. Hist. Colls.*, I (1877), 406–14.

Stebbins, C. B. "Father Winter and His Family." *Mich. Hist. Colls.*, VIII (1886), 178–94.

James Clyman, American Frontiersman, 1792–1881; the Adventures of a Trapper and Covered Wagon Emigrant as Told in his own Reminiscences and Diaries. Charles L. Camp, ed. (San Francisco, California Historical Society, 1928). Also in "Diaries and Memoranda of a Journey through the Far West, 1844 to 1846." *Cal. Hist. Soc. Quar.*, IV (1925), 307–60; V (1926), 44–84, 109–38, 255–82, 378–401.[11]

Schettler, Mrs. Eliza M. Scott. "Lights and Shadows from Pioneer Life." *Mich. Hist. Colls.*, XXXV (1907), 184–98.

A Western Pioneer or Incidents of the Life and Times of Alfred Brunson (2 vols., Cincinnati, Hitchcock and Walde; New York, Carlton and Lanahan, 1872). Extracts in "A Methodist Circuit Rider's Horseback Tour from Pennsylvania to Wisconsin, 1835," *Wis. Hist. Soc. Colls.*, XV (1900), 264–91.[12]

Bristol, Mrs. Mary Ann Brevoort. "Reminiscences of the Northwest." *Wis. Hist. Soc. Colls.*, VIII (1879), 293–308. Reprinted from the *Milwaukee Sunday Telegraph*, Mar. 30, Apr. 27, May 18, June 15, 1879.

"Journal of Priddy Meeks." *Utah Hist. Quar.*, X (1942), 145–223.

Tilly Buttrick, an Easterner, took a trip in 1812 down the Ohio to Cincinnati and Louisville. Early in 1815 he again descended the river to New Orleans and returned in 1817 by way of Cincinnati, Lower Sundusky, and Lake Erie to Detroit, Fort Erie, and Lower Sandusky Bay. His account of these adventures is generally dull in spite of several lively events. Bela Hubbard's "Memoir of Luther Harvey" relates experiences in Ohio and on Lake Erie during the War of 1812 and incidents as late as 1836. Chapter 12 mentions a book by Hubbard recounting events in 1837 and later. A readable tale by C. B. Stebbins summarizes a trip in 1812 from Connecticut up Lake Erie, and his settlement and life in Adrian, Michigan in 1848. A second narrative by Stebbins will be discussed in Chapter 12.

James Clyman, a mounted ranger in Ohio in the War of 1812, tells in one of his diaries of drifting westward in 1818 and of going to St. Louis in 1823 where he joined Ashley's expedition which ascended the Missouri and reached Green River in 1824. In 1827 he returned to St. Louis and later bought a farm near Danville, Illinois. As a soldier in the Black Hawk War he went to the Wisconsin frontier and later made two trips to the Far West, one in 1844 and one in 1848. The 1844–1846 diary shows his humor, common sense, and interest in literature.

In her narrative of happenings from 1812 to about 1860, Mrs. Eliza Schettler recounts events in Michigan and at Green Bay, including numerous experiences with Indians. The Reverend Alfred Brunson's long, interesting work tells of his trip from the East to Ohio in 1812 and his experiences in the War of 1812 on Lake Erie and at Detroit. Describes a trip by horseback from Meadville, Pennsylvania, to Prairie du Chien in 1835, and his ministerial life in Ohio and Michigan. Reminiscences of the War of 1812 and of Indians and pioneer experiences at Detroit over a long period make up the major part of Mrs. Mary Ann Bristol's narrative. Although Priddy Meeks took part in the Mormon migration to Utah at a much later date, his journal begins in 1812 and describes in well written detail his early life in Indian territory.

The Diary of Elbridge Gerry, Jr. Claude G. Bowers, ed. (New York, Brentano's, 1927). Extracts in *Mass. Hist. Soc. Procs.*, XLVII (1914), 523–28.[13]

Henry, Joseph. Diary, 1813. MS. Original owned by Mrs. S. Elizabeth Henry Goetter, Mansfield, O.; typed copies in the Rutherford B. Hayes Library, Fremont, O., and the Library of the Ohio Historical Society, Columbus.

"Diary of Capt. James Bonner." *West. Res. Hist. Soc. Pubs.*, II [No. 49] (1879), 103–4.[14]

"Robert Yost his Book." *Ohio Arch. Hist. Quar.*, XXIII (1914), 150–61.[15]

The Diary of Elbridge Gerry, Jr., is an interesting and detailed account of a horseback journey in Ohio and the East in 1813. Joseph Henry, who lived near St. Clairsville, Ohio, wrote a diary of a trip in September of 1813 by way of Delaware, Norton, Upper Sandusky, Tiffin, Fremont, and Fort Meigs, Ohio, to Detroit. Captain James Bonner's journal, hastily written, tells of events in the war during 1813–1814 and contains descriptions of northern Ohio settlements and notes on Indians. A similar military journal by Robert Yost relates interesting experiences in a march from southern Ohio to Detroit.

Journal of the Life and Religious Labours of Elias Hicks (New York, 1832).[16]

Howells, William Cooper. *Recollections of Life in Ohio, 1813–40* (Cincinnati, Arthur H. Clarke Co., 1895).[17]

Taliaferro, Maj. Lawrence. "Autobiography." *Colls. Minn. Hist. Soc.*, VI (1894), 189–255.[18]

Above average in interest is a journal by Quaker Elias Hicks, the famed abolitionist. It has notes on social life, reading, and speaking tours in the East and in Ohio during 1813–1820. William Cooper Howells, father of William Dean Howells, the novelist, has left a picture of his life in eastern Ohio during 1813–1840 in his *Recollections*, which reveals his high principles, buoyant spirit, humor, and literary interests. The autobiography of Lawrence Taliaferro, an Indian agent, covers the years 1813–40 and tells of a trip from the East to Detroit, of experiences in the northern Midwest, and of Indian affairs.

Laird, Charles Kendall. Autobiography, 1813–1859. About 249 pp. 2 MS. notebooks. Indiana Historical Society, Indianapolis.

In his notebooks, Charles K. Laird gives an interesting account of various trips by his parents and himself between Vermont and Indiana beginning in 1813 and of later journeys down the Ohio and Mississippi to New Orleans and Natchez and back. There are descriptions of men prominent in the early history of the region and entries as late as June 20, 1859.

Brown, Samuel R. *Views of the Campaigns of the Northwestern Army, &c. Comprising . . . View of the Lake Coast from Sandusky to Detroit.* [Alternate title: *Views on Lake Erie, Comprising a Minute and Interesting Account of the Conflict on Lake Erie– . . . View of the Lake Coast from Buffalo to Detroit*] (Troy, N. Y., Francis Adancourt, 1814).[19]

"James Callaway in the War of 1812. Diary." Edgar B. Wesley, ed. *Mo. Hist. Soc. Colls.*, V (1927), 74–77.[20]

A description of Lake Erie and the conflict there is contained in a book by Samuel R. Brown. Captain James Callaway, a Missourian, described Taylor's expedition against the Sac and Fox Indians and the Battle of Credit Rock in a hastily written but valuable diary.

Mills, Samuel J. and Daniel Smith. *Report of a Missionary Tour through that Part of the United States which Lies West of the Allegany Mountains; Performed under the Direction of the Massachusetts Missionary Society* (Andover, Flagg and Gould, 1815).[21]

"Narrative of Spoon Decorah." *Wis. Hist. Soc. Colls.*, XIII (1895), 448–62.

Samuel Mills, co-author of *A Correct View . . .*, mentioned earlier in this chapter, collaborated with another Eastern churchman, Daniel Smith, in writing a report of an additional missionary

tour in 1814–1815. The section of the work called "View of the Mississippi Territory" discusses the Midwest as a field for missionary endeavors. One of the few Middle Western narratives by an Indian, valuable and interesting for this reason, is that by Spoon Decorah, told to and written by the editor of the *Wisconsin Historical Society Collections*. It extends from 1814 until about 1888. Decorah remembered the British attack on Prairie du Chien and the Black Hawk War and expressed disapproval of the white man's action in moving the Indians across the Mississippi.

Cotton, Dr. John. "From Rhode Island to Ohio in 1815." *Journal of American History*, XVI (1922), 36–49, 249–60. Extracts in *Old Northw. Geneal. Quar.*, XIII (1910), 59–67.[22]

"Autobiography of Alvin P. Hovey's Early Life." Elfrieda Lang, ed. *Ind. Mag. Hist.*, XLVIII (1952), 71–84.[23]

Madox, D. T. *Late Account of the Missouri Territory, Compiled from Notes Taken during a Tour through that Country in 1815, and a Translation of Letters from a Distinguished French Emigrant. Written in 1817* (Paris, Ky., John Lyle, 1817).

John Cotton's account of his trip from Rhode Island down the Ohio to Franklintown in 1815 is a very interesting narrative. Descriptions of Indian mounds, towns, rivers, forests, a German tavern, and camp meetings make good reading. Although not born until 1821, Alvin Hovey recounted incidents in the journey of his father from Vermont to Indiana in 1815. D. T. Madox' *Late Account* is a collection of brief notes on the Missouri country.

"The Journals of Jules de Mun." Thomas M. Marshall, ed. *Mo. Hist. Soc. Colls.*, V (1928), 166–208, 311–26.[24]

Paddock, Gains. "The Spirit of '76 from the Green Mountains." *Jour. Ill. State Hist. Soc.*, XII (1920), 368–87.

"The Diary of Salome Paddock Enos." Introduction by Louise I. Enos. *Jour. Ill. State Hist. Soc.*, XIII (1920), 370–77.

Richardson, William. *Journal from Boston to the Western Country and down the Ohio and Mississippi Rivers to New Orleans, 1815–1816* (New York, Valve Pilot Corp., 1940).

One of Jules De Mun's journals, translated from the French, gives an account of a fur-trading expedition from St. Louis to the upper Arkansas River in 1815 and another tells of a second expedition from the same city to the lower part of the Kansas River the following year. Both are readable and interesting. Accounts of a trip in 1815 by covered wagon to Pittsburgh and then by flatboat down the Ohio, a winter in Cincinnati, a journey to St. Louis in 1816, and removal to Illinois make up the narrative of Gains Paddock as told by his grandson. The same events are included in the diary of Salome Paddock Enos, Paddock's daughter. The *Journal from Boston . . .* contains excerpts from William Richardson's journal of a trip down the Ohio and Mississippi to the South, published by his great-grandson.

Flint, Timothy. *Recollections of the Last Ten Years, Passed in Occasional Residences and Journeyings in the Valley of the Mississippi, from Pittsburg and the Missouri to the Gulf of Mexico, and from Florida to the Spanish Frontier; in a Series of Letters to the Rev. James Flint, of Salem, Massachusetts* (Boston, Cummings, Hilliard and Co., 1826).[25]

Johnston, George. "Reminiscences of Sault Ste. Marys, 1815." *Mich. Hist. Colls.*, XII (1888), 605–11.

Lockwood, James H. "Early Times and Events in Wisconsin." *Wis. Hist. Soc. Colls.*, II (1856), 98–196.

"Narrative by Louis B. Porlier." *Wis. Hist. Soc. Colls.*, XV (1900), 439–47.

In 1815, at the age of thirty-five, Timothy Flint, a Harvard graduate and at one time a teacher and Congregational clergyman, journeyed westward with his family to improve his health. He began a tour from Cincinnati through southern Indiana and Kentucky which became the basis for the first part of his clearly written and accurate book. Actual contact with the frontier made him change his romantic concept of nature. After a trip to New Orleans and up the Mississippi to St. Louis, he served almost six years as a missionary in the Missouri country, settling first at St. Charles and in 1822 at New Orleans. Although he was compelled to return to the East because of illness, he later spent several years in Cincinnati, where he edited the *Western Monthly Review* and became the open champion of the frontier. His novels and other books dealing with Western subjects helped give him a position as one of the first true Midwestern men of letters.

George Johnston's "Reminiscences" describe life in Upper Michigan and difficulties with Indians during 1815, 1816, and 1820. A story of a trip from New York state by way of the Great Lakes to Detroit, Green Bay, St. Louis, and Galena and facts about fur trading and dealings with Indians are contained in James H. Lockwood's narrative (1815-31). Louis Porlier's brief account tells of his birth at Green Bay and life in Wisconsin during 1815-1847.

Flower, George. Travels in the United States, 1816. 2 vols., 211 and 162 pp. MSS., partially published. Chicago Historical Society. Extracts in "The Mississippi Valley in 1816 through an Englishman's Diary," Otto L. Schmidt, ed., *Miss. Val. Hist. Rev.*, XIV (1927), 137-55.[26]

"A Journey from Baltimore to Louisville in 1816: Diary of William Newton Mercer." Edwin A. Davis and John C. L. Andreassen, eds. *Ohio Arch. Hist. Quar.*, XLV (1936), 351-64.[27]

"Diary of Asahel North on a Journey from Vermont to the Illinois Territory, 1816." Marcus North, ed. *Jour. Ill. State Hist. Soc.*, XV (1922-1923), 679-87.[28]

Thomas, David. *Travels through the Western Country in the Summer of 1816. Including Notices of the Natural History, Antiquities, Topography, Agriculture, Commerce and Manufactures* . . . (Auburn, N. Y., David Rumsey, 1819).[29]

Thompson, Amos. Unfinished Reminiscences of a Trip from Maine to Illinois, 1816. Copy. MS. Illinois State Historical Library, Springfield.

The Englishman, George Flower, son of the Richard Flower who helped Morris Birkbeck establish the English colony in Illinois, first visited the Midwest and South in 1816 and wrote a diary of his trip, with entries at Steubenville, Cincinnati, and other Ohio River towns. One of his translated letters probably helped encourage Norwegian emigration to the frontier. Narratives by Flower's father and others who settled in the English colony are discussed later in this chapter.

Proceeding in 1816 by stage, carriage, flatboat, and horseback, young William Mercer journeyed from Baltimore to Marietta, Cincinnati, and New Orleans. His is an informative diary. Cincinnati, he believed, had obtained its full growth. The diary of Asahel North records in an interesting but hastily written way a wedding trip from Vermont to the Illinois country in a prairie schooner. David Thomas's *Travels through the Western Country*, a work of great merit, is a description of an exploratory tour to the Wabash lands in the New Purchase. Thomas emphasized the growth of settlement in that region and gave information on such subjects as climate, prices, commerce, flora and fauna, and general conditions of the West.

Biddle, James W. "Recollections of Green Bay in 1816-'17." *Wis. Hist. Soc. Colls.*, I (1854; 1903 reprint), 49-68.[30]

Brown, Uria. Travel and Business Diary. *Maryland History Magazine*, X (1915), 263-83, 344-69; XI (1916), 42-49, 142-57, 218-37, 348-75.[31]

Joyes, Capt. Thomas. Diary and Notes, 1816-1817. MS. Listed in *Guide to Manuscript Materials of American Origin in the Illinois Historical Survey* (Urbana, 1951), p. 30.

Montule, Édouard de. *Voyage en Amérique, en Italie, en Siciel, et en Égypte, pendant les années 1816, 1817, 1818, et 1819* (Paris, Delauney, etc., 1821). Translated in part into English by Edward D. Seeber (Bloomington, Indiana University Press, 1951).

Buechler, Johann U. *Land- und Seereisen eines st. gallischen Kantonburgers nach Nordamerika und Westindien, über Amsterdam nach Baltimore, Pitzburg, Callipoli, Sensanetta, Neuvevay, die Gegend Wabasch am Ohio, Natschet, Battonrouge und New-Orleans am Mississippi etc., und wieder zurück nach Amsterdam, in den Jahren 1816, 1817, und 1818* . . . (St. Gallen, Zollikofer und Zühlin, 1819).

James Biddle, serving under a military appointment, has interesting recollections of events in Wisconsin in 1816-1817, including a description of Indian marriage customs. The diary of Uria Brown gives his impressions on a trip to settle land claims in Ohio and several Eastern states during the same years. In order to make a survey of desirable mill sites and townships, Captain Thomas Joyes, deputy surveyor of Louisville, Kentucky, journeyed with a party up the Mississippi, breaking ice along the way, to Fort Clark near Peoria, Illinois. The journal of Édouard de Montulé gives a Frenchman's impressions of the Midwest during 1816-19. After visiting New York and the West Indies, he traveled by boat from New Orleans to Louisville and by stagecoach and horseback to Frankfort, Lexington, Chillicothe, and then to the east. The twenty-four letters making up his narrative reveal an inquisitive mind and an interest in commonplace things. Johann Buechler's narrative gives a Swiss reaction to much the same region at the same time. A Dutch edition of his book appeared in the same year the original was published.

Birkbeck, Morris. *Notes on a Journey in America, from the Coast of Virginia to the Territory of Illinois, with Proposals for the establishment of a Colony of English* (Philadelphia, Caleb Richardson, 1817).

——— *Letters from Illinois* (Boston, Wells and Lilly, 1818).[32]

Morris Birkbeck, who was educated in the classics and was experienced in farming, brought his family with him from England and, with George Flower, founded the English settlement in Edwards County, Illinois. His travels down the Ohio River from Wheeling pleased him and turned him into one of the staunchest advocates of British settlement in the American West. In 1818, he became permanently estranged from Flower. As an opponent of slavery, he worked to retain Illinois' status as a free state until he drowned in the Fox River in 1825. Birkbeck's abilities to observe carefully and write well make his books valuable sources of information about the frontier. The first book ran through eleven editions in two years and the latter, which was translated into French and German in 1819, through seven English editions. Birkbeck was attacked by such persons as William Cobbett, who was in the pay of Eastern land speculators, as unreliable in his praise of the frontier. A caustic review of the *Notes on a Journey* . . . in *The Quarterly Review* (Vol. XIX, Apr., 1818) aroused distrust of his opinions. A letter by the poet Keats written January 15, 1820, reflects this attitude.

Chesebrough, Silas. "Journal of a Journey to the Westward." Peter S. McGuire, ed. *Amer. Hist. Rev.*, XXXVII (1931), 65-88.[33]

"Journal of Thomas Dean. A Voyage to Indiana in 1817." John C. Dean, ed. *Ind. Hist. Soc. Pubs.*, VI (1918), 273–345.[34]

Fearon, Henry Bradshaw. *Sketches of America. A Narrative of a Journey of Five Thousand Miles through the Eastern and Western States of America; Contained in Eight Reports Addressed to Thirty-nine English Families by whom the Author was Deputed, in June 1817, to Ascertain whether Any, and What Part of the United States would be Suitable for their Residence. With Remarks on Mr. Birkbeck's "Notes" and "Letters"* (London, Longman Hurst, Rees, Orme, and Brown, 1818).[35]

The diary of Silas Chesebrough details a trip from Connecticut to Ohio in 1817 to gain first-hand information about the Ohio country as a possible place of residence. His style is not literary but his observations are accurate. He writes, for instance, that all homes in Ohio were built of logs without nails. A journey to obtain land in Indiana for the Brothertown Indians in New York state is recorded in the 1817 journal of Thomas Dean, who traveled down the Ohio and up the Wabash, from Fort Harrison to the mouth of the Mississinewa River, walked from the fort to the White River country, and returned via Fort Wayne and Detroit to Buffalo. The descriptions of the country and of difficulties of travel are realistic.

In seeking a suitable location for thirty-nine English families, Henry B. Fearon, who had a very favorable impression of America when he arrived, became disillusioned by slavery, the high cost of property, and the lack of cleanliness, generosity, liberality, and comprehension of liberty or honor. Although he admitted that the country had no large standing army and possessed territory and growing wealth, he advocated emigration for few Englishmen other than mechanics, small farmers, and poor people. The title "Fearon's Falsehoods" was applied to the book by William Cobbett, the critic of Birkbeck's eulogistic volumes.

Flügel, J. G. "Pages from a Journal of a Voyage down the Mississippi to New Orleans in 1817." Felix Flügel, ed. *La. Hist. Quar.*, VII (1924), 414–40.[36]

Kimball, James. "A Journey to the West in 1817." *Essex Inst. Hist. Colls.*, VIII (1866), 226–50.

J. G. Flügel, a German, wrote a journal in English, French, and German, but only the English portion has been published. It describes the Mississippi River and southern Missouri as seen from his boat. James Kimball wrote a chatty diary on his way from the East to Ohio, with interesting observations on people and customs in such towns as Steubenville, Louisville, Athens, and Marietta.

Long, Maj. Stephen H. *Voyage in a Six-Oared Skiff to the Falls of Saint Anthony in 1817. Colls. Minn. Hist. Soc.*, II (1889, reprint of 1860–1867), 9–83.[37]

——— Journals of the Long Expedition of 1823. 4 vols. MSS. Minnesota Historical Society, St. Paul. The first volume has been published as *Voyage in a Six-Oared Skiff. . . .*

Major Stephen H. Long, superintendent of Indian affairs in the Northwest, made an exploratory trip from Prairie du Chien up the Mississippi to the Falls of St. Anthony and back down the river to St. Louis. He secured sketches of the upper Mississippi, selected sites for military purposes, and wrote a very readable diary full of descriptions of places, Indians, and antiquities. In 1819–20, he commanded an expedition to the Rocky Mountains, accounts of which were written by John R. Bell, Titian Ramsay Peale and Edwin James, which are mentioned later in this chapter. His unpublished journals cover an expedition under his command from Philadelphia to the Red River of the North and Fort Garry and return by way of the Great Lakes. An account of this expedition, based partly on Long's notes, appears in W. H. Keating's *Narrative . . .* , described in Chapter 9.

Newton, Lucy. "A journal or memorandum of my journey from Union, Ohio, to Mecanicksburg and from there to Anderson Towsnhip [Hamilton County]," 1817. 3 pp. MS. Listed in Biggert, *Guide*, No. 757.

Palmer, John. *Journal of Travels in the United States of America, and in Lower Canada, Performed in the Year 1817; Containing Particulars Relating to the Prices of Land and Provisions; Remarks on the Country and People, Interesting Anecdotes, and an Account of the Commerce, Trade and Present State of Washington, New York . . . Cincinnati, . . . &c. To Which Are Added a Description of Ohio, Indiana, Illinois and Missouri, and a Variety of Other Useful Information . . .* (London, Sherwood Neely and Jones, 1818).[38]

Storrow, Samuel Appleton. *Narrative of a Tour in the Summer of 1817 on the Shores of Lake Superior and Other Northern Lakes of the U. S. . . .* (n. p., 1818). Reprinted as "The North-West in 1817," *Wis. Hist. Soc. Colls.*, VI (1872), 154–87.

Waldo, Samuel Putnam. *The Tour of James Monroe, President of the United States, in the Year 1817; through the States of Maryland, Pennsylvania, New-Jersey, New-York, Connecticut, Rhode-Island, Massachusetts, New-Hampshire, Vermont, and Ohio . . . and Historical and Geographical Notices of the Principal Places through which he Passed . . .* (Hartford, Conn., F. D. Bolles and Co., 1818).[39]

The title of Lucy Newton's memorandum is self-explanatory. John Palmer, an Englishman, who traveled down the Ohio, evidently based his description of Indiana and Western territories upon information by S. R. Brown in the *Western Gazetteer* (No. 96). Samuel Storrow, judge-advocate in the American army, wrote a long narrative letter full of topographical descriptions of a tour in 1817 from Detroit to Fort Gratiot, Mackinac, Green Bay, Lake Winnebago, Fort Wayne, and Fort Meigs. Samuel P. Waldo related events in President James Monroe's tour of travel from Detroit through Ohio and several Eastern states.

Account of Robert Abbott of a Journey from Detroit to Vincennes, Indiana, and Return, Giving Places, Distances, Weather, and Expenses, 1817–1818. MS. Abbott Family Papers. Burton Historical Collection, Detroit.

Anonymous. "A Journey to the West in 1817." *Essex Inst. Hist. Colls.*, VIII (1866), 226–49.[40]

Fordham, Elias Pym. *Personal Narrative of Travels in Virginia, Maryland, Pennsylvania, Ohio, Kentucky, and of a Residence in the Indiana Territory, 1817–1818.* Frederic A. Ogg, ed. (Cleveland, Arthur H. Clark Co., 1906).[41]

Robert Abbott's account needs no comment. The anonymous diary is a lively account of a journey to Ohio and back to the East from September, 1817 to February, 1818, including interesting criticisms of the region.

Elias P. Fordham, a young Englishman who accompanied Birkbeck to America, wrote a series of letters to friends in England in 1817 and 1818. His extremely factual writing was never intended for publication. In traveling down the Ohio to Cincinnati, he found that the frontiersmen were not so hospitable as they had been described in the accounts he had read. He considered Indiana, which he crossed on horseback, a vast forest interrupted only by the Ohio and Wabash rivers. At the English prairie settlement at Shawneetown, Illinois, which contained cabins swarming with half-naked children, he found boys of eighteen building huts, marrying, and rearing children. Although he considered the frontiersmen's manners coarse and their drinking habits bad, he admired their superb masculinity. He discussed immigration and described trips down the Patoka to Kentucky and across the Wabash in search of lands. In all, he felt Birkbeck's writings gave an incomplete picture of America.

"Thomas Lippincott, a Pioneer of 1818 and his Diary." *Jour. Ill. State Hist. Soc.*, X (1917–1918), 237–55. Reprinted from *Presbytery Reporter*, Alton, Ill., Jan., 1870. Reprinted also in Mrs. Charles P. Noyes, ed. *A Family History in Letters and Documents* (St. Paul, Privately printed, 1919), 331–42.[42]

While traveling by flatboat with his wife and baby down the Ohio to Shawneetown and overland by horse and wagon through southern Illinois in 1817–1818, Thomas Lippincott wrote an interesting diary containing comments on travel conditions and places and people on the way. He mentions Steubenville, Marietta, Maysville, and Augusta.

Schoolcraft, Henry Rowe. *A View of the Lead Mines of Missouri; Including Some Observations on the Mineralogy, Geology, Geography, Antiquities, Soil, Climate, Population, and Productions of Missouri and Arkansaw, and Other Sections of the Western Country* . . . (New York, Charles Wiley and Co., 1819). Reprinted in part as *Journal of a Tour into the Interior of Missouri and Arkansaw, from Potosi, or Mine à Burton, in Missouri Territory, in a South-west Direction, toward the Rocky Mountains; Performed in the Years 1818 and 1819* (London, Sir Richard Phillips and Co., 1821).

———— *The Indian in his Wigwam, or Characteristics of the Red Race of America. From Original Notes and Manuscripts* (New York, W. H. Graham, 1848).

———— *Narrative Journal of Travels through the Northwestern Regions of the United States, extending from Detroit through the Great Chain of American Lakes to the Sources of the Mississippi River. Performed as a Member of the Expedition under Governor Cass. In the Year 1820* (Albany, N. Y., E. and E. Hosford, 1821). Slightly different version in *Summary Narrative of an Exploratory Expedition to the Sources of the of the Mississippi River* (Philadelphia, 1855). Chapter 15 is abridged as "Dubuque in 1820, August 7th," *Ia. Hist. Rec.*, XVI (1900), 100–06. Reprint of the entire journal, Mentor L. Williams, ed. (East Lansing, Michigan State University Press, 1953).

———— *Travels in the Central Portions of the Mississippi Valley: Comprising Observations on the Mineral Geography, Internal Resources, and Aboriginal Population* (New York, Collins and Hanney, 1825). Extract entitled "A Journey up the Illinois River in 1821," in Milo M. Quaife, ed., *Pictures of Illinois One Hundred Years Ago* (Chicago, R. R. Donnelley and Sons Co., 1918).

———— *Henry R. Schoolcraft—Expedition into the Indian Country.* (n. p. [Washington?], n. d. [1831?]).

———— Travel Notes and Journals relating to Indian Affairs (beginning in about 1831). In the Henry R. Schoolcraft Papers. MSS. Library of Congress.

———— *Narrative of an Expedition through the Upper Mississippi to Itasca Lake, the Actual Source of this River; Embracing the Exploratory Trip through the St. Croix and Burntwood (or Broule) River; in 1832. Under the Direction of Henry R. Schoolcraft* (New York, Harper and Bros., 1834).

———— and Allen. *Schoolcraft and Allen—Expedition to Northwest Indians. Letter from the Secretary of War, Transmitting a Map and Report of Lieut. Allen and H. B. [read R.] Schoolcraft's Visit to the Northwest Indians in 1832* (Washington, Gales and Seaton, 1834).

Schoolcraft, Henry R. Private Journal of Indian Affairs, 1837–?, H. R. Schoolcraft Papers. MS. Library of Congress.

———— *Personal Memoirs of a Residence of Thirty Years with the Indian Tribes on the American Frontiers . . . A. D. 1812 to A. D. 1842* (Philadelphia, Lippincott, Grambo and Co., 1851).[43]

In some ways the most important of all Midwestern travelers, Henry Rowe Schoolcraft was interested not only in exploration, but also in writing, business affairs, industry, mineralogy, geology, ethnology, Indian life, and history. His book, *Algic Researches*, a treatise on Indians and their myths and legends, was the main source of Longfellow's *Hiawatha*. So popular was his *Narrative Journal of Travels* . . . that it went through several editions, and other of his books were widely read.

Schoolcraft explored the Missouri mineral region and the Arkansas River basin in 1817 and 1818 and published a book on the trip, *A View of the Lead Mines of Missouri* . . . , which showed his keen observation and interest in Indians and other subjects. A description of a trip by keel boat down the Ohio and another of the Ozark Mountains together with further comments on Indians are contained in *The Indian and his Wigwam*. . . . As official geologist and mineralogist of the Cass expedition to search for the sources of the Mississippi, he accompanied Cass, governor of Michigan, and his party up the Lakes from Detroit in 1820. His *Narrative Journal* . . . of his trip is written in a somewhat stuffy "literary," style but is a very satisfactory record and gives an insight into Schoolcraft's personality. Additional versions of the same trip written by James Doty and Charles Trowbridge are mentioned in Chapter 9. Another expedition with Cass in 1821 took Schoolcraft from Detroit down the Wabash and Ohio to Shawneetown, by wagon to St. Louis, by river to Peoria, and by horseback to Chicago, where a treaty was negotiated with the Indians. This journey became the basis for *Travels in the Central Portion of the Mississippi Valley*. . . .

After a trip into the Indian country in about 1831, he produced *Henry R. Schoolcraft—Expedition into the Indian Country* and several unpublished travel notes and journals of approximately that year and later. *Narrative of an Expedition through the Upper Mississippi* . . . , is primarily devoted to comments on Indian life and character, and contains extracts from the manuscript journals of several fur traders. Promoted to superintendent of Indian affairs for Michigan in 1836, Schoolcraft began a private journal, at Mackinaw on October 1, 1837, relating to Indian matters, as does his *Personal Memoirs of a Residence of Thirty Years with the Indian Tribes*. Among other activities, he helped found the Michigan Historical Society and the Algic Society of Detroit. He wrote the *Algic Researches* (2 vols., New York, Harper and Brothers, 1839) and the massive, six-volume *Historical and Statistical Information Respecting . . . the Indian Tribes of the United States* . . . (Philadelphia, Lippincott, Grambo and Co., 1851–1857). Although he published nothing after 1857, his contributions to the literature of the frontier are obviously outstanding.

[Worth, Gorham A.] *Recollections of Cincinnati, from a Residence of Five Years, 1817 to 1821* (Albany, Charles Van Benthuysen, 1851). Reprinted in *Hist. Phil. Soc. of Ohio Quar. Pubs.*, XI (1916), 5–48.[44]

"Richard Smith and his Journal, 1817–1824." *Jour. Fr. Hist. Soc.*, XIII (1916), 49–58, 89–97, 129–39; XIV (1917), 15–25, 59–69, 108–18, 161–67.[45]

Adams, Philo. Diaries of two journeys, 1817, 1831. 96 pp. MS. Chicago Historical Society.

Parkison, Col. Daniel M. "Pioneer Life in Wisconsin." *Wis. Hist. Soc. Colls.*, II (1856), 327–64.

"Mrs. Adele P. Gratiot's Narrative." *Wis. Hist. Soc. Colls.*, X (1888), 261–75.

An unidentified author, probably Gorham A. Worth, traveled in 1817 from Philadelphia to Pittsburgh and down the Ohio to Cincinnati, where he lived for five years. He comments very frankly upon the faults and merits of the town in a well-written narrative. Extracts from the journal of Richard Smith, an Englishman who joined the Friends in Ohio, contains comments on trade, religion and narrates trips from 1817 to 1824. Philo Adams' diaries are of a trip from Middlebury, Vermont, to Ohio in 1817 and one from Lake Erie to Green Bay in 1831. After moving from Tennessee to Illinois in 1817, to Sangamon County in 1819, and to Wisconsin in 1829, Daniel Parkinson wrote a narrative containing interesting comments on frontier conditions and campaigns during the Black Hawk War, in which he took part. Mrs. Adele Gratiot's travels by boat and two-horse wagon to Illinois in 1825, her settlement at Gratiot's Grove, and an account of the horrors of the Black Hawk War and of a trip to Fort Snelling in 1837 are included in her narrative. Her family moved to the lead-mining regions of Missouri in 1841.

Chase, Philander. *Bishop Chase's Reminiscences; an Autobiography; Second Edition; Comprising a History of the Principal Events in the Author's Life to A. D. 1847* (2 vols., Boston, Dow, 1848).[46]
——— *Bishop Chase's Address Delivered Before the Convention of the Protestant Episcopal Church, Springfield, Illinois, June 16, 1845* (St. Louis, Davies, 1845).
Diary of William Sewall. John Goodell, ed. (Beardstown, Ill., Gordon and Feldman, 1930).[47]

A turning point in the life of Philander Chase came when he went to Ohio in 1817. In 1819 he again turned West as bishop of the Protestant Episcopal Church of Ohio. During the latter year he founded Kenyon College and in 1821 became president of Cincinnati College. He was made bishop of Illinois in 1835 and visited Chicago and other Illinois towns but later moved to Michigan. His *Reminiscences* consists mainly of extracts from letters and journals. His *Address* is his day-by-day record of travels in Illinois during 1843 and 1844. Robert S. Bailey's *The Church in the Wilderness*, to be mentioned in Chapter 12, describes the author's visit in 1839 to Chase's home near Peoria.

In his diary, William Sewall tells of pioneer life and various travels in the East and in Illinois during 1817–1846. His information on churches, schooling, farming, courtship, and local matters lacks sparkle but has valuable details.

The John Mason Peck Papers, 1817–1857. MS. partially published. Shurtleff College Library, Upper Alton, Illinois.
Forty Years of Pioneer Life. Memoir of John Mason Peck . . . edited from his Journals and Correspondence by Rufus Babcock (Philadelphia, American Baptist Publishing Society, 1864).[48]
Clark, George. "Recollections." *Mich. Hist. Colls.*, I (1878), 501–7.

Any story of the frontier church is incomplete without mentioning John Mason Peck. In 1817 he established the western mission at St. Louis and, after it was closed in 1822, he moved to Rock Spring, Illinois. As a missionary he rode by horse through Illinois, Indiana, and Missouri, enduring cold and hunger. In 1827 he helped establish Rock Spring Seminary, became editor of the *Western Watchman* in 1849, and held various pastorates until 1854, after which he retired to Rock Spring. *Forty Years of Pioneer Life* shows his importance as a missionary, pioneer, editor, and authority on the West. His complete papers have not been published.

The "Recollections" of George Clark, not to be confused with George Rogers Clark, covers a long period, from 1817 to 1876,

and includes accounts of visits to Maumee, Detroit, and Cleveland, fishing and gaming activities, and other events. It gives a good picture of early times, but the abrupt changes in subject detract from the flow of the narrative.

Billon, Frederic L. "Reminiscences of Our Removal to St. Louis." Dana O. Jensen, ed. *Mo. Hist. Soc. Bull.*, XII (1956), 278–84.
"The Original Diary of Mrs. Laura (Downs) Clark, of Wakeman, Ohio, from June 21, to October 26, 1818." *Firelands Pioneer*, New Series, XXI (1920), 2308–26.
Darby, William. *A Tour from the City of New-York to Detroit, in the Michigan Territory, Made between the 2d of May and the 22d of September, 1818 . . .* (New York, Kirk and Mercein, 1819).[49]
Edwards, Col. Abram. "A Western Reminiscence." *Wis. Hist. Soc. Colls.*, V (1868), 158–60.
Evans, Estwick. *A Pedestrian Tour, of Four Thousand Miles, Through the Western States and Territories, during the Winter and Spring of 1818 . . .* (Concord, N. H., Joseph C. Spear, 1819).[50]

A brief narrative by Frederic L. Billon tells of his Trip in 1818 with his father from Philadelphia to Pittsburgh, down the Ohio to Shawneetown, and by land across Illinois to St. Louis. "The Original Diary" gives details of life in the Firelands, Ohio, area in 1818, revealing the domesticity and the loneliness of a doctor's wife. William Darby was a surveyor and one of the country's leading geographers. His tour was made for the purpose of helping establish the boundary between the United States and Canada. His *Emigrant's Guide to the Western and Southwestern States . . .* (1819) and *View of the United States . . .* (1828) contain valuable geographical information. Colonel Abram Edwards' brief, well-written tale recounts events in a voyage by schooner in 1818 from Detroit to Mackinac, Green Bay, and Chicago. Edwards expressed the belief that the Midwest offered an inducement for settlement to New Englanders. More important than these is Estwick Evans' *A Pedestrian Tour of Four Thousand Miles*, competently written, detailed, informative, and very romantic in its attitude towards the West. So Chateaubriand-like was the author's approach that he wore buffalo skins and was accompanied by only two dogs during a part of his trip. "I wished to acquire the simplicity, native feelings, and virtues of savage life," he wrote. He traveled in 1818 from the East to Buffalo, through upper Ohio to Detroit, by way of the Lakes to Chicago, then to Pittsburgh, and finally down the Ohio.

Logan, John. *The Western Woodpecker, being the Journal of a Journey, Performed in the Months of February, March and April, 1818, from Georgetown, in the District of Columbia, to the Miami, in the State of Ohio, and back again* (Georgetown, D. C., the Author, 1818).
Miller, Andrew. *New States and Territories, or the Ohio, Indiana, Illinois, Michigan, North-Western, Missouri, Louisiana, Mississippi, and Alabama in their Real Characters, in 1818; . . . Collected from the Accounts of Gentlemen . . . and Personal Observation* (n. p. [Keene, N. H.?], n. d. [1819?]).
Stuart, Charles B. Notes on a Journey to the Western States in Company of Capt. R. N. Desha, 1818. 30 pp. MS. Illinois State Historical Library, Springfield.
Tanner, Edward. "Wisconsin in 1818." *Wis. Hist. Soc. Colls.*, VIII (1879), 287–92.

Logan's *The Western Woodpecker* is a pamphlet. Andrew Miller's *New States and Territories* is almost valueless. It was printed to help emigrants and includes the author's brief observations on the Midwest. The notes of Charles B. Stuart, a Virginian, relate incidents in a military Journey in 1818 from Washington, D. C., to St. Louis. Edward Tanner's story of a trip from St. Louis to Prairie du Chien and up the Wisconsin River is devoted mainly to topographical description and to an account of a meeting with Indians.

Harding, Benjamin. *A Tour through the Western Country, A.D. 1818 & 1819* . . . (New London, Conn., Samuel Green, 1819).

Hecke, J. Valentin. *Reise durch die Vereinigten Staaten von Nord-Amerika in den Jahren 1818 und 1819* . . . (2 vols., Berlin, H. Ph. Petri, 1820–1821).

Harris, William Tell. *Remarks Made during a Tour through the United States of America, in the Years 1817, 1818, and 1819. . . . In a Series of Letters to Friends in England* (Liverpool, H. Fisher, 1819).[51]

Hulme, Thomas. *Journal Made during a Tour in the Western Countries of America* (London, 1828). Forming Part III of William Cobbett's *A Year's Residence in the United States of America*. Reprinted in Thwaites, *Early Western Travels*, X, 17–84.[52]

Benjamin Harding, a surveyor, wrote a brief tract covering a tour in Illinois. J. Valentin Hecke's German book about a trip through America is somewhat unreliable. There are chapters on Indiana, Illinois, and other parts of the country. Harris was an Englishman who visited the English Settlement and Shawneetown. The tone of his letters was favorable to America in contrast to the attitudes expressed in the works of Fearon, Faux and others. Another favorable British view of America is contained in Thomas Hulme's *Journal Made during a Tour* . . . , describing a trip in 1818–1819. Hulme, an English farmer, found America in contrast to England, a free, happy, unostentatious land, and he condemned the travelers who had written malicious books. The diary, consisting of many jottings and incomplete sentences, has entries written at Evansville, Indiana; Princeton, Illinois; Birkbeck's settlement; and Chillicothe, Zanesville, and Steubenville, Ohio. The attitude of William Cobbett, the British critic mentioned in this chapter, had changed somewhat and he actually encouraged the settlement of America.

Flint, James. *Letters from America, Containing Observations on the Climate and Agriculture of the Western States, the Manners of the People, the Prospects of Emigrants, &c., &c.* (Edinburgh, W. and C. Taft, etc., 1822). Reprinted in Thwaites, *Early Western Travels*, Vol. IX.[53]

Nuttall, Thomas. *A Journal of Travels into the Arkansa Territory, during the Year 1819. With Occasional Observations on the Manners of the Aborigines* . . . (Philadelphia, Thomas H. Palmer, 1821). Reprinted in Thwaites, *Early Western Travels*, X, 17–84.[54]

James Flint and Thomas Nuttall, both British, visited the frontier during 1818–1820 and wrote significant observations. Flint, a scientific economist, was particularly interested in the Midwest and descended the Ohio from Pittsburgh late in 1818, seeing Cincinnati, Chillicothe, and Louisville and settling at Jeffersonville, Indiana, for several months before returning to the East by way of Cincinnati and Lake Erie. His pace is leisurely but his manner, as in his description and condemnation of slavery, is often digressive. His book was originally a series of letters and is obviously not literary in style.

Nuttall had studied botany and had accompanied John Bradbury on his Missouri River journey in 1809–1811. His *A Journal of Travels* includes a brief account of a trip down the Ohio in 1818 and then westward into the Arkansas Territory. Nearly every chapter of his book reflects his knowledge of natural history and interest in ethnology, giving a scientist's picture of the frontier.

Rafinesque, C. S. *A Life of Travels and Researches in North America and South Europe, or Outlines of the Life, Travels and Researches of C. S. Rafinesque, A.M., Ph.D.* . . . (Philadelphia, F. Turner, 1836).[55]

Another botanist, an American of French-German descent, one whose pedantry brought him much unfavorable criticism, was Constantine Samuel Rafinesque, who, although he first visited the United States in 1802, obtained information on the Midwest for his book, *A Life of Travels* . . . , from trips in 1818 and 1825. During 1818 he descended part of the Ohio and returned through Ohio to the East. After serving as professor of botany at a college in Kentucky, in 1825, he proceeded east by way of Cincinnati, Dayton, Mansfield, and Sandusky, ultimately settling in Philadelphia. His many works, largely scientific, show his wide learning but are marred by occasional inaccuracies.

Allen, Orisson. "Sketch of the First Settlement of Pontiac. . . ." *Mich. Hist. Colls.*, VI (1884), 384–86.

Stewart, Mrs. E. M. S. [Mrs. Electa M. (Bronson) Sheldon]. "Incidents in the Life of Mr. Eber Ward. . . ." *Mich. Hist. Colls.*, VI (1884), 471–73.

——— *Childhood Memories of Life in Detroit* (n. p., n. d.).

——— "Childhood's Recollections of Detroit," *Mich. Hist. Colls.*, XVIII (1892), 458–65.

——— "Early Settlement of Ann Arbor." *Mich. Hist. Colls.*, VI (1884), 443–46.

"Anecdotes of Major Daniel Ashby." *Glimpses of the Past*, VIII (1941), 105–47.

Van Cleve, Charlotte. *Ouisconsin, "Three Score Years and Ten"* (Minneapolis, Harrison and Smith, 1888).

Kellogg, Sheldon Ingalls. Autobiography, 1818–1858. MS. Listed in Biggert, *Guide*, No. 584.

Orisson Allen's account, extending to 1833, contains the tale of a trip up Lake Erie to Michigan in 1818 and describes early pioneer hardships and meetings with Indians. The town of Pontiac in 1819, Allen wrote, had one log house. Mrs. E. M. S. Stewart's narratives relate a similar trip to Michigan in the same year, her memories of Detroit, the settlement of Ann Arbor, and pioneer life to 1849. The experiences of a frontier hunter and Indian fighter who finally settled down as a farmer are well told in the "Anecdotes" (1818–1869) of Major Daniel Ashby. Such events as bee and bear hunting and surveying the big snow of 1830–1831 are given separate captions. Another trip up Lake Erie to Michigan in 1818 is included in *Ouisconsin* of Charlotte Van Cleve, an interesting autobiography. She later accompanied her husband to Green Bay and traveled up the Fox River to Lake Winnebago and then up the Mississippi. Although most of her later life was spent at Fort Snelling, she took trips to Cincinnati and elsewhere.

The autobiography of Sheldon Ingalls Kellogg tells of his life in New York State and records a trip to Cincinnati in 1818 and events there until 1858. Kellogg eventually moved to California, where he died in 1886.

Incidents and Events in the Life of Gurdon Saltonstall Hubbard; Collected from Personal Narrations and Other Sources, and Arranged by his Nephew, Henry E. Hamilton (Chicago, Rand McNally and Co., 1888). Reprinted as *The Autobiography of Gurdon Saltonstall Hubbard* (Chicago, R. R. Donnelley and Sons Co., 1911). Extracts in "Journey of Gurdon S. Hubbard . . . from Montreal to Mackinac and Chicago in

1818." *Mich. Hist. Colls.*, III (1881), 125–27, and "A Voyageur of 1818," *Mich. Hist. Colls.*, XIV (1890), 544–45.

Hubbard, Gurdon S. Reminiscences of Vermilion County, 1832. 12 pp. MS. An address delivered before the Old Settlers' Society at Danville which describes Chicago and his life as a trader with the Pottawatomie Indians in 1832. Chicago Historical Society.[56]

Journeying from Montreal to Chicago as a clerk for the American Fur Company, Gurdon S. Hubbard (1802–1886) became a pioneer merchant and meat packer. His autobiography tells of a trip to St. Louis, Cahokia, and Mackinac, of his residence in Danville, Illinois, from 1828 to 1834, and of his later life in Chicago. Since Hubbard was one of the last representatives in Illinois of the trader who carried on commerce through barter, his narrative furnishes a valuable picture of the end of this era. His prose is readable, though at times disconnected.

Anonymous. "Notes on the Missouri River and Some of the Native Tribes in the Neighborhood, By a Military Gentleman Attached to the Yellowstone Expedition in 1819." *Analectic Magazine*, I (April, May, 1820).[57]

Amphlett, William. *The Emigrants Directory to the Western States of North America; Including a Voyage out from Liverpool; the Geography and Topography of the Whole Western Country, . . . with Instructions for Descending the Rivers Ohio and Mississippi . . .* (London, Longman, etc., 1819).[58]

Brown, Gen. Jacob. "Memoranda of a Military Tour Commenced at Brownsville on Sunday the 30th of May 1819, to Several Ports and Garrisons on the Waters of the Western Lakes." *Buffalo Hist. Soc. Pubs.*, XXIV (1920), 295–323.[59]

Ernst, Ferdinand. *Bemerkungen auf einer Reise durch des Innere der Vereinigten Staaten von Nord-Amerika im Jahre 1819; besonders in Beziehung auf die an den Flüssen Sangömo und Onapischquasippi . . . im gedachten Jahre von den Indianern an den Congress abgetretenen Landstrichen; nebst einer Uebersetzung der Constitution des Illinois-Staats* (Hildesheim, Gerstenberg, 1820). Translated in part by E. P. Baker as "Travels in Illinois in 1819." *Ill. State Hist. Soc. Trans.*, 1903, VIII (1904), 150–65.

The "Notes . . . By a Military Gentleman" are about his trip from Fort Osage to Council Bluffs in 1819. William Amphlett, a Britisher, wished to inform his countrymen about America. His book contains information on Illinois. Jacob Brown records events in an expedition of observation in 1819 to various military posts on the Great Lakes—up Lake Erie to Detroit and then to Mackinac, Green Bay, and back. He includes notes on weather and scenery. Ferdinand Ernst was a German seeking land for a party of immigrant countrymen. He visited the English colony in Illinois in 1819 and later in the same year went to Kaskaskia, St. Louis, Edwardsville, Vandalia, and finally to New Orleans. He described the prairies realistically, and his partly translated book is an important source of information about the frontier.

Forsyth, Maj. Thomas. "Journal of a Voyage from St. Louis to the Falls of St. Anthony in 1819." *Wis. Hist. Soc. Colls.*, VI (1872), 188–215. Reprinted as "Fort Snelling. Col. Leavenworth's Expedition to Establish It, in 1819." *Colls. Minn. Hist. Soc.*, III (1870–1880), 139–67.[60]

Major Forsyth, an Indian agent, ascended the Mississippi by keel-boat in an expedition to establish a settlement at the mouth of St. Peter's River. His diary of the trip contains full descriptions of the river and of Indians. Later in the year he was promoted to a full agency and stationed near Rock Island, Illinois.

Hawkins, Rev. John Henry Willis. Journal. In William G. Hawkins, *Life of John H. W. Hawkins* (Boston, John P. Jewett and Co.; Cleveland, Henry P. Jewett; New York, Sheldon, Blakeman and Co., 1859), 23–191 *passim*,[61]

Lee, Gen. Alfred. "Central Ohio Seventy Years Ago. Adventures of John A. Quitman." *Mag. Amer. Hist.*, XIX (1888), 224–32.[62]

Narrative of Richard Lee Mason in the Pioneer West (New York, Charles F. Heartman, 1915). Reprinted from an early newspaper. Extracts relating to Indiana in Harlow Lindley, *Indiana as Seen by Early Travelers* (Indianapolis, 1916), pp. 235–38 [*Ind. Hist. Colls.*, IV (1916)].[63]

Wright, John S. *Letters from the West; or, a Caution to Emigrants; . . .* (Salem, N. Y., Dodd and Stevenson, 1819). Extracts in "Early Travel on the Ohio and its Tributaries," George B. Catlin, ed. *Mich. Hist.*, XX (1936), 153–61.

The Reverend John Hawkins' journal was written during a tour from Baltimore down the Ohio to Madison, Indiana, in 1819 and during his later years as a clergyman in the East. The narrative of General Alfred Lee is based on the letters of John A. Quitman, who described a trip down the Ohio by keelboat in 1819. Quitman stopped at Chillicothe and at Delaware, Ohio, where he began legal studies while holding a government clerkship. Richard Lee Mason had been offered bounty land near Alton, Illinois, and journeyed from Pennsylvania through Ohio, Kentucky, and Indiana in 1819 to locate it. Pleased with the West, he moved to St. Louis and took up a medical practice. His diary contains interesting comments on the state of civilization in this area. John S. Wright made a tour of inspection down the Ohio and through parts of the bordering states in 1819. Hoping to find a location, he was disgusted to learn that the most desirable land was owned by speculators. "Kidnapping of people of African blood is carried on with brutal ferocity where free blacks have settled," he observed. Although full of statistics, his book shows his powers of observation and satire.

Anonymous. Journal Kept by an Aide-de-Camp on 1819–1820 Journey. 4 pp., Typescript. In the Jacob Brown Papers. Burton Historical Collection, Detroit.

Atkinson, Col. Henry. Journal of the Advance Corps of the Military Branch of the Yellowstone Expedition, August 30, 1818, to July 10, 1820. MS. Listed in Mary C. Withington, comp. *A Catalogue of Manuscripts in the Collection of Western Americana Founded by William R. Coe, Yale University Library* (New Haven, 1952), No. 15.[64]

Leggett, Mary N. Journal of a Trip from Newark, N. J., to Edwardsville, Ill., September 21, 1819–January 2, 1820. 50 pp. MS. Illinois State Historical Library, Springfield.

The Journal Kept by an Aide-de-camp contains notations relating to Fort Niagara, Fort Erie, Put-in-Bay, Detroit, and Mackinac Island. The journal of Colonel Henry Atkinson is historically important. He was assigned command in 1819 of the Yellowstone Expedition of 1,100 men, which served as a warning to the British and Indians. Written mainly by Lieutenant Thomas Kavanaugh, it describes the journey, hunts for food along the way, counsels with the Indians, and life in the cantonments during the winter. The men reached Council Bluffs where a post was established, but failed to complete the expedition. Atkinson returned to St. Louis and took part in another Yellowstone expedition, that in 1825, mentioned in Chapter 9.

Faux, William. *Memorable Days in America: Being a Journal of a Tour to the United States, Principally Undertaken to Ascertain . . . the Condition and Probable Prospects of British Emi-*

grants; *Including Accounts of Mr. Birkbeck's Settlement in the Illinois* . . . (London, W. Simpkin and R. Marshall, 1823). Reprinted in Thwaites, *Early Western Travels*, XI, 16–305; XII, 11–138. Extracts relating to Indiana in Harlow Lindley, *Indiana as Seen by Early Travelers* (Indianapolis, 1916).[65]
Welby, Adlard. *A Visit to North America and the English Settlements in Illinois, with a Winter Residence at Philadelphia* . . . (London, J. Drury, etc., 1821).[66]

William Faux was another Englishman seeking to obtain information about America for British emigrants. After a trip to South Carolina, he traveled down the Ohio and visited Louisville, New Albion, Vincennes, Princeton, and the English settlement in Illinois in 1819–1820. Although his attitude in *Memorable Days in America* was at times satirical and as abusive as that of some of the other severe British critics, he tried to give a true picture of the West. He liked parts of the frontier, but almost everything in Indiana seemed wild and half savage to him. The men were "systematically unprincipled," he thought, and completely lacking in a sense of morals. His book is informal.

Adlard Welby, also an Englishman, was even more unfavorable to America than Faux. He found Ohio in 1819 a wilderness and saw disappointed emigrants returning east from Illinois. The Americans were blindly conceited, he decided, and lacked good will and benevolence. His book, nevertheless, contains much valuable information.

James, Edwin. *Account of an Expedition from Pittsburgh to the Rocky Mountains . . . under the Command of Major Stephen H. Long. From the Notes of Major Long, Mr. T. Say, and Other Gentlemen of the Exploring Party* (2 vols., Philadelphia, Carey and Lea, 1822–1823). Reprinted in Thwaites, *Early Western Travels*, vols. XIV–XVIII. Extract in Lloyd McFarling, ed., *Exploring the Northern Plains* . . . (Caldwell, Ida., 1955), pp. 80–92.[67]
"The Journal of Titian Ramsay Peale, Pioneer Naturalist." A. O. Weese, ed. *Mo. Hist. Rev.*, XLI (1947), 147–63; 266–84.[68]

Edwin James, a botanist like Nuttall, and Titian Ramsay Peale wrote accounts of the Stephen H. Long expedition to the Rocky Mountains in 1819–1820 which are valuable, partly, because Long himself left notes but no lengthy description of the expedition. The party, formed by order of J. C. Calhoun, Secretary of War, included several engineers and scientific men who set out for the upper Missouri in May, 1819. James' narrative gives a detailed picture of the trip from Pittsburgh down the Ohio and up the Mississippi to St. Louis. Of the five steamboats that tried to navigate up the Missouri only two reached the mouth of the Kaw. Although troops finally arrived at Council Bluffs, about three hundred of the men got scurvy and a hundred died. The book received unfavorable treatment from several commentators and discouraged Western migration.

The story of the completion of the expedition is told in the journals of Titian Ramsay Peale and John R. Bell. Peale was assistant naturalist and painter under Long. He recounts events in the river trip described by James and tells of Long's continued journey in 1820 up the bank of the Platte River to its sources. His journal is factual but rather carelessly written. Bell's diary will be discussed in Chapter 9.

Flower, Richard. *Letters from Lexington and the Illinois, Containing a Brief Account of the English Settlement in the Latter Territory, and a Refutation of the Misrepresentations of Mr. Cobbett* (London, C. Teulon for J. Ridgway, 1819).
———, Benjamin, and Morris Birkbeck. *Letters from the Illinois, 1820. 1821. Containing an Account of the English Settlement at Albion and its Vicinity, and a Refutation of Various*

Misrepresentations, those more particularly of Mr. Cobbett. By Richard Flower. With a Letter from M. Birkbeck; and a Preface and Notes by Benjamin Flower (London, C. Teulon for J. Ridgway, 1822). Reprinted in Thwaites, *Early Western Travels*, X, 85–169 and with *Letters from Lexington* . . . in E. E. Sparks, *The English Settlement in the Illinois* . . . (London, Museum Book Store, and Cedar Rapids, Ia., the Torch Press, 1907).[69]

Richard Flower, like his son, George Flower, played an important part in the early years of the English colony in Illinois. He was a British farmer who moved from Kentucky to Albion, Illinois, in the spring of 1819 and occupied a house which his son had built for him. His purpose in writing *Letters from Lexington and the Illinois* . . . was to refute William Cobbett's misrepresentation of America by giving a truer picture of the frontier and to encourage European people who were willing to work to emigrate. Although his frontier neighbors respected him, they distrusted his dignity and the freedom with which he expressed his opinions. The first edition of his book appeared in 1819, but his "letters" from Illinois date as late as August 20, 1821. He returned to England in 1824.

"Going West in 1820 including Extracts from the Journal of Jacob Richardson Jr., read before the Society, November 16, 1903, by George Richardson." *Hyde Park* (Mass.) *Historical Record*, IV (1904), 46–67.[70]
Little, James A. *Jacob Hamblin, A Narrative of his Personal Experience, as a Frontiersman, Missionary to the Indians and Explorer, Disclosing Interpositions of Providence, Severe Privations, Perilous Situations and Remarkable Escape* (Salt Lake City, Juvenile Instructor Office, 1861).
Woods, John. *Two years' Residence in the Settlement on the English Prairie, in the Illinois Country, United States, With an Account of its Animal and Vegetable Productions, Agriculture, &c., &c.* . . . (London, Longman, Hurst, Rees, Orme, and Brown, 1822). Reprinted in Thwaites, *Early Western Travels*, X, 177–357.[71]

The journal of 1819–1821 written by Jacob Richardson, Jr., partially published, lists events in a trip from New Hampshire down the Ohio to Arkansas. En route Richardson stopped at Shawneetown and Cave in Rock. He later became a schoolteacher in the South.

James A. Little's tale relates the frontier experiences of Jacob Hamblin, an explorer and Mormon missionary, from his birth at Salem, Ohio, in 1819 to his life in Salt Lake City in 1850. Includes trips to Nauvoo and Wisconsin, as well as other interesting events.

John Woods, like Richard Flower, was a British farmer who settled on the English prairie in 1819. His book gives a favorable view of conditions there and contains a full account of his life and much valuable information on social, economic, and political conditions in Illinois during 1819–1821. It includes notes on travel, agriculture, towns, and American customs.

White, James Haley. "Early Days in St. Louis." *Glimpses of the Past*, VI (1939), 5–13.
Tillson, Mrs. Christiana H. *Reminiscences of Early Life in Illinois by our Mother* (Amherst, Mass. [?], 1873). Reprinted as *A Woman's Story of Pioneer Illinois*, Milo M. Quaife, ed. (Chicago, R. R. Donnelley and Sons Co., 1919).
Childs, Col. Ebenezer. "Recollections of Wisconsin since 1820." *Wis. Hist. Soc. Colls.*, IV (1859), 153–95.
"Autobiography and Reminiscences of Philander Prescott." *Colls. Minn. Hist. Soc.*, VI (1894), 475–91.
Stow, Horace. Diary [i. e., Reminiscences], 1819–1895. MS.

largely unpublished. Owned by Mrs. Markley Bush, North Madison, Ind.; typed transcript, 35 pp., Indiana Historical Society. Extracts in Society of Indiana Pioneers, *Year Book, 1952* (Indianapolis), pp. 9–30.

James Haley White's narrative is a well-written, detailed account (1819–1822) of a trip down the Ohio by flatboat and up the Mississippi to St. Louis by steamboat in 1819. Mrs. Tillson's *Reminiscences* is an intimate and valuable account of life and travels in southern Illinois, 1819–1827. The "Recollections . . ." of Colonel Ebenezer Childs, covering the years 1819–1852, contains information on a trip to the Midwest from Massachusetts,

with comments on Detroit, Mackinaw, St. Louis, and Chicago, life in various towns, and encounters with Indians. Philander Prescott traveled west by steamer to visit his brother in Detroit in 1819, who then accompanied him farther west.

The partially published diary of Horace Stow includes reminiscences going back to 1807 in Vermont. It is an interesting account of travels from Olean, New York, in 1819, to Switzerland County, Indiana, and of many trips in early Indiana, including events up to 1896. The published extracts omit an anecdote concerning William Henry Harrison and incidents about the building of the Madison and Indianapolis Railroad.

Chapter 9

Midwestern Travel Tales of 1820–1825

There were no major wars to prevent the expansion of the American nation during Monroe's Administration (1817–1825), "The Era of Good Feeling." It was a period of continued growth for the West. Illinois was made a state in 1818 and Missouri in 1821. The settlement of the frontier was in full swing. The states of Ohio, Indiana, Illinois, and the territory of Michigan were beginning to offer some of the comforts of civilization to the traveler. Although narrators of various types appeared—visitors, settlers, missionaries, soldiers, and others—there were fewer important names among them than during preceding and later eras. The number of tales written was indeed large and the historical value of many of them is great, but few could be called outstanding.

The Journal of Captain John R. Bell. Harlin M. Fuller and LeRoy R. Hafen, eds. (Glendale, Calif., Arthur H. Clark Co., 1957).[1]
"Journal of Henry P. Benton." *Ind. Mag. Hist.*, XXXVII (1941), 387–95.[2]
Delafield, Maj. Joseph. *The Unfortified Boundary.* Robert McElroy and Thomas Riggs, eds. (New York, Privately printed, 1943).

Captain John R. Bell, like Titian R. Peale and Edwin James, described the Stephen Long expedition to the Rockies in 1820. Bell, in fact, was the official journalist of the expedition, and his diary is a day-by-day account of his trip from West Point, across Pennsylvania, down the Ohio, by horseback from St. Louis to Council Bluffs, and then a tour to the Rockies and his return to Washington by way of the South. His writing shows careful observation and contains good description. A deputy surveyor of public lands in Indiana, Henry P. Benton, wrote a readable diary recounting events in his journey in the spring of 1820 to survey lands where the Tippecanoe River empties into the Wabash River and his return across north central Indiana. He gives notes on weather, camps, and topography. *The Unfortified Boundary* is the diary of Major Joseph Delafield, a United States agent, who was sent in the same year to help determine the boundary between America and Canada. It contains an interesting description of customs in and around old Detroit and a visit to the islands of Lake Huron.

Doty, James Duane. "Official Journal, 1820. Expedition with Cass and Schoolcraft." *Wis. Hist. Soc. Colls.*, XIII (1895), 163–219.[3]
Trowbridge, Charles C. "With Cass in the Northwest in 1820." Ralph H. Brown, ed. *Minn. Hist.*, XXIII (1942), 126–48, 233–52, 328–48.[4]

Henry R. Schoolcraft's narrative of the exploring expedition under Governor Cass up the Great Lakes from Detroit has been discussed in Chapter 8. Accompanying the group was James Duane Doty, a lawyer and politician, who kept a diary describing the trip. Although impersonal and carelessly written, it shows close observations of nature, natural resources, and Indians. Doty explored what is now Wisconsin and later became the second governor of the Wisconsin Territory. Charles C. Trowbridge, a youth at this time but later an influential citizen of Detroit and author of *Detroit, Past and Present* (1864), wrote a diary of the same expedition, which is interesting in comparison with the more mature writing of Schoolcraft.

"The 1820 Journal of Stephen Watts Kearny, Comprising a Narrative Account of the Council Bluff–St. Peter's Military Exploration and a Voyage down the Mississippi River to St. Louis." Valentine Mott Porter, ed. *Mo. Hist. Soc. Colls.*, III (1908) 8–29, 90–131. Reprinted as "An Expedition across Iowa in 1820," *Ann. of Ia.*, 3rd Series, X (1912), 343–71.[5]

An expedition sent in 1820 from Council Bluffs to open a route between Camp Missouri, near Omaha, and Camp Cold Water, near Minneapolis, is described in the diary of Captain Stephen W. Kearny. Includes notes on forts, towns, and Indian villages, comments on geography, and some personal items. Kearny's conquest of New Mexico in 1846 will be mentioned in Chapter 14.

Keyes, Willard. "A Journal of Life in Wisconsin One Hundred Years Ago." *Wis. Mag. Hist.*, III (1920), 339–63, 443–65.[6]
Morse, Jedidiah. *A Report to the Secretary of War of the United States, . . . Comprising a Narrative of a Tour Performed in the Summer of 1820 . . .* (New Haven, S. Converse, etc., 1822).[7]

Willard Keyes' informative diary, carelessly written, tells of life in Wisconsin in 1820 and comments on water travel, Indians, sickness, schoolteaching, milling, and logging. Jedidiah Morse, called "the Father of American Geography," was sent West in 1820 to gain information about Indian trade, fur companies, and government trading posts. His is an official report, which contains historically valuable material on the Indians of Illinois and a description of Chicago.

Page, Karl G. *Darstellung der bürgerlichen Verhältnisse in dem Freistaaten von Nordamerika; nebst einer merkwürdigen Reise dahin . . .* (Bautzen, Lehmann [1830?]).
"The Journal of John Tipton." *Ind. Mag. Hist.*, I (1905), 9–15, 75–79. Reprinted from *Indianapolis News*, Apr. 17, 1879.[8]

Karl G. Page's book contains notes on a number of Midwestern settlements he visited in 1820. John Tipton, a pioneer born in Tennessee, came to Indiana in 1807 when twenty-one years old. In 1820 he was commissioned to locate a site for the state capital. Later he was prominent in state affairs. His journal of this trip, though poorly written, gives a good picture of early Indiana.

[Smith, Henry A.] Information on a trip in 1820. MS. Listed in Lucile M. Kane and Kathryn A. Johnson, *Manuscript Collections of the Minnesota Historical Society. Guide Number 2* (St. Paul, Minnesota Historical Society, 1955), No. 1343.

Tillson, John. Journal of a Journey from Boston across Illinois to Eastern Missouri, 1820. 21 pp. MS. Illinois State Historical Library, Springfield.

Worthington, W. C. D. Diary, 1820. MS. Library of Congress.

A MS. by Henry A. Smith or a member of his family gives information on a trip by wagon in 1820 from St. Louis through Indiana and Ohio. John Tillson's journal describes a journey beginning on June 27 and ending December 2, 1820. W. C. D. Worthington's diary recounts a journey through Missouri in the same year.

Hawley, Zerah. *A Journal of a Tour through Connecticut, Massachusetts, New York, the North Part of Pennsylvania, and Ohio, Including a Year's Residence in that Part of the State of Ohio, Styled New Connecticut, or Western Reserve. In which is Given a Description of the Country, Climate, Soil, Productions, Animals, Buildings, Manners of the People, State of Society, Population, &c. From Actual and Careful Observation* (New Haven, Conn., S. Converse, 1822).[9]

Smith, Daniel. Journal of a Voyage from Portsmouth, England, to New Orleans on Board the *Margaret*, 1820–1821. MS. Illinois State Historical Library, Springfield.

Zerah Hawley, an Easterner, first visited Ohio in September, 1820, and mentioned various Ohio towns in a series of letters dated as late as August 27, 1821. Their primary purpose was to discourage settlement in the Western Reserve by making absurd and improbable representations. They include interesting descriptions of the manners and dress of Ohioans and of crops, trade, and scenery. Daniel Smith was an Englishman bound for the Birkbeck colony in Illinois. His journal, begun in 1820, ends at Shawneetown in March, 1821.

West, Rev. John. *The Substance of a Journal During a Residence at the Red River Colony, British North America, and Frequent Excursions Among the North-West American Indians in the Years 1820, 1821, 1822, 1823* (London, L. B. Seeley and Son, 1824). Extracts in *Nor. Dak. Hist. Soc. Colls.*, III (1910), 439–90.[10]

A smoothly flowing narrative by an English minister, the Reverend John West, describes a trip to and from Winnipeg and the Red River Colony and a considerable amount of travel in the Northwest during 1820–1823. Gives information on Indians and comments on missionaries, religion, and the frontier and its hardships.

Hall, James. *Letters from the West; Containing Sketches of Scenery, Manners, and Customs; and Anecdotes Connected with the First Settlement of the Western Sections of the United States* (London, H. Colburn, 1828).[11]

The first Midwesterner to become what could be called a professional man of letters, with the possible exception of Timothy Flint, was James Hall, novelist, journalist, editor, and travel narrator. He was born in Philadelphia in 1793, served in the army for over five years, practiced law in Pittsburgh for two years, and in April, 1820, descended the Ohio for the purpose of continuing legal practice in the West. His *Letters from the West* . . . recounts events on this trip and exhibits interest in scenery and river life. He settled in Shawneetown, Illinois, where

he became district attorney and editor and part owner of the *Illinois Gazette*. The latter part of the *Letters* is more than a commonplace travel narrative. It has interesting observations on people, manners, and places and includes animated tales; but it does not mention events after 1825, when he began to emerge as a writer. He lived in Vandalia for five years before moving to Cincinnati in 1833, and later visited Detroit, Green Bay, and Lake Superior. Such of his writings as *Kentucky, The Harpe's Head, The Romance of Western History*, and *Legends of the West* give an accurate picture of the frontier, and his life proved that it was possible for a talented man to make writing a profession in the Midwest.

Finley, Rev. James Bradley. *Life among the Indians; or, Personal Reminiscences and Historical Incidents Illustrative of Indian Life and Character*. D. W. Clark, ed. (Cincinnati, Cranston and Curts; New York, Hunt and Eaton, 1857).[12]

Ellis, Gen. Albert G. "Recollections of Rev. Eleazar Williams." *Wis. Hist. Soc. Colls.*, VIII (1879), 322–69.[13]

The Reverend James B. Finley was a Methodist missionary to the Indians. His *Life among the Indians* . . . contains incidents from his autobiography, discussed in Chapter 5. The early part of the *Life* . . . is about Indians in the Midwest before his time. Graphically relates interesting events during 1820–1827 such as camp meetings; the emphasis is, of course, religious. Finley also wrote *History of the Wyandott Mission* (1840) and *Sketches of Western Methodism* (1856). The "Recollections of Rev. Eleazar Williams" (1820–1832) is insignificant as a narrative but is possibly historically important because Williams may have been the lost dauphin of France. The story tells of the removal of a group of Indians from Oneida, New York, to Green Bay, Wisconsin. Ellis wrote that Williams spoke the Mohawk language well but English badly. Ellis's narrative of his own life will be described later in this chapter.

Spencer, J. W. *Reminiscences of Pioneer Life in the Mississippi Valley* . . . (Davenport, Ia., Griggs, Watson, and Day, 1872). Reprint ed. by Milo M. Quaife (Chicago, R. R. Donnelley and Sons Co., 1942).

Ross, Harvey L. *The Early Pioneers and Pioneer Events of the State of Illinois including Personal Recollections of the Writer; of Abraham Lincoln, Andrew Jackson, and Peter Cartwright, together with a Brief Biography of the Writer* (Chicago, Eastman, 1899).

Fonda, John H. "Early Reminiscences of Wisconsin." *Wis. Hist. Soc. Colls.*, V (1868), 205–92.[14]

The Life and Adventures of James P. Beckwourth, Mountaineer, Scout, and Pioneer, and Chief of the Crow Nation of Indians . . . Written from his own Dictation, by T. D. Bonner (New York, Harper, 1856).[15]

J. W. Spencer's *Reminiscences* briefly chronicles a trip from the East via St. Louis to Illinois in 1820. It covers various journeys in the Midwest, including one to Rock Island, Illinois, in 1828, and describes Chief Black Hawk and the Black Hawk War, as well as events as late as 1838. Harvey L. Ross's *The Early Pioneers . . . including Personal Recollections* . . . tells of his trip from New Jersey to Illinois in 1820 and of travel in various parts of the latter state during the years 1820–1840. Ross remembered Andrew Jackson, Peter Cartwright, and Lincoln. John H. Fonda proceeded by way of the Illinois River from St. Louis to Chicago in 1820. In 1825, after descending the Ohio and visiting Santa Fé, he went to Wisconsin. He narrates, in a spirited manner, his hunting and fishing experiences, activities in the Black Hawk War, and adventures as late as 1848.

The life of James P. Beckwourth, a hunter and raconteur, gives an account of his visit to the lead region of Illinois in 1820, his part in a fur-trading expedition organized in 1823, and his life among the Crow Indians. The style is inflated and bombastic.

Growing Up with Southern Illinois, 1820 to 1860, from the Memoirs of Daniel Harmon Brush. Milo M. Quaife, ed. (Chicago, R. R. Donnelley and Sons Co., 1944).

"Narrative of Peter J. Vieau." *Wis. Hist. Soc. Colls.,* XV (1900), 458–69.

Baird, Elizabeth Thérèse. "Reminiscences of Early Days on Mackinac Island." *Wis. Hist. Soc. Colls.,* XIV (1898), 17–64.

———— "Reminiscences of Life in Territorial Wisconsin." *Wis. Hist. Soc. Colls.,* XV (1900), 205–63.

———— "Indian Customs and Early Recollections." *Wis. Hist. Soc. Colls.,* IX (1882), 303–26.

Much detail about Lake Erie, Ohio, Indiana, and southern Illinois is contained in the writing of Daniel H. Brush, an Easterner, which forms a continuous narrative of events from 1820 to 1860. Peter Vieau's tale, written by the editor of the *Wisconsin Historical Society Collections,* is unimportant but recounts incidents in the fur trade during 1820–1880. Mrs. Elizabeth T. Baird's narratives are extremely interesting accounts of such pioneer experiences as dog sledging, syrup making, and Indian encounters. Included is a story of a man who sought and found a brother who had been stolen by the Indians. Her article on life in territorial Wisconsin (1824–1842) describes a trip from Mackinac Island to Green Bay. Most vivid of all is her tale of the Indian massacre at Prairie du Chien in "Indian Customs and Early Recollections."

Northwest Coast of America, May 15, 1826 . . . Mr. [Francis] Baylies, from the Select Committee . . . made the following report: [Baylies' 2nd Report.] 19th Congress, 1st Session, House of Representatives. Report 213, Serial 142.[16]

"From England to Illinois in 1821. The Journal of William Hall." Jay Monaghan, ed. *Jour. Ill. State Hist. Soc.,* XXXIX (1946), 21–67, 208–53.

Teas, Thomas Scattergood. "From *Journal of a Tour to Fort Wayne and the Adjacent Country in the Year 1821*. . . ." In Harlow Lindley, ed. *Indiana as Seen by Early Travelers* (Indianapolis, Indiana Historical Commission, 1916), pp. 246–55.[17]

A report by Francis Baylies gives an account of a purported trip in 1821 by S. A. Ruddock from Council Bluffs to the mouth of the Columbia, up the Platte, south to Santa Fé, and then westward. William Hall, an Englishman, wrote a rather lengthy journal of his trip in 1821 from England to America and down the Ohio to Shawneetown, Illinois. He included the story of Morris Birkbeck's drowning. A long and factual journal, it shows Hall's appreciation of nature. The extract from the journal of Thomas S. Teas tells of events in a two-week journey by foot from Philadelphia to northern Indiana and return. There are comments on encounters with friendly Indians and long descriptions of scenery and towns.

"The Journals of Capt. Thomas Becknell from Boone's Lick to Santa Fé and from Santa Cruz to Green River." *Mo. Hist. Rev.,* IV (1910), 65–84.

The Journal of Jacob Fowler, Narrating an Adventure from Arkansas through the Indian Territory, Oklahoma, Kansas, Colorado, and New Mexico . . . *1821–22.* Elliott Coues, ed. (New York, F. P. Harper, 1898).[18]

Memoirs of William Forster. Benjamin Seebohm, ed. (2 vols., London, 1865). Extracts relating to Indiana in Harlow Lindley, *Indiana as Seen by Early Travelers,* 256–68.[19]

Ogden, George W. *Letters from the West, Comprising a Tour through the Western Country and a Residence of Two Summers in the States of Ohio and Kentucky; originally Written in Letters to a Brother* (New Bedford, Mass., Melcher and Rogers, 1823). Reprinted in R. G. Thwaites, ed. *Early Western Travels, 1748–1846* (32 vols., Cleveland, Arthur H. Clark Co., 1904), Vol. XIX.[20]

Ellis, Gen. Albert G. "Fifty-four Years' Recollections of Men and Events in Wisconsin." *Wis. Hist. Soc. Colls.,* VII (1876), 207–68.

Captain Becknell displays an eye for nature, familiarity with literature, and an ability to write good prose in his journals, which narrate an expedition in 1821 from Missouri to Santa Fé. This established the Santa Fé Trail. Major Jacob Fowler's journal relates incidents in a journey through what is now Oklahoma, Kansas, and Colorado in 1821–1822. It shows keen observation and a realistic outlook. William Forster was a ministering British Quaker who came to America in 1820 and traveled in the Midwest during 1821–1822 and 1845. Although he often used the word "backwoods," he wrote realistically and apparently appreciated the scenery of the prairies. There are well-phrased comments on travel, religious affairs, and work.

A more important book than the preceding is Ogden's *Letters from the West.* Ogden, a Quaker merchant from Massachusetts, undertook in 1821 a business journey to the Western country, where he remained for two years. Though much of his volume consists of letters plagiarized from travel accounts by Estwick Evans and others, several realistic observations were evidently based upon an actual residence in Ohio and Kentucky. The "Recollections" of General Albert G. Ellis, editor of the previously listed tale by Eleazar Williams, is a smoothly phrased story of a trip in 1821 from the East by way of the Great Lakes, Detroit, and Mackinac to Green Bay and of life and people in Green Bay. A later journey to New York and back is mentioned.

Anonymous. "A Diary of 1822." *Penna. Mag. Hist. Biog.,* XLIX (1925), 61–74.[21]

Reminiscences of Parmenas Taylor Turnley. From the Cradle to Three-Score and Ten . . . (Chicago, Donohue and Henneberry, 1892).

James Watson Webb's Trip Across Illinois in 1822. Frank E. Stevens, ed. (Sycamore, Ill., Sycamore Tribune Print, 1924).

The anonymous "Diary of 1822" covers a trip from Pennsylvania to New Lisbon, Ohio, and back. It notes the large number of taverns in comparison with the few houses and stores in the towns and describes the scenery. Turnley gives a detailed insight into the Chicago of about 1822. James W. Webb's "Trip" is a brief account of his walk west from Chicago in the winter of 1822, during which he was half frozen. An Indian companion led him back to Chicago.

DeForest, David Curtis. Grand Tour to the Western Country. June 10–August 20, 1822. MS. Yale University Library, New Haven, Connecticut.[22]

Graham, George. Journal, 1822. Notebook, 69 pp. MS. Historical and Philosophical Society of Ohio, Cincinnati.

A successful merchant and consul to Argentina, David C. DeForest, visited various places in Ohio during the summer of 1822 and wrote a diary of his trip. A man of considerable culture, he endowed the DeForest scholarships at Yale College and established a prize in English. The 1822 notebook of George Graham describes his trip from Stoystown, Pennsylvania, down the Ohio Valley and Mississippi River to New Orleans. He became a pioneer industrial and civic leader of Cincinnati.

Blane, William. *An Excursion through the United States and Canada during the Years 1822–23. By an English Gentleman* . . . (London, Baldwin, Cradock, and Joy, 1824).[23]

Wilhelm, Paul, Duke of Wuerttemberg. *Erste Reise nach dem Nördlichen Amerika in den Jahren 1822 bis 1824* . . . (Stuttgart and Tübingen, J. G. Cotta, 1835). English translation by William G. Bek in *Sou. Dak. Hist. Colls.*, XIX (1938), 7–474.[24]

Meeker, Moses. "Early History of the Lead Region of Wisconsin." *Wis. Hist. Soc. Colls.*, VI (1872; 1908 reprint), 271–96.[25]

Condemning the attitude of Thomas Ashe, William Blane, also an Englishman, visited the Birkbeck settlement in Illinois and the Rappist colony of New Harmony in Indiana in 1822–1823 and wrote one of the best and most unbiased English books about the West. His trip took him from Vincennes to St. Louis and New Harmony.

Also just, but at the same time critical in approach, is the narrative of Paul Wilhelm, who shipped from Hamburg to New Orleans in 1822, ascended the Mississippi and Missouri as far as present lower South Dakota, and returned by the same route. The English translation is long and detailed but readable. A pioneer lead-miner and physician, Moses Meeker, born in New Jersey in 1790, made trips from Cincinnati to Galena, Illinois, by horseback in 1821 and by keelboat in 1823. His narrative is mainly about the lead region of Wisconsin during 1822–1825 rather than about the details of travel.

Baird, Henry S. "Recollections of the Early History of Northern Wisconsin." *Wis. Hist. Soc. Colls.*, IV (1859), 197–221.

"A Home in the Woods. Oliver Johnson's Reminiscences of Early Marion County." Related by Howard Johnson. *Ind. Hist. Soc. Pubs.*, XVI (1951), 137–234.

Interweaving history with description, a brief narrative by Henry Baird tells of Indians and conditions at Green Bay and in northern Wisconsin during 1822–1855. Written in picturesque, interesting language, Oliver Johnson's "Home in the Woods" is an intimate account of early Marion County, Indiana, beginning in 1822: cabin building, shooting matches, country fairs, fights, hunts, and other pioneer activities.

Beltrami, G. Constantino. *La Découverte des Sources du Mississippi et de la Rivière Sanglante. Description du Cours Entier du Mississippi* . . . (New Orleans, Benjamin Levy, 1824). English version: *A Pilgrimage in Europe and America, Leading to the Discovery of the Sources of the Mississippi and Bloody River; with a Description of the Whole Course of the Former, and of the Ohio* (2 vols., London, Hunt and Clarke, 1828).[26]

A political refugee and traveler from Italy, Constantino Beltrami by chance fell in with the expedition of Major Stephen Long at Fort St. Peter in 1823 and accompanied it for a time. Treated harshly by Long, he left the expedition and explored independently, discovering what he claimed was the northernmost source of the Mississippi which he named "Lake Julia."

Brown, Col. Richard. "Memorandum Book of events hapned [sic] from the commencement of building a boat," 1823. MS. In the Nessly-DeSellem Collection of family papers. Listed in Elizabeth Biggert, comp. *Guide to the Manuscript Collections in the Library of the Ohio State Archaeological and Historical Society* (Columbus, 1953), No. 753.

Codd, Matthew. Diary of a Journey in America, 1823. MS. Buffalo Historical Society, New York.

Jouett, Matthew H. Diary of letters written in 1823. 43 pp., MS. transcript. Durrett Collection, University of Chicago.[27]

Smith, Benjamin R. Memorandum of a journey, 1823. 114 pp. MS. Indiana University Library, Bloomington.

Whitlock, William C. Journal of a Journey, 1823. Original MS. in private hands. 10 pp. Typed copy made for his granddaughter. Listed in Biggert, *Guide*, No. 1092.

In addition to the journal of 1823 by Stephen H. Long, mentioned in Chapter 8, at least five other Midwestern travel narratives were written during the year. Colonel Richard Brown's "memorandum book" relates events during a boat trip on the Ohio River from Steubenville to Maysville, Kentucky. Matthew Codd's diary is an extensive narrative of Midwestern travel. A well-known Kentucky painter, Matthew H. Jouett, wrote his "letters" while he was traveling on the Mississippi River. A keelboat trip from Pittsburgh to Cincinnati makes up a large part of a memorandum book by Benjamin R. Smith, who started west from Rhode Island in August. He ended his narrative on October 7, 1823. Whitlock's brief journal covers a journey from Virginia to Union County, Illinois.

Hebert, William. *A Visit to the Colony of Harmony, in Indiana, in the United States of America, recently Purchased by Mr. Owen for the Establishment of a Society of Mutual Co-operation and Community of Property, in a Letter to a Friend; to which are Added, Some Observations on that Mode of Society, and on Political Society at Large: also, a Sketch of the Formation of a Co-operative Society* . . . (London, George Mann, 1825). Reprinted in *Ind. Hist. Colls.*, III (1916), 327–59.

William Hebert was another Englishman who visited New Harmony and wrote a letter about it. Since he was particularly interested in Robert Owen's social experiment, the chief value of his work lies in the full discussion of the religious and social conditions that existed in the colony during the latter half of 1823. The book should be compared with Robert Dale Owen's autobiography, mentioned near the end of this chapter.

Keating, William Hypolitus. *Narrative of an Expedition to the Source of St. Peter's River, Lake Winnepeek, Lake of the Woods, etc. Performed in the Year 1823* (2 vols., Philadelphia, H. C. Carey and I. Lea, 1824). Extract in *Nor. Dak. Hist. Soc. Colls.*, III (1910), 491–97.[28]

Keating based much of his narrative of Stephen Long's expedition of 1823 upon Long's own unpublished notes (see Chapter 8), and on the notes of Thomas Say, but he himself was the "literary journalist" of the party and wrote of what he himself had observed. As he was a professor of mineralogy at the University of Pennsylvania, he paid particular attention to the copper deposits in the Lake Superior Region, but he gives much interesting matter about Ohio, Indiana, Illinois, Chicago, Prairie du Chien, and the Wisconsin-Minnesota area. The work is lengthy and rather monotonous in spite of valuable information about Indians and settlers.

"Diary of James Kennerly, 1823–1826." Edgar B. Wesley, ed. *Mo. Hist. Soc. Colls.*, VI (1928), 41–97.[29]

Postl, Karl. [Charles Sealsfield.] *Die Vereinigten Staaten von Nordamerika, nach ihrem politischen, religiösen, and gesellschaftlichen Verhältnisse betractet; mit eines Reise durch den westlichen Theil von Pennsylvanien, Ohio, Kentucky, Indiana, Illinois, Missuri, Tennessee, das Gebiet Arkansas, Mississippi und Louisiana* . . . (2 vols., Stuttgart and Tubingen, Cotta, 1827). English versions: *The Americans as they are; Described in a Tour through the Valley of the Mississippi* (London, Hurst, Chance, and Co., 1828) and *The United States of North America as They Are* (London, W. Simpkin and R. Marshall, 1828).[30]

A diary by James Kennerly, an Easterner who resided at St. Louis before he moved to Council Bluffs, devotes much space to business affairs and the weather. Although poorly written, it provides a good picture of events at an army post.

Karl Postl, writing under the pseudonym "Charles Sealsfield," was a Moravian novelist who visited the south and southwestern parts of the United States in 1823–1824, remained in a town near Pittsburgh from 1824 until late 1825, and returned to New Orleans in 1826. His *Die Vereinigten Staaten . . .* contains no offensive remarks about the Midwest unless his unfavorable comments on colleges in the area can be considered derogatory. The work had a direct influence upon German immigration. The English translation was rather widely known.

Hall, Baynard Rush. *The New Purchase, or Seven and a Half Years in the Far West* (New York, D. Appleton and Co.; Philadelphia, G. S. Appleton, 1843).[31]

Later to become one of the first professors in Indiana, Baynard Rush Hall in 1823 journeyed westward and located near Gosport. He began teaching in the seminary which developed into Indiana University, but was disappointed with the West. His book about these experiences gives a very interesting picture of the rude state of civilization and culture in Bloomington, Indiana, about 1826. One writer, Agnes M. Murray, says it is the only distinguished early work written in this area.

Royall, Mrs. Anne Newport. *Sketches of History, Life, and Manners in the United States, by a Traveller* (New-Haven, Conn., the Author, 1826).
——— *Mrs. Royall's Southern Tour, or, Second Series of the Black Book* (3 vols., Washington, 1830–31).[32]

An American propagandist, novelist, playwright, and author of several travel books, Mrs. Anne Newport Royall saw most of the United States during 1823–1830. She wrote in order to make a living and, although she was observant, her narratives show the faults of hasty composition. Her best travel book, *Sketches of History, Life, and Manners, in the United States . . . ,* indicates that she touched Ohio in 1823, and Vol. III of her *Southern Tour* contains comments on the numerous towns in Indiana, Missouri, and Illinois which she visited in 1830. A biographer, Sarah H. Porter, points out that Mrs. Royall went to see her mother and brother in Indiana in 1831 and traveled to Cincinnati and later descended the Mississippi River. Although almost forgotten today, she is to be remembered not so much for her books as for her editorial attacks upon what she believed was wrong, especially the graft she exposed wherever she found it.

Autobiography of Peter Cartwright, the Backwoods Preacher. W. P. Strickland, ed. (Cincinnati, Cranston and Curts; New York, Hunt and Eaton, 1856).[33]

Naively self-glorifying and unsatisfactory as a record of his life, the *Autobiography of Peter Cartwright* is, nevertheless, written with great verve and depicts social and religious conditions in the Midwest during the author's lifetime. Cartwright explored part of Illinois in 1823 and settled in Sangamon County the following year. He traveled extensively on his circuits and attended numerous conferences. His popularity on the frontier was due to some of those characteristics admired by the Westerner—self-confidence, ruggedness, and directness of approach.

Crawford, Rev. R. C. "Reminiscences of Pioneer Ministers of Michigan." *Mich. Hist. Colls.,* XVII (1892), 226–38.
——— "Reminiscences of Pioneer Life in Michigan." *Mich. Hist. Colls.,* IV (1883), 41–53.
——— "Reminiscences of Seventy Years in Michigan." *Mich. Hist. Colls.,* XXVI (1896), 585–93.

——— "Fifty-two Years of Itinerant Life in the Michigan Conference of the M. E. Church." *Mich. Hist. Colls.,* XXII (1894), 266–81.

The four relatively brief narratives of the Reverend R. C. Crawford when grouped together make up the story of his life in Michigan from his arrival there from Canada in 1825 to 1895. "Reminiscences of Pioneer Ministers" recounts the travels and activities of various preachers in Michigan during 1823–1848. "Reminiscences of Pioneer Life in Michigan" and "Reminiscences of Seventy Years in Michigan" give, in a spirited manner, interesting incidents in the life of a pioneer preacher. "Fifty-two Years of Itinerant Life in the Michigan Conference" is distinctly religious in tone, however, and is less rewarding than are the others.

Reminiscences of Levi Coffin, the Reputed President of the Underground Railroad . . . (Cincinnati, Western Tract Society, 1876).[34]
Church, Jeremiah. *Journal of Travels, Adventures, and Remarks, of Jerry Church* (Harrisburg, Pa., 1845). Reprinted at Harrisburg (Aurand Press, 1933).

According to his *Reminiscences . . . ,* Levi Coffin in 1823 visited a Quaker settlement in Sangamon County, Illinois, and in 1826 moved to Newport (now Fountain City), Indiana, where he opened a store and lived for more than twenty years. Jeremiah Church traveled down the Ohio River with a friend in about 1823, stayed a few weeks in Ohio, and returned East. A later trip took him to Cincinnati, where he met a man who exhibited wax figures in Kentucky and Indiana. Nearly a year's stay in Cincinnati, a sojourn at the home of a friend on the Big Miami River, a return to Cincinnati, a trip south in 1830 and up the Mississippi to St. Louis later, and travels in Illinois, Michigan, and Indiana as late as 1833 make up the remainder of his life in the Midwest. His narrative is written in a fresh, lively manner and is one of the most interesting and intimate records of the period.

Coffin, Charles. "North Carolina to Indiana in 1824." *Bull. Fr. Hist. Soc.,* III (1909), 91–95.
——— "Personal Reminiscences of Charles F. Coffin of Wayne County, Indiana, from 1824 to 1833." *Ind. Hist. Soc. Colls.,* III (1916), 532–35.
Woodward, Arthur. "Adventuring to Santa Fé." *New Mex. Hist. Rev.,* XVII (1942), 288–93. Reprinted from the *Missouri Intelligencer,* Aug. 5, 19, 1825.

Charles Coffin's article is a clearly written little story which quotes from his father's journal and tells how the family traveled from North Carolina to Indiana by two-horse wagon in 1824, averaging twenty to thirty miles per day. Following the Wilderness Road, the family reached the Ohio River and then proceeded to Wayne County, Indiana. The father taught school for a while at Milton, Indiana. Coffin's "Personal Reminiscences" describes other pioneer customs and hardships.

One of the few Midwestern travel tales written in a humorous vein is Arthur Woodward's account of a trip in about 1824 from Boone's Lick, Missouri, to Santa Fé and back. He parodies the Biblical style, including divisions into chapters and verses.

"Diary of Mrs. Joseph Duncan." [Elizabeth Caldwell Smith.] *Jour. Ill. State Hist. Soc.,* XXI (1928–1929), 1–91; additional in *Ill. State Hist. Soc. Trans.,* No. 26 (1919), 126–27, 164–67, 177–78.[35]
Marmaduke, Meredith Miles. "Journal of a Trip from Franklin, Missouri, to Santa Fé, New Mexico in 1824." *Mo. Hist. Rev.,* VI (1911), 1–10. Reprinted from *Missouri Intelligencer,* with

notes by F. A. Sampson, Sept. 2, 1825. Reprinted in A. B. Hulbert, ed. *Southwest on the Turquoise Trail* ([Colorado Springs], the Stewart Commission of Colorado College, [Denver] Public Library, 1933), 69–77.[36]

"Diary of William Owen, from November 10, 1824, to April 20, 1825." Joel W. Hiatt, ed. *Ind. Hist. Soc. Pubs.*, IV (1906), 1–134.[37]

The diary of Mrs. Elizabeth C. Duncan, wife of Governor Joseph Duncan of Illinois, whose own diary is discussed in Chapter 10, is a rather dull account of her early school life in Newark and domestic and social life in Illinois during 1824–1825. Much emphasis upon travel appears in the journal of Meredith Marmaduke, one-time governor of Missouri. It contains brief notes on stage coaches and on people and customs in New Mexico. Another picture of life in New Harmony, Indiana, is contained in the diary of the Scotchman William Owen, son of Robert Owen, who traveled from the East by way of the Ohio and Wabash rivers to his father's settlement in 1824. The entries are well written and historically valuable. Later Owen visited Cincinnati and then returned to the East.

"The Diaries of Donald MacDonald, 1824–1826." *Ind. Hist. Soc. Pubs.*, XIV (1942), 147–379.

Another figure in the New Harmony experiment was Donald MacDonald, described by Robert Dale Owen in *Threading My Way*. He voyaged from Britain to America in the same ship with Robert Owen and Robert Dale Owen and made two trips down the Ohio to New Harmony, one in 1824–1825 and one in 1825–1826. His style is vivid and his work should be considered with that of Blane, Hebert, the Owens, Paul Brown, Karl Bernhard, and Duclos, all mentioned in this chapter, to obtain a comprehensive picture of the New Harmony experiment.

Duden, Gottfried. *Bericht über eine Reise nach den westlichen Staaten Nord-Amerika's und einem mehrjährigen Aufenthalt am Missouri (in den Jahren 1824, 25, 26 und 1827), in Bezug auf Auswanderung und Uebervolkerung; oder, Das Leben im Innern der Vereinigten Staaten, und dessen Bedeutung für die häusliche und politische Lage der Europäer* . . . (Elberfeld, Lucas, 1824). Translated by William G. Bek in "Gottfried Duden's 'Report,' 1824–1827," *Mo. Hist. Rev.*, XII (1917), 1–21, 81–89, 163–79, 258–70; XIII (1918), 44–56, 157–81, 251–81. Extracts translated by Alice H. Finch, *Mo. Hist. Rev.*, XLIII (1949), 334–43; XLIV (1949), 21–30.[38]

German-born Gottfried Duden traveled down the Ohio and up the Mississippi to St. Louis. After spending some time there he settled in Montgomery County, Missouri. Pleased with the fertility of the soil and believing that people in the Atlantic states envied the West, he wrote a glowing account of his New World experiences during 1824–1827 which had a tremendous influence in encouraging the tide of German immigration. Although most of the German immigrants were at first disappointed, they usually became accustomed to the new land. Several of Duden's followers also wrote diaries, which are mentioned in Chapter 11.

Johnston, George. *Journal in the North West, 1824–1827.* MS. Library of Congress.

Lamb, Rev. C. A. "Reminiscences by C. A. Lamb." *Mich. Hist. Colls.*, V (1884), 46–51.

——— "Incidents in Pioneer Life in Clinton County." *Mich. Hist. Colls.*, I (1877), 149–51.

Journal Kept by David Douglas during His Travels in North America, 1823–1827 . . . (London, W. Wesley & Son, 1914). Extracts edited by Sir W. J. Hooker in *Companion to the Botanical Magazine* (London), II (1835–1836), 79–182; *Oreg. Hist. Soc. Quar.*, VI (1905), 76–97, 206–27, 288–309, 417–49.[39]

George Johnston's journal is in the form of letters written from the Great Lakes region. The Reverend C. A. Lamb in his "Reminiscences . . ." records incidents in his trip from Detroit through much of Michigan in 1824. His narrative covering 1829–1853 describes travel from Buffalo to Detroit and Bloomfield, Michigan. Both accounts are well told and contain religious sentiments. A journey to the Columbia River beginning in 1824 is related in the journal of David Douglas, an English horticulturist who traveled by way of the Red River settlement and York Factory and returned to England in 1829. A second trip in 1830 included another visit to the Northwest.

Pattie, James O. *Personal Narrative during an Expedition from St. Louis, through the Vast Regions between that Place and the Pacific Ocean* . . . Timothy Flint, ed. (Cincinnati, John Wood, 1831). Reprinted in R. G. Thwaites, ed. *Early Western Travels*, Vol. XVIII, and also edited by Milo M. Quaife (Chicago, R. R. Donnelley and Sons Co., 1930).[40]

Encouraged by Timothy Flint, James O. Pattie, a native of Kentucky, wrote a narrative of a trading and trapping expedition beginning in 1824 which took him westward from St. Louis. His party ascended the Missouri to Council Bluffs, proceeded as far as the Platte, and then turned south. He records interesting encounters with Indians and one with a grizzly bear in a factual and smoothly flowing tale. Pattie eventually went to the Far West but returned penniless to Cincinnati in 1830.

Kennerly, William Clark. *Persimmon Hill, A Narrative of Old St. Louis and the Far West.* [Edited and rewritten by Elizabeth Russell.] (Norman, University of Oklahoma Press, 1948).

Soper, Mrs. Sarah E. "Reminiscence of Pioneer Life in Oakland County." *Mich. Hist. Colls.*, XXVIII (1900), 399–408.

Kedzie, Robert Clark. "Recollections of Pioneer and Professional Life in Michigan." *Mich. Hist. Colls.*, XXIX (1901), 526–58.[41]

The narrative of his birth at a fort on the Missouri River, removal to St. Louis and life in this town, and various trips from there is contained in *Persimmon Hill*, the story of William C. Kennerly's life (1824–1863). His tale of a trip in 1843 will be mentioned in Chapter 13. Mrs. Sarah Soper's reminiscences go back to a boat trip in 1824 from Buffalo to Ashtabula, Ohio, and then to central Ohio and Detroit. Difficulties of pioneer life as late as 1867, such as cabin building and bear hunting, are interestingly told. The recollections of Robert C. Kedzie cover the years 1824–97. They include his traveling up the Erie Canal and Lake Erie to the mouth of the River Raisin, his removal to Kedzie Grove, his college days, medical practice, and numerous other events after 1850. Kedzie became a professor at Michigan State Agricultural College.

Anonymous. "Journal of the Atkinson-O'Fallon Expedition." Russell Reid and C. G. Gannon, eds. *Nor. Dak. Hist. Quar.*, IV (1929), 5–56.[42]

Ashley, William. "The Ashley Narrative." In *The Ashley-Smith Explorations and the Discovery of a Central Route to the Pacific 1822–1829. With the Original Journals.* Harrison C. Dale, ed. (Cleveland, Arthur H. Clark Co., 1918), pp. 117–61; reprinted at Glendale, Cal., 1941).[43]

Sibley, George Champlin. *Journal.* Kate L. Gregg, ed. (Albuquerque, University of New Mexico Press, 1952).

The Atkinson-O'Fallon expedition went from St. Louis up the Missouri to the mouth of the Yellowstone River in 1825. The anonymous "Journal" gives a detailed picture of troop movements and mileage. Colonel Atkinson's journal of the 1819 expedition to the Yellowstone, mentioned in Chapter 8, should be compared with it. William Ashley, a fur trader, explorer, and later a United States congressman, composed a journal in the form of a long, well-written letter to Atkinson, relating events in his 1825 trip up the Platte to the Rockies and his return to Council Bluffs and the East. George Champlin Sibley's narrative is a lengthy account of travel from St. Louis to Santa Fé in the same year.

Lavasseur, A. *Lafayette in America in 1824 and 1825; or, Journal of a Voyage to the United States . . .* John D. Godman, trans. (2 vols., Philadelphia, Carey and Lea, 1829).[44]

Loomis, Chester A. *A Journey on Horseback through the Great West, in 1825 . . .* (Bath, New York, Plaindealer Press, 182–?).

The Marquis de Lafayette's secretary, A. Lavasseur, accompanied the celebrated Frenchman on his tour of America in 1825 and wrote one of the most interesting Midwestern travel tales of the decade. He recorded keen and detailed observations on the old French communities visited, described St. Louis and Kaskaskia, and included an account of a shipwreck on the Ohio in which Lafayette might have lost his life.

Chester A. Loomis's *A Journey on Horseback . . .*, an unimportant pamphlet, is evidently a reprint of a narrative that originally appeared in a newspaper. Loomis visited Elyria, Columbus, Zanesville, Vermillion, Kaskaskia, Vandalia, Sandusky, and other towns in 1825.

Reed, Rev. Isaac. *The Christian Traveller. In Five Parts. Including Nine Years and Eighteen Thousand Miles* (New York, J. and J. Harper, 1828). Extracts in *Jour. Ill. State Hist. Soc.*, V (1912), 279–84. Quoted in *Ill. Hist. Soc. Trans.*, No. 22 (1916), 74–76.[45]

Williams, William. "Extracts from a Pioneer's Note-Book." *Mag. West. Hist.*, X (1889), 177–82, 397–400.

Greenup, Christopher H. *Journal of a Trip to Washington and Richmond in 1825.* 14 pp., transcript. Durrett Collection, University of Chicago.

A Presbyterian preacher, Isaac Reed, went to Paris, Illinois, in 1825 to organize a church there and wrote a valuable book, *The Christian Traveller*, about his travels in Indiana, Kentucky, and Illinois. "Perhaps no book of this kind," says Professor Rusk, "contains a franker statement of the moral and cultural conditions then found in the smaller towns of Indiana and Kentucky." William Williams is not to be confused with other men of the same name. The extracts from his notebook describe a trip from Buffalo to Painesville, Ohio, in 1825.

Bernhard, Karl, Duke of Saxe-Weimar-Eisenach. *Reise durch Nord Amerika in den Jahren 1825 und 1826 . . .* (2 vols., Weimar, Hoffman, 1828). English translation: *Travels through North America, during the Years 1825 and 1826* (2 vols., Philadelphia, Carey, Lea and Carey, 1828).[46]

Brown, Paul. *Twelve Months in New-Harmony; Presenting a Faithful Account of the Principal Occurrences which have Taken Place there within that Period; Interspersed with Remarks* (Cincinnati, William Hill Woodward, 1827).

Karl Bernhard toured America from 1826 to 1828 and made rather flattering remarks about the Midwest. He ascended the Mississippi to St. Louis and proceeded by river to New Harmony.

He quoted most of the descriptions of the towns he passed through, however, from the *Western Navigator*. Another visitor to the Rappist community was Paul Brown who, in 1825, descended the Ohio from Pittsburgh to Louisville, walked across Kentucky to Tennessee, and in 1826 set out from Nashville to join Owen. His *Twelve Months in New-Harmony* shows a growing dissatisfaction with this sociological experiment.

"Diary and Recollections of Victor Colin Duclos." *Ind. Hist. Soc. Colls.*, III (1916), 536–47.

Hunt, Mrs. Millicent. "A Puritan Wife on the Frontier." Horace Adams, ed. *Miss. Val. Hist. Rev.*, XXVII (1940), 67–84.

Essex, James Cartwright. "Excerpts from an Autobiography." *Glimpses of the Past*, I (1934), 52–59.

Victor C. Duclos, a Frenchman, voyaged to Philadelphia, descended the Ohio from Pittsburgh to Mount Vernon, Indiana, in 1825, and joined the New Harmony colony. His readable but unfinished diary and recollections contain a minute description of this settlement and of events as late as 1833. Mrs. Millicent Hunt's Midwestern diary emphasizes her spiritual experiences from late 1825 until November 16, 1833, but mentions travel by sleigh to the River Raisin early in 1827. The published portions of James C. Essex's autobiography chronicle a trip from Kentucky to St. Louis and contain readable descriptions of pioneer activities during 1825–1836.

Owen, Robert Dale. *Threading my Way. Twenty-Seven Years of Autobiography* (London, Trübner and Co., 1874).[47]

The autobiography of Robert Dale Owen, the son of Robert Owen, contains much valuable information on his life in the Midwest as well as a criticism (in his Paper No. IX) of his father's New Harmony experiment. British by birth, Robert Dale lived in Indiana for many years, beginning in 1825, and in 1842 became a United States congressman from that state.

Life and Confessions of John D. Lee, the Mormon, with a Full Account of the Mountain Meadows Massacre, and Execution of Lee (Philadelphia, Barclay, c. 1877).

Journals of John D. Lee. Charles Kelly, ed. (Salt Lake City, Western Printing Co., 1938).[48]

Stevens, Sherman. "Sketch of Early Pioneer Life." *Mich. Hist. Colls.*, VII (1886), 93–98, 394–98.

"Reminiscences of Frederick Chouteau." *Kans. State Hist. Soc. Trans.*, VIII (1904), 423–34.[49]

The books on John Doyle Lee tell of his Midwestern travel experiences beginning in 1825, his joining the Mormons in Missouri in 1838, his return with them to Illinois in 1839, and his life as a Mormon missionary in the Middle West as late as 1846. He had eighteen wives and sixty-four children.

Sherman Stevens' "Sketch" narrates his trip from Buffalo by way of Lake Erie to Detroit and the difficulties of pioneer life in Michigan during 1825–1850. He studied the Indian language and took a camping trip with an Indian companion. Frederick Chouteau, Indian agent, reached Clay County, Missouri, in 1825 and in his narrative included a description of a keelboat trip with his brother to St. Louis. Although a disconnected account, it has interesting observations on Indian customs.

Chapter 10

Midwestern Travel Narratives of 1826–1831

The opening of the Erie Canal in 1825 and the building of other canals and railroads greatly facilitated the settlement of the Midwest. Its increasing importance was symbolized by the presence of Andrew Jackson in the White House from 1829 to 1837. Keelboats and commercial boats dotted the Ohio River, and travel on the Mississippi increased tremendously. The completion of the National Pike from Cumberland to Wheeling was an event of great importance.[1] It is no small wonder that English travelers like William Bullock, Basil Hall, and Mrs. Frances Trollope visited the frontier during the 1820's.

More frontier tales and a larger number of stories about the trans-Mississippi Midwest were written during 1826–1831 than in previous eras of equal length. Although several important travel writers visited the region at this time, many of the tales are slight and insignificant. Yet by placing all of them together, the reader can obtain a detailed and accurate picture of the times.

McKenney, Thomas Loraine. *Sketches of a Tour to the Lakes, of the Character and Customs of the Chippeway Indians, and of Incidents Connected with the Treaty of Fond du Lac . . .* (Baltimore, Fielding Lucas, Jr., 1827). Extracts in "The Indian Chief Pontiac, and the Siege of Detroit." *Mich. Hist. Colls.*, VI (1884), 504–12.

——— *Memoirs, Official and Personal; with Sketches of Travels among the Northern and Southern Indians; Embracing a War Excursion, and Descriptions of Scenes Along the Western Borders* (2 vols., New York, Paine and Burgess, 1846).[2]

Thomas McKenney's *Sketches of a Tour to the Lakes . . .* is written in the form of narrative letters and is a valuable and detailed picture of Indian life on the Great Lakes. McKenney arrived at Niagara Falls on June 13, 1826, and by June 16 was at Detroit, which he said was beautiful. On July 4 he was at Sault Ste. Marie, where he stayed several days before proceeding to Grand Island and the American Fur Company establishment at Fond du Lac, where he helped arrange a treaty with the Indians. He returned homeward by way of Mackinac Island, Lake Huron, Detroit, and Lake Erie late in the summer of the same year. His *Memoirs, Official and Personal* contains an account of a later journey down the Mississippi from Prairie du Chien in 1827. Interest in the Indian is reflected not only in these books but also in his *History of the Indian Tribes of North America . . .* (1836–1844).

Henshaw, Mary Catherine. Journal of a Tour, 1826–1827. 65 pp. MS. Henry E. Huntington Library, San Marino, California.

Power, Nathan. "Book of Record, 1826–1873." Photostatic copy of MS. Michigan Historical Collections, University of Michigan, Ann Arbor.

Knapp, S. B. Memorandum and Account of Life in Michigan, 1826–1905. 14 pp., typescript. In the Abner Pease Knapp Papers. Burton Historical Collection, Detroit.

Mary Catherine Henshaw's journal covers a tour from Middlebury, Vermont, to Green Bay, Michigan Territory, September 4, 1826 to August 17, 1827. A short account of a trip from New York to Michigan in 1826 and very brief records of other trips made by Nathan Power or his wife from 1826 to 1873 are included in his "Book of Record." The content of S. B. Knapp's Memorandum is obvious from the title.

Cross, William H. "Early Michigan." *Mich. Hist. Colls.*, X (1888), 54–57.

Richards, F. S. "Eighty Years in Michigan." *Mich. Hist. Colls.*, XXXVIII (1912), 365–69.

"Reminiscences of Mrs. George Palmer." *Mich. Hist. Colls.*, VII (1886), 564–66.

A brief tale by William H. Cross describes the building of a house at Tecumseh, Michigan, and other pioneer experiences during 1826–1831. More interesting is P. S. Richards' story of a stormy trip on Lake Erie in 1826 while he was journeying from New York state to Detroit. Richards' father entered the Michigan wilderness to locate some government land, built a house at Rawsonville and after some experiences with Indians and bears in the neighborhood, moved to Ypsilanti. He records events as late as about 1887. The "Reminiscences" of Mrs. George Palmer covers a similar trip to Detroit and gives a good description of Indian life.

Bullock, William. *Sketch of a Journey through the Western States of North America, from New Orleans, by the Mississippi, Ohio, City of Cincinnati and Falls of Niagara, to New York, in 1827 . . .* (London, John Miller, 1827). Reprinted in R. G. Thwaites, ed. *Early Western Travels, . . .* (32 vols., Cleveland, Arthur H. Clark Co., 1905), Vol. XIX.[3]

A learned English showman, traveler, and lecturer, William Bullock, entered the United States in 1827 at the mouth of the Mississippi and ascended this river and the Ohio to Cincinnati. During a previous visit in 1822, he had purchased an estate on the Kentucky shore where he planned to attract a colony of Englishmen. His narrative is brief but gives details of frontier life. He was amazed by the magnificence of the Ohio above Louisville and wrote enthusiastic descriptions of the countryside and Cincinnati. Mrs. Frances Trollope, who met him in this city, noted in her *Domestic Manners of the Americans* that he seemed out of place on the frontier. The publication of his book drew the attention of many Englishmen to the Ohio Valley. Included in the work are extracts about Cincinnati written by various authors in 1826.

"The Diary of John Corcoran." Charles Van Ravenswaay, ed. *Mo. Hist. Soc. Bull.*, XIII (1957), 264–74.

Judah, Dr. Samuel Bernard. "A Journal of Travel from New York to Indiana in 1827." *Ind. Mag. Hist.*, XVII (1921), 338–52.[4]

Keeney, Salmon. "Salmon Keeney's Visit to Michigan in 1827." Helen Everett, ed. *Mich. Hist.*, XL (1956), 433–46.

Pickering, Joseph. *Inquiries to an Emigrant: Being the Narrative of an English Farmer from the Year 1824 to 1830, During Which Period He Travelled the United States and Canada with a View to Settle as an Emigrant . . .* (3rd ed., London, Effingham Wilson, 1832).

Snelling, William Joseph. "Early Days at Prairie du Chien and the Winnebago Outbreak of 1827." *Wis. Hist. Soc. Colls.*, V (1868), 123–58. Reprinted from *Colls. Minn. Hist. Soc.*, 1857.[5]

Whiting, Capt. Henry. "A Visit to the Cave in Put-in-Bay Island." Under the title "The Saustawraytsees" in Henry R. Schoolcraft, *The American Indians . . .* (1850). Reprinted in *Northw. Ohio Quar.*, XI (1939), 12–16.

Plummer, John Thomas. Diary of a Journey from Richmond, Indiana, to New Haven, Connecticut. October 16–30, 1827. MS. owned by Lawrence J. King, Richmond, Ind.; photostatic copy, Yale University Library.

The diary of John Corcoran gives an account of a trip from the Red River in Hudson's Bay Territory to St. Louis in 1827. It comments on hardships, hunting, and other matters. Dr. Samuel B. Judah journeyed in the same year from the East to Cleveland, Columbus, Dayton, Cincinnati, and Vincennes to visit his son. His diary, though hastily written, has an interesting list of prices: corn, twelve and one-half cents per basket; turkeys, eighteen and three-quarters cents a pound; and beef, two to three cents a pound. He remarked that whiskey was drunk like water but said he saw few drunkards. Salmon Keeney records a trip from Pennsylvania through northern Ohio to Detroit, Ann Arbor, and other places in Michigan and back by way of Detroit and Buffalo. He gives descriptions of topography and settlements.

Joseph Pickering, an English farmer, touched Michigan in 1827 and described the Detroit River in the latter part of his book. Snelling's "Early Days at Prairie du Chien . . ." has reflections on the justice of the Indians. He later published a book of short stories in which he makes one of the first pleas for a realistic attitude in fiction. While en route to Buffalo from Detroit in 1827, Captain Whiting visited the cave on Put-in-Bay Island in Lake Erie.

Palmer, Friend. "Detroit in 1827 and Later On." *Mich. Hist. Colls.*, XXXV (1907), 272–83.

———— *Early Days in Detroit; Papers Written by General Friend Palmer, of Detroit, Being his Personal Reminiscences of Important Events and Descriptions of the City for Over Eighty Years* (Detroit, Hunt and June, 1906).[6]

Friend Palmer came to Michigan by steamer with his mother and sisters in 1827 and in "Detroit in 1827 and Later On" (1827–1832) described Detroit as a town without paved streets and scarcely any sidewalks. His *Early Days in Detroit* is a lengthy volume and contains much information about early Michigan and the Indians.

Farnsworth, Benjamin Stow. Diary, 1820–1842. In the Benjamin Stow Farnsworth Papers. MS. Burton Historical Collection, Detroit.

Benjamin S. Farnsworth's diary begins in 1820, but he did not see the Midwest until 1827 when he arrived by boat from Buffalo on November 10. He returned to Massachusetts in September, 1828, but on December 1, 1836, again started for Detroit, this time to establish himself in business. He made a third trip to and from Boston in 1837. His diary contains lengthy descriptions of Detroit and nearby towns and of business and family life as late as 1842.

Cooke, Col. Philip St. George. *Scenes and Adventures in the Army; or, Romance of Military Life* (Philadelphia, Lindsay and Blakiston, 1857).

———— "A Journal of the Santa Fé Trail." William E. Connelley, ed. *Miss. Val. Hist. Rev.*, XII (1925), 72–98, 227–55.[7]

Colonel Cooke's book gives a valid picture of army life on the frontier. After graduating from West Point, Cooke began a trip westward in 1827. Traveling by way of the Ohio and the Mississippi, he reached Fort Snelling, the Falls of St. Anthony, and Galena in 1828. He returned to St. Louis and took other trips, one up the Missouri to Fort Leavenworth and part way up the Platte. After the Black Hawk War, he marched to Oregon by way of the Platte, Fort Laramie, and the Rockies. His book, divided into chapters but partly in diary form, is lively and contains interesting comments on the places he visited. The "Journal of the Santa Fé Trail" is his official military journal of May to July, 1843, of the expedition of a detachment of U. S. Dragoons from Leavenworth to protect traders on the annual trip from Missouri to Mexico via Santa Fé.

"Narrative of Morgan L. Martin." *Wis. Hist. Soc. Colls.*, XI (1888), 385–415.[8]

Seymour, C. B. "Early Days in Old Washtenaw County." *Mich. Hist. Colls.*, XXVIII (1900), 391–99.

A readable narrative by Morgan L. Martin relates events in a trip to Green Bay by way of the Great Lakes and Detroit in 1827, a visit to Galena, Illinois, in 1828, one to Chicago to attend a treaty council in 1833, another to the second Wisconsin state constitutional convention at Madison in 1847, and incidents as late as 1872. C. B. Seymour's brief, well-written narrative describes his early schooling, a journey from Buffalo to Detroit in 1827, and a trek into the western wilderness.

Anonymous. "Heads and Tales of a Voyage to and from America, and a Tour There in 1827 and 1828." MS. Vol. IV, 182 pp., January 28–November 24, 1828, relates to voyage down the Ohio and Mississippi rivers. Illinois State Historical Library, Springfield.

Anonymous. Travel Narrative, 1828. In the David L. Porter Papers. MS. Burton Historical Collection, Detroit.

Pitcher, Zina. Diary of expedition in the Michipicoten River region. May 18–23, 1828. 18 pp. MS. Burton Historical Collection, Detroit.

———— Diary of expedition along west end of Lake Superior. July 10–August 3, 1828. 28 pp. MS. Burton Historical Collection, Detroit.[9]

"The Heads and Tales of a Voyage . . ." tells of travel down the Ohio and Mississippi Rivers to New Orleans in 1828. The Travel Narrative describes a journey from the East by way of the Erie Canal and Lake Erie to Detroit.

Zina Pitcher was an army man, naturalist, and physician who, shortly after receiving his M. D. from Middlebury College in 1822, was stationed in Michigan, where he served for eight years at Detroit, Saginaw, and Sault Ste. Marie. His diaries recount events during expeditions in the Lake Superior Region in 1828. The second expedition of 1828 was with Schoolcraft, McKenney, and others for the purpose of searching for copper and studying Indian customs and the geography.

The English Party's Excursion to Paris . . . ; to Which Is Added, a Trip to America, etc.; etc., etc., by J. B., Esq., Barrister-at-law . . . (London, Longmans, 1850).[10]

Baillie, Col. John. "An Englishman's Pocket Note-Book in 1828. What He Saw in America." *Mag. of Amer. Hist.*, XIX (1888), 331–38, 422–28, 511–12; XX (1888), 61–64.[11]

Brunson, Mrs. Catherine Calkins. "A Sketch of Pioneer Life among the Indians." *Mich. Hist. Colls.*, XXVIII (1900), 161–63.

Edwards, Maj. Abraham. "A Sketch of Pioneer Life." *Mich. Hist Colls.*, III (1881), 148–51.

"J. B." (John Baillie?) records in rather dull travel notes a trip to America and down the Ohio and Mississippi in 1828. Colonel John Baillie, Orientalist and at one time member of Parliament, describes a similar journey down these rivers in the same year and shows an obvious appreciation of nature. Mrs. Catherine C. Brunson's realistic sketch of life among the Michigan Indians in 1828 includes an account of an Indian attack upon a white man. Major Edwards' "Sketch" is another brief tale of life in Michigan in this year. He describes a trip from Detroit to western Michigan by covered wagon to find a home on the frontier.

Hall, Basil. *Travels in North America in the Years 1827 and 1828* (3 vols., Edinburgh, Cadell and Co., etc., 1829).[12]

Hall, Mrs. Basil (Margaret Hunter). *The Aristocratic Journey . . .* (New York, London, G. P. Putnam's Sons, 1931).

An Englishman with aristocratic prejudices, Captain Basil Hall believed that the American political system was imperfect. In April, 1828, he ascended the Mississippi and Ohio to Louisville, traveled to St. Louis, and crossed Illinois and Indiana to Cincinnati, reaching Pittsburgh by way of the Ohio and returning to England. Since he failed to appreciate the Middle West, it was not strange that when his book appeared, he became a prime target for the American critics.[13] His wife accompanied him on this visit and wrote a series of narrative letters which contains some of the most adverse criticisms of America ever written. She commented on bad manners and bad hotels in the West but liked the appearance of the prairies and the banks of the Mississippi.

"Journal of Isaac McCoy for the Exploring Expedition of 1828." Lela Barnes, ed. *Kans. Hist. Quar.*, V (1936), 227–77, 339–77.

"Isaac McCoy's Second Exploring Trip in 1828." John F. McDermott, ed. *Kans. Hist. Quar.*, XIII (1945), 400–62.[14]

Massey, H. "Traveling on the Great Lakes When Detroit Was Young." *Mich. Hist. Colls.*, VII (1886), 131–33.

Journal of the Life, Labours and Travels of Thomas Shillitoe (London, 1839). Reprinted in *Friends' Library* (Philadelphia, Joseph Rakestraw, 1839), III, 342–478.[15]

"Major Alfonso Wetmore's Diary of a Journey to Santa Fé, 1828." *Mo. Hist. Rev.*, VIII (1914), 177–97. Reprinted in A. B. Hulbert, ed. *Southwest on the Turquoise Trail* ([Colorado Springs], the Stewart Commission of Colorado College, [Denver] Public Library, 1933), 182–95. First published as *Sen. Exec. Doc. 90*, 22nd Congress, 1st Session.[16]

Isaac McCoy was a Michigan Baptist missionary who in 1828 accompanied some Indians from Michigan to St. Louis for the purpose of exploring locations for settlement west of the Mississippi. His diaries, consisting mainly of jottings and personal notes, show his concern over the drunken behavior of the Indians and recount his trip with the Indians to the Neosho River and south of Fort Gibson.

A brief narrative by H. Massey tells of a boat trip from Buffalo to Detroit in 1828. A lengthy, well-written journal by an English Quaker, Reverend Thomas S. Shillitoe, an old man at the time, describes a trip from England to America, down the Ohio River to Cincinnati, later to Indiana, and return to the East, all in 1828. In the United States he tried to heal the schism which existed between the Quakers and the seceders who called themselves Hicksites after Elias Hicks, whose work is mentioned in Chapter 8. Major Wetmore's diary, actually part of a narrative letter to the Secretary of War, gives an account of a journey, also in 1828, from Franklin, Missouri, to Santa Fé. Poorly written. Wetmore was editor, lawyer, and writer.

Trollope, Mrs. Frances (Milton). *Domestic Manners of the Americans* (2 vols., London, Whittaker, Treacher, and Co., 1832). Reprint edited by Donald Smalley (New York, Alfred A. Knopf, 1949). Extracts in "American Audience 1829 . . . ," *Drama* (1950), pp. 231–33.

———— Notes for *Domestic Manners of the Americans*, 1828–1830, 3 vols. MSS. largely unpublished. Indiana University Library, Bloomington.[17]

One of the two or three best-known criticisms of the United States in this period is Mrs. Trollope's *Domestic Manners of the Americans*. Since her husband had done poorly in business, she and part of the family journeyed from England by way of New Orleans to Cincinnati in 1828, and, to retrieve their fortunes, decided to open a bazaar there. She was favorably impressed by the scenery she saw along the banks of the Mississippi and Ohio, but her business venture collapsed and she soon became disillusioned. Although she probably tried to take a fair view of America, she failed because of her snobbishness and innate obstinacy.[18] Her famous son, the novelist Anthony Trollope, said in his *Autobiography* that when she decided to write a book about the New World, she almost immediately received a considerable sum from the publishers, even though she had never before earned a shilling. "Whatever she saw she judged, as most women do, from her own standing point . . . The Americans were to her rough, uncouth, and vulgar,—and she told them so," he said. "Her volumes were very bitter, but they were very clever, and they saved the family from ruin."[19] No less than four editions appeared before 1833, and the book was translated into both French and Spanish. Her notebooks show that she was very conscious of Basil Hall's work when she wrote her own, and later she received encouragement from Hall regarding the publication of her book.[20]

Domestic Manners of the Americans is extremely interesting and rewarding reading. Such incidents from American life as watermelon eating, revival meetings, and the disappointing behavior of a servant girl are well told, and Mrs. Trollope's remarks are not entirely unfavorable. Most of the notes to the book remain unpublished.

Needless to say, the reactions to her criticisms were violent. The Reverend Calvin Colton, whose narrative will be described later in this chapter, wrote an ill-humored rebuttal in *The Americans, By an American in London* (1833). *The Edinburgh Review* of July, 1832, upon reviewing Mrs. Trollope's book, asked for a peace between England and America;[21] *Blackwood's Magazine* criticized certain parts of her work unfavorably,[22] and *The American Quarterly Review* suggested that her mistakes were not so much the result of her inclinations as the fault of her education.[23] F. W. Shelton in *The Trollopiad* (1837) celebrated her fame in crude couplets.[24] Travel narrators Charles A. Murray, C. D. Arfwedson, Henry Tudor, and James Stuart, to be discussed in Chapters 10 and 11, commented unfavorably upon her or her writing. As Professor Rusk has said, "No other English writer, with the exception of Scott and Byron, was as well known throughout the West and none was so sordidly hated."[25] Since she had not yet obtained success as a novelist, she was judged by this one book.

Short, Rich. *Travels in the United States of America, through the States of New-York, Pennsylvania, Ohio, Michigan Territory . . . With Advice to Emigrants . . .* (2nd ed., London, Richard Lambert, 183–?).[26]

Caswall, Rev. Henry. *America, and the American Church* (London, J. G. and F. Rivington, 1839).

———— *The City of the Mormons; or, Three Days at Nauvoo, Ill., in 1842* (London, F. Rivington, 1842). Probably first published in the *Irish Ecclesiastical Journal* and reprinted in the *Museum of Foreign Literature*, XLV (1842), 901–6.[27]

Rich Short, an Englishman, briefly described two westward trips, one in 1828 and another in 1831, in his *Travels in the United States. . . .* It is a feeble and obscure work, bitter towards the author's neighbors in Michigan where he attempted farming. In contrast, Reverend Henry Caswall was a sympathetic English observer who visited numerous Ohio towns during his tour of 1828–1833 and formed a generally favorable opinion of the inhabitants. His *America and the American Church*, which, of course, emphasizes the religious phase of his trip, was begun as a series of letters but is partly divided into chapters. A second voyage to America in 1842 gave him an opportunity to observe the territory between St. Louis and Nauvoo, Illinois.

Blair, James I. Diary. 1828–1835. MS. New Jersey Historical Society, Newark.

Letts, Mrs. Albina (Brockway). "Ye Olden Tyme." Reminiscences of Pioneer Experiences of Letts Family in Illinois, Black Hawk War, Land Sales in Chicago, etc. 1828–1835. 31 pp., typescript. Chicago Historical Society.[28]

James I. Blair's diary tells of Western and Southern trips. "Ye Olden Tyme" was dictated to Mrs. Albina Letts by David Letts, who rode horseback from Ohio to settle in Illinois in 1828. For his horse he was offered forty acres of land where the heart of Chicago now stands. He made two trips back and forth to Ohio before finally settling near Cedar Point, Illinois, in 1830. He went to Bloomington, Illinois, in 1831, moved to Fort Wilburn on the Illinois River at the outbreak of the Black Hawk War, returned to his farm after hostilities ceased, moved to other towns, saw a land sale in Chicago, and became school commissioner of Peru. Several interesting incidents in the lives of his children are included in this well-written and historically valuable document.

Gilbert, Oliver. "Pioneer Reminiscences." *Wis. Mag. Hist.*, XIV (1930), 182–92.

Mitchell, Mary. "Reminiscences of the Early Northwest." *Wis. Hist., Soc. Procs.*, L (1902), 173–89. Condensed from reminiscences in the *Menominee* (Mich.) *Herald*, Oct. 16, 18, 20, 1899.

Mazzuchelli, Samuel Charles. *Memorie Istoriche ed Edificanti d'un Missionario Apostolico dell'ordine dei Predicatori . . . negli Stati-Uniti d'America* (Milan, Boniardi-Pogliani, 1844). English translation in *The Young Eagle* (St. Clara Academy, Wis., 1898); English translation published at Chicago (W. F. Hall Printing Co., 1915).[29]

A very factual but readable narrative of 1828–1842 by Oliver Gilbert describes an 1828 trip from Kentucky down the Ohio and up the Mississippi. He was at Prairie du Chien during part of the Black Hawk War, delivered government dispatches to General Dodge at Dodgeville, Wisconsin, and later, as a trader with the Indians, he opened a store with his brother at Prairie du Chien. Mary Mitchell's reminiscences, which cover the same years, tell of her life at Green Bay and of occasional visits to Chicago. Rare among Midwestern travel tales is one by the Italian-born Samuel Charles Mazzuchelli, architect, missionary, and linguist. He arrived in Kentucky in 1828 and proceeded to Ohio, where, upon being ordained to the priesthood in 1830, he departed for Mackinac. Three years later he made Green Bay his headquarters, in 1835 established the first church in the Prairie du Chien area, and in 1843 visited Nauvoo and attempted to convert Joseph Smith. His book includes accounts of trips to Galena, Dubuque, Davenport, and St. Louis.

LaRonde [Ronde, de La], John T. "Personal Narrative." *Wis. Hist. Soc. Colls.*, VII (1876), 345–65.

Clark, Satterlee. "Early Times at Fort Winnebago." *Wis. Hist. Soc. Colls.*, VIII (1879), 309–21.

Davidson, W. "Personal Narrative." *Wis. Hist. Soc. Colls.*, V (1868), 317–20.

LaRonde was born in France and was employed by the Indian Department of the United States government as an interpreter. He describes his journey from Canada to the Sault in 1828, from there to the Mississippi River, a winter at River St. Croix, a trip to Mackinaw and Portage, Wisconsin, and several interesting events as late as 1844. Satterlee Clark, whose tale covers the years from 1828–49, tells of arriving at Green Bay, of building Fort Winnebago, and of events in the Black Hawk War. Davidson relates the life of a prospector at Galena, Mineral Point, and other settlements in Wisconsin during 1828–1855.

Atwater, Caleb. *Remarks Made on a Tour to Prairie du Chien; thence to Washington City, in 1829* (Columbus, Ohio, Jenkins and Grover, 1831).[30]

In 1829 President Jackson appointed Caleb Atwater one of three commissioners to arrange a treaty with the Winnebago and other Indians. His descriptions of the Mississippi River, the lead region of northern Illinois, and the Indians are of value, and the book contains his prophetic remarks about the future growth of new states. He was a prolific author, the first advocate of soil conservation, an early historian, and a pioneer in education.

"Notes by Amos Bancroft M.D. of a trip from Groton [Mass.] to Ohio in 1829." MS. Original and a copy annotated by Charles K. Bolton. Listed in Elizabeth Biggert, comp. *Guide to the Manuscript Collections in the Library of the Ohio State Archaeological and Historical Society* (Columbus, 1953), No. 160.

Shannon, S. P. MSS., including letters, 1829. 42 pp. Chicago Historical Society.

Dr. Bancroft's notes need no comment. S. P. Shannon gives an account of a winter spent with the Fox and Sac Indians in the northern part of Illinois.

Dewey, F. A. "From Buffalo to Michigan in 1829." *Mich. Hist. Colls.*, IX (1886), 161–66.

Riley, Maj. Bennet. "Journal." Fred S. Perrine, ed. *New Mex. Hist. Rev.*, III (1928), 267–300.[31]

Van Arsdale, Mrs. P. "A Pioneer Story." *Annals of Iowa*, 3rd Series, XIII (1922), 279–303.

F. A. Dewey's trip took him by way of Lake Erie to Detroit and Ypsilanti and return to the East by land during cold weather. His well-written tale emphasizes the hardships of travel. Major Riley's "Journal" is an official military journal assigned to him but evidently written by Lieutenant James F. Izard on his behalf. It gives an account of an exepedition in

1829 from Jefferson Barracks, Missouri, by way of Fort Leavenworth and the Santa Fé Trail to the crossing of the Arkansas River, and relates interesting Indian encounters; the entries are often mere fragmentary jottings. Mrs. Van Arsdale wrote a readable narrative of a pioneer Dutch family's trek from Detroit westward, probably in 1829.

Beeson, Jacob. Diary, 1829–1830. 98 pp. MS. William L. Clements Library, University of Michigan, Ann Arbor.

Williams, Annabelle. Journal of a Trip from Philadelphia to Cleveland. 3 vols. MSS. in the Annabelle Williams Manuscripts, 1829–1831. Listed in Paul Bleyden, comp. *Guide to the Manuscript Collections in the Historical Society of Pennsylvania* (Philadelphia, Historical Society of Pennsylvania, 1949), No. 715.

Jacob Beeson's diary records a journey from Uniontown, Pennsylvania, to Louisiana and Alabama by way of the Ohio and Mississippi rivers. Annabelle Williams' journal is lengthy.

Duncan, Joseph. Diary. *Ill. Hist. Soc. Trans.*, No. 26 (1919), 180–87. Extract (Feb.–July, 1829) in *Tenn. Hist. Mag.*, VII (1922), 245–49.[32]

Löwig, Gustav. *Die Freistaaten von Nord-Amerika. Beobactungen und praktische Bemerkungen für auswandernde Deutsche* . . . (Heidelberg and Leipzig, K. Gross, 1833).

The diary of Joseph Duncan, at one time governor of Illinois, contains much information on his public life and on personal activities and affairs in Kentucky, where he was born, and in Illinois during 1829 and 1830. Some of the same period is covered in the diary of his wife, Mrs. Elizabeth C. Duncan, who is mentioned in Chapter 9. Gustav Löwig's *Die Freistaaten von Nord-Amerika* . . . was another one of the books written to give information to prospective German emigrants. Löwig visited the Eastern cities and descended the Ohio to the Mississippi, traversed part of Illinois, and passed St. Louis. There are observations on the soil and prices of crops in the Midwest and high praise for the beauty of the Ohio Valley.

Brownell, Thomas Church. Missionary Journal. *Protestant Episcopal Church History Magazine*, VII (1938), 303–22.[33]

Sturtevant, Julian Monson. *An Autobiography.* J. M. Sturtevant, Jr., ed. (New York, Chicago, Toronto, Fleming H. Revell Co., 1896).[34]

Brown, Ebenezer Lakin. "Autobiographical Notes." A. Ada Brown, ed. *Mich. Hist. Colls.*, XXX (1906), 424–94.[35]

Waldo, William. "Recollections of a Septuagenarian." *Glimpses of the Past*, V (1938), 62–94.

"Autobiography of Clarissa E. G. Hobbs." *Jour. Ill. State Hist. Soc.*, XVII (1925), 612–714.

An Episcopal bishop, Thomas Church Brownell, made a trip in 1829 at the request of the Episcopal Missionary Society from the East to Cincinnati, Louisville, the South, and back. He wrote notes on preaching, people, and places during two journeys to New Orleans, one in 1829 and 1830 and another in 1834 and 1835. Julian M. Sturtevant, a Congregational minister who had studied at Yale, took a similar journey down the Ohio in the same years and proceeded to St. Louis and Jacksonville, where he helped found Illinois College, of which he later became president. His *Autobiography* is detailed and generally well written. Ebenezer Lakin Brown's "Notes" record a trip in 1829 by way of Lake Erie to Detroit, by stage to Ypsilanti and Ann Arbor, and then to the town of Schoolcraft, Michigan. They include his experiences in the Black Hawk War and various trips and events as late as 1886. William Waldo describes characters and incidents of the Santa Fé trade route over a long number of

years beginning in 1829. He mentions such important figures as Pike, Sublette, and Jedediah Smith. An even longer time (1829–1923) is covered in the autobiography of Clarissa E. G. Hobbs, who tells of her birth in 1829 and her father's trip west from New England, including his hardships and encounters with Indians. The style is straightforward and unpretentious.

Anonymous. "Fort Tecumseh and Fort Pierre Journal and Letter Books." Charles E. DeLand, ed. *Sou. Dak. Hist. Colls.*, IX (1918), 69–167.[36]

Anonymous [Bache, Lieut. Robert or Robert Baird]. *View of the Valley of the Mississippi; or, The Emigrant's and Traveller's Guide to the West; containing a General Description of that Entire Country; and also Notices of the Soil, etc.* . . . (Philadelphia, H. S. Tanner, 1832).[37]

Colton, Rev. Calvin. *Tour of the American Lakes, and among the Indians of the Northwest Territory, in 1830* . . . (2 vols., London, Frederick Westley and A. H. Davis, 1833). Extracts in "Remarkable Instance of Capital Crime," and "Lake St. Clair," *Mich. Hist. Colls.*, VI (1884), 103–5, 418–20.[38]

The anonymous Journal relates events at Fort Tecumseh and Fort Pierre in South Dakota during 1830. The anonymous *View of the Valley of the Mississippi* is often attributed to Robert Baird but is probably by Lieutenant Robert Bache. It was written to inform travelers and prospective settlers about the Mississippi Valley. The author claimed that much of his information was based upon personal observation. The first ten chapters present a general view of the region and Chapters 11–24 contain geographical, statistical, and historical descriptions of much the same area. The remainder of the book describes colleges, religious sects, and steamboat travel. Reverend Calvin Colton, a journalist, politician, and author, wrote his *Tour of the American Lakes* with the purpose of giving a picture of the region. It includes an account of the last case of capital punishment in Michigan. Colton defended the theory that the Indians were descendants of the ancient Israelites.

Conkey, William. "A Journey from Massachusetts to Illinois in 1830." *Ill. State Hist. Soc. Trans.*, 1906, XI (1906), 214–18.

"A Diary Written by Captain Hiram Henshaw." In Mabel Henshaw Gardiner and Ann Henshaw Gardiner, *Chronicles of Old Berkeley* (Durham, N. C., Seeman Press, 1938), pp. 282–314.[39]

"Mrs. Caroline Phelps' Diary." J. T. Phelps Ewan, ed. *Jour. Ill. State Hist. Soc.*, XXIII (1930), 209–39.[40]

"Diary of Colonel Richard Ware Wyatt on Horseback Trip to the Western Country in 1830." *Ky. Hist. Soc. Reg.*, XXXIX (1941), 106–15.[41]

William Conkey traveled with an emigrant party up Lake Erie from Buffalo to the Maumee River and by wagon through Indiana and the Grand Prairie of Illinois. His narrative, well-written, contains an appreciation of nature but is brief and below average in interest. Captain Henshaw's diary covers a journey from West Virginia through southern Ohio to Kentucky on business in 1830. There are jottings on weather, scenery, farming, mills, towns, visits, and expenses. Mrs. Caroline Phelps of Lewistown, Illinois, wrote a diary in 1830 about everyday happenings. She comments on Indians and a flood and an explosion. Colonel Richard W. Wyatt's diary relates incidents on his trip down the Ohio and into Ohio, Indiana, Illinois, and Missouri and return to Kentucky. The work is readable but some of the entries are mere jottings.

"Benj.[amin] Herr's Journal, 1830." *German-American Annals*, V (1903), 8–31.[42]

Loomis, Elisha. "Diary of Trip Rochester to Mackinac Island." Philip P. Mason, ed. *Mich. Hist.*, XXXVII (1953), 27–41.

"[James] McCall's Journal of a Visit to Wisconsin in 1830." *Wis. Hist. Soc. Colls.*, XII (1892), 170–204.[43]

Northrup, Enos. "First Trip to Michigan." *Mich. Hist. Colls.*, V (1884), 69–70.

—— "Traveling Three Hundred Miles to Mill . . ." *Mich. Hist. Colls.*, V (1884), 405–6.[44]

Simpson, Frances. "Journey for Frances." Introduction by Grace Lee Nute. *The Beaver* (Dec., 1953), 50–54; (Mar., 1954), 12–17; (Summer, 1954), 12–18.

Benjamin Herr wrote detailed and descriptive touristic notes on a trip through much of New York state to Buffalo, by water to Sandusky, by stage to Cincinnati, and return to the East. Elisha Loomis, of Rochester, New York, having decided to become a teacher at the mission at Mackinac Island in 1830, set out with his wife and children and recorded his observations on the trip and on the founding of Detroit. A well-written diary, decidedly religious in tone. James McCall, appointed commissioner to settle differences between Indian tribes, records in an official journal, in legal-sounding language, a trip from Detroit to Green Bay and return in 1830. Exceedingly brief are the narratives by Enos Northrup which describe the Maumee swamp, his trip, also in 1830, from Hinckley, Ohio, to Gull Prairie, Michigan Territory, and his trip in Michigan in 1831 with two yoke of oxen and his return by horseback and boat. Frances Simpson gives a good insight into modes of travel in 1830. She describes Lake Superior, a canoe trip in Canada, and the trading posts on the Rainy River.

Taylor, Judge Lester. "Notes taken . . . while appraising school lands that give us free public schools," 1830. 77 pp., typescript. Listed in Biggert, *Guide*, No. 1001.

Fitch, Asa. Diary, December 1, 1830–February 20, 1831. MS. Yale University Library, New Haven, Connecticut.[45]

Chase, Salmon Portland. Diaries and a memorandum book: Diary, January 1, 1829–March, 1854 [no entries for the period 1843–1849]; Diary, March 1, 1845–September 30, 1859; Memorandum book, 1844–1859. MSS. Library of Congress.[46]

The "Notes" by Judge Lester Taylor, an Ohio state legislator from Claridon, Ohio, describe a trip on the Ohio River and the Erie Canal. The diary of Asa Fitch, entomologist and professor of natural history in the Rensselaer School (now Rensselaer Polytechnic Institute) at Troy, New York, was kept at Greenville and Vandalia, Illinois, during the winter of 1830–1831. Parts of the elaborate diaries of Salmon P. Chase, American statesman and jurist, have been printed,[47] but several Midwestern items remain unpublished. The first is a diary of his journey in March, 1830, by way of Wheeling to Cincinnati. Subsequently he made references to trips from the latter city to Columbus, Louisville, and other nearby places during 1830 to 1859.

Hamilton, Thomas. *Men and Manners in America. By the Author of Cyril Thornton, etc.* (Philadelphia, Carey, Lea and Blanchard, 1833).[48]

"From England to Ohio, 1830–1832: The Journal of Thomas K. Wharton." James H. Rodabaugh, ed. *Ohio Hist. Quar.*, LXV (1956), 1–27, 111–51.[49]

Stuart, James. *Three Years in North America* (2 vols., Edinburgh, Robert Cadell, etc., 1833).[50]

Extracts from the Journal and Letters of Hannah Chapman Backhouse . . . (London, R. Barrett, 1858), pp. 78–185.[51]

Busby, Joseph. "Recollections of Pioneer Life in Michigan." *Mich. Hist. Colls.*, IX (1886), 118–27.

After visiting several Eastern cities and Cincinnati and descending the Ohio and Mississippi in 1830–1831, Thomas Hamilton presented his unfavorable opinion of the United States in a minor book, *Men and Manners in America.* He had a good sense of humor, but he echoed Mrs. Trollope's satirical tone and warned England against imitating American institutions, although he admitted that he might be guilty of British prejudice.

In 1830, as a boy of sixteen, Thomas K. Wharton voyaged with his family from England to America and traveled by way of Buffalo and Lake Erie to Sandusky. His Journal records life in such towns as Dayton, Springfield, Columbus, and Zanesville during 1831 and 1832. It is well-written. Wharton transcribed it in 1854 and added his recollections.

James Stuart, another British subject, followed Mrs. Trollope's route along the Mississippi but contradicted her criticisms and, in contrast to Hamilton, defended the frontier. His *Three Years in North America* contains many observations on agriculture and social conditions during his trip from 1830 to 1832 and was popular enough to go through three editions in two years.

A partially published Quaker journal (1830–1835) by Hannah C. Backhouse, born at Norwich, England, records a voyage to America and includes comments on Ohio and Indiana. There are pleasant notes on scenery, people, and institutions. Joseph Busby's narrative, short but smoothly written, tells of a stay in the United States beginning in 1830 and continuing to about 1846. After reaching New York from England, Busby traveled by lake steamer to Detroit and by foot to Ypsilanti. He describes Detroit in 1832 and tells of moving to Saginaw, where he helped build his father's house.

"Daniel Lake Collins's Diary." In Arthur Adams and Sarah A. Risley, *A Genealogy of the Lake Family* (Hartford, Conn., privately printed, 1915), pp. 280–93.[52]

Jewett, Mrs. A. L. "Pioneer Life in 1830." *Mich. Hist. Colls.*, VI (1884), 426–30.

Marsh, Rev. Cutting. "Extracts from Marsh's Journal, During the Black Hawk War." *Wis. Hist. Soc. Colls.*, XV (1900), 60–65.[53]

Kinzie, Juliette Augusta (Magill). *Wau-bun, the "Early Day" in the North-west. By Mrs. John H. Kinzie of Chicago* (New York, Derby and Jackson; Cincinnati, H. W. Derby and Co., 1856). Reprint, Milo M. Quaife, ed. (Chicago, R. R. Donnelley and Sons Co., 1932).

Miller, Albert. "Reminiscences." *Mich. Hist. Colls.*, VII (1886), 388–94.

The narrative of Daniel Collins, New Jersey farmer and surveyor, details a trip from the East by way of the Ohio Canal to Akron, thence to Dover, Columbus, and other Ohio towns, into Kentucky and Indiana, and down the rivers to New Orleans from 1830 to 1831. Originally a diary, most of it is re-written in narrative form and contains interesting notes on scenery, social life, and economic conditions. Mrs. A. L. Jewett's "Pioneer Life . . . ," covering the same years, describes her trip from Vermont to Saginaw, Michigan, by boat and wagon, and her experiences in the wilderness as the wife of a surveyor.

The partially published journal of the Reverend Cutting Marsh, Congregational missionary to the Stockbridge Indians, tells of his reaching Detroit from the East in 1830 and of incidents in the Black Hawk War in the Michigan Territory. Many entries are mere jottings, and the tone of the work is religious.

Mrs. Juliette A. Kinzie's *Wau-bun* has been mentioned as an Indian captivity tale in Chapter 3, but part of her work is an account of a trip from Detroit to Mackinac, Green Bay, Fox River, Lake Winnebago, Rock River, Dixon, and Chicago and life at some of these places from 1830 to 1833, including incidents in the Black Hawk War. Another tale of 1830–1833 is Judge Albert Miller's "Reminiscences," a factual story of a winter at Flint and residence at Grand Blanc.

Pilcher, Rev. Elijah H. "Forty Years Ago." *Mich. Hist. Colls.*, V (1884), 80–89.
"The Journal of Charles Ballance of Peoria." Ernest E. East, ed. *Jour. Ill. State Hist. Soc.*, XXX (1937), 70–84.[54]
"Reminiscences of James E. R. Harrell." Fred Lockley, ed. *Oreg. Hist. Soc. Quar.*, XXIV (1923), 186–92.
Manly, William Lewis. *Death Valley in '49* (New York, Santa Barbara, Wallace Hebberd, 1894). Reprinted at Chicago (R. R. Donnelley and Sons Co., 1927).
"Chapters from the Autobiography of an Octogenarian (Miss Emily V. Mason), 1830–1850." *Mich. Hist. Colls.*, XXXV (1907), 248–58.
Thomas, N. M. "Reminiscences." *Mich. Hist. Colls.*, XXVIII (1900), 533–36.
"Diary of William M. Campbell." *Glimpses of the Past*, III (1936), 138–50.[55]
"Reminiscences of Jesup W. Scott." In H. S. Knapp, *History of the Maumee Valley* (Toledo, Blade Mammoth Printing and Publishing House, 1873), pp. 537–44.
Smith, Edwin S. "Pioneer Days in Kalamazoo and Van Buren." *Mich. Hist. Colls.*, XIV (1890), 272–80.
Hinman, John F. "My First Journey to Michigan, with Other Reminiscences." *Mich. Hist. Colls.*, XIV (1890), 563–71.

Elijah H. Pilcher describes a trip by horseback from western Virginia to Michigan and various religious conferences and events, 1830–1838. The diary of Charles Ballance (1830–1838) relates his visits to several Illinois towns and describes Peoria, where he lived. James E. R. Harrell's "Reminiscences" (1830–1847) includes a tale of a trip with three yoke of oxen from Six-Mile Prairie in Illinois to the Dalles in the Far West in 1847. William Manly narrates a long trek from Vermont to Cleveland and Michigan, where he and his father built two log houses, a later trip farther west and the return to Michigan, a journey to Chicago and Wisconsin, and a trip across Iowa to Fort Laramie and Death Valley (1830–1849). Long but well-written. The "Autobiography" of Emily V. Mason, sister of the governor of Michigan, tells of life in Detroit and various trips out of the Midwest. N. M. Thomas's brief story records travel by foot across southern Michigan into northern Illinois and Indiana. The diary of William M. Campbell, a lawyer in St. Charles, Missouri, gives detailed descriptions of various parts of Missouri and Illinois noted on a business and prospecting trip in 1830. Not all the entries are dated and many are mere jottings. "Reminiscences of Jessup W. Scott," well-written, chronicles his moving from South Carolina to Ohio in 1830, to Florence, Ohio, and to Perrysburg and Toledo in 1832. Edwin S. Smith's narrative contains a well-told account of a trip from Detroit to Michigan towns farther west in 1832 and later and of difficulties with the Indians. John F. Hinman's account contains details of a boat trip from Buffalo to Detroit, probably in 1830, and reminiscences of events as late as 1857.

O'Ferrall [Ferrall], Simon Ansley. *A Ramble of Six Thousand Miles through the United States of America* (London, E. Wilson, London, 1832). Reprinted at Bowling Green, O. (Historical Publications Co., 1919).[56]
"The Journey of Lewis David Von Schweinitz to Goshen, Bartholomew County in 1831." Adolf Gerber, trans. *Ind. Hist. Soc. Pubs.*, VIII (1927), 205–85.[57]
Suppiger, Joseph. *Reisebericht der Familie Köpfli & Suppiger nach St. Louis am Mississippi und Gründung von New-Swit-*

zerland, im *Staate Illinois* (Sursee [Schnyder'sche buckdruckerei], 1833). Translated extracts in "Swiss Emigrants Seek Home in America." Leo G. Titus, ed. *Hist. Phil. Soc. of Ohio Bull.*, XIV (1956), 167–85.
Vigne, Godfrey Thomas. *Six Months in America* (2 vols., London, Whittaker, Treacher and Co., 1832).[58]

A Ramble of Six Thousand Miles through the United States . . . by Simon A. O'Ferrall, another British observer, is largely descriptive. He traveled from Buffalo by way of Lake Erie to Sandusky, and thence to Columbus, Cincinnati, New Harmony, Illinois, and St. Louis. His interesting comments on a revival meeting near Cincinnati, on the English settlement in Illinois, and on causes for the failure of the New Harmony experiment lend value to the book. A botanist, pioneer mycologist, and Moravian clergyman, Lewis D. Von Schweinitz traveled to Indiana to establish a church at Hope and to restore his health. His journal, occasionally interesting, describes the trip down the Ohio to Madison, Indiana, across part of Indiana, and his return to Pennsylvania. Joseph Suppiger was one of the few Swiss travelers to visit the frontier at this time. His diary tells of a journey in 1831 from New York to Buffalo, Zanesville, and the Muskingum River and down the Ohio, up the Illinois, part way by land to Chicago, and down the Mississippi. Godfrey Vigne, another Englishman, descended the Ohio in 1831 and visited Maysville, Cincinnati, Lexington, Sandusky, Detroit, Green Bay, and Canada, all of which he describes.

Tocqueville, Alexis Charles Henri Maurice Clérel de. *DeTocqueville's Voyage en Amérique*. R. Clyde Ford, ed. (Boston, D. C. Heath and Co., 1909).[59]

Alexis de Tocqueville, author of *Democracy in America* (Paris, 1836, 1840) which is one of the fairest analyses of American institutions, voyaged from France to the United States in 1831 with his friend, Gustave de Beaumont, to examine penal establishments. He visited Detroit, Saginaw, and the Michigan wilderness, descended the Ohio and Mississippi, and noted the restlessness of the pioneer. He betrays a rather sentimental attitude toward the charm of Indian life, somewhat like that of Chateaubriand.

Old-age Recollections of Mrs. Marietta (Rumsey) Crittenden, 1831. MS. Burton Historical Collection, Detroit.
Rogers, Obadiah. Diary of Journey from New Braintree, Massachusetts, to Tecumseh, Michigan, 1831. 2 pp. MS. Michigan Historical Collections, University of Michigan, Ann Arbor. Typed copy in the Obadiah Rogers Papers, Burton Historical Collection, Detroit.

The recollections of Mrs. Marietta Crittenden, written in her old age, tell of the migration of her family from Vermont to Michigan in 1831, when she was only six years old. Obadiah Rogers (1792–1873) kept a diary during 1831–1837 which contains a brief description of his journey in 1831 to Michigan.

The Narrative of Giles Bryan Slocum (n. p., n. d.).
Thompson, Rev. O. C. "Observations and Experiences in Michigan Forty Years Ago." *Mich. Hist. Colls.*, I (1877), 395–402.
Tudor, Henry. *Narrative of a Tour in North America; Comprising Mexico, the Mines of Real del Monte, the United States, and the British Colonies; with an Excursion to the Island of Cuba. In a Series of Letters, Written in the Years 1831-2* (2 vols., London, James Duncan, 1834).[60]

The Giles Bryan Slocum narrative covers a trip by steamer from Saratoga County, New York, to Michigan and visits to Monroe, Michigan, and Perrysburg and Maumee, Ohio (1831–1832). It gives a good insight into frontier life and is in a readable style.

Reverend O. C. Thompson's account describes a similar steamer trip to Detroit in 1831. It mentions early Detroit and Western settlements and an interesting hike into the wilderness. In 1832 Thompson became principal of the academy at Ann Arbor.

Henry Tudor, a Britisher, has been mentioned in this chapter as an unfavorable critic of Mrs. Trollope's *Domestic Manners.* On the basis of his tour during 1831–1832 he found Mrs. Trollope unfair in her judgments and ridiculed her "sublime tone of disdainful superiority."

"Autobiography of Rev. William H. Brockway, of Albion." *Mich. Hist. Colls.*, III (1881), 158–60.

Hall, Rev. Sherman. "Extracts from the Journal of Mr. Hall." *Miss. Her.*, XXIX (1833), 410–14, 472–73; XXX (1834), 24–27.[61]

Stone, Alvan and David Wright. *Memoir of Alvan Stone, of Goshen, Mass., By David Wright* . . . (Boston, Gould, Kendall and Lincoln, etc., 1837).

Washburn, Amasa Cornwall. Diary. *1944 Yearbook of the Society of Indiana Pioneers.*[62]

The brief autobiography of the Reverend William H. Brockway, an Eastern clergyman, mentions travel by way of Lake Erie to Detroit and other events during 1831–1833. Appointed missionary by the American Board of Commissioners for Foreign Missions, the Reverend Sherman Hall, in a diary of the same years, described his trip from Mackinac along the south shore of Lake Superior. He established a mission at Lapointe, the first mission among the Chippewa since the time of the Jesuits. Alvan Stone, a young Baptist, went to Illinois in 1831, partly through the influence of John Mason Peck, taught school in several places, and died in 1833. A large part of his memoir, written by David Wright, consists of extracts from his diary. The diary of Amasa C. Washburn chronicles a journey from Putney, Vermont, to Blooming Grove, Illinois, in 1831 and return in 1833. An interesting section describes a canoe trip through Indiana on the St. Joseph and Kankakee rivers.

O'Bryan, William. *A Narrative of Travels in the United States of America, with Some Account of American Manners and Polity, and Advice to Emigrants and Travellers Going to that Interesting Country* (London, For the Author, 1836).[63]

William O'Bryan, an English minister, migrated to America in 1831 and preached in many places, but failed to establish a church. His diary, written from August, 1831, to June, 1834, records travel in Ohio, personal adventures, comments on manners and institutions, and advice to settlers. It is more varied than most diaries of this type.

Chase, Enoch. Reminiscences. MS. Partially published. Listed in Alice E. Smith, comp. *Guide to the Manuscripts of the Wisconsin Historical Society* (Madison, State Historical Society of Wisconsin, 1944), No. 121. Extracts in James S. Buck, *Pioneer History of Milwaukee* . . . (2 vols., Milwaukee, Swain and Tate, 1890), I, 49–52.

Narrative of the Adventures of Zenas Leonard, a Native of Clearfield County, Pa. who Spent Five Years in Trapping for Furs, Trading with the Indians, &c., &c., of the Rocky Mountains; Written by himself (Clearfield, Pa., D. W. Moore, 1839). Extract in Charles Neider, *The Great West* (New York, Coward-McCann, 1958).[64]

Leaving his home in Vermont in 1831, Enoch Chase traveled westward by schooner and stage to Coldwater, Michigan, where he practiced medicine and taught school until he moved to Milwaukee in April, 1835. His partly unpublished reminiscences describe the pioneer men and women of Milwaukee. He writes of Indian troubles, local rivalries, government organization, and the development of industries. Part of the narrative of Zenas Leonard was stolen by Indians but later replaced by Leonard. Started when he was twenty-two, his diary contains several good descriptions of nature and accounts of interesting incidents. He describes eating buffalo meat, making boats of buffalo skins, and encountering Indians. Since he was gone four years, his parents thought he was lost, but he eventually returned to Pennsylvania and later settled at Sibley, Missouri.

Driggs, Alfred L. "Early Days in Michigan." *Mich. Hist. Colls.*, X (1888), 57–60.

Gregg, Josiah. *Commerce of the Prairies: or the Journal of a Santa Fé Trader, During Eight Expeditions across the Great Western Prairies, and a Residence of Nearly Nine Years in Northern Mexico* (2 vols., New York, Henry G. Langley, 1844). Reprinted in Thwaites, *Early Western Travels*, Vols. XIX–XX; reprint, Milo M. Quaife, ed. (Chicago, R. R. Donnelley and Sons Co., 1926) and Max L. Moorhead, ed. (Norman, University of Oklahoma Press, 1954).

Diary and Letters of Josiah Gregg. Southwestern Enterprises, 1840–1847. Maurice G. Fuller, ed. (Norman, University of Oklahoma Press, 1941).[65]

Alfred L. Driggs' brief narrative gives a picture of pioneer Detroit, Jackson, and White Pigeon and emphasizes pioneer difficulties from 1831 to 1836. Included is an account of a visit to Chicago and the building of a saw mill. Josiah Gregg's *Commerce of the Prairies* is one of the books devoted to the Great Plains region and the Santa Fé Trail. Besides giving an account of the origin of the Trail, it relates events in Gregg's journeys in the spring of 1831 from Independence, Missouri, up the Arkansas River, on to Santa Fé and Mexico, and his return in 1840. Gregg was born in Tennessee but moved to Independence and became one of the early Santa Fé traders. He was a doctor by profession but was interested in history and wrote well. His work went through several editions.

Burlend, Mrs. Rebecca. *A True Picture of Emigration; or, Fourteen Years in the Interior of North America; Being a Full and Impartial Account of the Various Difficulties and Ultimate Success of an English Family Who Emigrated from Berwick-in-Elmet, near Leeds, in the Year 1831* (London, G. Berger, etc., 1848). Reprint, Milo M. Quaife, ed. (Chicago, R. R. Donnelley and Sons Co., 1936).

Porter, Rev. Jeremiah. Journals. 18 booklets, each about 50 pp. MS. Partially published. Chicago Historical Society.

———— "Mackinac to Sault Ste. Marie by Canoe in 1831." *Mich. Hist.*, XXX (1946), 466–75; additions in "A Missionary in Early Sault Ste. Marie." Lewis Beeson, ed. *Mich. Hist.*, XXXVIII (1954), 321–70.

———— "Sketches of a Pioneer Ministry." *Mich. Hist. Colls.*, IV (1883), 84–88.

Mrs. Rebecca Burlend, an Englishwoman who journeyed by way of the Mississippi River to Pike County, Illinois, with her husband and children, wrote an excellent description of frontier life from 1831 to 1845. Later the family bought an eighty-acre farm near the present town of Detroit, Illinois. She evidently related the account to her son, Edward Burlend, who recorded and arranged it. The Journals of Jeremiah Porter, the preacher-founder of the Presbyterian church in Chicago, record life in the Midwest from 1831 to 1848. The published portions consist of a long journal of a boat trip from Buffalo to Detroit and one from Mackinac to the Sault, of work among the Indians, experiences in the Black Hawk War, and life in early Chicago. Part of the writing is in diary form and part is straight narrative, with emphasis upon religious activities.

Nossaman, Mrs. Sarah W. "Pioneering at Bonaparte and Near Pella." *Ann. of Ia.*, 3rd Series, XIII (1922), 441–53.

Little, Frank. "Early Recollections of the Indians about Gull Prairie." *Mich. Hist. Colls.*, XXVII (1897), 330–38.

Little, James A. *From Kirtland [Ohio] to Salt Lake City* (Salt Lake City, James A. Little, 1890).

"The Narrative of Samuel W. Pond." Theodore C. Blegen, ed. *Minn. Hist.*, XXI (1940), 15–32, 158-75, 272–83.[66]

Jerome, Edwin. "Incidents in the Black Hawk War." *Mich. Hist. Colls.*, I (1877), 48–51.

Willard, Samuel. "Personal Reminiscences of Life in Illinois—1830 to 1850." *Ill. State Hist. Soc. Trans.*, 1906, XI (1906), 73–87.

Personal Recollections of John M. Palmer; the Story of an Earnest Life (Cincinnati, R. Clarke Co., 1901).[67]

Mrs. Sarah W. Nossaman's narrative is a rather monotonous rehearsal of the troubles of pioneers in Iowa during 1831 and later. Frank Little's tale (1831–c. 1851) describes a trip up Lake Erie to Detroit, interior Michigan and Indiana, and the Black Hawk uprising. The story of the Mormon migration from Ohio to Salt Lake City is related in James Little's book, one of many such accounts. It covers events during 1831–1847 and 1852. Samuel W. Pond, a Congregational missionary to the Indians, wrote an unpretentious, straightforward narrative of travels in Minnesota and elsewhere in the Midwest during 1831 and later. He studied the Indians and, after a visit to the East in 1837, took charge of the Lake Harriet Mission in 1839. He composed several books on the Sioux language and established a mission at Shakopee (which he called Prairieville), Minnesota.

Edwin Jerome's narrative, beginning in 1831, tells of an interesting journey from Detroit past Chicago to Galena, of events in the Black Hawk War, and of a murder in Galena. A well-written tale is Samuel Willard's account of a trip from Boston and Pittsburgh, by river past St. Louis, and of life at Alton and Carrollton. Willard noted the broad vowels of Midwestern speech and commented on such things as crops and railroads. John McAuley Palmer, who later became governor of Illinois, went to that state in 1831 when he was fourteen years old: His *Personal Recollections* tells of this and many other trips in different parts of Illinois, of pioneer conditions, and of events as late as 1900.

Chapter 11

Irving, Bryant, Hoffman, Martineau, and

Other Writers on the Midwest—1832–1835

With a population somewhat over thirteen million by 1832, the United States had pushed its frontiers to southern Michigan, northern Indiana and Illinois, and the west bank of the Mississippi. The westward tide of migration was briefly checked by prosperity and the rise of new industries in the Atlantic states,[1] but with Andrew Jackson in the White House (1829–1837), for the first time in history a representative of the West was President. Furthermore, the decline of westward expansion was only temporary. Improved transportation, the lure of fortune-making by speculation in the West, and curiosity over frontier conditions all helped to bring about an increase in the number of visitors and settlers.

A comparison of the tales mentioned in this chapter with those of preceding chapters shows an obvious increase in the number of well-written Midwestern travel books. Works by such writers as Washington Irving, John Treat Irving, Patrick Shireff, Charles J. Latrobe, John D. Caton, Charles Fenno Hoffman, Michel Chevalier, Sir Charles Murray, Harriet Martineau, George Featherstonhaugh, and Mrs. Eliza W. Farnham rank high in the literature of travel. In addition to these, a large number of brief and minor tales appeared, written by people of varied interests and nationalities, English, Scotch, German, French, Swedish, and Swiss. The Midwest was fast becoming a populated land, what Walt Whitman called "a newer garden of creation";[2] and the wilderness of the roaming Indian, plentiful wild life, log cabin, and keelboat was soon to disappear.

Anonymous. "A Diary of the Black Hawk War." *Ia. Jour. Hist.*, VIII (1910), 265–69.[3]

Gratiot, Henry. "A Journal of Events and Proceedings with the Rock River Band of Winnebago Indians." Milo M. Quaife, ed. *Miss. Val. Hist. Rev.*, XII (1925), 396–407.[4]

Parkinson, Jr., Peter. "Notes on the Black Hawk War." *Wis. Hist. Soc. Colls.*, X (1888), 184–212.

In addition to the tales beginning before 1832, which include information on the Black Hawk War, three of the known narratives of this war are concerned only with the events of 1832. Greedy for desirable lands held by the Indians, the whites occu-

pied an Indian village at the mouth of the Rock River in Illinois, and the Indians, led by Black Hawk and aided by Kickapoo and Pottawatomie warriors, vowed revenge. The governor of the state called out the militia and the Indians fled west of the Mississippi. In the spring of 1832, Black Hawk and his band returned, massacred nearly a score of whites, carried off two young women, and killed several settlers. Later the Indians were defeated, however, and Black Hawk was captured.[5]

The anonymous diary is by an Indian and gives in a brief, styleless form details of the Black Hawk War and notes on Indian affairs in 1832. Henry Gratiot, a sub-Indian agent, describes the activities of the Winnebago Indians at Rock River in the war. His journal includes some interesting Indian speeches. Peter Parkinson narrates a boy's experiences in Colonel Dodge's squadron and the defeat of the Indians at the Battle of Bad Axe and comments on Dodge's heroism.

Bliss, Col. John H. "Reminiscences of Fort Snelling." *Colls. Minn. Hist. Soc.*, VI (1894), 335–53.

Boutwell, Rev. William T. "Extracts from the Journal of Mr. Boutwell." *Missionary Herald*, XXX (1834), 132–36, 177–80, 222–23, 259–62. Reprinted in *Colls. Minn. Hist. Soc.*, I (1902 reprint of 1850–1856 Vol.), 121–40.[6]

Colonel John R. Bliss's "Reminiscences . . ." relates incidents in a trip from Meadville, Pennsylvania, down the Ohio from Pittsburgh, and up the Mississippi to Prairie du Chien and Fort Snelling in 1832. The extracts from Reverend William T. Boutwell's journal give a good picture of the upper Great Lakes. Boutwell accompanied Henry R. Schoolcraft from Mackinac across Lake Superior and through the Ojibwa country to the headwaters of the Mississippi. There are observations and jottings on nature, topography, and forts.

Copley, Alexander. Travel Diary, 1832. MS. In the Alexander Copley Papers, 1814–1881. Listed in *Guide to Manuscript Collections in Michigan* (Michigan Historical Collections, University of Michigan; Detroit, Historical Records Survey Project, 1941). Vol. I, No. 114.

"Journal of a Pioneer Missionary—the Rev. Lemuel Foster." Matthew Spinka, ed. *Jour. Ill. State Hist. Soc.*, XXI (1928), 183–99.

Hoskins, Nathan, Jr. *Notes upon the Western Country, Contained within the States of Ohio, Indiana, Illinois, and the Territory of Michigan: Taken on a Tour through that Country in the Summer of 1832* (Greenfield, Mass., James P. Fogg, 1833).[7]

Alexander Copley kept a diary on a trip in 1832 from Dayton, Ohio, to the St. Joseph River region. The Reverend Lemuel Foster, born in Connecticut in 1799, drove twelve hundred miles to Jackson, Illinois, in 1832. His journal, tinged with religious sentiments, describes the founding of several churches and the growth of Illinois. The *Notes upon the Western Country* of Nathan Hoskins, Jr., the Vermont historian, is based on his reading and on his own observations of the eastern Midwest in 1832.

Irving, Washington. *A Tour on the Prairies. By the Author of the Sketch Book* (Philadelphia, Carey, Lea, and Blanchard, 1835). Reprinted by the University of Oklahoma Press, 1956. Extracts in F. A. Sampson, "Washington Irving, Travels in Missouri and the South," *Mo. Hist. Rev.,* V (1910), 15–33, and in Joseph B. Thoburn, "Centennial of the Tour on the Prairies," *Chrons. of Okla.,* X (1932), 426–33.
The Journals of Washington Irving. William P. Trent and George S. Hellman, eds. (3 vols., Boston, Bibliophile Society, 1919), Vol. III.
The Western Journals of Washington Irving. John F. McDermott, ed. (Norman, University of Oklahoma Press, 1944).[8]

Washington Irving, whose reputation as a writer had preceded him to the frontier,[9] set out with James Kirke Paulding, Charles J. Latrobe, and two other travelers to attend a meeting of Indian tribes in Arkansas in 1832. He took a steamboat down the Ohio, left Cincinnati on September 3, and on September 14 passed through St. Louis, where he located one of his nephews, visited a gambling house, listened to French spoken in the streets, and drove out to see Chief Black Hawk, held captive at Jefferson Barracks. From Missouri he proceeded into the Southwest. *A Tour on the Prairies* records these experiences. It is the first work by a major American writer based upon the Midwestern frontier. Irving called it "a simple narrative of everyday occurrences."[10] It is certainly not a great book, but in it the motley life of border Indians, trappers, Negroes, and creoles is faithfully presented. The trip undoubtedly engendered an interest in the West, which resulted in such books as *Astoria* (1836) and *The Adventures of Captain Bonneville* (1850).

McCormick, William R. "A Trip from Detroit to the Saginaw Valley over Fifty Years Ago." *Mich. Hist. Colls.,* VII (1886), 271–77.
"Diary of Aaron Miller." *Ohio Arch. Hist. Quar.,* XXXIII (1924), 67–79.[11]
Pavie, Théodore. *Souvenirs Atlantiques. Voyage aux États-Unis et au Canada* (2 vols., Paris, Roret, 1833).
Whittlesey, Charles. "Recollections of a Tour through Wisconsin in 1832." *Wis. Hist. Soc. Colls.,* I (1855; 1903 reprint), 64–85.
———— "Two Months in the Copper Region." In *Fugitive Essays, Upon Interesting and Useful Subjects Relating to the Early History of Ohio* . . . (Hudson, O., Sawyer, Ingersoll and Co., 1852), pp. 282–344. Reprinted from the *National Magazine,* Feb., 1846.

A brief but entertaining narrative by William R. McCormick tells of his experiences with two Indians he had hired to paddle his canoe up the Flint River in Michigan. They got drunk. The factual but illiterate diary of Aaron Miller describes a trip he and one of his brothers made by horseback into Ohio in 1832 for the purpose of locating wheat land and new homes for five of the brothers, their return to Virginia, and their migration to Highland County, Ohio. The second volume of Théodore Pavie's *Souvenirs Atlantiques* tells of a trip down the Ohio to Cincinnati, Louisville, and Illinois. Whittlesey's "Recollections" are of Mackinaw, Green Bay, the Fox River, Lake Huron and Lake Michigan, Fort Winnebago, Galena, and Fever River. He recalls the cruel treatment the Indians received from the whites during the Black Hawk War. He is the author of the account of Lord Dunsmore's march to the Ohio in 1774, mentioned in Chapter 4.

Whittlesey also wrote a good article about a trip to the copper region along the south coast of Lake Superior in 1845.

Oregon; or, A Short History of a Long Journey from the Atlantic Ocean to the Region of the Pacific by Land; Drawn up from the Notes and Oral Information of John B. Wyeth, One of the Party Who Left Mr. Nathaniel J. Wyeth, July 28th, 1832, Four Days' March Beyond the Ridge of the Rocky Mountains, and the Only One Who Has Returned to New England (Cambridge, Mass., J. B. Wyeth, 1833). Reprinted in R. G. Thwaites, ed. *Early Western Travels* . . . (32 vols., Cleveland, Arthur H. Clark Co., 1905), XXI, 1–106.[12]
The Correspondence and Journals of Captain Nathaniel J. Wyeth, 1831–6 . . . In *Sources of the History of Oregon,* F. G. Young, ed. (Eugene, Oreg., 1899), I, 155–219, 221–56. The first journal is reprinted in *The Call of the Columbia,* Archer B. Hulbert, ed. ([Colorado Springs], Stewart Commission of Colorado College, [Denver] Public Library, 1934), pp. 112–53.[13]

John B. Wyeth, cousin of the better-known Nathaniel J. Wyeth, has left a record in *Oregon* of his trip down the Ohio from Pittsburgh in 1832, his impressions of Cincinnati, St. Louis, and Independence, his ascent of the Missouri, later events in the Rocky Mountains, his separation from his cousin, and his return to New England. Nathaniel's account of exploration from Independence into Kansas and Nebraska, up the Platte, and to the Pacific in 1832–1833 has been published in the original journal form. Reverend Jason Lee, Reverend Cyrus Shepard, and John K. Townsend, all to be discussed in this chapter, wrote travel narratives about their parts in Wyeth's second (1834) expedition.

Alexander, Sir James Edward. *Transatlantic Sketches, Comprising Visits to the most Interesting Scenes in North and South America* . . . (2 vols., London, Richard Bentley, 1833).
Ball, John. "Across the Continent Seventy Years Ago." *Oreg. Hist. Soc. Quar.,* III (1902), 82–106.[14]
Campbell, Robert. "A Journey to Kentucky for Sheep." *Nor. Dak. Hist. Quar.,* I (1926), 35–45.[15]
Shirreff, Patrick. *A Tour Through North America; Together with a Comprehensive View of the Canadas and United States. As Adopted for Agricultural Emigration* (Edinburgh, Oliver and Boyd, etc., 1835).[16]
Tower, Mrs. Prudence. "The Journey of Ionia's First Settlers." *Mich. Hist. Colls.,* XXVIII (1900), 145–48.

Sir James E. Alexander, an Englishman, ascended the Mississippi and Ohio from New Orleans, probably in 1832 and continued up the Ohio to Wheeling and then to Lake Erie and Buffalo. He made favorable comments about America, particularly Cincinnati, where he had met Timothy Flint. John Ball's article contains extracts from his journal of 1832–1833 of his trip with the first Wyeth expedition across the Midwest to Oregon and includes notes of moderate interest on Indians, scenery, natural history, and climate. More readable is Robert Campbell's diary of a trip by horseback from the Red River Colony to Kentucky and return, all in 1832–1833. A careful British observer, Patrick Shirreff, wrote an interesting and informative book, *A Tour through North America,* about agriculture in Canada and the United States and his journey to Detroit, Niles, Chicago, Springfield, Jacksonville, St. Louis, Cincinnati, Perrysburg, his return to Detroit, and trip to New York. His observations on Chicago are interesting: "Chicago consists of about 150 wood houses, placed irregularly on both sides of the river, over which there is a bridge." Mrs. Prudence Tower's narrative describes incidents during a trip from Buffalo up Lake Erie to Detroit, the Indians at Ionia, Michigan, and the hardships of pioneer life during 1832–33.

Eyre, John. *The Christian Spectator: being a Journey from England to Ohio, two years in that State, Travels in America, &c. . . .* (Albany, N. Y., J. Munsell, 1838). Reprinted with *The European Stranger* as *Travels in America* (New York, R. Craighead, 1851).

——— *The European Stranger in America* (New York, Folson's Book Store, 1839).

The Diary of Barton Griffith, Covington, Indiana, 1832–1834, Now Edited and Published for the First Time by Permission of his Great Great Nephew, J. Barton Griffith (Crawfordsville, Ind., R. E. Banta, 1932).

Griffiths, D., Jr., *Two Years' Residence in the New Settlements of Ohio, North America: With Directions to Emigrants* (London, Westley and Davis, etc., 1835).

Maximilian, Prince of Wied. *Travels in the Interior of North America, in the Years 1832, 1833, and 1834.* Trans. from the German *Reise in das innere Nord-America . . .* (Coblenz, 1839–41) by H. Evans Lloyd (London, Ackerman and Co., 1843). Extract in Lloyd McFarling, ed. *Exploring the Northern Plains . . .* (Caldwell, Ida., 1955), pp. 55–65.[17]

Myers, Frederick. *Garrison Life at Fort Dearborn, 1832–1834.* 207 pp. MS. Chicago Historical Society.

The two years, 1832–1834, John Eyre spent in Ohio made a very favorable impression upon him, which he recorded in *The Christian Spectator*. A continuation of this work, *The European Stranger in America*, describes his trip from Ohio to New York. Intimate personal reflections appear in the diary of young Barton Griffith (1832–1834), who moved from Pennsylvania to Covington, Indiana, and became manager of the first business house there. Just before his death he took a trip down the Mississippi by way of Indianapolis, Rushville, Terre Haute, Vincennes, Louisville, Evansville, Shawneetown, the Cumberland River, and Paducah. An Englishman with a similar surname, D. Griffiths, Jr., visited America during the same years to study conditions for British emigrants. He found the Western Reserve New Settlements the most suitable place for settlers. His book, though brief, contains valuable descriptions of manners and customs. Griffiths visited an interesting Protestant meeting at Vermillion, Ohio, and took a trip to Detroit in 1833, a settlement he described as "a thriving town, and very much frequented by Indians."

Maximilian, Prince of Wied, came to America principally to see the Rocky Mountains, but he spent the winter of 1832–33 at New Harmony and undertook extensive excursions into the nearby regions. In the spring he traveled by way of the Ohio, Mississippi, and Missouri to the Rockies, and returned to St. Louis in 1834. The prince, who was a naturalist, wrote valuable, detailed information about people and settlements and effective descriptions of nature.

The manuscript of Frederick Myers contains comments on the country and frontier life from 1832 to 1834 and a record of all vessels sailing to various Lake Michigan ports.

"Journal of Ebenezer Mattoon Chamberlain 1832–5." Louise Fogle, ed. *Ind. Mag. Hist.*, XV (1919), 232–59.[18]

Gibbs, Mary V. "Glimpses of Early Michigan Life in and about Kalamazoo." *Mag. of Amer. Hist.*, XXIV (1890), 457–64.

Ebenezer M. Chamberlain's diary covers a journey from Maine to Indiana in 1832 and events during 1832–1835. En route he visited Cincinnati, which he praised highly. He taught school for a time near Connersville. He reached Elkhart on November 20, 1832, and opened a school there, but he found that section of the country unpleasant because of its lack of civilization. His style is flowery and he is often sentimental. Mary V. Gibbs's narrative describes scenery, Indians, pioneer hardships, and social life in Michigan during the same years.

"Bishop [John Baptist] Purcell's Journal, 1832–1836." *Cath. Hist. Rev.*, V (1919), 239–55.[19]

Catlin, George. *North American Indians, Being Letters and Notes on their Manners, Customs, and Conditions, Written during Eight Years' Travel and Adventure among the Wildest Tribes of Indians in North America, 1832–1839* (London, 1851). (Several other editions and titles.) Extracts in "The Far West in 1832," *Mag. of Amer. Hist.*, XXV (1891), 86, and in McFarling, *Exploring the Northern Plains*, pp. 46–52.[20]

"Extracts from the Diary of Rev. Moses Merrill, a Missionary to the Otoe Indians from 1832 to 1840." *Neb. Hist. Soc. Trans. Reports*, IV (1892), 160–91.[21]

The administrator of the Catholic diocese of Ohio, Bishop John B. Purcell, a man greatly interested in education, journeyed down the Ohio to Cincinnati by riverboat in 1832 and wrote a brief diary of events as late as 1836. It is religious and personal in tone but has amusing comments on nuns, bigotry, and drunkenness.

George Catlin, the well-known ethnologist, artist, and author of *Life Among the Indians . . .* (1867), spent the years from 1832 to 1840 traveling in the Midwest and Far West and gathered his letters during this period into a book, *North American Indians*, which relates incidents on his trips up the Missouri in 1832 and to other parts of the frontier. It includes an account of the Leavenworth-Dodge expedition to the Pawnee Pict village in 1834, which he accompanied. The extracts from the journal of the Reverend Moses Merrill describe work among the Otoe Indians in the Platte River country during the same years. Merrill, a native of Sedgwick, Maine, expressed disgust with the Indians, especially with their drunkenness. His journal has no literary merit but gives details of Otoe life and customs and includes his adventures and personal affairs.

Nicollet, Joseph Nicholas. *Journals and Reports, 1808–1840.* MSS. Library of Congress, Washington, D.C. Extracts in *House Document 52*, 28th Congress, 2nd Session (1844–1845); reprinted in "Nicollet and Frémont." *Sou. Dak. Hist. Colls.*, X (1920), 69–129. Extracts in McFarling, *Exploring the Northern Plains*, pp. 175–87.[22]

Joseph N. Nicollet, French scientist and descendant of the early explorer, Jean Nicolet, voyaged to New Orleans in 1832, ascended the Mississippi, and at St. Louis met the Chouteau family, who encouraged his plans for exploration. His first expedition was a trip up the Mississippi in 1836 to find its source. In 1838, accompanied by John C. Frémont, he headed an expedition for a survey of the upper Missouri, and in 1839 he made a second survey of the Missouri, reaching Devil's Lake in North Dakota. Some of his unpublished diaries of these expeditions are among the most interesting of his papers.

Bryant, William Cullen. "Illinois Fifty Years Ago." In *Prose Writings of William Cullen Bryant.* Parke Godwin, ed. (New York, D. Appleton and Co., 1889), II, 3–22.

——— *Letters of a Traveller; or, Notes of Things Seen in Europe and America* (New York, G. P. Putnam; London, Bentley, 1850). Reprinted from the *New York Post*.[23]

America's earliest poet of distinction, William Cullen Bryant, in 1832 traveled by way of the Ohio and Mississippi and across the prairies to Jacksonville, Illinois, to visit his brothers.[24] In letters to his wife, printed as "Illinois Fifty Years Ago," he described his trip. He wrote to Richard Henry Dana about life on the prairies—sleeping in log houses, eating corn bread and honey, and riding horseback across the wilderness. On one occasion he met a group of Illinois volunteers hurrying to take part in the Black Hawk War but did not know then that their leader was Abraham Lincoln. He was favorably impressed by the frontier and wrote two poems about it, "The Hunter of the Prairies" and "The Prairies," the latter of which is probably the earliest good description of the West in verse. His mother, Mrs. Peter Bryant, moved to Princeton, Illinois, in 1835,[25] where the members of his family gradually reassembled. Bryant visited these relatives on several other occasions, in 1841, in 1845, and in 1846, when he traveled to Chicago by way of the Great Lakes and went by stage to Princeton, a trip interestingly described in his *Letters of a Traveller.* His enthusiasm for the region undoubtedly influenced such Western writers as Timothy Flint and William D. Gallagher.[26]

Hess, John W. "John W. Hess Wiith the Mormon Battalion." *Utah Hist. Quar.,* IV (1931), 47–55.[27]

"Reminiscences of William H. Packwood." Fred Lockley, ed. *Oreg. Hist. Soc. Quar.,* XVI (1915), 33–54.

Autobiography of the Late Col. George T. M. Davis, Captain and Aid-de-Camp Scott's Army of Invasion (Mexico), from Posthumous Papers. Published by his Legal Representatives (New York, Jenkins and McCowan, 1891).

"Extracts from Meeker's Journal." In Douglas C. McMurtrie and Albert H. Allen, *Jotham Meeker, Pioneer Printer of Kansas* (Chicago, Eyncourt Press, 1930), pp. 45–126.[28]

Potter, Theodore E. "A Boy's Story of Pioneer Life in Michigan." *Mich. Hist. Colls.,* XXXV (1907), 393–412.

Collyer, Robert. *A Man in Earnest; Life of A. H. Conant* (Boston, 1868). Abridged in *Augustus Conant . . .* (Boston, American Unitarian Association, 1905), 31–55 *passim.*[29]

Turner, Jesse W. "Reminiscences of Kalamazoo." W. H. Woodward, ed. *Mich. Hist. Colls.,* XVIII (1892), 570–88. Reprinted from *Kalamazoo Telegraph,* 1883.

McMaster, S. W. *Sixty Years on the Upper Mississippi. My Life and Experiences* (Rock Island, Ill., 1893).

Extracts from the journal and autobiography of John W. Hess, a Mormon, record the trip from Ohio to Ray County, Missouri, in 1832, removal to Nauvoo, Illinois, because of religious persecution, and the journey westward, where he enlisted in the army and went to Fort Leavenworth and then to Santa Fé. "Reminiscences of William H. Packwood" tells of the writer's birth in Illinois in 1832, his enlistment in the Mounted Rifles in 1848, and his march with the men to Leavenworth the following year. The group crossed the Kaw in open flatboats and forded the South Platte. The autobiography by Colonel George T. M. Davis is an interesting book, describing, among events as late as 1852, a trip from Illinois to New York and the author's participation in the Mexican War. The published parts of the missionary journal of the Reverend Jotham Meeker consist of jottings covering a trip to Independence, Missouri, and to Shawnee, Kansas, in 1833. At the latter town he taught the Indians. He taught and worked among them for eighteen years at Ottawa, Kansas, where he died in 1855, a sincere and devoted missionary.

An interesting story of boyhood life in Michigan, 1832–c. 1852, is Theodore E. Potter's "A Boy's Story." It gives an account of a trip from Saline to Ypsilanti, a visit to Lansing, and various experiences such as hunting for honey and meeting Indians. Robert Collyer's biography of Augustus Hammond Conant covers Conant's life in the Midwest from 1832 to 1861 and includes a private diary. Born in Vermont, Conant made his first trip through Illinois in 1836, later settling near Chicago. A good narrative about a journey from Buffalo up Lake Erie to Detroit and then to Bronson, Michigan, and interesting incidents of pioneer

and Indian life (1832–   ) is Jesse Turner's "Reminiscences of Kalamazoo." S. W. McMaster's book is a satisfactory account of experiences in St. Louis and on the upper Mississippi. The sixty years begin in 1832.

Anonymous. Journal of a Trip from New Hampshire into Illinois in 1833. 99 pp. MS. Chicago Historical Society.

Goddard, Abner S. Diary, 1833. In the Orrin F. Smith and Family Papers. Listed in Grace Lee Nute and Gertrude W. Ackermann, comps. *Guide to the Personal Papers in the Manuscript Collection of the Minnesota Historical Society* (St. Paul, 1935), No. 233.

Lyman Family Narrative, 1833. 7 pp. MS. Listed in *Guide to Manuscript Materials of American Origin in the Illinois Historical Society* (Urbana, 1951), p. 41.

Felch, Alpheus. Diary. June–July, 1833. MS. Burton Historical Collection, Detroit.[30]

Wilson, Benjamin. Narrative of an Overland Journey to California, 1833. 67 pp. MS. Huntington Library, San Marino, Calif.; photostatic copy in the Newberry Library, Chicago. Listed in Ruth L. Butler, comp. *A Check List of Manuscripts in the Edward E. Ayer Collection* (Chicago, 1937), No. 1008.

Several journals of trips in 1833 from the Eastern states to Illinois remain unpublished. A well-written anonymous one, probably by a young storekeeper, records a visit to Chicago and travels in the Fox River country to Galena. The diary of Abner S. Goddard records a trip from Pennsylvania to Illinois. The Lyman Family Narrative is a brief account of an eight-week wagon trip by the five Lyman brothers (Dr. John, Azel, Alver, Ezra, and Cornelius) from New York to Sangamon County, Illinois. The diary by Alpheus Felch, who was to become a lawyer, senator, and governor of Michigan, gives a descriptive sketch of his journey from Maine to Detroit and mentions later travel to Monroe, Michigan, and Cincinnati. Benjamin Wilson's narrative was dictated to Hubert Howe Bancroft

"Diary of Jabez Kent Botsford." In Eli H. Botsford, *Adventures in Ancestors* (n. p., 1936), pp. 61–75.[31]

"Diary of George David. A Trip from London to Chicago in 1833." R. P. Mason, ed. *Mich. Hist.,* XVIII (1934), 53–66.[32]

Published extracts from the diary of Jabez K. Botsford, a young man at the time, describe a journey westward in 1833, by packet on the Erie Canal and then by lake steamer to Chicago. There are jottings on the growth of Cleveland, on Indians at Detroit, and on the weather. The "Diary of George David" is an extract which relates events in an Englishman's trip from London by way of Sandusky and Perrysburg, Ohio, and Oak Openings, Somerfield, Tecumseh, and White Pigeon, Michigan, to Chicago. It gives several interesting descriptions.

Anonymous. "Reminiscences of Wisconsin in 1833." *Wis. Hist. Soc. Colls.,* X (1888), 231–34.

Haynes, Harvey. "A Trip from Rome [N. Y.] to Mackinaw in Territorial Days with Powder and Clothing for Soldiers at the Fort." *Mich. Hist. Colls.,* XIII (1889), 520–25.

Irving, John Treat. *Indian Sketches Taken During a U. S. Expedition to Make Treaties with the Pawnee and Other Tribes of Indians in 1833* (2 vols., Philadelphia, Carey, Lea and Blanchard, 1835). Reprinted by the University of Oklahoma Press, Norman, 1955.[33]

"Reminiscences of Wisconsin in 1833," a brief narrative by an unidentified soldier, relates events in a journey begun in 1832 from Chicago to Dixon's Ferry and down the Rock River to Rock Island, Illinois, to Fort Hamilton and then north to Fort Winnebago, following the Wisconsin River to Helena. Cholera raged in the army camp where the author stayed. Harvey Haynes was an adventurous youth, who made his trip in 1833.

A nephew of Washington Irving and an author in his own right, John Treat Irving expressed a gentlemanly and urbane concern about Indians in his *Indian Sketches Taken During a U. S. Expedition,* which is similar in attitude to another one of his works, *The Hunter of the Prairie* (1837). The former includes a well-written account of his trip in 1833 from St. Louis to Independence, Leavenworth, and on into the prairies, and contains much information about Indian life and customs.

A Voice from the West. Rev. Bela Jacob's Report of his Tour in the Western States, Performed in the Spring and Summer of 1833. Presented to the Executive Committee of the Western Baptist Educational Association . . . (Boston, J. Howe, 1833).[34]

Latrobe, Charles Joseph. *The Rambler in North America, 1832–1833* (2 vols., London, R. B. Seeley and W. Burnside, 1835). Extracts in "A River Trip in 1833," *The Palimpsest,* II (1921), 244–63.[35]

Stewart, Sir William George Drummond. *Edward Warren* (London, G. Walker, 1834).

Weston, Richard. *A Visit to the United States and Canada in 1833; with the View of Settling in America, Including a Voyage to and from New-York* (Edinburgh, Richard Weston and Sons; Glasgow, Richard Griffin and Co., 1836).[36]

A Baptist minister, the Reverend Bela Jacobs, wrote a very brief book about his Western trip in 1833, noting educational and religious conditions. He traveled from Shawneetown, Illinois, by way of Kaskaskia to St. Louis, visited Alton and Edwardsville, and returned across Illinois to Vincennes.

The Rambler in North America, by Charles Joseph Latrobe, the well-known British traveler, is a work generally impartial in attitude and gay in mood. He went to America with his friend, Count Albert Pourtales, and after spending about a year in the East and South, visited Chicago in 1833. Like Washington Irving, whom he joined on his frontier tour, he sought to improve relations between England and America.

Sir William Drummond Stewart's book describes his trip to and in the Rocky Mountains in 1833, his adventures as a hunter, and gives his impressions of the Indians of the West. His journey of 1843 will be mentioned in Chapter 13. Richard Weston, a Scotchman, after seeing Illinois and Cincinnati, attacked the Westerners as savages and found nothing to admire in the United States, thus renewing the unfavorable criticisms of America by Europeans.

"John Dean Caton's Reminiscences of Chicago in 1833 and 1834." Harry E. Pratt, ed. *Jour. Ill. State Hist. Soc.,* XXVIII (1935), 5–25.[37]

Hoffman, Charles Fenno. *A Winter in the West; by a New Yorker . . .* (2 vols., New York, Harper and Bros., 1835). Extracts in "Winter Scenes in Early Michigan," "Michigan as Seen by an Early Traveler," "Winter Scenes on the Frontier," *Mich. Hist.* IX (1925), 72–94, 220–48, 413–37, 547–68.[38]

Chicago's first lawyer, John Dean Caton, in 1833 at the age of twenty-one left New York for Chicago and wrote an account of the trip. He describes logs laid across the streets in Chicago, sand hills along Michigan Avenue, and a boarding house where seven beds and fourteen people were crowded into one room. He attended the first political convention held in Illinois, that at Ottawa on March 4, 1834. His narrative is extremely well written and expresses great enthusiasm for the state of Illinois.

One of the most valuable of all travel books about the American frontier is Charles Fenno Hoffman's *A Winter in the West.* Hoffman was a New York editor and novelist who went west

in 1833–1834 for his health. He traveled by stage from Pittsburgh to Cleveland, by boat to Detroit, by horseback and four-horse wagon to Chicago, and by sled and coach to St. Louis. His generous praise of the West was undoubtedly motivated by his desire to answer the British critics who had attacked the region. Although emulating de Tocqueville's fervor and occasionally becoming poetic, he was far from being blind to the unfavorable aspects of the frontier. The monotony of the prairie around LaPorte, Indiana, for example, depressed him. Among the more interesting parts of his book are accounts of a quaint New Year's ball and a wolf hunt.

Gilbert, John. Diary, 1833–1837. MS. Burton Historical Collection, Detroit.

Kellogg, Miner Kilbourne. Journal, 1833–1837. 44 pp. MS. notebook. Historical and Philosophical Society of Ohio, Cincinnati.

Keep, Rev. John. Autobiography, 1781–1866. MS. Library of Congress.[39]

John Gilbert, who was affiliated with the Baptist church, wrote a diary of his move as a young man from Cortland to Oswego, New York, and thence to Detroit and Mount Clemens, Michigan. The notebook by Miner Kilbourne Kellogg, an artist in Cincinnati and Cleveland, is primarily devoted to travel in Ohio, Indiana, and Kentucky during the same years. The Reverend John Keep moved to Cleveland in 1833. The following year he was elected a trustee of Oberlin College, where he spent most of the remainder of his life.

Merrill, Rev. S. P. "Early Life in Nebraska." *Neb. Hist. Soc. Trans. Reports,* V (1893), 205–40.

The Life of Jonathan Baldwin Turner by his daughter Mary Turner Carriel (Jacksonville, Ill., 1911).[40]

Cleaver, Charles. *Early Chicago Reminiscences* (Chicago, Fergus Historical Series, No. 19, 1882).

——— Extracts from articles in the *Chicago Tribune.* In *Reminiscences of Chicago During the Forties and Fifties* (Chicago, R. R. Donnelley and Sons Co., 1913).

Arends, Friedrich. *Schilderung des Mississippithales; oder, des Westens der Vereinigten Staaten von Nordamerika; nebst Abriss meiner Reise dahin* (Emden, Woortman, 1838).

"Diary of Rev. Jason Lee." *Oreg. Hist. Soc. Quar.,* XVII (1916), 116–46, 240–66, 397–430. Extracts in *Christian Advocate* (New York), Oct. 3, 30, 1834, and in A. B. Hulbert, *The Oregon Crusade . . .* ([Colorado Springs], Stewart Commission of Colorado College, [Denver] Public Library, 1935), pp. 147–60, 167–84.[41]

The letters of the Reverend S. P. Merrill, some of which contain journals, tell about Moses Merrill and missionary activities among the Nebraska Indians during 1833–1835. *The Life of Jonathan Baldwin Turner* covers events in the Midwest during the same years. Turner was a professor at Illinois College who in 1835 took a trip to observe the Indians of the upper Mississippi. Charles Cleaver, who arrived in Chicago with his family from England in October 1833, soon became one of the town's first businessmen. His *Reminiscences* include accounts of trips to Milwaukee, Springfield, Galena, St. Louis, and Peru from 1835 to *c.*1843. He liked Chicago but hated the slavery system.

A German, Friedrich Arends, came to Missouri in 1833, stayed in America until 1838, and wrote a book about the Mississippi Valley. It is based on his observations and on the accounts by Darby, Hall, Flint, and Peck. A missionary to Oregon, the Reverend Jason Lee, accompanied by his brother Daniel Lee, passed through the Midwest on his way from Canada to Liberty, Missouri, and then to Fort Vancouver. His diary gives a personal and unusual picture of life on the trail from 1833 to 1838.

Withey, Mrs. Marion L. H. (S. L.) "Personal Recollections and Incidents of the Early Days of Richland and Grand Rapids." *Mich. Hist. Colls.*, V (1884), 434–39.

—— "Personal Recollections of Early Days in Kent County." *Mich. Hist. Colls.* XXXIX (1915), 345–52.

Packard, Silas Sadler. *My Recollections of Ohio. A Paper Read before the Ohio Society of New York . . .* (New York, Ohio Society of New York, 1890). Reprinted in *Mag. West. Hist.*, XIII (1891), 396–406, 564–79.[42]

Bussey, Cyrus. "Cyrus Bussey's Boyhood." *Ia. Jour. Hist.*, XXX (1932), 513–31.[43]

Forty Years a Fur Trader on the Upper Mississippi; the Personal Narrative of Charles Larpenteur, 1833–1872. Elliott Coues, ed. (New York, F. P. Harper, 1898).[44]

Muench, Frederick. "The Followers of Duden. Frederick Muench." William G. Bek, trans. *Mo. Hist. Rev.*, XVIII (1924), 415–37, 562–84.

Memoirs of Gustav Koerner, 1809–1896; Life-Sketches Written at the Suggestion of his Children; Edited by Thomas J. McCormack (2 vols., Cedar Rapids, Ia., Torch Press, 1909).[45]

Fifty Years in Iowa; Being the Personal Reminiscences of J. M. D. Burrows, Concerning the Men and Events, Social Life, Industrial Interests, Physical Development, and Commercial Progress of Davenport and Scott County, During the Period from 1838 to 1888 (Davenport, Ia., Glass and Co., 1888). Reprinted at Chicago (R. R. Donnelley and Sons Co., 1942). Extracts in "A Pioneer Journey," *The Palimpsest*, IV (1923), 300–6.

"The Reminiscences of James Holt: A Narrative of the Emmett Company." Dale L. Morgan, ed. *Utah Hist. Quar.*, XXIII 1955), 1–33.

The two narratives by Mrs. Marion L. H. Withey record her trip by boat from Buffalo to Detroit and by ox team to Richland, Michigan, and other happenings from 1833 to 1838. That first published tells of her reading *The Leather Stocking Tales* on winter nights, of her early education, of the death of her father, and of several interesting pioneer customs. The second describes fever, ague, and wolves, visits to an Indian camp where the Indians waited for specie payment, and an Indian dance in the late winter of 1837. Silas Packard writes in a sprightly manner of a trip in 1833 on the Erie Canal and Lake Erie when he was only seven years old, of pioneer life and hardships, and of backwoods schooling. He drove to Kentucky in 1845, where he taught school for two and a half years, and then moved to Cincinnati and Fredonia, Ohio. Cyrus Bussey in 1833, at the age of four, moved with his family from Ohio to Indiana, in 1855 removed to Iowa, and later took part in the Civil War. His narrative covers his life from 1833 past 1850.

Charles Larpenteur, a Frenchman, after working in St. Louis for several years, became a clerk of the Rocky Mountain Fur Company and from 1833 spent most of his life in the fur trade of the Missouri Valley. After the death of his first wife, an Indian woman, he married another Indian. His narrative covers these and other events as late as 1872, when he died. Two Germans who moved to the Midwest in 1833 and wrote accounts of their lives were Frederick Muench and Gustav Koerner. The former, like Hermann Steines, Gert Boebel, and Herman Garlichs, to be mentioned later in this chapter, was influenced by Gottfried Duden's favorable impressions into moving to Missouri, where he wrote an account of his hardships, of farming and other activities from 1833 to 1872. Koerner, later to become a jurist, statesman, and historian, lived at Belleville, Illinois, took a law course at Transylvania University, and later returned to Belleville. His memoirs, covering events in the Midwest as

late as 1836, give a valuable picture of conditions. He realized that Duden's optimism about Missouri had unfortunately led to the disappointment of a number of German settlers.

In *Fifty Years in Iowa* J. M. D. Burrows chronicles his trip by steamer to the Wisconsin region in 1833, his return to Cincinnati, where he sold his property, and his trip in 1841 through Indiana and Illinois to Iowa, where he lived until 1888. His book of reminiscences gives a good insight into the times. The narrative of James Holt, written in good prose, tells of the author's birth, removal to Illinois in 1833, conversion to Mormonism, return to Tennessee in 1844, trips west in 1846 and 1847, and settlement in Iowa until 1852, when he set out for Salt Lake City.

Abdy, Edward Strutt. *Journal of a Residence and Tour in the United States of North America, from April, 1833, to October, 1834* (3 vols., London, J. Murray, 1833).[46]

Heywood, Robert. *A Journey to America in 1834.* Mrs. Mary (Heywood) Haslam, ed. (Cambridge, Eng., Privately printed, 1919).[47]

Edward S. Abdy, a fellow of Jesus College, Cambridge University, wrote generally unfavorable, even caustic, comments about America and slavery. He traveled by steamer from Louisville to Madison, Indiana, and Cincinnati and to the East by way of Hillsborough, Zanesville, Wheeling, and Pittsburgh, walking from Hillsborough to Bainbridge, Ohio. His notes on social institutions and his favorable opinion of Cincinnati hospitality are interesting. Robert Heywood, of Lancashire, sailed from Liverpool to New York and visited Cincinnati, Louisville, and Columbus. His diary contains comments on these and other places and descriptions of several eminent people.

Arfwedson, C. D. *The United States and Canada, in 1832, 1833, and 1834* (2 vols., London, Richard Bentley, 1834).[48]

Bromme, Traugott. *Reisen durch die Vereinigten Staaten und Ober-Canada* (3 vols., Baltimore, C. Scheld and Co.; Dresden, Walther, 1834–1835).

Koch, Louis and M. Beyer. *Amerikanische Reisen . . .* (4 vols., Leipzig, Müller, 1839–1841).

Neidhard, Karl. "Reise nach Michigan . . . im Sommer 1834." *Amerikanisches Magazin* (Altona and Leipzig), May, 1835. Translated by Frank X. Baum. Robert B. Brown, ed. *Mich. Hist.*, XXXV (1951), 32–84.

"The Followers of Duden: Selections from Hermann Steines' Diary." William G. Bek, trans. *Mo. Hist. Rev.*, XIV (1919–1920), 56–59, 436–46.[49]

C. D. Arfwedson, a Swede, took a trip up the Mississippi and Ohio rivers to Louisville, Cincinnati, and Wheeling in 1834. The Midwest impressed him very favorably. He gave high praise to Cincinnati but called Mrs. Trollope's bazaar an "absurd compound of every species of architecture."

Four German travel accounts of the frontier were written during the same year. Traugott Bromme went from St. Louis across Illinois to obtain information for immigrants. Louis Koch and M. Beyer describe a river trip from the East to the same city. A careful and detailed analysis of the problems of migrating Germans, especially those in southern Michigan, appears in Karl Neidhard's narrative of his trip by way of Lake Erie to Detroit. Hermann Steines also gives advice to would-be German immigrants and describes life in Missouri.

Allis, Rev. Samuel. "Forty Years among the Indians and on the Eastern Borders of Nebraska." *Neb. Hist. Soc. Trans. Reports,* II (1887), 133–66. Extracts in *Miss. Her.*, XXXII (1836), 68–70.[50]

Kemper, Jackson. "Journal of an Episcopalian Missionary's Tour to Green Bay, 1834." *Wis. Hist. Soc. Colls.*, XIV (1898), 394–449.[51]

"Mission to the Western Indians.—Journal of Rev. J. Kerr." *Christian Advocate* (Philadelphia), XII (1834), 517–19.[52]

The Journal of Cyrus Shepard's Trip across the Plains in 1834. 213 pp. MS. Partially published, the major part in Z. A. Mudge, *The Missionary Teacher: A Memoir of Cyrus Shepard* (New York, Lane and Tippett, 1848).[53] Listed in Mary C. Withington, comp. *A Catalogue of Manuscripts in the Collection of Western Americana Founded by William R. Coe, Yale University Library* (New Haven, 1952), No. 421.

Several journals were written in 1834 by missionaries to the Indians. Reverend Samuel Allis, a Baptist missionary, kept one of his trip in 1834 from the East to St. Louis and the territory occupied by the Kickapoo and Pawnee Indians in the present states of Kansas and Nebraska. His "Forty Years among the Indians" exhibits his religious interests and carries his narrative down to 1846. Although Bishop Jackson Kemper had visited Ohio as early as 1812, his travel journals cover a trip by way of the Great Lakes to the Indian mission near Green Bay, Wisconsin, and later trips to be mentioned in Chapters 12 and 13. The entries are detailed and contain interesting comments on religion, society, education, scenery, Indians, and personal life. Reverend J. Kerr wrote brief notes about work among the Shawnee Indians in the summer of 1834 and observations on the difficulties of missionary life on the frontier. Cyrus Shepard, a missionary with the Wyeth expedition of 1834, went as far as Oregon. His journal is carefully written.

Anderson, William Marshall. "Anderson's Narrative of a Ride to the Rocky Mountains in 1834." A. J. Partoll, ed. *Frontier and Midland*, XIX (1938), 54–63. Reprinted from the *Circleville Democrat and Watchman*, Sept. 29, Oct. 13, 1871. Reprinted as No. 27 of *Sources of Northwest History* (Missoula, Mont., University of Montana), 12 pp.; reprinted at New York (Edward Eberstadt and Sons, 1951).[54]

Jarrett, David. Travel Diary. *Montgomery County* (Penna.) *Historical Society Sketches*, VI (1929), 121–36.[55]

Parker, Amos Andrew. *Trip to the West and Texas, Comprising a Journey of Eight Thousand Miles, through New-York, Michigan, Illinois, Missouri, Louisiana and Texas, in the Autumn and Winter of 1834-5. Interspersed with Anecdotes, Incidents and Observations . . .* (Concord, N. H., White and Fisher, 1835).[56]

Townsend, John Kirk. *Narrative of a Journey across the Rocky Mountains, to the Columbia River, and a Visit to the Sandwich Islands, Chili, &c.* (Philadelphia, Henry Perkins, 1839). Reprinted in Thwaites, *Early Western Travels*, XXI, 107–369. Extracts in *Waddie's Select Circulating Library*, Part II (1835), 427–32, and in A. B. Hulbert, ed. *The Call of the Columbia* (Colorado Springs and Denver, 1934), 188–226.[57]

Wheelock, T. W. "Col. Henry Dodge and his Regiment of Dragoons on the Plains in 1834. Journal of the Campaign." *Ann. of Ia.*, 3rd Series, XVII (1930), 173–97.

William M. Anderson, of Louisville, was a guest of the Sublette Expedition of 1834 and accompanied it from Independence, Missouri, following the Kaw, Blue, and Platte rivers and returning by way of Council Bluffs and St. Louis to Louisville. Only a small part of his brief but racy diary of the trip is about the Midwest. The diary of David Jarrett describes an overland journey from Montgomery County, Pennsylvania, to Ohio and the West in the same year. There are notes on towns, roads, inns, distances, and the countryside.

Amos Parker's *Trip to the West and Texas* and John K. Townsend's *Narrative of a Journey* . . . are mainly about regions south and west of the Middle West. Parker's book, however, tells of extensive travel in Michigan, northern and central Illinois, and Missouri and contains descriptions of historical value. Townsend recounts travel in 1834 from Pittsburgh to St. Louis and Independence and a trip with Wyeth, Sublette, and Nuttall up the Platte. He expresses keen appreciation of nature and comments on Indian and wild life. Wheelock's journal includes experiences with Indians. It is unimportant.

Chevalier, Michel. *Lettres sur l'Amérique du Nord . . .* (2 vols., Paris, Charles Gosselin and Co., 1836). English trans. *Society, Manners and Politics in the United States; being a Series of Letters in North America . . .* by Thomas Gamaliel Bradford from the third Paris ed. (Boston, Weeks, Jordan and Co., 1839).[58]

Michel Chevalier came to the United States to inspect public works for the French minister of the interior and visited the Midwest in 1834 and 1835. He called Cincinnati, where he met General William Henry Harrison, "a large and beautiful town." He held that pioneers should not be judged by the same standards used for judging Europeans and believed that the Americans had accomplished much.

Anonymous. "A Journal of Marches by the First United States Dragoons 1834–1835." Louis Pelzer, ed. *Ia. Jour. Hist.*, VII (1909), 311–78.[59]

Dunbar, Rev. John. "Extracts from the Journal of Mr. Dunbar." *Missionary Herald*, XXXI (1835), 343–49, 376–81, 417–21.[60]

——— "The Presbyterian Mission among the Pawnee Indians in Nebraska, 1834 to 1836." *Kans. State Hist. Soc. Colls.*, XI (1910), 323–32.[61]

"The Journal of Hugh Evans, Covering the First and Second Campaigns of the United States Dragoon Regiment in 1834 and 1835." Fred S. Perrine, ed. *Chrons. of Okla.*, III (1925), 175–215.

——— "Hugh Evans' Journal of Colonel Henry Dodge's Expedition to the Rocky Mountains in 1835." Fred S. Perrine, ed. *Miss. Val. Hist. Rev.*, XIV (1927), 192–214.[62]

The anonymous author of "A Journal of Marches" was an officer of the Dragoons. The marches were made in the upper Mississippi Valley to Indian villages. The first part consists of brief notes and the second records Colonel Kearny's march from Fort Des Moines to an Indian village in Minnesota. A Presbyterian missionary, the Reverend John Dunbar, traveled from the East to St. Louis, Leavenworth, and on to Grand Pawnee village. His diary, written in a good style, mentions interesting details of Pawnee customs and habits. "The Journal of Hugh Evans" chronicles a march from Jefferson Barracks to Fort Gibson, in Oklahoma, for the purpose of making a treaty with the Indians. Evans, a sergeant, also kept a journal of a march from Fort Leavenworth to the Rockies in 1835, which contains descriptions of the Kansas country and Indian villages.

Sleight, Morris. Journals and Letters, 1834–1835. 4 vols. MS. Chicago Historical Society.

Goodrich, Enos. "Across Michigan Territory Sixty Years Ago." *Mich. Hist. Colls.*, XXVI (1896), 228–35.

——— "Pioneer Sketch of Moses Goodrich and His Trip to Michigan in February, 1836, with His Brother Levi." *Mich. Hist. Colls.*, XVII (1892), 480–90.

Winsor, Z. G. "Early Settlement of Ottawa County." *Mich. Hist. Colls.*, IX (1886), 234–37.

Morris Sleight's four volumes cover his trip through the Midwest to California. Enos Goodrich's "Across Michigan Territory . . ." tells of a journey in 1834 by boat to Detroit, by foot to near Ann Arbor, by stage to Chicago, and return to Detroit by way of the Great Lakes and Mackinaw the following year. His other article describes a trip later in 1836 with his brother from Buffalo through Canada to Detroit, Lapeer, and Thread Creek, Michigan. Z. G. Winsor's brief narrative recalls early days in Grand Haven, Michigan, and trade with the Indians in 1834 and 1835.

Murray, Sir Charles Augustus. *Travels in North America during the Years 1834, 1835, 1836. Including a Summer Residence with the Pawnee Tribe of Indians, in the Remote Prairies of the Missouri* (2 vols., New York, Harned and Bros., 1839). Extracts in "A Visit to Dubuque in 1835," *Ann. of Ia.*, 3rd Series, XXII (1940), 410–11, and in A. B. Hulbert, ed. *Pioneer Roads and Experiences of Travelers* (2 vols., Cleveland, A. H. Clark Co., 1904), Vol. II.[63]

Shout, Mary E. "Reminiscences of the First Settlement at Owosso." *Mich. Hist. Colls.*, XXX (1906), 344–52.

Rogers, George. *Memorandum of the Experience, Labors, and Travels of a Universalist Preacher, Written by Himself* (Cincinnati, John A. Gurley, 1845).

Griswold, Joseph M. "Some Reminiscences of Early Times in Brooklyn, Jackson County, Michigan." *Mich. Hist. Colls.*, XXVI (1896), 256–61.

Rodolf, Theodore. "Pioneering in the Wisconsin Lead Region." *Wis. Hist. Soc. Colls.*, XV (1900), 338–89.

Nowlin, William. *The Bark Covered House, or Back in the Woods Again; Being a Graphic and Thrilling Description of Real Pioneer Life in the Wilderness of Michigan* (Detroit, the Author, 1876). Reprint, Milo M. Quaife, ed. (Chicago, R. R. Donnelley and Sons Co., 1937).

Goebel, Gert. *Laenger als ein Menchenleben in Missouri* (St. Louis, C. Witter, 1877). English trans. William G. Bek, "The Followers of Duden. Gert Goebel." *Mo. Hist. Rev.*, XVI (1922), 289–307, 343–83, 522–50; XVII (1922), 28–56, 331–39.

Merrill, Henry. "Pioneer Life in Wisconsin." *Wis. Hist. Soc. Colls.*, VII (1876), 367–402.

Sir Charles Augustus Murray was another Englishman to write a book making light of Mrs. Trollope's criticisms. Cincinnati three or four years after she saw it, he said, was far different from the place she had described. In 1835 he traveled to St. Louis by river, proceeded to Galena, Illinois, where he saw the lead mines, ascended the Missouri to Liberty, "the last western village in the United States," and continued westward on horseback. Mark Twain in *Life on the Mississippi* cites Murray's *Travels in North America* for its appreciation of the Mississippi River.[64]

Mary E. Shout's "Reminiscences" is concerned with the life of her mother: an account of her mother's trip through Canada to Detroit and pioneer hardships in various places in Michigan from 1834 to 1836. George Rogers made several trips to the West, the first from Pennsylvania to Cincinnati and back by horse in 1834. Other trips took him to Highland County, Wilmington, and Waynesville, Ohio; St. Louis and Troy, Missouri; Alton, Illinois; and Indiana and Michigan as late as 1844. His book is autobiographical, part narrative and part diary. Joseph M. Griswold's tale is of a trip by way of Lake Erie to Toledo and by cart and oxen into Michigan and life there from 1834 to 1846. He includes interesting lists of prices and comments on early settlers. Theodore Rodolf writes of travel from Switzerland by way of St. Louis to Wisconsin in 1834 when he was a youth of

seventeen. Visits to Milwaukee and other places and events as late as 1848 are described. It is a well-written narrative by a man whose native language was not English.

The Bark Covered House is William Nowlin's lengthy story of his journey from the East by way of Lake Erie to Detroit and interior Michigan and of such adventures there as building a house in the woods and being visited by a bear and by Indians, adventures taking place over a long time-span, 1834–1873. A German immigrant, Gert Goebel, influenced like Muench, Steines, Garlichs, and Rieger by Gottfried Duden to settle in Missouri, relates events in his life in that state from 1834 to about 1876 and gives an analysis of American society and agricultural conditions. Henry Merrill's article is a detailed account of a trip beginning in 1834 from Utica by way of the Great Lakes and up the Fox River to Fort Winnebago, across the prairies to Mineral Point, Wisconsin, and the Mississippi River, and the return East. In 1839 he went to St. Louis and eventually settled at Portage, Wisconsin.

Alling, Prudden. "An Adventurous Journey to Chicago in 1835." *Firelands Pioneer*, New Series, XX (1918), 2016–24.[65]

"Journal of Cyrus P. Bradley." *Ohio Arch. Hist. Quar.*, XV (1906), 207–70.[66]

Field, A. D. "Illinois and its Mammoth City. Sketches of Chicago." *National Magazine*, XII (1858), 347–50, 407–11.

Prudden Alling, a native of New York state, describes a journey by coach from Norwalk, Ohio, to near Ottawa, Illinois, by way of Detroit, Ypsilanti, and Chicago. His diary is incomplete. His comments on high Chicago land prices are interesting. Cyrus Parker Bradley, a college student, of Concord, New Hampshire, writes a lively account of a summer holiday tour down the Ohio from Pittsburgh to Cincinnati, across Ohio, and into Michigan in 1835. A good sense of humor and familiarity with literature are evident, while religion, drunkenness, filth, and profanity elicit caustic comments. A. D. Field's narrative is a brief sketch of a trip from the East to Chicago, also in 1835.

Gilman, Chandler Robbins. *Life on the Lakes; Being Tales and Sketches Collected during a Trip to the Pictured Rocks of Lake Superior* (2 vols., New York, George Dearborn, 1836).[67]

Hoby, James and F. A. Cox. *The Baptists in America; a Narrative of the Deputation from the Baptist Union in England, to the United States and Canada . . .* (London, Ward, 1836).[68]

Smith, Mrs. Julia Talbot. "Reminiscences of Detroit." *Mich. Hist. Colls.*, XXXV (1907), 682–83.

Chandler Robbins Gilman's *Life on the Lakes* is a collection of letters and touristic notes tracing his trip from the East in 1835 to Cleveland, Sandusky, and Detroit, by way of the Great Lakes to Chicago, to Ottawa and Peoria by post coach, and on to Alton and St. Louis by steamboat. Ralph L. Rusk says that it is unusual among books of Western travel for its humor and the charm of its style. There are many comments on settlers and Indians and enthusiastic descriptions of the shores of Lakes Huron and Superior.

The Baptists in America is a report to the Baptist Union of England about churches and religious conditions in America by two Britishers. They made a trip in 1835 through part of Indiana and Illinois, including New Harmony and the English settlement, and make interesting comments on slavery. Mrs. Julia T. Smith's two pages tell of a journey from New York to Detroit in the same year.

"Captain [Lemuel] Ford's Journal of an Expedition to the Rocky Mountains." Louis Pelzer, ed. *Miss. Val. Hist. Rev.*, XII (1926), 550–79.

——— "A Summer on the Prairie." *Army and Navy Chronicle*, II (1836), 277–78, 292–93, 311–12, 321–22, 337–38, 363–64, 369–70, 385–86; III (1836), 1–2, 17–18, 30–31. Reprinted in A. B. Hulbert. *The Call of the Columbia*, pp. 228–305.[69]

Kingsbury, Lieut. Gaines Pease. "Journal of the March of a Detachment of Dragoons, under the Command of Colonel Dodge, During the Summer of 1835." *Senate Executive Documents* 209, 24th Congress, 1st Session (1836). Also in *American State Papers, Military Affairs*, VI, 130–44.[70]

Parker, Rev. Samuel. *Journal of an Exploratory Tour beyond the Rocky Mountains, under the Direction of the A[merican] B[oard] C[ommissioners] F[oreign] M[issions] Performed in the Years 1835, '36, and '37* (Ithaca, N.Y., the Author, 1838).[71]

"Journal and Report by Dr. Marcus Whitman of his Tour of Exploration with Rev. Samuel Parker in 1835 Beyond the Rocky Mountains." *Oreg. Hist. Soc. Quar.*, XXVIII (1927), 239–57. Slightly different text in A. B. and D. P. Hulbert, eds. *Marcus Whitman, Crusader* (Denver, Denver Public Library, 1936), I, 146–65.[72]

Reed, Andrew and James Matheson. *A Narrative of the Visit to the American Churches, by the Deputation from the Congregational Union of England and Wales* (2 vols., London, Jackson and Walford, 1835). Selections in Andrew and Charles Reed, eds. *Memoirs of the Life and Philanthropic Labours of Andrew Reed* . . . (London, 1863).[73]

"Diary of General Robert Patterson." *Journal of American History*, I (1907), 653–68.[74]

Captain Lemuel Ford's diary covers a march of about sixteen hundred miles through Nebraska, Colorado, and Kansas from May to September, 1835. It is the basis for his narrative, "A Summer on the Prairie." Most of it is devoted to descriptions of events and sights along the way, such as buffalo and antelope seen near the Platte. Similar is a journal by Lieutenant Gaines P. Kingsbury, which chronicles a march of Dragoons from Fort Leavenworth up the South Platte, south to the Arkansas River and Santa Fé Trail, and their return to the Fort.

Reverend Samuel Parker accompanied the well-known Marcus Whitman to Oregon. His book is mainly about the Far West but it gives an account of a trip down the rivers from Pittsburgh to Point Girardeau and Ste. Genevieve, up the rivers to St. Louis, Leavenworth, and Council Bluffs, and westward up the Platte into the Black Hills and Rocky Mountains. Since Parker's main purposes were to become acquainted with the remote Indian tribes, learn their attitude towards teachers of Christianity, and select sites for missions, there is much about religion and Indians in his book. The journal of Dr. Marcus Whitman, important missionary to the Indians of the Far West, covers the same trip but begins at a later date. Like Parker, he was sent to the West by the Board of Commissioners for Foreign Missions and wrote mainly about religion and the Indian.

Two English clergymen, Andrew Reed and James Matheson, like Hoby and Cox were deputized to visit the United States in 1835. Their book criticized the West and consequently met with the disapproval of such Western publications as *The Western Monthly Magazine*.[75]

General Robert Patterson wrote a diary, only partially published, of a trip from his home in Philadelphia down the Ohio to Iowa and the upper Mississippi country in 1835. Detailed descriptions of people, customs, crops, towns, and hotels make the work valuable, although many of the entries are merely jottings.

Roberts, Amelia. Journal, 1835. 1 vol. MS. Illinois State Historical Library, Springfield.

Giddings, David. Diary, 1835–1836. MS. Listed in Alice E.

Smith, comp. *Guide to the Manuscripts of the Wisconsin Historical Society* (Madison, 1944), No. 253.

Tatham, G. N. Journal, 1835–1836. 40 pp. MS. Illinois State Historical Library, Springfield.

Amelia Roberts' journal covers a trip from New York to Illinois in 1835. David Giddings traveled from New York state to Chicago and Green Bay. His diary of the trip contains observations on the size and condition of the settlements en route. G. N. Tatham's journal covers a business trip through Illinois and Michigan.

"Selections from the Autobiography of John Gage." *Vineland Historical Magazine*, IX (1924), 177–83, 188–91, 216–20; X (1925), 29–31, 47–51, 66–68, 229–32.[76]

John Gage made an extensive tour in the East and Michigan during 1835–1836. He visited the principal towns, including Chicago, where he built the first steam flour mill west of Buffalo. His "Autobiography" is interesting. He comments on the stagecoach trip across southern Michigan and shows an interest in the natural resources of the region.

Martineau, Harriet. *Retrospect of Western Travel* (3 vols., London, Saunders and Otley; 2 vols., New York, Harper and Bros., 1838).

——— *Society in America* . . . (2 vols., New York and London, Saunders and Otley, 1837). Extracts in Henry Brown, "The Present and Future Prospects of Chicago," *Fergus Historical Series*, No. 9, and "Harriet Martineau's Travels in and Around Michigan, 1836," *Mich. Hist.*, VII (1923), 49–99.[77]

"The books of Harriet Martineau," says Professor Rusk, "contained probably the most important view of the West by an English author during the last years of the pioneer period."[78] Miss Martineau, who was charmed by much of what she saw, wrote in a readable style which at times grew poetic in the description of nature and places. Her 1835 visit took her down the Ohio to Cincinnati, a town which fascinated her so much that in *Retrospect of Western Travel* she wrote that she would prefer that city to any other large one in the United States as a place to live. She commented on Dr. Daniel Drake, and she called Mrs. Trollope's bazaar the one great deformity of the city.[79]

In 1836 when she again journeyed west by coach from Michigan to LaPorte, Indiana, she was stopped en route to Chicago at Michigan City by bad roads. *Society in America* is more critical than *Retrospect*. . . . The houses in Chicago seemed to her shabby and insignificant, the inns intolerable, and the people land mad. Yet she found the town busy and prosperous, and she noted the fertility of the soil of the region and enjoyed the sight of Lake Michigan.[80] As a student of English radical thought, she was sympathetic towards American legislation, but she condemned American literature. Although some of her remarks wounded the vanity of Americans,[81] her books were favorable in the main and belong to the literature of Anglo-American reconciliation.[82]

Featherstonhaugh, George William. *A Canoe Voyage up the Minnay Sotor; with an Account of the Lead and Copper Deposits in Wisconsin; of the Gold Region in the Cherokee Country; and Sketches of Popular Manners* . . . (2 vols., London, R. Bentley, 1847).[83]

Hesse, Nicholas. *Das Westliche Nord-Amerika, in besonderer Beziehung auf die deutschen Einwanderer, etc.* (Paderborn, 1838). Translated excerpts in "Nicholas Hesse, German Visitor to Missouri, 1835–1837." William G. Bek, trans. *Mo. Hist. Rev.*, XLI (1946–47), 19–44, 164–83, 285–304, 373–90; XLII (1947–48), 34–49, 140–52, 241–48.

Lawrence, James H. "Pioneer Recollections." *Mich. Hist. Colls.,* XVIII (1892), 360–73.

George W. Featherstonhaugh was a British geologist. His book, well-written, describes a geological reconnaissance in America from 1835 to 1837.[84] After reaching Pittsburgh he went by land to Cleveland and by water to Detroit, where he stayed from late July to early August 1835, and proceeded up the Great Lakes by steamer to Mackinac and Green Bay, then to Fox River, Fort Snelling, Galena, St. Louis, and the Wisconsin and Mississippi rivers before returning to the East. Comments on topography, scenery, mineralogy, manners, customs, and Indian life show his varied interests.

The tale of Nicholas Hesse, written in his log house on the Osage River in Missouri, expressed his disappointment with the Midwest, thus tending to discourage possible settlers. He made an excursion into the interior of the state, noting such things as climate, wild life, and possibilities for farming. James H. Lawrence's "Pioneer Recollections" covers the years 1835–37 and contains interesting comments on pioneer hardships and encounters with Indians.

Levinge, Sir Richard George Augustus. *Echoes from the Backwoods; or, Sketches of Transatlantic Life* . . . (2 vols., London, Colburn, 1846).[85]

Farnham, Mrs. Eliza Woodson Burhans. *Life in Prairie Land* . . . (New York, Harper and Bros., 1846).[86]

The Life of Rev. John Clark by Rev. B. M. Hall with an Introduction by Bishop Morris (New York, Carlton and Porter, 1856).

Garlichs, Hermann. "The Followers of Duden. Herman Garlichs—Theologian." William G. Bek, trans. *Mo. Hist. Rev.,* XVIII (1923), 36–54.

Janes, Henry F. "Early Reminiscences of Janesville." *Wis. Hist. Soc. Colls.,* VI (1872), 426–35.

Beardsley, A. M. "Reminiscences and Scenes of Backwoods and Pioneer Life." *Mich. Hist. Colls.,* XXVIII (1900), 137–41.

Williams, Rev. W. B. "Personal Reminiscences." *Mich. Hist. Colls.,* XXII (1894), 526–41.

A British writer, soldier, and sportsman, Sir Richard Levinge, made two trips to America, one in 1835 and another in 1839. His first journey took him from Buffalo to Cleveland, across Ohio to the Ohio River, Cincinnati, Louisville, and down the Mississippi. On his second trip he went west, to Detroit, Chicago, and the nearby prairies. His *Echoes from the Backwoods* contains interesting descriptions of the Midwest during these visits.

Although some of its details are fictitious, Mrs. Eliza W. Farnham's *Life in Prairie Land,* covering experiences from 1835 to 1841, is an important book. After moving from New York state to Illinois in 1835, when she was twenty years old, she married Thomas Jefferson Farnham in the following year. They moved to New York in 1841, proceeded to California in 1849, and returned to New York in 1856. During her travels down the Ohio and through the Great Lakes and elsewhere, she showed an exuberant love of the West and nature. The Reverend B. M. Hall's biography of the Reverend John Clark, Methodist missionary among the Indians at Green Bay and later an elder of the Chicago District, tells of events in the Midwest during the same years, including a trip around the end of Lake Michigan, an account of Chicago in 1837, and a later trip by way of St. Louis to Texas.

Hermann Garlichs was another German follower of Duden, the Missouri pioneer. His narrative (1835–1849) centers on religious interests and activities in Missouri. Henry F. Janes's "Reminiscences" record his travel from Ohio to Indiana and Wisconsin. He made land claims near Racine, undertook a difficult journey to Rock Prairie, Wisconsin, and built the first cabin in Janesville, Wisconsin, all during 1835–1849. A. M. Beardsley's tale (1835–1870) relates happenings on a trip west by way of Cleveland, Sandusky, and Fort Meigs to West Constantine, Michigan, where he built a cabin. In 1838 he rode by rail from Ypsilanti to Detroit and New York state, and later returned to West Constantine. Reverend W. B. Williams' "Personal Reminiscences" is a readable narrative of travel to Detroit by way of Lake Erie about 1835 and of pioneer customs and hardships in Michigan after 1850.

Chapter 12

Midwestern Travel Tales by Flagg, Marryat,

Mrs. Jameson, Mrs. Kirkland, and Others—1836–1840

The last half of the 1830's, which included the last years of Jackson's administration and the major part of Van Buren's, was a critical period for America. The fear of losing Oregon to Britain, the difficulty with Mormons in Missouri beginning in 1833, the Panic of 1837 and the nation-wide business disaster, the quarrel with Mexico over American shipping, the slavery problem and the annexation of Texas, and the Panic of 1839 with the consequent financial plight of several Midwestern states were some of the events which temporarily hindered western expansion.[1] The number of frontier travel narratives written during these years continued to grow, however, and several important ones appeared.

By 1840 Ohio and Indiana claimed a significant percentage of the total population; and Michigan, Illinois, Missouri, and the territories of Wisconsin and Iowa swelled the figure. More varied types of people were settling in the region than before, and a greater variety of types of travel narratives were being written. Although many of the accounts were brief and unimportant, a larger number of tales of literary merit were being produced because the frontier was attracting noted people. It was not, however, the Old West of the French priests, the early trappers and explorers, and the Indian wandering in his own domain. It was a better world in many ways, but with the breaking of the ground for agriculture, roads, and cities, the felling of forests, and building of bridges, the frontier began to disappear, and the romance of the early days also was lost except for written records such as are here described.

Anonymous. Diary, 1836. 12 pp. MS. New York Public Library.

Anonymous. Journal of a Trip to the Western Country, August–September, 1836. Approximately 40 pp. MS. Illinois State Historical Library, Springfield.

Bridge, H. Journal, March–April, 1836. 70 pp. MS. Illinois State Historical Library.[2]

Chandler, Sarah. Diary, 1836. MS. Listed in *Guide to the Western Historical Manuscripts Collection* (*University of Missouri Bulletin*, Library Series No. 22; Columbia, 1952), No. 99.

[Larwill, Joseph H.] Journal of a Journey, August–October, 1836. Approximately 40 pp. MS. Illinois State Historical Library.

Unpublished narratives of 1836 record travels in Ohio, Illinois, Missouri, and Wisconsin Territory. The 12-page anonymous diary was kept on a journey by rail and canal from New York to Pittsburgh and by boat to St. Louis and Dubuque in the Wisconsin Territory, where the writer became a clerk. The anonymous journal describes a trip from Baltimore through Ohio, Illinois, and Missouri. H. Bridge's journal covers a trip from New Orleans by way of Louisville and Cincinnati to Columbia, Pennsylvania. The diary of Sarah Chandler includes an account of a journey from Virginia to Casper County, Missouri. Joseph H. Larwill is probably the author of a journal describing a trip from Wooster, Ohio, to Kentucky, Illinois, and Missouri.

Ferguson, Judge C. F. "Reminiscences of a Journey to Indianapolis in the Year 1836." *Ind. Hist. Soc. Pubs.*, II (1893), 349–57.

Minor, Lucian. "A Journey to the West in 1836." *Mass. Hist. Soc. Procs.*, 2nd Series, VII (1891–1892), 263–94.[3]

In 1836, when still a small boy, C. F. Ferguson took a trip by steamboat from Charlestown, Indiana, to Madison, Indiana, by stage to Indianapolis, and back to Charlestown by horseback. He recorded it in his "Reminiscences," with comments on later politics in Indianapolis. Lucian Minor, a professor at William and Mary College, gives an account of travel from Virginia to the junction of the Ohio and the Wabash. He writes well and mentions scenery, social life, and literary figures.

Davidson, James D. Journal. *Jour. Sou. Hist.*, I (1935), 345–71. Extracts in "Diary during Visits to Indiana," *Ind. Mag. Hist.*, XXIV (1928), 130–36.[4]

"Diary of Charles Dehault Delassus from New Orleans to St. Louis, 1836." John F. McDermott, ed. *La. Hist. Quar.*, XXX (1947), 359–438.

"Journal of Lewis Birdsall Harris, 1836–1842." *Southwestern Historical Quarterly*, XXV (1921), 63–71, 131–46.[5]

"A Yankee School Teacher in Louisiana, 1835–1837; The Diary of Caroline B. Poole." James A. Padgett, ed. *La. Hist. Quar.*, XX (1937), 651–79.[6]

James D. Davidson's journal records a trip in 1836 down the Ohio and Mississippi rivers. Cincinnati, Louisville, and Madison and Greensburg, Indiana, impressed him favorably. A part of Charles D. Delassus' diary of a ten-day trip up the Mississippi from New Orleans in the same year, describes life in southern Missouri and St. Louis. Lewis B. Harris's journal of travel from New York to Texas includes entries written aboard a steamboat descending the Ohio River in 1836. His style is smooth, and the work shows appreciation of scenery. Less important is the diary of Caroline B. Poole, who ascended the Mississippi from New

Orleans to Louisville, also in 1836; her jottings include mention of picking blackberries along the Illinois side of the river.

Flagg, Edmund. *The Far West: or, a Tour Beyond the Mountains, Embracing Outlines of Western Life and Scenery; Sketches of the Prairies, Rivers, Ancient Mounds, Early Settlements of the French, etc., etc.* (2 vols., New York, Harper and Brothers, 1838).[7]

One of the most colorful descriptions of the Midwest during the latter part of the frontier period is Edmund Flagg's *The Far West*, an elaboration of a series of letters, "Sketches of a Traveller," originally published in the *Louisville Journal* in 1836. In the summer and autumn of this year Flagg descended the Ohio and part of the Mississippi and visited St. Louis and Edwardsville, Upper Alton, Vandalia, Kaskaskia, Salem, and several other Illinois towns. Although he traveled no farther west than this region, the title of his book shows that he considered it a distant place. The work is a classic of its kind, even though the outlook is very romantic and highly colored. It is detailed, well written, often dramatic and poetic, and filled with references to literature and history. Particularly valuable are the comments upon the old French towns along the Mississippi.

Foster, Suel. "Recollections of Early Times in Iowa." *Ia. Hist. Rec.*, I (1885), 157–58.
Kellogg, Amherst Willoughby. "Recollections of Life in Early Wisconsin." *Wis. Mag. Hist.*, VII (1924), 473–98; VIII (1924), 88–110, 221–43.
Lea, Lieut. Albert M. *Notes on the Wisconsin Territory . . .* (Philadelphia, Henry S. Tanner, 1836). Reprinted in *Ann. of Ia.*, 3rd Series, XI (1913), 115–67, and as *The Book that Gave Iowa Its Name* (Iowa City, State Historical Society, 1935).[8]
Longyear, Mrs. Margaret. "The Settlement of Clinton County." *Mich. Hist. Colls.*, XXXIX (1915), 360–64.
"Reminiscences of Richard Mott." In H. S. Knapp, *History of the Maumee Valley* (Toledo, Blade Mammoth Printing and Publishing House, 1871), pp. 545–58.
Palmer, Strange M. "Western Wisconsin in 1836." *Wis. Hist. Soc. Colls.*, VI (1872), 297–307.
Smith, Isaac T. "Early Settlement of Rock County." *Wis. Hist. Soc. Colls.*, VI (1872), 416–25.
Stewart, Catharine. *New Homes in the West* (Nashville, Cameron and Fall, 1843).
A Journey in 1836 from New Jersey to Ohio, Being the Diary of [Mrs.] Elizabeth Lundy Willson. William C. Armstrong, ed. (Morrison, Ill., Shawver Publishing Co., 1929).
Wrede, Friedrich W. von. *Lebensbilder aus den Vereinigten Staaten von Nordamerika und Texas . . .* (Cassell, Printed by the author, 1844).

The two pages of Suel Foster's "Recollections" record visiting Davenport, Rockingham, Montevideo, other Iowa towns, and an Indian village in 1836. Amherst Willoughby Kellogg's "Recollections of Life in Early Wisconsin" describes his journey in 1836, when he was a young boy, from Buffalo to Detroit by way of Lake Erie and by team and wagon to Chicago and then to Wisconsin. He depicts in fluent prose simple family pioneer life. Lieutenant Lea, after whom the town of Albert Lea, Minnesota, was named, wrote notes which are largely topographical descriptions of the Wisconsin Territory. Another lake trip from Buffalo to Detroit in 1836 and travels through parts of Indiana, Illinois, Wisconsin, and Michigan are the subjects of Mrs. Margaret Longyear's brief tale. Disappointed with Detroit, she moved to Dewitt, Michigan, where she endured many pioneer discomforts. A three-day stage ride in 1836 from Columbus to Maumee, Ohio, and a lengthy description of early Toledo make up the

"Reminiscences of Richard Mott." A very readable account of a trip in the same year by lumber wagon from Galena through Elk Grove and Belmont to Mineral Point, Wisconsin, of life at the last named town, and a journey by steamer to Prairie du Chien and finally to Rock Island appears in Strange M. Palmer's narrative. Isaac T. Smith's tale, partly in diary form containing humorous touches, is about travel and travel difficulties in Wisconsin in 1836 as far as Rock River. Catharine Stewart's *New Home in the West* tells of trips from Chicago to Galena and down the Mississippi, also in 1836. She has good descriptions of the country and settlements. Mrs. Willson chronicles a journey in the same year from the East to Buffalo, Lake Erie, Conneaut, Ashtabula, Cleveland, Upper Sandusky, Delaware, Zanesville, and return by way of western Virginia. Friedrich von Wrede's narrative contains information on St. Louis and Illinois, which he visited in 1836.

Logan, James. *Notes of a Journey through Canada, the United States of America, and the West Indies* (Edinburgh, Fraser and Co.; London, Smith, Elder and Co., 1838).[9] .

Leaving Edinburgh on May 30, 1836, James Logan voyaged to Quebec and traveled by way of Montreal to Detroit, which he described as "a neat little place, having a population of nearly 9000." He proceeded to Mackinaw in a schooner, visited the Sault and Gros Cape on Lake Superior, and continued on to Chicago, Peru, and St. Louis, up the Ohio to Cincinnati, across Ohio to Ashtabula, and later to the East and South. His book contains an interesting account of this trip. Comments on the mania for land speculation in Chicago give an insight into economic conditions of the times.

DeSellem, John L. Diary. "Nonsense [sic] or Scribling [sic] of a Voyager, Nov. 20th 1836" to January 1, 1837. MS. in the Nessly-DeSellem Collection. Listed in Elizabeth Biggert, comp. *Guide to the Manuscript Collections in the Library of the Ohio State Archaeological and Historical Society* (Columbus, 1953), No. 753.
Switzler, William Franklin. Travel Sketches, 1836–1837. Typed copies. MSS. Listed in *Guide to the Western Historical Manuscripts Collection*, No. 526.[10]
Mason, Charles. Diary, 1829–1882. MS. Library of Congress.[11]

John L. DeSellem's diary was kept when he was a flatboatman traveling from Pittsburgh to Memphis during 1836 and 1837. It includes a description of Cincinnati. William F. Switzler, born in 1819 and author of several books on Missouri history, moved from Kentucky to a Missouri farm, where he grew up. His travel sketches give accounts of journeys from Missouri to the South in 1836–1837. Springfield, Missouri, he called a "poor place" of some eight or ten cabins. Charles Mason went west on a tour of observation in 1836, and in 1837 was appointed public prosecutor of Des Moines County, Wisconsin Territory. His diary, extending over a long period, mentions later law practice in Washington, D. C., and residence at Burlington, Iowa.

Lenz, T. W. *Reise nach Saint Louis am Mississippi; nebst meinen, während eines vierzehnmonatlichen Aufenthaltes i. d. J. 1836 und 1837, theils im Missouristaate, theils in Illinois gemachten Beobachtungen und Erfahrungen* (Weimar, Voight, 1838).
Rieger, Rev. Johann Georg Joseph. "The Followers of Duden. Joseph Rieger—Colporteur." William G. Bek, trans. *Mo. Hist. Rev.*, XVIII (1924), 212–49.[12]

T. W. Lenz, a German, is the author of a travel book in his native language about a trip to St. Louis by way of the Ohio and Mississippi and visits to nearby places in Illinois. Reverend Johann G. J. Rieger, born in Bavaria, was attracted to Missouri by the enthusiasm of Duden. His first mission field was Alton, Illinois. His diary, in German, of his life as a Christian missionary in Illinois, Iowa, and Missouri (1836–1869), has been partially translated and published.

Gray, Rev. William Henry. "Journal of a Trip from the Columbia River to Utica, N. Y." *Whitman College Quarterly*, XVI (1913).
—— "Gray's Journal of 1838." *Pac. Northw. Quar.*, XXIX (1938), 277–82.[13]
Chase, Rev. Supply. "A Pioneer Minister." *Mich. Hist. Colls.*, V (1884), 52–60.
Woodard, Rev. S. C. "Reminiscences of the Early Itinerancy." *Mich. Hist. Colls.*, XIV (1890), 553–60.

The first journal of William Henry Gray, a native of New York state, narrates a journey from Reverend H. H. Spalding's location on the Columbia River to Utica, New York, beginning on December 28, 1836, and continuing to October 16, 1837. The second journal, actually in the form of a letter but printed as a narrative and copied from an original journal, gives an account of the author's progress from Independence, Missouri, up the Kaw and Platte rivers, and on to Oregon. The entries are brief.

The narrative of the Reverend Supply Chase, a minister in Pontiac and vicinity, is divided into topics and includes notes on the town of Pontiac, frontier hospitality, the Patriot War, a trip on the Great Lakes, and other events during 1836–1838. Another narrative of life in Michigan is that by S. C. Woodard, a pioneer Methodist minister who traveled to Detroit by steamer from New York state in 1836. The tale is brief and less interesting than many others but covers a long time.

Plumbe, John, Jr. *Sketches of Iowa and Wisconsin, Taken during a Residence of Three Years in those Territories* (St. Louis, Chambers, Harris and Knapp, 1839). Reprinted at Iowa City (State Historical Society of Iowa, 1948), and as "Iowa," *Ann. of Ia.*, 3rd Series, XIV (1925), 481–537, 595–617.[14]
Stebbins, C. B. "Story of Another Pioneer." *Mich. Hist. Colls.*, V (1884), 125–37.
"The Diary of Martin McLeod." Grace Lee Nute, ed. *Minn. Hist.*, IV (1922), 351–439. Extracts in John H. Stevens, *Personal Recollections of Minnesota and Its People* (Minneapolis, Tribune Job Printing, 1890), 345–57.[15]

Sincere appreciation of nature is apparent in *Sketches of Iowa and Wisconsin* (1836–1839) by John Plumbe, Jr., who as a young man migrated to Dubuque, which was nominally his home the remainder of his life. C. B. Stebbins' "Story of Another Pioneer" (1836–1840), supplements the earlier narrative mentioned in Chapter 8 and relates events in a trip from Buffalo by way of Toledo to Detroit in 1836 and life in Michigan. The diary of Major Martin McLeod, actually an account of a filibustering expedition in Minnesota in 1836 and other events as late as 1841, is hastily written but contains some original expressions and shows his familiarity with Shakespeare and other poets.

Wiley, Oren. "The Journal of a Vermont Man in Ohio, 1836–1842." LeRoy P. Graf, ed. *Ohio Arch. Hist. Quar.*, LX (1951), 175–99.
Ball, Lucy. "Early days in Grand Rapids." *Mich. Hist. Colls.*, XXXVIII (1912), 92–104.
Barlow, William. "Reminiscences of Seventy Years." *Oreg. Hist. Soc. Quar.*, XIII (1912), 240–86.
Barber, Edward W. "Recollections and Lessons of Pioneer Boyhood." *Mich. Hist. Colls.*, XXXI (1902), 178–227.
Towner, Mrs. Julia Belle. "My Mother's Girlhood." *Mich. Hist. Colls.*, XXXV (1907), 180–84.

Hoyt, William C. "Early Recollections." *Mich. Hist. Colls.*, V (1884), 61–63.
Hoyt, Mrs. Mary M. "Early Recollections of Pioneer Life in Michigan and the Founding of Yankee Springs." *Mich. Hist. Colls.*, XXX (1906), 289–302.
Hazelton, George H. "Reminiscences of Seventeen Years Residence in Michigan, 1836–1853." *Mich. Hist. Colls.*, XXI (1894), 370–418.
Hoppin, Ruth. "Personal Recollections of Pioneer Days." *Mich. Hist. Colls.*, XXXVIII (1912), 410–17.
Spalding, William Witter. "Early Days in Duluth." *Mich. Hist. Colls.*, XXIX (1901), 677–97.
Lafever, Margaret. "Story of Early Day Life in Michigan." *Mich. Hist. Colls.*, XXXVIII (1912), 672–77.

Oren Wiley left Vermont for Ohio in 1836 and visited Sandusky, Detroit, and southern Ohio. His journal shows his literary interests and contains praise for the West. Lucy Ball's narrative relates events in the life of her father in the Midwest during 1836–1843: his journey by steamboat from Buffalo to Toledo and Detroit and return to Troy, New York, the trip back to Michigan, life at Grand Rapids, and the early days of the Michigan legislature. William Barlow's "Reminiscences" is a chatty, enjoyable tale describing a trip from Indiana to Illinois in 1836, house building near Farmington, and a trek to Oregon by way of Quincy and the Platte River in 1846. Edward W. Barber's narrative extends from 1836 to 1847. As a boy he went from Buffalo to Detroit and in 1839 traveled by oxen and wagon to Vermontville, Michigan. Later his father made several trips to Michigan. Barber mentions various pioneer ventures such as clearing land and building fences. Similar Michigan experiences are recorded in several other tales, including Mrs. Julia B. Towner's brief story of 1836–1848. William C. and Mrs. Mary M. Hoyt wrote narratives of Michigan life. The former's briefly chronicles a steamboat journey by way of Lake Erie to Detroit, by stagecoach to Niles, and events of 1836–1852; and the latter's tells of travel by covered wagon from New York state to Detroit, of taking an Indian trail to the west from there, and mentions incidents in pioneer life. George H. Hazelton's "Reminiscences" mentions a lake journey to Detroit, the return to the East, the trip back to Michigan, and military and business experiences. Ruth Hoppin describes Indian customs and pioneer hardships in Michigan from 1836 to about 1856. William W. Spalding descended the Ohio in 1836, reached Peru, Illinois, later moved to other Illinois towns, and, hearing of the discovery of copper on Lake Superior, went north in 1845. The latter part of his account describes Indians and life on the Lake as late as 1888. Margaret Lafever expresses disappointment over conditions she and her father found in Michigan in 1836. They came by covered wagon from New York state to Detroit, Dexter, and Eaton Rapids, Michigan. She sympathized with the Indians driven from their homes, tells of a friendship with an Indian, and mentions pioneer work and the death of her parents.

Anonymous. Journal of a Traveler, October 5–19, 1837. 35 pp. MS. Illinois State Historical Library, Springfield.
—— Journal, May 17–30, 1837. MS. in the Mark Morris Papers. Burton Historical Collection, Detroit.
Warren, Elihu. Diary, 1837. 3 pp., typed copy. MS. Listed in Alice E. Smith, comp. *Guide to the Manuscripts of the Wisconsin Historical Society* (Madison, 1944), No. 711.
Williams, Thomas Hale. An Account of a Journey, 1837. Typed copy, made from original MS. Listed in Lucile M. Kane and Kathryn A. Johnson, comps. *Manuscript Collections of the Minnesota Historical Society. Guide Book Number 2* (St. Paul, 1955), No. 1611.

The anonymous journal of a traveller was by a Philadelphia merchant of a trip from Philadelphia to Frankfort, Kentucky. The second anonymous journal describes a voyage from Rochester, New York, to Detroit. Elihu Warner's brief diary recounts a journey by keelboat from Canfield, Ohio, to Prairie du Chien with a group of immigrants. Thomas H. Williams' account covers a journey from New England to Alton, Illinois.

"Diary of Philip Johnson Buckner, M.D." *Wm. and Mary Coll. Hist. Mag.*, 2nd Series, XXIII (1943), 69–84.

Clark, John Alonso. *Gleanings by the Way* (Philadelphia, W. J. and J. K. Simon; New York, R. Carter, 1842).

Hall, Frederick. *Letters from the East and from the West* (Baltimore, F. Taylor and William M. Morrison, etc., 1840).[16]

The Diary of Lucy Ann Higbee (Cleveland, O., Privately printed, 1924).[17]

Smith, William Rudolph. *Observations on the Wisconsin Territory; Chiefly on that Part Called the "Wisconsin Lead District"* . . . (Philadelphia, Carey and Hart, 1838).

——— *Incidents of a Journey from Pennsylvania to Wisconsin Territory . . . , to Which Are Added Gen. Smith's Autobiography, 1787–1808, Letters . . . Brief Biographical Sketch, 1787–1868* (Chicago, W. Howes, 1927). Journal reprinted as "Journal of William Rudolph Smith." *Wis. Mag. Hist.*, XII (1928–1929), 192–220, 300–21.[18]

Dr. Philip Johnson Buckner, grandson of Captain Philip Buckner, mentioned in Chapter 7, wrote a diary consisting of numerous jottings made on a trip in 1837 from a river point in Kentucky past Cincinnati to Rodney, on the Mississippi River. *Gleanings by the Way* is compiled from extracts from a journal that Clark kept during a tour down the Ohio in the same year, up the Mississippi, and across northern Illinois in a lumber wagon. Frederick Hall's letters make up a travel tale of a journey from Wheeling down the Ohio to Zanesville, the Muskingum River, Lancaster, Ohio University, back to the Ohio River, and to Marietta College, the Ohio Canal, and Kentucky, all in 1837. The diary of Miss Lucy Ann Higbee, of Trenton, New Jersey, records incidents in a journey in 1837 from Richmond, Virginia, to Ohio by stage and steamer.

More important than these are the journal and autobiographical sketch of William R. Smith, distinguished Wisconsin pioneer. Appointed to negotiate a treaty with the Chippewa Indians, he left his home in Pennsylvania in 1837 and proceeded by river from Pittsburgh to Prairie du Chien. An account of this and part of the return journey is included in his clearly written narrative.

Jameson, Mrs. Anna Brownell. *Winter Studies and Summer Rambles in Canada* (3 vols., London, Saunders and Otley, 1838). Extracts in "Impressions of Detroit, 1837," "Detroit to Mackinac Island, 1837," "Impressions of Mackinac Island, 1837," and "Impressions of Sault Ste. Marie, 1837," *Mich. Hist.*, VIII (1924), 51–76, 140–69, 349–91, 486–533.[19]

Dye, Mrs. Richard. "Coming to Michigan." *Mich. Hist. Colls.*, VIII (1886), 260–65.

Journal of Thomas Nye Written during a Journey between Montreal and Chicago in 1837. Hugh McLellan, ed. (Champlain, N. Y., Moorsfield Press, 1932).[20]

One of the better known professional British authors to visit the Middle West was Irish-born Mrs. Anna B. Jameson. Her enjoyable travel book describes her trip in 1837 to Detroit, Mackinac Island, and the Sault. She was favorably impressed by the Michigan city but hated the heat. She included an account of the Pontiac War.

Mrs. Richard Dye's brief and somewhat sentimental tale tells of a lake trip in the same year from the East to Detroit and then

to Pontiac where she established a wilderness home. Thomas Nye, a lawyer, voyaged from his home in Montreal to Chicago by steamer and returned to Detroit by land with his bride, and then proceeded by steamer to Cleveland and overland to Montreal, all from October to December, 1837. His journal of this trip consists mainly of brief notes but contains good pictures of a prairie fire and of various inns.

Duffield, George C. "Coming into Iowa in 1837." *Ann. of Ia.*, 3rd Series, VI (1903), 1–8.

——— "An Iowa Settler's Homestead." *Ann. of Ia.*, VI (1903), 206–20.

Espinosa, J. Manuel. "Memoir of a Kentuckian in New Mexico, 1848–1884." *New Mex. Hist. Rev.*, XIII (1937), 1–13.

Log City Days; Two Narratives on the Settlement of Galesburg, Illinois. The Diary of Jerusha Loomis Farnham . . . (Galesburg, Knox College, Centenary Publications, 1937).[21]

Lillybridge, Dr. C. "Journey of a Party of Cherokee Emigrants." Grant Foreman, ed. *Miss. Val. Hist. Rev.*, XVIII (1931–1932), 232–45.[22]

"The Journal of Mrs. Peter Martineau." Summarized by Bell Hooker. *Wis. Mag. Hist.*, XVII (1933), 72–76.

Noonan, J. A. "Recollections of Wisconsin in February, 1837." *Wis. Hist. Soc. Colls.*, VII (1876), 409–12.

"Diary of John Peake." Harold F. Crookes, ed. *Jour. Ill. State Hist. Soc.*, VIII (1915), 114–31.[23]

Duffield's two articles describe a trip from the East to Iowa, the building of a log cabin, and give his interesting impressions of Iowa in 1838. The memoir of J. Manuel Espinosa includes mention of Judge Samuel Ellison's trip in 1837 from Kentucky to Cincinnati and his three-month stay there to recruit men for a trip to Texas and New Mexico. Mrs. Jerusha L. Farnham's diary includes an account of her travel in 1837 from Troy, New York, to the Gale Colony at Log City, Illinois. Dr. C. Lillybridge, a New York physician, accompanied a group of emigrating Cherokees down the Ohio and Mississippi rivers into the Southwest in the same year. His journal is impersonal but unusual. The journal of Mrs. Peter Martineau describes her removal from the East to New Albany, Indiana, in 1837 and later trips from Bloomington, Indiana, to Indianapolis, Toledo, and the East and a steamboat voyage from Buffalo to Chicago. J. A. Noonan recollects a surveying trip and towns on the way from Green Bay to Mineral Point, Wisconsin, and Milwaukee. The diary of John Peake, a native Virginian, mentions travel in Illinois, also in 1837; rather dull.

Rynning, Ole. *Sandfaerdig Beretning om Amerika, til Oplysning og Nytte for Bonde og Menigmaad; Forsattet af en Norsk, som kom derover i Juni maaned 1837* (Christiania, Guldberg and Dzwonkowski, 1839). Original, reprinted and edited, and English translation by T. C. Blegen, as *Ole Rynning's True Account of America* (Minneapolis, Norwegian-American Historical Association, "Travel and Description Series," Vol. I, 1926); translation only in *Minn. Hist. Bull.*, II (1917), 221–69.[24]

Wette, Ludwig de. *Reise in den Vereinigten Staaten und Canada im Jahr 1837* (Leipzig, Weidmann, 1838).

Ole Rynning, a Norwegian immigrant leader, settled in Illinois in 1837. He and three companions journeyed from Chicago to the Beaver Creek region in the Iroquois country, where they started a settlement, which was devastated by malaria. In a blizzard Rynning lacerated and froze his feet. While ill he wrote his *Sandfaerdig Beretning om America*, which greatly encouraged Norwegian immigration since he firmly believed that the United States would become a place of refuge for financially destitute Europeans. A German, Ludwig de Wette, includes in his book an account of a trip up the Mississippi River to St. Louis and across Illinois to Vincennes.

Hobart, Nathaniel. Letters in the Form of a Diary, 1837–1838. Photostatic copy of MS. Yale University Library, New Haven, Conn.

Garrioch, Peter. Journal. 1837–1847. Typescript edited by Rev. George Gunn; a fragment of MS. journal by Garrioch. Manitoba Provincial Library, Winnipeg.[25]

———— "Peter Garrioch at St. Peter." *Minn. Hist.*, XX (1939), 119–28.[26]

Monroe, Charles, Autobiography, 1837–1867. 11 pp. MS. Monroe Papers. Burton Historical Collection, Detroit.

Nathaniel Hobart wrote a series of letters on a journey "West and South" in 1837 and a second journey to the Northwest in May, 1838. He visited such cities as Wheeling, Cincinnati, Louisville, St. Louis, and New Orleans. Peter Garrioch, teacher and free trader in furs, relates his wanderings from the Red River Settlement over the plains and fur trade centers in Minnesota, Dakota, and Manitoba. The published portion of his journal describes a journey by cart and canoe from the Red River Colony to St. Peter, in what is now Minnesota, and negotiations with the Chippewa. The autobiography of Charles Monroe, written at Hillsdale, Michigan, in 1875, gives an account of several walking tours in New York state and in the Middle West to Chicago and includes events as late as 1867, when the author took possession of property at Jonesville, Michigan.

A Trip to the Prairies and in the Interior of North America. . . . Travel Notes by Count Francesco Arese, Now First Translated from the Original French by Andrew Evans (New York, The Harbor Press, 1934). Extracts in "The Middle West in 1837 . . . ," Lynn M. Case, ed., *Miss. Val. Hist. Rev.*, XX (1933), 381–99.

Daubeny, Dr. Charles G. Bridle. *Journal of a Tour through the United States and in Canada, Made During the Years 1837–38 . . .* (Oxford, T. Combe, 1843).[27]

"Diary of the Rev. James-Hanmer Francis, 1837–1838." Winifred L. Holman, ed. *Ohio Arch. Hist. Quar.*, LI (1942), 41–61.[28]

An Italian count, Francesco Arese, wrote travel notes in French describing his trip in 1837 and 1838 down the Ohio, up the Mississippi to St. Louis, up part of the Missouri, and across the plains to Green Bay, Wisconsin, and his return to New York by way of the Great Lakes. His literary style, ability to relate events interestingly, and favorable attitude towards Cincinnati and other Midwestern localities deserve mention. Dr. Charles G. Daubeny, a professor of chemistry and botany at Oxford University, descended the Ohio and Mississippi by steamer, ascended the latter river to St. Louis, and returned to the East by way of the Ohio. He makes a valid criticism of American character. Much of his volume is devoted to scientific matters. Leaving his home in Connecticut, the Reverend James-Hanmer Francis traveled to northern Ohio and made a horseback trip to Adrian and Niles, Michigan, through northern Indiana into Illinois, and from Chicago back to Niles and Ohio. His diary is rather fragmentary and mentions his preaching activities during these travels.

Marryat, Frederick. *A Diary in America, with Remarks on its Institutions* (2 vols., Philadelphia, Carey and Hart, 1839). Part Second (3 vols., London, Longman, Orme, Brown, Green, and Longmans, 1839). Extracts in "An English Officer's Description of Wisconsin in 1837," *Wis. Hist. Soc. Colls.*, XIV (1898), 137–54, and "Captain Marryat in Minnesota, 1838," *Minn. Hist.*, VI (1925), 168–84.[29]

Frederick Marryat, the English novelist, was at the full tide of his popularity when he visited the United States in 1837 and 1838, but because of his somewhat flippant attitude and lack of faith in the permanent benefits of democracy he was not well received. He called the Mississippi "the Great Sewer," for example, and said the flies in the lower part of St. Louis "on a moderate calculation, are in many parts fifty to the square inch." He was not entirely unfair, however, for he described the beauty of the moon shining on the great river and found Cincinnati more pleasant than did Mrs. Trollope. His trip took him into the Midwest from Detroit, by way of the Great Lakes and Illinois to St. Louis, up the Ohio by steamboat to Cincinnati, and back to the East.

Smith, Joshua Toulmin. *Journal in America, 1837–1838.* Floyd B. Streeter, ed. (Metuchen, N. J., C. F. Heartman, 1925; forming No. 41 of Heartman's Historical Series).[30]

"Journal of Salmon Stebbins, 1837–1838." *Wis. Mag. Hist.*, IX (1925), 188–212.[31]

An Englishman, Joshua T. Smith, voyaged from England to Detroit and in his journal expressed disappointment in not finding a Utopia in the United States. He commented at length on American "barbarians," wildcat money, and the Canadian rebellion, and he lectured on phrenology at Ann Arbor and Detroit, successfully according to Henry R. Schoolcraft. After settling for a time at the latter city, he moved to the East. Samuel Stebbins was an itinerant preacher who traveled to Wisconsin from northern New York state.

Kirkland, Mrs. Caroline Matilda. *A New Home—Who'll Follow? or, Glimpses of Western Life* (New York and Boston, F. S. and J. B. Francis, 1839). Reprinted as *A New Home, or Life in the Clearings,* John Nerber, ed. (New York, G. P. Putnam's Sons, 1953).[32]

Memorable for its realistic picture of frontier Michigan life is Mrs. Caroline M. Kirkland's *A New Home—Who'll Follow?* a narrative employing so many of the techniques of fiction that it is difficult to classify. With her husband she moved from the East to Detroit in 1835 and in 1837 to Pinckney, Michigan, a town about twenty miles from Ann Arbor. There they remained until 1843 and there she made her observations. Although her literary fame is but slight today, Edgar Allen Poe called her one of America's best writers, with "a province of her own," in which she had few equals.[33] Unquestionably, her narrative is an important source for an objective and authoritative picture of frontier life in the 1830's and is a forerunner of the realist movement in American literature. Her son, Joseph Kirkland, the novelist, learned the principles of objective realism from her, and he in turn has influenced Hamlin Garland and others. Mrs. Kirkland's purpose was to set down the whole truth as she saw it, and her work was an exposé which offended her Michigan neighbors. In a style both vivacious and original she described such varied events as a frontier forest fire, a backwoods political rally, a trip to Detroit, and a siege of malaria. Her sense of humor and her use of understatement are noticeable.

Hubbard, Bela. *Memorials of a Half-Century in Michigan and the Lake Region* (New York and London, G. P. Putnam's Sons, 1888).

Coonc, Elizabeth Ann. "Reminiscences of a Pioneer Woman." *Wash. Hist. Quar.*, VIII (1917), 14–21.

"Reminiscences of James Jory." H. S. Lyman, ed. *Oreg. Hist. Soc. Quar.*, III (1902), 271–86.

"William A. Trubody's Narrative." Charles L. Camp, ed. *Cal. Hist. Soc. Quar.*, XVI (1937), 122–43.

Taylor, Rev. George. "First Visit to Michigan." *Mich. Hist. Colls.,* VI (1884), 15–17.

Bela Hubbard, author of "Memoir of Luther Harvey," mentioned in Chapter 8, wrote a story of his life in the Midwest, *Memorials of a Half-Century* . . . , in which he tells of a geological expedition in Michigan to Saginaw, canoe journeys on Lake Huron in 1837, and a trip in 1840 from Mackinac by way of the Sault to Ontonagon, LaPointe, and other places on Lake Superior. Elizabeth Coonc's "Reminiscences" begins with her Midwestern experiences in 1837 and includes a trip from Pike County, Illinois, by ox team along the Oregon Trail in 1846 and 1847. James Jory, a Britisher, made a very interesting trek from St. Louis to Illinois to avoid the evils of the slavery system and from Independence across the plains to the Far West, 1837–1847. His "Reminiscences" are well written with occasional humorous touches. William Alexander Trubody's narrative covers the same years and begins with a trip down the Ohio and up the Missouri, settlement at Dover, Missouri, and a journey in 1847 to the Far West with a band of a hundred immigrant wagons. The brief narrative of the Reverend George Taylor, who became a Methodist minister in Detroit, relates events on a journey from Rochester by way of Lake Erie to Detroit and to Ypsilanti by four-horse stage.

Keyes, Elisha W. "Early Days in Jefferson County." *Wis. Hist. Soc. Colls.,* XI (1888), 416–34.[34]
Forty Years on the Frontier as Seen in the Journals and Reminiscences of Granville Stuart, Gold-Miner, Trader, Merchant, Rancher and Politician. Paul C. Phillips, ed. (2 vols., Cleveland, Arthur H. Clark Co., 1925). Extracts in "Boyhood on the Frontier," *The Palimpsest,* VII (1926), 213–29.[35]
Woodman, Elias S. "Early Recollections." *Mich. Hist. Colls.,* XVIII (1892), 455–58.
Van Antwerp, Ver Planck. "Reminiscences of Early Iowa." *Ia. Jour. Hist.,* LII (1954), 343–64.
Hayes, Mrs. A. M. "Reminiscences of Pioneer Days in Hastings." *Mich. Hist. Colls.,* XXVI (1896), 235–41.
Riggs, Rev. Stephen Return. *Mary and I. Forty Years with the Sioux* (Chicago, W. G. Holmes, 1880).
——— "Journal of a Tour from Lac Qui Parle to the Missouri River." *Miss. Her.,* XXXVII (1841), 179–86. Reprinted in *Sou. Dak. Hist. Colls.,* XIII (1926), 330–44.[36]
"Autobiography of Rev. William Hamilton." *Neb. Hist. Soc. Trans. Reports,* I (1885), 60–73.

The narrative of Elisha W. Keyes describes how, as a boy in 1837, he went by steamboat from Buffalo to Detroit, by covered wagon to Milwaukee, and continued to the present site of Lake Mills, Wisconsin, where his father built a log house. It relates pioneer hardships and Indian activities. *Forty Years on the Frontier* mentions Stuart's birth in 1834, a trip from Virginia to Princeton, Illinois, in 1837, his prairie schooling, life on the farm, and journey to California in 1852. Elias S. Woodman's "Early Recollections" (1837–1860) tells of a trip from Buffalo to Detroit and life at Novi, Michigan. Ver Planck Van Antwerp's "Reminiscences" describes a trip in 1837 from the Wabash River to Fort Snelling and includes an account of the Missouri-Iowa War in 1839–1840 and events as late as 1868. Mrs. A. M. Hayes' "Reminiscences" (1837–1873) tells of a boat trip to Detroit, a land journey to Ann Arbor, and settlement at Hastings, Michigan. The book of the Reverend Stephen R. Riggs discusses his missionary work among the Sioux. In 1837 he and his wife went to Lac Qui Parle, in Minnesota, and in 1843 he opened a new station at Traverse des Sioux, where he stayed until 1846. He returned to Lac Qui Parle and remained there until the mission building burned in 1854. He mentions travels from Ohio to New

England, to St. Louis, and up the Mississippi. Another minister who journeyed west was the Reverend William Hamilton, whose autobiography (1811–1884), in the form of a long letter, details his trip in 1837 from Pittsburgh down the Ohio, up the Missouri, and into the Indian country. He remarks sympathetically on the white man's shameful treatment of the Indian.

Hatheway, Franklin. "Surveying in Wisconsin in 1837." *Wis. Hist. Soc. Colls.,* XV (1900), 390–98.
Fifty Years in Camp and Field, Diary of Major-General Ethan Allen Hitchcock, U. S. A. W. A. Croffut, ed. (New York and London, G. P. Putnam's Sons, 1909).[37]
"Letter of William-Henry Everest." In *Everest Genealogy,* Winifred L. Holman, ed. (Concord, N. H., Rumford Press, 1955), pp. 410–11.
Webber, Mrs. Betsey. "Early Recollections." *Mich. Hist. Colls.,* XVIII (1892), 428–33.

Although Franklin Hatheway first went to Wisconsin from the East in 1835, his narrative does not begin until he returned to that state for surveying purposes in 1837. He also .went to Wisconsin in 1843 and later lived in Cleveland and Chicago. The diary of Major-General Ethan Allan Hitchcock gives an account of his trip to the Indian bureau in St. Louis in 1837, of visiting Jefferson Barracks in 1843, and of later experiences in the Mexican and Civil wars. William-Henry Everest's letter, written in 1942, tells of the William Andrew Everest family's move from New York state to the Western Reserve in 1837 and of later trips to Lake Ontario, Cleveland, and Niagara Falls. Mrs. Betsey Webber relates an encounter with Indians, a riding experience and life in pioneer Michigan (c. 1837–1838). Her tone is religious and her style is colloquial.

Beebe, Silas. "A Trip from Utica, New York, to Ingham County, Michigan." *Mich. Hist. Colls.,* I (1877), 187–92.
Blanchard, William C. Journal of a Tour, 1838. MS. The William C. Blanchard Papers. Burton Historical Collection, Detroit.
Hill, Jediah. "A Journey from Ohio to New Jersey in 1838." 6 pp.; typed from a total of 20 pp., MS. Original in private hands. Listed in Biggert, *Guide,* No. 516.
Shute, Robert C. Diary of a Trip, May 20–August 2, 1838. Listed in Biggert, *Guide,* No. 934.

"A Trip from Utica . . ." is an extract from the narrative of Silas Beebe, told partly by his son, and relates incidents on the trip by way of Lake Erie to Maumee, Toledo, and Detroit in 1838. William C. Blanchard's journal, written in the summer of 1838 when he was twenty, describes a tour from Boston by way of Niagara Falls to Michigan. Jediah Hill's journey began in Hamilton County, Ohio. Robert C. Shute's trip was from Camden, Ohio, to Barnesville, Ohio.

"Charles Minton Baker's Journal from Vermont to Wisconsin." *Wis. Mag. Hist.,* V (1921–1922), 391–401.
Kemper, Bishop Jackson. "A Trip through Wisconsin in 1838." *Wis. Mag. Hist.,* VIII (1925), 423–45.[38]
Kingman, John. *Letters Written while on a Tour to Illinois and Wisconsin, in the Summer of 1838* (Hingham, Mass., J. Farmer, 1842).

Charles M. Baker traveled from Hortonville, Vermont, to Wisconsin in 1838 and settled at Lake Geneva. His journal exaggerates the romantic aspects of the frontier, e.g., the following jotting: "Hail thou fair & fertile West, thou world of floods & forests of bright rivers & green prairies, thou art henceforth my home." Bishop Jackson Kemper, mentioned also in Chapters 11 and 13, wrote a diary of a trip from Dubuque to Fond du Lac. John Kingman's *Letters* comprise a brief journal of his tour.

Bird, Robert Montgomery. *Peter Pilgrim: or a Rambler's Recollections. By the Author of "Calavar," "Nick of the Woods," &c.*... (2 vols., Philadelphia, Lea and Blanchard, 1838).[39]

Robert Montgomery Bird was a well-known Western playwright, novelist, and editor. His *Peter Pilgrim* is a collection of realistic travel sketches. His familiarity with the frontier is evinced by his knowledge of the Indian, of Mississippi River steamboat travel, and of Mammoth Cave, all of which he describes in detail.

Baker, John W. "Western Travels." Harry R. Stevens, ed. *Hist. Phil. Soc. of Ohio Bull.*, VI (1948), 127–55.

Polke, William. "Journal of an Emigrating Party of Pottawattomie Indians, from Twin Lakes, in Marshall County, Ia. [Indiana], to Their Home on the Osage River in the We[stern] Territory." *Ind. Mag. Hist.*, XXI (1925), 316–36.[40]

Jones, Abner D. *Illinois and the West, with a Township Map* ... (Philadelphia, W. Marshall and Co., 1838).

Swartzell, William. *Mormonism Exposed, being a Journal of a Residence in Missouri from the 28th of May to the 20th of August, 1838*... (Pekin, O., Published by the author, 1840).[41]

Young, Dr. John A. "Traveling in the Middle West in 1838." *Ann. of Ia.*, 3rd Series, XIX (1933), 139–45.[42]

Zimmerman, Eduard. "Travel into Missouri in October, 1838." Trans. by William G. Bek from the German. *Mo. Hist. Rev.*, IX (1914), 33–43.

Castelnau, Francis, Comte de. *Vues et Souvenirs de l'Amérique du Nord* (Paris, A. Bertrand, 1842).

Deming, Ebenezer. [Maj. Walter Wilkey, pseud.] *Western Emigration; Narrative of a Tour to & One Year's Residence in "Edensburgh" (Illinois) by Major Walter Wilkey, an Honest Yeoman of Mooseboro, State of Maine. A More Humorous and Interesting "Traveller's Guide to the West," Was Never Before Published, and by Which It Will Be Perceived that the Famous "Maine-pine-swamp Speculation," Has been Completely Outdone!* ... (New York, G. Clariborne, and Others, 1839). Reprinted in *Mag. Hist.*, VII (1914), 849–80.[43]

A diary by John W. Baker records a trip down the Ohio and into Illinois past Joliet and his return to the East by way of the Great Lakes in 1838. He noted that the grass and weeds on the prairie grew as high as the stage in which he was riding. William Polke's journal describes the difficult trek a group of emigrating Indians made from Twin Lakes, Indiana, to the Osage River in 1838. Abner D. Jones in *Illinois and the West* tells of a trip in the same year through parts of Indiana, Illinois, and Missouri.

William Swartzell, at one time a Mormon deacon, wrote *Mormonism Exposed*, which is an interesting revelation of the persecution suffered by the Mormons in Missouri. Dr. John A. Young's diary is a rather amusing but hastily written record of travel from Chillicothe, Ohio, to Monmouth, Illinois, in order to begin medical practice, and of a later trip to St. Louis. Edmund Zimmerman, a German, visited St. Louis and in his narrative commented unfavorably on the lack of distinction between classes and on the heat, cholera, and fever there during the summer but expressed appreciation of nature and the hospitality of the people. He mentioned Duden's book and its influence on fellow Germans. A work by a Frenchman, Francis, Comte de Castelnau, contains notes on Illinois and the West in 1838.

Written in a humorous vein is a strange pamphlet called *Western Emigration*, by Ebenezer Deming, telling of a trip by way of Cleveland and Detroit to Illinois. He described and debunked a town he called "Edensburgh," where he said he stayed for a year, probably in 1838. He ridiculed New Englanders foolish enough to consider moving to the West. The work is original and satirical and is written in a natural and refreshing style.

Olmsted, David. Incomplete autobiographical sketch, 1838, 1840. MS. Listed in Grace Lee Nute and Gertrude W. Ackermann, comps. *Guide to the Personal Papers in the Manuscript Collection of the Minnesota Historical Society* (St. Paul, Minnesota Historical Society, 1935), No. 193.[44]

Dougherty, Peter. Travel Diaries, 1838–1842. 2 vols. MSS. Listed in *Guide to Manuscript Collections in Michigan, Michigan Historical Collection, University of Michigan* (Detroit, Historical Records Survey Project, 1941), Vol. I, No. 139.[45]

Jenks, M. H. Diary, 1838, and Notes, *c.* 1842–*c.* 1845. MSS. Indiana Historical Society, Indianapolis.

Pratt, Rev. William Moody. Diary, 1838–1891. MS. Indiana Historical Society. University of Kentucky Library, Lexington, has 90 typed pages copied from MS. owned by Julian K. Dale, Terre Haute, Ind.

David Olmsted's autobiographical sketch contains information about his family and relatives and about a journey in 1838 from Vermont by way of Lake Erie, Indiana, and Chicago to Wisconsin and an exploring trip through northern Iowa in 1840. The first volume of the travel diaries of Peter Dougherty, a Presbyterian missionary to the Michigan area between 1838 and 1871, is an account of a trip (June 19, 1838–June 30, 1839) from New York City to Mackinac Island and Grand Traverse Bay, a return to New York for supplies, and a trip back to the island. The second volume is about a later journey (August 19, 1840–August 1, 1842) from New York to Mackinac. The two manuscripts of M. H. Jenks consist of a diary covering travel (May 10–June 3, 1838) from Philadelphia down the Ohio River, up the canal to Richmond, Indiana, across Ohio, and return to the East and of interesting notes of a trip to St. Louis, Galena, and Chicago. The latter trip, which is recorded in barely legible pencil notes, mentions North Bend and General Harrison, Nauvoo, Joseph Smith, and the Mormon Temple. Reverend William Moody Pratt, frontier Baptist preacher, left a readable diary which was begun in 1838 when he was twenty-one and which he continued until 1891. Pratt served in churches scattered throughout Indiana and Kentucky and in his diary mentions travels and events in church life.

"The Journal of Henry B. Miller." Thomas M. Marshall, ed. *Mo. Hist. Soc. Colls.*, VI (1931), 213–87.[46]

Gerstner, Clara von. *Beschreibung einer Reise durch die Vereinigten Staaten von Nord-America in den Jahren 1838 bis 1840, in Gessellschaft des Ritters Frank Anton von Gerstner* ... (Leipzig, J. C. Hinrichs, 1842).

"Journal of Cyrus Sanders." *Ia. Jour. Hist.*, XXXVII (1939), 52–88.[47]

"The History and Journal of the Life and Travels of Jesse W. Crosby." *Ann. of Wyo.*, XI (1939), 145–218.[48]

The Autobiography of Joseph Jefferson (New York, Century Co., 1897?) Reprinted as "Joseph Jefferson, Chicagoan" in Mabel McIlvaine, comp., *Reminiscences of Chicago During the Forties and Fifties* (Chicago, R. R. Donnelley and Sons Co., 1913).[49]

"Recollections of Benjamin Franklin Bonney." Fred Lockley, ed. *Oreg. Hist. Soc. Quar.*, XXIV (1923), 36–55.

Autobiography of Selah Hibbard Barrett, the Self-educated Clergyman ... (Rutland, O., The Author, 1872).[50]

"Recollections of Judge Francis Springer." *Ann. of Ia.*, 3rd Series, II (1897), 569–85.

The diary of Henry B. Miller, a young Pennsylvanian, relates events in a trip to Iowa and Illinois, various activities in St.

Louis, and a journey to Natchez (1838–1839). It contains much trivial matter but has an interesting description of the Mississippi. Clara von Gerstner's trip through the United States included travel up the Mississippi and Ohio rivers. Cyrus Sanders journeyed from Cincinnati by water to Vincennes and by stage from there to Iowa, returned to Ohio by way of St. Louis, and went back to Iowa, all between 1838 and 1845. His diary of these and other events is especially interesting because of its literary allusions and comments on such subjects as gambling, tavern life, and pioneer hardships. The diary of Jesse W. Crosby, converted to Mormonism at the age of eighteen, includes mention of a trip in 1838 to Kirtland, Ohio, to join the main body of the church and a journey with the Mormons to Missouri by horse team, then to Nauvoo, and in 1847 to the Great Salt Lake Valley.

Joseph Jefferson was a well-known actor who in his autobiography records his boyhood trip in 1838 from Albany by way of Lakes Erie and Huron to Illinois, where he accompanied his father, also an actor, on a tour of Burlington, Quincy, Peoria, Pekin, and Springfield. Later he followed the American army to Mexico and did not return to New York until 1849. Benjamin F. Bonney, after spending the first part of his life in Illinois, in 1845 began a trek by wagon from Independence to Oregon. His interesting narrative begins in 1838 and ends in about 1877. Travel in Ohio is recorded in the autobiography of Selah H. Barrett, a self-educated Methodist who undertook religious work in various parts of America and Canada. Her record begins in 1838 and ends in 1872. Judge Francis Springer describes a trip in 1838 from Maine by way of the Ohio and Mississippi to Burlington, Iowa, and later events.

Milburn, William Henry. *Ten Years of Preacher-Life; Chapters from an Autobiography* (New York, Derby and Jackson, 1859).[51]

Frémont, Col. John Charles. *Memoirs of My Life* (2 vols., Chicago, Belford, Clarke and Co., 1887). Extracts in "Frémont's Story, 1838–1839." *Sou. Dak. Hist. Colls.*, X (1920), 71–97, and in "Pathfinding in Iowa," *The Palimpsest*, IX (1928), 176–84.

———— *Report of the Exploring Expedition to the Rocky Mountains in the Year 1842, and to Oregon and North California in the Years 1843–'44* (Washington, Gales and Seaton, 1845). Often reprinted, usually as *Narrative of the Exploring Expedition. . . .* Extracts in Lloyd McFarling, ed. *Exploring the Northern Plains . . .* (Caldwell, Ida., Caxton Printers, 1955), pp. 107–17.[52]

Exploring with Frémont; the Private Diaries of Charles Preuss, Cartographer for John C. Frémont on his First, Second, and Fourth Expedition to the Far West. Ed. and trans. from the German by Erwin G. and Elizabeth Gudde (Norman, University of Oklahoma Press, 1958).

William Henry Milburn, author and minister, relates in *Ten Years of Preacher-Life* how he left Philadelphia for Jacksonville, Illinois, in 1838, later made two trips to Chicago, and in 1843 became an itinerant Methodist preacher. In 1844 he went to St. Louis, where he lived for nine months, traveled by boat from Wheeling to Cincinnati in 1845, moved to Baltimore the following year, and in 1848 went south because of poor health. His book throws light on social and religious conditions of the time.

John C. Frémont's life-story is important because of his eminence as an adventurer and explorer. His autobiography is written in readable prose and contains accurate and eloquent descriptions of the prairies and mountains. During 1838 and 1839 with Joseph C. Nicollet, he explored much of the country between Fort Pierre on the Missouri and Fort Snelling on the Mississippi. In 1842 he undertook an exploring expedition to the Rocky

Mountains, the diary and report of which is said to have influenced Longfellow's *Evangeline*. This and an expedition to the Rockies in 1843–1844 are recorded in the detailed diary in German of Charles Preuss. Frémont's *Notes of Travel in California . . .* (1846), written with Lieutenant Colonel William Henry Emory, is mentioned in Chapter 14.

"Bugle." "Buffalo to Chicago in 1839." *United Service Journal and Naval and Military Magazine*, Mar., Apr., 1848. Reprint, Fred Landon, ed. *Inland Seas*, IV (1948), 168–72.

Bailey, Robert S. *The Church in the Wilderness; Narrative of a Visit to the Right Rev. Philander Chase, Bishop of Illinois . . .* (Charleston, Illinois, Miller, 1839).

Gould, J. "Wanderings in the West in 1839." *Ind. Mag. Hist.*, XXX (1934), 71–103. Reprinted from *New England Farmer*, 1840. Section on Illinois reprinted and edited with same title by Earl W. Hayter, *Jour. Ill. State Hist. Soc.*, XXXIII (1940), 389–411.

A person using the name of "Bugle" wrote a spirited narrative of life aboard ship from Buffalo to Chicago in 1839. Entirely different in content is Robert S. Bailey's tale of a trip to Peoria, Illinois, to visit Philander Chase, who at the time was building Jubilee College near that town. "Wanderings in the West," by J. Gould, describes his descent of the Ohio River and his visit to Illinois and Wisconsin. Although Marietta, Ohio, reminded him of his native New England, he disliked the sloughs of Illinois and some of the infamous characters there. The narrative reveals good observation and is written in a readable, conversational style.

Oakley, Obadiah. Journal. In LeRoy R. and Ann W. Hafen, eds. *To the Rockies and Oregon, 1839–1842* (Glendale, Calif., Arthur H. Clark Co., 1955), pp. 26–64.

Smith, Sidney. Diary. In L. R. and A. W. Hafen, *To the Rockies and Oregon*, pp. 64–93.

Shortess, Robert. Narrative. In L. R. and A. W. Hafen, *To the Rockies and Oregon*, pp. 95–120. Reprinted from *Oreg. Pion. Assn. Trans.*, 1896.

Clarke, S. A. "Reminiscences of Joseph Holman." In L. R. and A. W. Hafen, *To the Rockies and Oregon*, pp. 123–34.

Kelly, Sarah Maria S. "Narrative by Amos Cook." In L. R. and A. W. Hafen, *To the Rockies and Oregon*, pp. 135–43. Reprinted from an interview in *The Oregonian*, June, 1890; also in H. W. Scott, *History of the Oregon Country* (Cambridge, Riverside Press, 1924), pp. 309–14.

A group of settlers went from Peoria, Illinois, to Oregon in 1839 and several of them composed accounts of the trek. The journal of Obadiah Oakley begins at Independence, Missouri, and, in well-written diary entries, describes the trip across the prairies and the wild life and Indians encountered along the way. Sidney Smith's diary begins eight days west of Independence. The narrative of Robert Shortess is in clear, interesting prose. The brief reminiscences of Joseph Holman as told by S. A. Clark were the result of an interview in 1878. Like it is Amos Cook's narrative.

LaBar, Hannah Rees. Diary, May 23–July 4, 1839. 6 pp. typed copy. MS. Listed in Alice E. Smith, *Guide to the Manuscripts of the Wisconsin Historical Society*, No. 378.

Russell, Roswell Philip. Information on a Journey up the Mississippi, 1839. MS. owned by Coral L. Colbrath, Duluth; 1 volume and 1 reel of microfilm, Minnesota Historical Society, St. Paul. Listed in Kane and Johnson, *Manuscript Collections of the Minnesota Historical Society. Guide Book Number 2*, No. 1343.

A brief diary by Hannah R. LaBar traces an emigrant journey from Stroudsburg, Pennsylvania, to Wisconsin, listing distances, and names of settlements, and giving other information. The manuscript by Roswell P. Russell gives information of a trip up the Mississippi River with Alexander Graham with a description of stops at various points along the way.

"Diary of Asahel Munger and Wife [Eliza]." *Oreg. Hist. Soc. Quar.*, VIII (1907), 398–405.[53]

Wislizenus, Dr. Adolphus. *Ein Ausflug nach den Felsen-Gebirgen im Jahre 1839* (St. Louis, W. Weber, 1840). English version by Frederick A. Wislizenus is entitled *A Journey to the Rocky Mountains in the Year 1839. Translated from the German, with a Sketch of the Author's Life* . . . (St. Louis, Missouri Historical Society, 1912). Also in *Senate Miscellaneous Document 26*, 30th Congress, 1st Session. Extract in McFarling, *Exploring the Northern Plains*, pp. 95–105.

—— *Memoir of a Tour in Northern Mexico, Connected with Col. Doniphan's Expedition, in 1846 and 1847* (Washington, Tippin and Streeper, 1848).[54]

A diary by Asahel Munger and his wife Eliza describes a trip from Oberlin, Ohio, by way of the Platte River to Oregon from May to September, 1839. Their comments on religion and the friendly Indians are interesting as is their criticism of the fur companies. The book of Adolphus Wislizenus, a German author and physician, gives an account of his arrival in New York in 1835, his practice as a country physician at Mascoutah, Illinois, and his travel up the Missouri River to Westport in April, 1839, where he joined a fur-trading party to the Rocky Mountains, returning by way of the Santa Fé trail to St. Louis. His second narrative describes his departure from St. Louis to take part in the Doniphan expedition to New Mexico.

Farnham, Thomas Jefferson. *Travels in the Great Western Prairies, the Anahuac and Rocky Mountains, and in the Oregon Territory* (Poughkeepsie, Killey and Lossing, 1841). Reprinted in R. G. Thwaites, ed. *Early Western Travels* . . . (32 vols., Cleveland, Arthur H. Clark Co., 1906), Vols. XXVIII and XXIX.[55]

"Some Account of a Journey to the Cherokees in 1839–1840; Being Extracts from the Journal of David E. Knowles." *Bull. Fr. Hist. Soc.*, VI (1915), 70–78; VII (1916), 15–21, 42–50.[56]

"Journal of E. Willard Smith while with the Fur Traders, Vasquez and Sublette, in the Rocky Mountain Region." *Oreg. Hist. Soc. Quar.*, XIV (1913), 250–79. Reprinted as "With Fur Traders in Colorado, 1839–1840 . . . ," *Colorado Magazine*, XXVII (1950), 161–88; extracts in *Ann. of Wyo.*, XI (1939), 33–41; also in L. R. and A. W. Hafen, *To the Rockies and Oregon*, pp. 151–95.[57]

As captain of nineteen young men who went to the Oregon Territory to try to settle the dispute with England over the region, Thomas Jefferson Farnham wrote a lengthy and interesting narrative of the trip which is unreliable, however, because of the personal opinions he expressed. Beginning in 1839, the group traveled from Independence, Missouri, to the Osage River, Council Grove, the Arkansas River, and farther west. Joseph Holman wrote a narrative of this expedition which can be found in S. A. Clarke's *Pioneer Days of Oregon History* (Portland, J. K. Gill, 1905) and elsewhere. During the summer of 1846 Farnham visited Mexico and returned by ascending the rivers to Peoria, but he left no known account of the trip.

David E. Knowles, a Quaker, wrote a diary on a journey in 1839 and 1840, mainly by horse and coach, from his home at East Farnham, Quebec, through Cincinnati, Indiana, and St. Louis to Cherokee missions and Friends' meetings in the Mid-

west. The journal is readable and decidedly religious in tone. A fur-trading expedition from Independence to the Far West, commanded at the start by Sublette and Vasquez, is described in the rather interesting 1839–1840 journal of E. Willard Smith, an architect and engineer living in Washington, D. C.

Bostwick, Alanson. Diary and Account of a Journey, 1839, 1841. MS. Listed in *Guide to Manuscript Materials of American Origin in the Illinois Historical Survey* (Urbana, 1951), p. 4, and in Nute and Ackermann, *Guide to the Personal Papers in the Manuscript Collections of the Minnesota Historical Society*, No. 291.

Cravath, Miles. Diaries, 1839–1841. MSS. Listed in Smith, *Guide to the Manuscripts of the Wisconsin Historical Society*, No. 155.

Alanson Bostwick, a schoolteacher, made a journey from his home in Winchester, Illinois, to Chicago and return in the summer of 1839 and a trip in 1841 from New York to Springfield, Illinois. The diaries of Miles Cravath describe his life at Courtlandville, New York, an overland journey by wagon from there to join his brother at Whitewater, Wisconsin, and pioneer life in the vicinity of Whitewater after May, 1840. His manuscripts include a diary kept by his father, Prosper Cravath, describing a trip by canal and the Great Lakes to Milwaukee.

Wahn und Ueberzeugung; Reise des Kupferschmiede-Meisters Friedrich Höhne in Weimar über Bremen nach Nord-Amerika und Texas in den Jahren 1839, 1840, und 1841 . . . (Weimar, Hoffman, 1844).

Naumann, Jakob. *Jacob Nauman's Reise nach den Vereinigten Staaten von Nordamerika, siebenjähriger Aufenthalt in denselben, und Rückkehr nach Deutschland—Mittheilungen für Auswanderungelustige, mit Gewerbe, besonderes Beziehung auf Ackerbau, Handel und Gewerbe; herausgegeben von Prof. Friedrich Bülau* (Leipzig, J. C. Hinrichs, 1850).

Meeker, Ezra. *Ox-Team Days on the Oregon Trail*. Howard R. Driggs, ed. (Yonkers-on-Hudson, N. Y., World Book Co., 1922).[58]

"Reminiscences of Mrs. Frank Collins, Nee Martha Elizabeth Gilliam." Fred Lockley, ed. *Oreg. Hist. Soc. Quar.*, XVII (1916), 358–72.

Two narratives by Germans describe trips in America during 1839 and later. Friedrich Höhne's book tells of a trip down the Ohio and Mississippi and Jacob Naumann's also relates events of a descent of the Ohio. He also mentions travel up the Mississippi, visits among Germans in Illinois, and the return journey.

Ezra Meeker as a boy traveled with his family in 1839 from the wilds of Ohio to Lockland, near Cincinnati, walked from this city to Attica, Indiana, and later traveled to Iowa and the West. His book is an entertaining story of the joys of a pioneer boyhood. Although the reminiscences of Mrs. Frank Collins are mainly devoted to Oregon, they mention her trip through the Midwest with an emigrant train.

Brewster, Edward. "From New York to Illinois by Water in 1840: Diary of My Trip West." Lewis Beeson, ed. *Mich. Hist.*, XXXII (1948), 270–89.

Buckingham, James. *The Eastern and Western States of America* (3 vols., London, Fisher, 1842).

Comfort, Elwood. "Philadelphia to Michigan: 1840." Philip P. Mason, ed. *Mich. Hist.*, XXXVIII (1954), 397–409.

"Diaries of S. H. Laughlin, of Tennessee, 1840, 1843." *Tenn. Hist. Mag.*, II (1916), 43–85.[59]

"Diary of Anna R. Morrison, Wife of Isaac L. Morrison." Miriam M. Worthington, ed. *Jour. Ill. State Hist. Soc.*, VII (1914), 34–50.[60]

Rabb, Mrs. Kate (Milner). *A Tour Through Indiana in 1840; the Diary of John Parsons of Petersburg, Va.* (New York, Robert M. McBride Co., 1920). Reprinted from a series of articles in the *Indianapolis Star.*[61]

Ricord, Jacob. "Recollections of Indian Life on Old Man's Creek in 1840." *Ia. Hist. Rec.,* VIII (1892), 370–73.

Steele, Mrs. Eliza R. *A Summer Journey in the West* (New York, John S. Taylor and Co., 1841).

"Life and Journal of John Sutherland." Ella Lonn, ed. *Miss. Val. Hist. Rev.,* IV (1917), 362–70.[62]

Wills, Rev. William Henry. "A Southern Traveler's Diary in 1840." *Publications of the Southern Historical Association,* VII (1903), 349–52, 427–32; VIII (1904), 23–39, 129–38.[63]

After buying five hundred acres of government land in Illinois in 1839, Edward Brewster and his family traveled by steamboat and lake steamer to build a farm there. He wrote a rather rambling diary of the trip. An Englishman, James Silk Buckingham, an ex-member of Parliament, visited the Midwest in 1840 and wrote a lengthy analysis. Volume three contains interesting descriptive matter pertaining to a journey down the Ohio, then up the Mississippi and Illinois rivers, across the Illinois prairies and his return to the East by way of the Great Lakes. Although critical, the book endeavors to be impartial. A diary by Elwood Comfort, a Quaker, whose manuscripts will be mentioned later in this chapter, tells of a trip from Philadelphia to Cleveland, Toledo, and Vermontville, Michigan, a settlement he and his family founded and named. The 1840 diary of S. H. Laughlin, Tennessee politician and journalist, describes travel to Cincinnati and up the Ohio River to Wheeling. The journal by Mrs. Anna R. Morrison gives an account of a journey from New York to Jacksonville, Illinois, during November and December, 1840.

Perhaps the most unusual of all American travel diaries is Mrs. Kate M. Rabb's *A Tour Through Indiana in 1840.* This is the story of "John Parsons" as told in the form of a fictitious diary of travel from Petersburg, Virginia, to Wheeling, down the Ohio to Cincinnati and Madison and then to Richmond, Indianapolis, Logansport, Crawfordsville, Terre Haute, and Vincennes. Parsons is described as a handsome, intelligent boy, a college graduate, only twenty-three at the time he wrote the diary; but the many literary touches could hardly have been written by such a youth. What Mrs. Rabb actually wrote was historical fiction based upon her reading and knowledge of the frontier.

Brief and unimportant is Jacob Ricord's "Recollections." Mrs. Eliza R. Steele's *A Summer Journey* . . . is a notebook of descriptions and observations made during a trip in 1840 through the Great Lakes to Chicago, across Illinois to Peoria, and on the Illinois, Mississippi, and Ohio rivers. "The Life and Journal of John Sutherland," a twenty-one-year-old Indiana farmer attending a Whig gathering at the battlefield of Tippecanoe in late May, 1840, consists of extracts from his hastily written notes which are brief but of historical value. A North Carolina minister, Reverend William Henry Wills, wrote a rather good diary, a small part of which describes a trip down the Ohio past Cincinnati and Cairo to the South and return. The comments on social habits, institutions, and places are spirited and amusing.

Pitezel, John H. Journal, *ca.* 1840. MS. Garrett Biblical Institute, Evanston, Illinois.

DuBois, ———. Diary on the Midwest, 1840–1843. MS. New York Public Library.

Smith, Rev. George Nelson. Journals, 1840–1879. MSS. Library of Congress. A copy of the diary for 1840–1845 is in the Burton Historical Collection, Detroit.

Comfort, Elwood. Diary of Accounts, 1840. 172 pp.; Diary of a journey from Tecumseh, Michigan, to Philadelphia, 1848. 60 pp. MSS. In the Elwood Comfort Papers, 1837–1848. Listed in *Guide to Manuscript Collections in Michigan,* Vol. I, Entry 100.

Hillhouse, Capt. William. Diary, 1840–1844. MS. Listed in *Guide to Manuscript Collections in Iowa,* Vol. I (Des Moines, 1940), p. 30.

Wilkinson, Rev. Asbury. Diary, Nov. 7, 1840–May 30, 1853. 7 vols. of notebooks, totalling 1244 pp. MSS. Indiana Historical Society Library, Indianapolis.

John H. Pitezel, a Methodist missionary to the Michigan upper peninsula, wrote a journal about 1840 of events which seems to have been used as a basis for his book, *Lights and Shades of Missionary Life . . . during Nine Years Spent in the Region of Lake Superior* (Cincinnati, Western Book Concern, 1860). A diary by a man named DuBois describes a journey during 1840–1843 from the East to New Orleans, up the rivers to Wheeling, and from there to Ashtabula and then his return east. Includes miscellaneous prose and poetry. The journals of the Reverend George Nelson Smith are accounts by another missionary to the Indians in Michigan. The two diaries of Elwood Comfort need no comment. Captain William Hillhouse's diary contains comments on a trip through Iowa, on witnessing Indian treaties by chiefs of the Sac and Fox tribes, on business with various Mississippi River steamboat captains, and on other interesting events in the early history of the Iowa Territory. The diary of Asbury Wilkinson, a Methodist circuit rider in southern Indiana, although almost entirely about services and activities of Methodist Episcopal churches in that area, gives interesting information on other preachers, locally important persons, and Asbury University.

Brown, William. *America: A Four Years' Residence in the United States and Canada: Giving a Full and Fair Description of the Country, as it Really Is, with the Manners, Customs, & Character of the Inhabitants* . . . (Leeds, the Author, 1849).

Haraszthy de Mokcsa, Count Agoston. *Utazás Eiszakamerikában* (2 vols., Pest, Hungary, 1844). Extract in English in "Haraszthy's Wisconsin Experience." Stephen Kliman, trans. *Wis. Mag. Hist.,* XXIII (1939), 182–206.[64]

Lanman, Charles. *Essays for Summer Hours* (Boston, Hillard, Gray and Co., 1841).

——— "The West in 1842–44." *Mag. Hist.,* XIX (1914), 193–203.

——— "Prairie du Chien." *Mag. Hist.,* XXI (1915), 105–9.

——— "The Voyageur." *Mag. Hist.,* XX (1915), 135–40.

——— *A Summer in the Wilderness; Embracing a Canoe Voyage up the Mississippi and around Lake Superior* (New York, D. Appleton and Co.; Philadelphia, G. S. Appleton, 1847).

——— *Adventures in the Wilds of the United States and British American Provinces* (2 vols., Philadelphia, J. W. Moore, 1856).

——— "Lake Winnipeg." *Mag. Hist.,* XXI (1915), 113–16.[65]

An Englishman's interest in American customs is shown in William Brown's *America,* which describes events beginning in about 1840 and contains an account of a trip from Buffalo to Cleveland and Berea, Ohio, where Brown saw a camp meeting. A Hungarian nobleman, Count Agoston Haraszthy, came to the United States in 1840 and traveled by way of the Great Lakes to Wisconsin, where he founded Sauk City. His two-volume travel narrative describes the trip. The work shows his appreciation of the beauty of the Lakes and contains descriptions of Madison, Milwaukee, and other places in his adopted land. In 1849 he went to San Diego.

The writings of Charles Lanman, author, artist, and traveler, include numerous touristic sketches of travel in the northern Midwest. His *Essays for Summer Hours* describes Michigan and the wilderness region of about 1840. "The West in 1842–44" is an account of Indians at the Falls of St. Anthony, the customs of the Sioux, and fur trapping in this region. "The Voyageur," a romantic piece evincing Lanman's appreciation of the northern atmosphere, relates a trip in 1845 to the headwaters of the Mississippi and along the shores of Lake Superior by canoe. "Prairie du Chien" briefly describes the town of that name and tells of his visit to an Indian lodge. His *Adventures in the Wilds . . .* was compiled from his earlier works, including *A Summer in the Wilderness;* the first volume recounts events on a trip from St. Louis to Nauvoo, Prairie du Chien, the Falls of St. Anthony, Lake Superior, Sault Ste. Marie, and Mackinaw, and the second volume tells of travel on the Ohio River. "Lake Winnipeg" describes Chippewa customs Lanman observed during a visit in 1846.

Pancoast, Charles Edward. *A Quaker Forty-Niner.* Anna P. Hannum, ed. (Philadelphia, University of Pennsylvania Press, 1930).

Starin, Frederick J. "Diary of a Journey to Wisconsin in 1840." *Wis. Mag. Hist.,* VI (1922), 73–94, 207–32, (1923), 334–45.[66]

"Autobiography of Abel Mills." *Jour. Ill. State Hist. Soc.,* XIX (1926), 94–209.

Manford, Erasmus. *Twenty-five Years in the West* (Chicago, E. Manford, 1867).

DeSmet, Pierre-Jean. *Letters and Sketches, with a Narrative of a Year's Residence among the Indian Tribes of the Rocky Mountains* (Philadelphia, M. Fithian, 1843).

——— *Life, Letters, and Travels of Father Pierre-Jean de Smet. . . .* Hiram M. Chittenden and Alfred T. Richardson, eds. (4 vols., New York, F. P. Harper, 1905).[67]

Howe, W. P. "Fifty-two Years in Iowa." *Ann. of Ia.,* 3rd Series, I (1894), 566–73.

A Quaker Forty-Niner is the lengthy and interesting autobiography of Charles E. Pancoast, a Philadelphia Quaker. It relates his travels in 1840 by river to St. Louis, a trip into Illinois in 1841, and a trek to the Far West with the gold seekers of 1849. Frederick Starin, a native of New York state, journeyed by way of the Great Lakes to Milwaukee, walked to East Troy, and proceeded by wagon to Whitewater, Wisconsin, and later to Madison and Fort Madison. His diary gives a valuable picture of early settlements in southern Wisconsin and makes fair reading. Abel Mills' autobiography describes his journey as a child with his parents down the Ohio to Putnam County, Illinois, in the spring of 1840. Planting crops, making bricks for a house, and seeing numerous rattlesnakes are among the experiences he mentions. Erasmus Manford was a Universalist preacher whose book tells of many preaching tours in Illinois beginning in 1840. Although the book contains much theological matter, it includes descriptions and local data.

The works of Pierre-Jean DeSmet give a realistic insight into the unselfish life and labors of this important Jesuit missionary. They begin in 1840, describe a trip up the Missouri River and across the present state of Nebraska, and continue until 1873, the date of DeSmet's death. He worked among the Indians from St. Louis to Puget Sound and Altrabasca, collecting valuable information on Indian manners, customs, warfare, legends, and traditions. Also to be mentioned is W. P. Howe's narrative of a trip in 1840 from Ohio to Iowa by two-horse wagon and his recollections of later events.

Chapter 13

Midwestern Travel Accounts by Dickens,

James K. Paulding, Margaret Fuller, Francis Parkman,

and Others—1841–1845

Although bankrupt or badly in debt in 1840–1841, the newer American states and territories continued to grow. Emigrants from eastern America, Canada, and Europe made their way to Buffalo and left there for the West, according to one account, at the rate of twelve hundred a day.[1] The city of Cleveland, with its thriving business district, attracted many, but others proceeded to Sandusky, Toledo, and Detroit. The Central Railroad was in operation to Ypsilanti, cars ran from Adrian to Monroe by 1840, and the Erie and Kalamazoo, the first railroad built in Ohio, ran thirty-four miles. If the travelers proceeded to Chicago, they found the streets of this settlement unpaved, but there were pretty cottages built north of the Chicago River and a ferry boat operated by ropes to carry passengers across it. Milwaukee was only seven years old when Margaret Fuller saw it in 1843, but by 1846 it was incorporated into a city. The old French towns in Illinois, however, remained much the same. After the National Pike or Cumberland Road was completed between Wheeling and Springfield, Illinois, in 1838, no highway was more often traveled by wagons, stagecoaches, and mail-coaches. Travel down the Ohio River was still popular, and the large river towns were thriving, Cincinnati boasting a population of over forty-six thousand in 1842. St. Louis, the western terminus for most river travel, also prospered. To the west lay Independence and the Indian country, which did not yet attract large numbers of visitors.[2]

English, Swedish, German, Scotch, Norwegian, and native American travelers visited the Midwest from 1841 to 1845. Marches of United States dragoons, the Oregon emigration of 1843, journeys on the Santa Fé Trail, overland expeditions, and the Mormon migration were events recorded in more than one narrative. These years saw an influx of distinguished visitors such as Dickens, Paulding, and Margaret Fuller, among others. A comparison of the content of the later tales with those by the French priests, fur traders, and other early travelers reveals two great differences: pictures of relatively settled regions, especially east of the Mississippi, as against accounts of the primitive wilderness; and numerous polished tales and books as against many crudely written and fragmentary records.

Morleigh [pseud.]. *Life in the West; Back-wood Leaves and Prairie Flowers: Rough Sketches on the Borders of the Picturesque, the Sublime, and Ridiculous, Extracts from the Note Book of Morleigh in Search of an Estate* (London, Saunders and Otley, 1842).

Oliver, William. *Eight Months in Illinois. With Information to Immigrants* (Newcastle upon Tyne, William A. Mitchell, 1843). Reprinted at Chicago (Walter M. Hill, 1924).

Simpson, Sir George. *Narrative of a Journey Round the World, During the Years 1841 and 1842* (2 vols., London, Henry Colburn, 1847).[3]

Three works by British writers describe Midwestern travel during 1841. Morleigh voyaged from England to America and visited Cleveland, Detroit, Goderich, Mackinaw, Chicago, Racine, and the Fox River country. He narrates events in a sprightly manner and in dialog. William Oliver's *Eight Months in Illinois,* written to give information to emigrants, relates events in a trip from England to New York and Pittsburgh, by river to St. Louis, and across Illinois and Indiana to Columbus, Cleveland, Buffalo, and farther east. Sir George Simpson's *Narrative of a Journey Round the World . . .* describes a trip from London to Boston and Montreal and up the Great Lakes to the Sault and Lake Superior.

Negus, Charles. "Early Times in Iowa." *Ann. of Ia.,* 1st Series, X (1872), 80–96, 161–75; XII (1874), 81–103, 195–218.

Smith, Ophia D. "A Trip to Iowa in 1841. [Excerpts from the Journal of Alfred West Gilbert]." *The Palimpsest,* XVII (1936), 329–41.

Swan, Lansing B. *Journal of a Trip to Michigan in 1841* (Rochester, George P. Humphrey, 1904). Extract in "Seeing Michigan in 1841," *Mich. Hist.,* XVIII (1934), 93–113.[4]

Gale, George. Diary, 1841. MS. Listed in Alice E. Smith, comp. *Guide to the Manuscripts of the Wisconsin Historical Society* (Madison, 1944), No. 246.

The diary of Charles Negus describes Fairfield, Iowa, relates a weird dream, and includes a narrative of the life of Thomas Dickey. Ophia D. Smith narrates Alfred West Gilbert's trip from Cincinnati to Iowa in 1841. Gilbert was a young surveyor who wrote a journal of travel by steamer to Keokuk and visits to several Iowa and Illinois towns. A diary by Lansing B. Swan records his journey in the same year from Rochester to Buffalo, by boat to Detroit, by rail to Ypsilanti, by wagon to Ann Arbor, by stage to Kalamazoo, and then to Niles and St. Joseph, Michigan, and his return by way of the Great Lakes and Detroit. The narrative is brief and realistic. It reveals an appreciation of nature and has amusing comments such as the following: "But for ugly looking women Michigan assuredly excels, as well as in dirty taverns and good looking 'school marms.'"

George Gale's short diary is that of a trip from New York to Milwaukee and Walworth County, Wisconsin.

Bidwell, John. *A Journey to California With Observations about the Country, Climate and the Route to This Country* (Weston, Mo.?, 1842?). Reprint, H. I. Priestley, ed. (San Francisco, John Henry Nash, 1937); also in Charles C. Royce, *John Bidwell, Pioneer, Statesman, Philanthropist* (Chico, Calif., 1906), pp. 8–37.[5]

"Diary of John Findlay Torrence, 1841." *Ky. Hist. Soc. Reg.*, VII (1909), 59–65.

Williams, Joseph. *Narrative of a Tour from the State of Indiana to the Oregon Territory in the Years 1841–2* (Cincinnati, the Author, 1843). Reprinted at New York (Cadmus Book Shop, 1921) and in LeRoy R. and Ann W. Hafen, eds. *To the Rockies and Oregon, 1839–1842* (Glendale, Calif., Arthur H. Clark Co., 1955), pp. 207–86.[6]

John Bidwell, of New York City, was with the first emigrant train to California and wrote an important diary of his journey by wagon from Independence, Missouri, along the Kansas and Platte rivers to Fort Laramie and farther west in 1841. His comments on the country, natural history, crops, weather, and social conditions are impersonal. The diary of John F. Torrence, well-written, describes a trip up the Ohio River to Pennsylvania with General William Henry Harrison. The diary by Joseph Williams, a sixty-three-year-old Methodist preacher, is an account of an early wagon train trek in 1841 from Ripley County, Indiana, to Indianapolis, Terre Haute, St. Louis, Westport, and up the Kaw to the Far West and return. It is religious in tone, historically valuable, realistic, and makes good reading.

Thacker, W. H. "An Account of a Party Perishing in a Blizzard in Northern Illinois." *Jour. Ill. State Hist. Soc.*, VI (1914), 517–22.

Sage, Rufus B. *Scenes in the Rocky Mountains and in Oregon, California, New Mexico, Texas, and the Grand Prairies* (Philadelphia, Carey and Hart, 1846). Reprint edited by LeRoy R. and Ann W. Hafen (Glendale, Calif., Arthur H. Clark Co., 1956).

Unonius, Gustaf. *Minnen fraen en sjuttonaerig vistelse i nordvestra Amerika.* [Memoirs.] (2 vols., Uppsala, Sweden, W. Schultz, etc., 1861, 1862). Translated by Nils W. Olsson as *A Pioneer in Northwest America, 1841–1858* (2 vols., Minneapolis, University of Minnesota Press, 1950).[7]

Byers, S. H. M. "Out West in the Forties." *Ia. Hist. Rec.*, V (1889), 365–74.

Diary and Letters of Rutherford Birchard Hayes. . . . Charles R. Williams, ed. (5 vols., Columbus, Ohio State Archaeological and Historical Society, 1922–1926).[8]

W. H. Thacker's narrative describes how men and horses were frozen in northern Illinois during the great blizzard of 1841–1842. Rufus B. Sage's *Scenes in the Rocky Mountains . . .* is a spirited, detailed story of his hunting and trapping expeditions beginning in 1841 in Kansas and Nebraska, on to Fort Platte, then on to the Rockies, and his return to Arkansas in 1844. The

English translation of the work of Gustaf Unonius, a Swedish minister, covers seventeen years of his memoirs. For twelve dollars, he traveled from New York to Chicago. He was impressed by the wide avenues of Detroit but found nearly everything in Mackinac old and fallen into disrepair. He eventually settled as a farmer in Wisconsin Territory. Disappointment with America is evident, however, in much of his book. "Out West in the Forties," by S. H. M. Byers, describes a trip in 1841 down the Ohio and up the Mississippi to Burlington, Iowa, and later life on the isolated Iowa prairie: weather, scenery, wild animals, and hardships of pioneer life. Rutherford B. Hayes, nineteenth President of the United States, began his personal diary at Kenyon College, Ohio, in 1841 and continued it until his death. Recorded are events in his student life at Columbus and Gambier, Ohio, his work in Cincinnati, and his years as governor of the state.

Dickens, Charles. *American Notes for General Circulation* (2 vols., London, Chapman and Hall, 1842).[9]

The most distinguished visitor to the Midwest before 1850 was Charles Dickens, whose fiction had already appeared in several frontier periodicals. At thirty years of age, already so famous that he was denied all privacy, he decided to visit America, primarily to inspect Cairo, Illinois, because of his heavy and unwise investment in Illinois bonds. The bonds had been sold by Darius B. Holbrook, who had organized the Cairo City and Canal Company, and who, in Europe, had advertised Cairo as "a grand city at the junction of the Mississippi and Ohio rivers." Dickens' disappointment in this town may account, in part, for his unfavorable opinion of the United States expressed in his *American Notes*, his summary of his 1842 trip.[10]

After reaching Pittsburgh, Dickens and his wife traveled by steamboat down the Ohio, stopping at Cincinnati and Louisville, and arrived at St. Louis on April 11, 1842, where he had been invited to be honor guest at a public dinner. The following day he and nine other young men toured Looking Glass Prairie, Illinois, and stopped at Belleville. Dr. J. F. Snyder, a boy at the time of Dickens' visit, remembered having seen him and maintained that *American Notes* shows the author's deliberate emphasis upon the unfavorable aspects of the trip. To Dickens, Belleville was "a small collection of wooden houses, huddled together in the very heart of the bush and swamp." Snyder was unimpressed by the celebrity's appearance and noted his bored yet amused attitude.[11] Dickens ate luncheon at the Mansion House in Belleville[12] and proceeded to Lebanon. Although he enjoyed a late afternoon picnic, he pronounced the prairies desolate and uninteresting. After a night at the Mermaid Hotel, he arose at five in the morning and walked around the town before the party returned to St. Louis. The Planters' House, where he stayed in St. Louis, reminded him of an English hospital, and the town seemed to him to be hot and humid, with vast rivers and tracts of unhealthful swampland around it.

On his return trip he described the Mississippi as "that intolerable river dragging its slimy length and ugly freight abruptly off towards New Orleans." Although Cairo was to him a "detestable morass," he found the country between Cincinnati and Columbus beautiful and luxuriant and Columbus itself, where he was given a reception, clean and pretty. He traveled by stagecoach from Cincinnati to Tiffin, by rail to Sandusky, which he reached on April 23, and thence by steamboat to Buffalo.

His satirical style did not, of course, win friends for him in America, but the favorable comments he made are often overlooked. *American Notes* was reprinted many times. He deplored American bad manners, including the practice of spitting in public. Detestable were the institution of slavery, already abolished in England, and the American political system. At least he called attention to the Midwest as had no previous visitor, and this first American tour gave him material which he utilized in *Martin Chuzzlewit.*

Haller, Maj. Granville Owen. Journal of a Scout, Sunday, April 10, 1842–Monday, April 25, 1842. MS. Pacific Northwest Collection, University of Washington Library, Seattle.[13]

Paxton, Mrs. Eliza Bailey. Journal of a Journey from Washington County, Pa., to Richland County, Ohio, 1842. 11 pp. MS. Listed in Elizabeth Biggert, comp. *Guide to the Manuscript Collections in the Library of the Ohio State Archaeological and Historical Society* (Columbus, 1953), No. 832.

Rice, Justin. Diary, September 5–October 4, 1842. MS. Three-page typed excerpt from his journal describing journey from Mackinac Island to La Pointe, 1842, in the Francis Raymond Papers. Burton Historical Collection, Detroit.

Major Haller's journal mentions certain events in his life as a scout in the Midwest. Mrs. Eliza Bailey Paxton describes Cadiz, Wooster, Mansfield, and other Ohio towns and mentions talk in the state of abolition. Justin Rice's diary covers his journey and the period of negotiations with the Chippewa Indians at La-Pointe, Wisconsin, to obtain title to their land in that vicinity. A treaty was signed on October 4, 1842, with Robert Stuart acting as agent for the United States government.

Journal of Medorem Crawford. An Account of his Trip Across the Plains with the Oregon Pioneers of 1842 . . . (Eugene, Ore., Star Job Office, 1897). Reprint in "Sources of the History of Oregon," *Oreg. Hist. Soc. Pubs.,* I, Part I (1897), 5–28.[14]

Hastings, Lansford Warren. *The Emigrants' Guide to Oregon and California, Containing Scenes and Incidents of a Party of Oregon Emigrants* . . . (Cincinnati, George Conclin, 1845). Reprint ed. Charles Henry Carey (Princeton, Princeton University Press, 1932).[15]

Lang, John D. and Samuel Taylor, Jr. *Report of a Visit to Some of the Tribes of Indians, Located West of the Mississippi River* (Providence, Knowles and Vose, 1843).[16]

Paulding, James Kirke. "Illinois and the Prairies." *Graham's Magazine,* XXXIV (1849), 16–25. Reprinted as "A Tour of Illinois in 1842," Mentor L. Williams, ed., *Jour. Ill. State Hist. Soc.,* XLII (1949), 292–312.

———— Sketch of the Great Lakes. *The Columbian Lady's and Gentleman's Magazine,* I (1844), 258–66. Reprint ed. M. L. Williams, *Mid-America,* XXXII (1950), 67–79.[17]

A native of New York, Medorem Crawford kept a journal of a trip from Havana, New York, to St. Louis and overland with Elijah White's party to Oregon from March to October, 1842. It is mainly statistical, with miscellaneous notations and an expense record. A more interesting account of part of the same trip appears in the narrative of Lansford W. Hastings, who did not join the White caravan until it reached Elm Grove, Kansas, but who took command because of dissatisfaction with White's management. The train split in two but consolidated again upon reaching Fort Laramie.

After ministering to the Indians, two Quakers, John D. Lang and Samuel Taylor, Jr., wrote a report of their trip to the Southwest in 1842 and made recommendations for the treatment of the Indians. They traveled by various means from the East to Cleveland and Detroit, across Michigan to the mouth of the St. Joseph River, from there to Chicago, Galena and Dubuque, then across the prairies, down the Mississippi to St. Louis, and then to St. Charles, Westport and Shawnee. From there they went on horseback to the Kickapoos above Fort Leavenworth and to various other Indian tribes in Kansas, Oklahoma, and Arkansas.

James Kirke Paulding, novelist, author and friend of Washington Irving, in his "Illinois and the Praries" tells of a seven-thousand-mile tour through the South and West in 1842 with Martin Van Buren. This included a steamboat trip up the Illinois River, a ride to Chicago by horseback, and a voyage by way of the Great Lakes to Detroit and Niagara. In *John Bull in America; or, the New Munchausen* (1825), Paulding makes one of his English fictional characters extremely critical of the manners and reading habits of the frontiersman.

Russel, Elizabeth Everitt. "Hunting Buffalo in the Early Forties." *Journal of American History,* XVIII (1924), 137–48.

Hamilton, William T. *My Sixty Years on the Plains* . . . (New York, Forest and Stream Publishing Co., 1905). Reprint ed. E. T. Sieber (Columbus, O., Long's College Book Co., 1951).

Salzbacher, Dr. Joseph. *Meine Reise nach Nord Amerika im Jahre 1842; mit Statistische Bemerkungen über die Zustände der katholischen Kirche bis auf die neuste Zeit* . . . (Vienna, Wimmer, Schmidt and Leo, 1845).

Scott, Rev. James Leander. *A Journal of a Missionary Tour through Pennsylvania, Ohio, Indiana, Illinois, Iowa, Wiskonsin and Michigan; comprising a concise description of different Sections of the Country: Health of Climate, Inducements for Emigration, with the embarrassments; the Religious condition of the People; Meetings Connected with the Mission; and of the Great Western Prairies* (Providence, R. I., the Author, 1843).[18]

Aitken, W. A. *A Journey up the Mississippi River from Its Mouth to Nauvoo, the City of the Latter Day Saints* (Ashton, Eng., Williamson, 1843?).[19]

Elizabeth E. Russel's article narrates a trip from St. Louis to and from the Yellowstone in 1842 made by her father, a fellow traveler in the party of Sir Drummond Stewart, a Scotchman, mentioned in Chapter 11, who had come to America to hunt buffalo. She mentions the Missouri River, Westport, and the Kansas and Nebraska plains. Much the same route was covered by another Scotchman, W. T. Hamilton, who settled in St. Louis with his father and started westward in 1842, events mentioned at the beginning of his autobiography. Joseph Salzbacher, a German Catholic prelate, describes a trip by river to St. Louis, across Illinois by stage to Vincennes, and back to the East. The *Journal* of the Reverend James L. Scott, Seventh-day Baptist missionary, is a useful and historically valuable diary of travels in 1842 through Ohio into Iowa, Wisconsin, and Michigan. He comments on the climate, scenery, emigration prospects, and religion. W. A. Aitken, an Englishman, describes a journey, probably in 1842, up the Mississippi to Nauvoo, Illinois, and a visit to the Mormon colony there.

Burnett, Peter Hardeman. *Recollections and Opinions of an Old Pioneer* (New York, D. Appleton and Co., 1880). Chapters 3–6 reprinted in *Oreg. Hist. Soc. Quar.,* V (1904), 64–99. Abridged in George Wilkes, *An Account and History of the Oregon Territory* . . . (London, William Lott, 1846).[20]

Lyman, H. S. "Reminiscences of William M. Case." *Oreg. Hist. Soc. Quar.,* I (1900), 269–95.

"Journal of Leonard E. Harrington." *Utah Hist. Quar.,* VIII (1940), 1–64.[21]

"Oscar Canfield's Pioneer Reminiscences." *Wash. Hist. Quar.,* VIII (1917), 251–60.

Regan, John. *The Emigrant's Guide to the Western States of America; or, Backwoods and Prairies; Containing a Complete Statement of the Advantages and Capacities of the Prairie Lands* . . . (2nd ed., Edinburgh, Oliver and Boyd, etc., etc., 1852).

Marshall, William Rainey. "Reminiscences of Wisconsin—1842 to 1848." *Mag. West. Hist.*, VII (1888), 247–50.[22]

"Journal of Paul Nelson Spofford (1842–1848)." Samuel T. Moore, ed. *Mich. Hist.*, XXIX (1945), 327–34.

Grange, Mattie Munsell. "Michigan Memories." *Mich. Hist.*, XXXVIII (1954), 116–40.

King, John Lyle. Diary, 1842–1874. 11 vols., about 350 to 900 pp. per vol. MSS. Indiana Historical Society Library, Indianapolis.

An early California and Oregon pioneer, Peter H. Burnett, wrote a historically valuable account of his trip by ox-team along the Platte River Valley and farther west in 1842 and 1843. He mentions the scarcity of fuel and the killing of buffalo and antelope along the way. H. S. Lyman's "Reminiscences of William M. Case," well-written, covers events in a trip to Platte City, Missouri, in 1842 and to Omaha in 1844. More interesting is his "Reminiscences of Hugh Cosgrove," to be described in Chapter 14. Leonard E. Harrington's journal (1842–1846) gives an account of a journey to Nauvoo, a later trip on the Mississippi and Ohio rivers and by canal to Cleveland and Buffalo, his return to Nauvoo, and a final trek with the Mormon group to Salt Lake City. He puts much emphasis on preaching and educational work in the Mormon church. Oscar Canfield's narrative (1842–1847) records a trip from the East to the Far West, but only a few sentences are about the Midwest.

A Scotchman, John Regan, immigrated to the United States in 1842 and in *The Emigrant's Guide to the Western States of America* writes extensive notes on his travels in Missouri, Iowa, and Illinois during 1842–1847. From New Orleans he ascended the Mississippi to St. Louis and settled at Ellisville, Illinois. He devotes long, chatty chapters to climate, agriculture, schools, trade, and travels in Illinois. The "Reminiscences" of William R. Marshall, later governor of Minnesota, gives a brief account of his search for copper along the St. Croix River in Wisconsin and mentions other events of his young manhood. Paul Nelson Spofford narrates his trip from New York to Detroit, Sault Ste. Marie, Chicago, Galena, and the Mississippi River in 1842 and events in 1848. Mattie Munsell Grange describes her father's journey to Michigan in 1842, his settlement at Kalamazoo, her birth in 1846, and later incidents.

The eleven-volume diary of John Lyle King, a lawyer in Madison, Indiana, gives details of social life in and about Madison. King's style is somewhat literary. The information about people, places, and events is historically valuable.

Anonymous. Journal of an Expedition of U. S. Dragoons from Fort Leavenworth, 1843. MS. In the Philip St. George Cooke Papers. Burton Historical Collection, Detroit.

Shaw, A. C. R. Diary, 1843. MS. Copy. Listed in *Guide to the Manuscript Collections of the Oregon Historical Society* (Portland, Oregon Historical Records Survey, 1940), No. 403.

Waldo, Daniel. "Critiques. Narrative and remarks, 1843." 3 pp. MS. Listed in Mary C. Withington, comp. *A Catalogue of Manuscripts in the Collection of Western Americana Founded by William R. Coe, Yale University Library* (New Haven, Yale University Press, 1952), No. 499. Quoted briefly in Hubert H. Bancroft, *History of Oregon* . . . (2 vols., San Francisco, The History Co., 1886–1888), I, 403, 405, and in Clifford M. Drury, *Marcus Whitman* . . . (Caldwell, Idaho, The Caxton Printers, 1937), pp. 332, 342.

The anonymous author of the "Journal" seems to have been a soldier in an expedition of United States dragoons sent to protect traders on the Santa Fé Trail. The diary by A. C. R. Shaw covers a trip from Illinois to Missouri during July and August,

1843. The brief manuscript of Daniel Waldo tells of his participation in the 1843 emigration to Oregon in order to improve his health.

Adams, Ephriam. *The Iowa Band* (Boston, Congregational Publication Society, 1870).

Anonymous. "Journal of a Steamboat Voyage from St. Louis to Fort Union." In Hiram M. Chittenden, *The American Fur Trade of the Far West* . . . (3 vols., New York, F. F. Harper, 1902), III, 984–1003. Reprint by Academic Reprints (Stanford, Calif., 1954).

"The Journal of John Boardman." *Utah. Hist. Quar.*, II (1929), 99–121.[23]

Clark, Julius T. "Reminiscences of the Chippewa Chief; Hole-in-the-Day." *Wis. Hist. Soc. Colls.*, V (1869), 378–86.

The Iowa Band describes missionary activity in early Iowa and tells of the movement of the Band, a troop of ten young Andover graduates sponsored by the Home Missionary Society, across northern Illinois in 1843. The steamboat of the "Journal of a Steamboat Voyage" was the *Omega*, and Audubon and his party were among the passengers. The entries begin on April 25, 1843, and contain interesting observations on travel, Indians, and the fur trade. "The Journal of John Boardman" relates the story of a wagon train bound for Oregon in the same year. Boardman started from Shawnee Mission, Kansas, and joined the Oregon group, traveling up the Blue and Platte rivers. Julius T. Clark recalls a trip in 1843 from Madison by steamboat to the Sault and LaPointe and dealings with the Chippewa tribe and Chief Hole-in-the-Day.

Fuller, Sarah Margaret [Marchesa d'Ossoli]. *Summer on the Lakes in 1843* (Boston, C. C. Little and J. Brown; New York, C. S. Francis and Co., 1844).[24]

Clarke, Sarah Freeman. "A Visit to Wisconsin in 1843." Nils W. Olsson, ed. *Wis. Mag. Hist.*, XXXI (1948), 452–60.

The well-known writer, transcendentalist, leader in the feminist movement, and friend of Ralph Waldo Emerson, Margaret Fuller, was invited to tour the Midwest in 1843 by one of her acquaintances, James Freeman Clarke, who believed that she needed a vacation from the strain of Boston life and sent her fifty dollars to help defray expenses. Clarke, his sister, and Miss Fuller journeyed to Niagara Falls and by way of the Great Lakes to Chicago. Later Miss Fuller visited her uncle at Oregon, Illinois, passing through Fox River, Geneva, Galena, Hazelwood, Kiskwaukee, and Belvidere on the way. In spite of the carpet of spring flowers, the prairies at first seemed desolate and dull to her, and she deplored the dearth of genius among Westerners; but in Chicago she enjoyed walking along the shores of Lake Michigan and, having found a new beauty in the region, left it regretfully. The Midwest inspired several poems before she left Illinois. Her *Summer on the Lakes* describes her impressions of such places as Milwaukee, Mackinaw, the Sault, and St. Joseph's Island. It is a pleasant and well-written travelogue. Sarah Freeman Clarke's "A Visit to Wisconsin" is in the form of a letter relating events during the trio's wagon ride from Chicago to Wisconsin. Brief and somewhat whimsical.

Up the Missouri with Audubon; the Journal of Edward Harris. John F. McDermott, ed. (Norman, University of Oklahoma Press, 1951).[25]

John James Audubon, whose journals have been previously described in Chapter 7, proposed that his friend and fellow ornithologist, Edward Harris, a Philadelphian, join him on a trip up the Missouri River in 1843. Harris consequently took a river steamer from Wheeling down the Ohio and traveled by way of Cincinnati, Edwardsville, Illinois, and St. Louis to Independence and farther west. Among the many entries, both long and short, one of the most interesting is an account of a buffalo hunt. He mentions later travel from Louisville to New Orleans.

Johnson, Overton and William H. Winter. *Route across the Rocky Mountains, with a Description of Oregon and California* (Lafayette, Ind., John Semans, 1846). Reprinted in *Oreg. Hist. Soc. Quar.,* VII (1906), 62–104, 163–210, 291–327; reprint ed. Carl L. Cannon (Princeton, Princeton University Press, 1932).[26]

Kennerly, William Clark. "My Hunting Trip to the Rockies in 1843." *Colorado Magazine,* XXII (1945), 23–38.[27]

Field, Matthew C. *Prairie and Mountain Sketches.* Kate L. Gregg and John F. McDermott, eds. (Norman, University of Oklahoma Press, 1957).

Lennox, E. H. *Overland to Oregon. History of the First Emigration to Oregon in 1843.* Robert Whitaker, ed. (Oakland, Cal., Privately printed, 1904).

Nesmith, James W. "Diary of the Emigration of 1843." *Oreg. Hist. Soc. Quar.,* VII (1906), 329–59.[28]

"William T. Newby's Diary of the Emigration of 1843." Harry N. M. Winton, ed. *Oreg. Hist. Soc. Quar.,* XL (1939), 219–42.[29]

Penter, Samuel. "Recollections of an Oregon Pioneer of 1843." *Oreg. Hist. Soc. Quar.,* VII (1906), 56–61.

The History of Oregon, Geographical and Political. By George Wilkes, . . . To Which Is Added a Journal of the Events of the Emigrating Expedition of 1843 . . . by a Member of the Oregon Legislature . . . (New York, W. H. Colyer, 1845).[30]

During the early 1840's the United States encouraged the settlement of Oregon in order to keep it from the British. In addition to Daniel Waldo's unpublished narrative, mentioned earlier in this chapter, several other tales of the Oregon emigration of 1843 have been preserved. Overton Johnson and William H. Winter were two young men from Indiana with Western land fever. Their journey began in Independence, Missouri, in the latter part of May, 1843, and took them across the Kansas prairies and up the North Platte River to Fort Laramie and thence West. They showed appreciation of the natural beauty of the region. In "My Hunting Trip to the Rockies," William C. Kennerly describes for Bessie A. Russell the William Drummond Stewart expedition of 1843 from St. Louis to Kansas Landing and Westport by boat and by horse to Fort Laramie and return. It is well written: accounts of a buffalo hunt and fear of attack by Indians are interesting parts. The same trip is recorded in the *Prairie and Mountain Sketches* by Matthew C. Field, London-born New Orleans newspaper man. E. H. Lennox relates in *Overland to Oregon* the history of the first Oregon emigration party in 1843. He joined Marcus Whitman, Applegate, and others. James W. Nesmith, a young man from Maine, writes of the same emigration. He describes traveling from Independence under the leadership of Dr. Elijah White, appointed Indian agent in Oregon, and his (Nesmith's) eventual abandonment of the White group to join the Whitman party. Hunting deer and antelope for food and avoiding Indian attacks were necessary duties. William T. Newby's diary notes his difficult trip from southwest Missouri to Westport and up the Platte with the Oregon emigrants. Samuel Penter, after living in Tennessee and Arkansas, moved to Missouri in 1842 and left for Oregon the following year with two horses, a small wagon, and a cow. He describes his trip up the Platte. George Wilkes' journal is a combination of narrative and diary forms.

Kemper, Jackson. "Bishop Jackson Kemper's Visit in Minnesota in 1843." Grace L. Nute, ed. *Minn. Hist.,* VII (1926), 264–73.[31]

Lapham, Increase Allen. "A Winter's Journey from Milwaukee to Green Bay, 1843." *Wis. Mag. Hist.,* IX (1925), 90–97.[32]

"Journal of James Darwin Maxwell." Doris M. Reed, ed. *Ind. Mag. Hist.,* XLVI (1950), 73–81.[33]

Young, John Edward. "From Central Illinois to the Shenandoah Valley in 1843." Mrs. Frederick L. Hamil, ed. *Jour. Ill. State Hist. Soc.,* XXV (1932), 167–89.[34]

Patton, Rev. William. "Journal of a Visit to the Indian Mission, Missouri Conference." *Mo. Hist. Soc. Bull.,* X (1954), 167–80.

"Journal of Pierson Barton Reading." *Society of California Pioneers Quarterly,* VII (1930), 148–98.[35]

"A Fragmentary Journal of William L. Sublette." *Miss. Val. Hist. Rev.,* VI (1919), 99–110.[36]

Gerstäcker, Friedrich Wilhelm Christian. *Streif- und Jagdzüge durch die Vereinigten Staaten Nord-Amerika . . .* (2 vols., Dresden, 1844, reprinted, Leipzig, Arnold, 1856).[37]

Bishop Jackson Kemper, whose earlier tales have been mentioned in Chapters 11 and 12, wrote two narrative letters about his visit to Fort Snelling to consider founding a mission there. Increase Allen Lapham describes a walk from Milwaukee to Green Bay. His brief account is rather didactic in tone but contains descriptions of scenery, weather, and Indians. James D. Maxwell's diary tells of travel in the fall of 1843 from Bloomington, Indiana, by way of Lafayette, Toledo, and Lake Erie to Philadelphia. Also going east in this year was John Edward Young, who set out on horseback from his home near Alton, Illinois, to visit his grandfathers in Kentucky and Virginia. Although poorly written, his diary of the trip is an interesting record. Reverend William Patton served in various ministerial circuits in Missouri. His journal of 1843 tells of a trip from Booneville, Missouri, to Marshall and Independence, and mentions meeting Indians and visiting the Shawnee Central Meeting House in Kansas. Pierson B. Reading, a native of New Jersey, wrote a journal of his 123-day journey from Westport by way of Fort Boise to Monterey, California, in 1843. More important than any of these men was William L. Sublette, fur trader, merchant, and roamer of the West, who wrote of an 1843 hunting trip in Missouri with Sir William Drummond Stewart, mentioned in Chapter 11. Sublette left Westport on May 27, 1843, but the diary covers only about three hundred miles of travel.

No later than 1843 Friedrich Gerstäcker left Germany and supported himself in the United States by whatever work he could obtain. He wrote a diary of his adventures which, when published in Germany, won him immediate literary fame. His first American trip took him from New York to Cleveland, Canton, St. Louis, and farther west. His *Streif-und Jagdzüge* is a long work and reveals a traditional German outlook. He wrote several novels and other books based upon his knowledge of America, including *Die Flusspiraten des Mississippi* (Leipzig, 1848; English translation, *The Pirates of the Mississippi*, London, G. Routledge and Co., 1850), which has a Midwestern setting.

Davis, John. "A Diary of the Illinois-Michigan Canal Investigation, 1843–1844." Guy A. Lee, ed. *Ill. State Hist. Soc. Trans., 1941,* XLVIII (1943), 38–72.

Bishop [Henry Benjamin] *Whipple's Southern Diary, 1843–1844.* Lester B. Shipper, ed. (Minneapolis, University of Minnesota Press, 1937).[38]

Parrish, Rev. Edward Evans. "Crossing the Plains in 1844." *Oreg. Pion. Assn. Trans.,* 16th Annual Reunion (1888), 82–122.[39]

Salter, William. *Sixty Years and Other Discourses, with Reminiscences* (Boston and Chicago, The Pilgrim Press, 1907).

———— "My Ministry in Iowa, 1843–1846." Philip D. Jordan, ed. *Ann. of Ia.*, 3rd Series, XIX (1935), 539–53, 592–613; XX (1935), 2s–49. A memoir based on this in *Ann. of Ia.*, 3rd Series, VII (1906–1907), 592–607, and reprinted in *Jackson County Annals* (Ia.), No. 4 (1907), 42–54. Summarized and quoted in "The Discovery of William Salter's Almanac Diary," *Ann. of Ia.*, 3rd Series, XVII (1930), 466–69.[40]

The Journal of Theodore Talbot. Charles H. Carey, ed. (Portland, Ore., Metropolitan Press, 1931). Summary in *Oreg. Hist. Soc. Quar.*, XXX (1929), 326–38.[41]

Platt, Mrs. Elvira G. "Some Experiences as a Teacher among the Pawnees." *Kans. State Hist. Soc. Colls.*, XIV (1915–1918), 784–94.

———— "Reminiscences of a Teacher among the Nebraska Indians, 1843–1885." *Neb. Hist. Soc. Trans. Reports,* III (1892), 125–43.

Larpenteur, August L. "Recollections of the City and People of St. Paul, 1843–1898." *Colls. Minn. Hist. Soc.*, IX (1901), 363–94.

John Davis's diary tells of a trip from Wheeling by river to St. Louis and thence to Chicago to investigate the possibilities of constructing a canal to connect Lake Michigan and the Mississippi River system. It includes descriptions of nature and topography. Bishop Henry B. Whipple as a young man visited the South and West to improve his health and wrote a diary about his journey in 1843 and 1844 up the Mississippi to St. Louis and up the Ohio and overland from Ohio to the East. His observations are acute and show his interest in social and religious conditions. He became the first Protestant Episcopal bishop of Minnesota and an important reformer of the United States Indian system. Another clergyman, the Reverend Edward E. Parrish, wrote a rather interesting diary (1843–1845) of a pioneer trek to Oregon in 1844, with comments on Ohio, Kentucky, Missouri, and the Great Plains. The Reverend William Salter, a member of "the Iowa Band," described earlier in this chapter, preached in various Iowa towns in that year and became missionary pastor in Maquoketa, where he served during parts of the years 1844 to 1846, frequently riding the circuit and preaching. His *Sixty Years and Other Discourses* is a book of reminiscences covering most of his life, but the events of 1843 to 1846 appear in diary form also in "My Ministry in Iowa. . . ."

Lieutenant Theodore Talbot's journal is the story of his adventures from April to October, 1843, with the John C. Frémont expedition which was mapping territory from Missouri to the Oregon coast. It includes an account of Talbot's steamboat trip from Wheeling to St. Louis, where he met Frémont, and a section dealing with the Gold Rush period and later, 1847–1852. Mrs. Elvira G. Platt and her husband joined the Reverend John Dunbar and started a school for the Pawnee Indians in territory now a part of Kansas and Nebraska. She wrote two narratives of her experiences, one covering the years from 1843 to 1847 and the other beginning in 1843 and extending to 1883. Dealing mainly with events other than travels is "Recollections of . . . St. Paul," by August L. Larpenteur, an Easterner who moved to Minnesota.

Buck, I. E. Journals, 1843, 1845. 6 pp. MS. Listed in Biggert, *Guide*, No. 217.

Sharpe, James M. "J. M. Sharpe, Private journal from March 1, 1843, to Feb. 10, 1848." 63 pp. MS. Listed in Withington, *A Catalogue of Manuscripts in the Collection of Western Americana*, No. 420.

I. E. Buck's journals of travel tell of his going from Delaware, Ohio, to Cincinnati in 1843 to see the laying of the corner-

stone of the Mount Ida Observatory there and of a journey from Delaware to Upper Sandusky, Ohio, in 1845. James Sharpe sought his fortune as a traveling merchant by buying merchandise in Cincinnati and trading in Indiana, St. Louis, Independence, Keokuk, Nauvoo, and other towns on the Mississippi, Missouri, and Red rivers. He wrote a journal of his wanderings, which includes an interesting account of Joseph Smith, the Mormon.

Allen, Capt. James. "Report and Journal of Captain James Allen's Dragoon Expedition in the Territory of Iowa in the Summer of 1844." Jacob Van der Zee, ed. *Ia. Jour. Hist.*, XI (1913), 68–108. Reprinted from House Document 168, 29th Congress, 1st Session, 1845–1846. Extracts relating to South Dakota in *Sou. Dak. Hist. Colls.*, IX (1918), 347–68.

———— "The Dragoons in the Iowa Territory, 1845." Robert Rutland, ed. *Ia. Jour. Hist.*, LI (1953), 57–78, 156–82.[42]

Letts, Allie M. "The Search for a Shilling. A True Story of Territorial Days in Iowa." *Ann. of Ia.*, 3rd Series, I (1893), 38–46.

Baxter, Henry. "Rafting on the Alleghany and Ohio, 1844." *Penna. Mag. Hist. Biog.*, LI (1927), 27–78, 143–71, 207–43.[43]

Lewis, Rev. George. *Impressions of America and the American Churches . . .* (Edinburgh, W. P. Kennedy, etc., 1845).

Wait, William Bell. *River, Road and Rail; William Richardson's Journey from Louisville to New York in 1844* (Patterson, N. J., Federal Printing Co., 1942).

Captain James Allen's journal of the expedition of the First Dragoons contains extensive description of the land and shows his interest in protecting the rights of the Indians. His diary of 1844–1845 mentions weather and military activities in the region which is now Iowa and South Dakota. Allie M. Letts also describes early days in Iowa Territory. Her narrative tells the story of a youth who became lost on his way to Burlington, Iowa.

An interesting insight into the life of a river raftsman appears in the diary of Henry Baxter. He steered his father's lumber down the Ohio River to sell it wherever he could find a market and then returned to Pittsburgh by steamer. The entries are long and contain observations on nature, weather, towns, industries, social life, religion, and literature and they give an excellent picture of the culture of the times. Another river traveler in 1844 was the Reverend George Lewis, British clergyman, whose *Impressions of America and the American Churches* contains a brief account of a trip up the Mississippi to St. Louis and by stage across Illinois to Vincennes. William Bell Wait's book needs no comment.

Harris, N. Sayre. *Journal of a Tour in the "Indian Territory," Performed by Order of the Domestic Committee of the Board of Missions of the Protestant Episcopal Church, in the Spring of 1844, by their Secretary and General Agent* (New York, Daniel Dana, Jr., 1844).[44]

Wharton, Maj. Clifton. "The Expedition of Major Clifton Wharton in 1844." *Kans. State Hist. Soc. Colls.*, XVI (1923–1925), 272–305.[45]

"Reminiscences of Honorable John Minto, Pioneer of 1844." H. S. Lyman, ed. *Oreg. Hist. Soc. Quar.*, II (1901), 119–254.

N. Sayre Harris undertook an inspection of missionary posts in Indian Territory, visiting the Choctaw, Seminole, Cree, Cherokee, Osage, and other tribes. His journal, interesting but hastily written, describes his trip from the East and New Orleans up the Mississippi as far north as Fort Leavenworth. He criticizes the work of the missions and proposes schools for the Indians as a means of building up the church. Major Clifton Wharton's visit to Indians farther north was entirely different in purpose: to warn the savages that they must treat the white people well and to show that the American government could punish them if they did not. His diary records his march from Leavenworth to Pawnee villages on the Platte River and to the country of the Otoes, Pottawatomies, Ioways, and Sioux on the Missouri River, and return. Some of the entries are fragmentary.

John Minto, an Easterner who journeyed to the Far West in 1844, tells a rather spirited tale of a trip to Oregon. His narrative includes his journey down the Ohio and up the Missouri and South Platte and contains interesting dialog.

Gause, Eli. Diary, October 18–November 11, 1844. MS. notebook, handsewn. Indiana Historical Society Library, Indianapolis.

McNeely, William. Journal of a Trip to the Far West, c. 1844. MS. Illinois State Historical Library, Springfield.

Putnam, Israel Ward. Journal, 1844–1845. MS. Listed in Biggert, *Guide,* No. 866.

Spalding, William Witter. Diary, 1844–1848. MS. Michigan Historical Collections, University of Michigan, Ann Arbor.

Eli Gause, a Quaker who moved from Ohio to Spiceland, Indiana, in 1834, kept a journal and expense account of an 1844 trip from Henry County, Indiana, to attend a Quaker meeting in Baltimore. The manuscript is barely legible. William McNeely relates a trip to the Far West and return to Wayne County, Illinois.

The journal of Israel Ward Putnam describes a trip from Belpré, Ohio, to Hamilton College, and gives an insight into student life there. William Witter Spalding's interesting diary relates events on a trip with D. S. Cash from State Diggins, Wisconsin Territory, to Michigan in 1844 and a journey by steamboat and canoe from Galena, Illinois, by way of the Mississippi, St. Croix, and Brule rivers to Copper Harbor and the mouth of the Ontonagon River during the spring and summer of 1845. The complete diary continues to 1848.

Koch, Albert C. *Reise durch einen Theil der Vereinigten Staaten von Nordamerika in den Jahren 1844 bis 1846* (Dresden and Leipzig, Arnold, 1847).

The Trapper's Guide; a Manual of Instructions for Capturing all Kinds of Fur-bearing Animals, and Curing their Skins; with Observations on the Fur Trade, Hints on Life in the Woods, and Narratives of Trapping and Hunting Excursions: by S. [amuel] Newhouse, and Other Trappers and Sportsmen. . . . J. H. Noyes, ed. (Wallingford, Conn., the Oneida Community, 1865).[46]

Grinnell, Josiah Bushnell. *Sketches of the West, or the Home of the Badgers . . .* (Milwaukee, I. A. Hopkins, 1845).

Webb, James Josiah. *Adventures in the Santa Fé Trade, 1844–1847.* Ralph P. Bieber, ed. (Glendale, Cal., Arthur H. Clark Co., 1931).

A travel narrative by a German, Albert C. Koch, gives an account of a trip down the Ohio and up the Mississippi on the way to Iowa Territory. Newhouse's *The Trapper's Guide* includes narratives of hunting excursions during 1844–1845 into the country around Chicago and mentions a trip up the north branch of the Chicago River to Mud Lake, about twelve miles distant. Josiah B. Grinnell's *Sketches of the West* is a series of narrative letters describing his travels through the Wisconsin Territory, where he visited Milwaukee, Racine, Madison, and other places during 1844–45. The second edition contains additional letters written in 1846 from other Wisconsin towns. His attitude was favorable and he foresaw the future growth of the region. James J. Webb

describes, in a vividly written narrative, a trip from St. Louis to Santa Fé in 1844, his return in 1845, and another trip in 1846.

Guadal P'a, the Journal of Lieutenant J.[ames] W. Abert, from Bent's Fort to St. Louis in 1845. H. Bailey Carroll, ed. (Canyon, Texas, Panhandle-Plains Historical Society, 1941).[47]

Anonymous. "The Dragoons in the Iowa Territory, 1845." Robert Rutland, ed. *Iowa Jour. Hist.,* LI (1953), 157–82.

Sumner, Capt. Edwin Vos. "Captain Edwin V. Sumner's Dragoon Expedition in the Territory of Iowa in the Summer of 1845." Jacob Van der Zee, ed. *Iowa Jour. Hist.,* XI (1913), 258–67. Reprinted from *United States Senate Documents,* 1st Session, 29th Congress, No. 1 (1845–1846), pp. 217–20.[48]

Lieutenant James W. Abert's journal covers an exploratory expedition by the Corps of Topographical Engineers. It contains scientific details and notes on the journey. Abert's notes, written during the Kearny expedition of 1846, are mentioned in Chapter 14. The anonymous author, a soldier, of "The Dragoons in the Iowa Territory" describes the march of the Dragoons northward from Fort Des Moines over twelve hundred miles of the Iowa Territory, much of it in the Sioux country. Some of his wording is picturesque and much of it is in diary style. The same trip is described in Captain James Allen's narrative of 1845, previously mentioned in this chapter, and in Captain Edwin Sumner's journal. Sumner explained the white man's law to the Indians in order to stop the Red River halfbreeds from hunting in United States territory.

Duerst, Mathias. "Diary of One of the Original Colonists of New Glarus [Wis.], 1845." Translated by John Luchsinger from the German. *Wis. Hist. Soc. Colls.,* XV (1900), 292–337.[49]

James, Thomas H. *Rambles in the United States and Canada during the Year 1845, with a Short Account of Oregon, by Rubio* [pseud.] (London, J. Ollivier, 1846).

A leader of a colony of Swiss emigrants, Mathias Duerst, wrote an interesting and informative narrative about his voyage in 1845 from Europe and his trip overland to St. Louis, Illinois, and Wisconsin, where he settled. Thomas H. James, an Englishman, was unfavorably impressed by America. His book relates incidents in his journey by way of the Ohio and Mississippi to St. Louis and return. Well written.

Anonymous. "A Walk on the Streets of St. Louis in 1845. By a Traveler." *Mo. Hist. Soc. Colls.,* VI (1928), 33–40. Reprinted from the *St. Louis Business Directory for 1847.*

Greenough, William W. "Tour to the Western Country." *Mass. Hist. Soc. Procs.,* XLIV (1911), 339–54.

Groff, R. B. "Early Experience in Iowa." *Ann. of Ia.,* 1st Series, IX (1871), 693–700.

Waugh, Alfred S. *Travels in Search of the Elephant. The Wanderings of Alfred S. Waugh, Artist. . . .* John F. McDermott, ed. (St. Louis, Missouri Historical Society, 1951).

Everett, Philo M. "Story of Philo Everett's Trip from Jackson, Michigan, to Marquette in 1845." R. A. Brotherton, ed. *Inland Seas,* I (Oct., 1945), 23–28; II (Jan., 1946), 45–49.

——— "Recollections of the Early Explorations and Discovery of Iron Ore on Lake Superior." *Mich. Hist. Colls.,* XI (1888), 161–74.

Marvill, Lewis. "First Trip by Steam to Lake Superior." *Mich. Hist. Colls.,* IV (1883), 67–69. Reprinted from the *Detroit Free Press and Tribune,* Mar. 26, 1882.

Moore, Nathaniel F. *Diary of a Trip from New York to the Falls of St. Anthony in 1845.* Stanley Pargellis and Ruth L. Butler, eds. (Chicago, Newberry Library, University of Chicago Press, 1946).[50]

Sears, George W. *Woodcraft* (New York, Forest and Stream Publishing Co., 1884). Reprinted under the nom de plume "Nessmuk," *Mich. Hist. Mag.*, XV (1931), 634–44.

Thayer, George W. "From Vermont to Lake Superior in 1845." *Mich. Hist. Colls.*, XXX (1906), 549–66.

Bagley, Calvin C. "Western Trip." *Wis. Mag. Hist.*, XXXVII (1954), 237–39.

The anonymous traveler writes interesting descriptions of various streets of St. Louis. William W. Greenough also saw St. Louis during a tour in 1845 from the East to Chicago, Rockford, Freeport, Galena, Quincy, and Missouri; his is a valuable and readable narrative. R. B. Groff describes touching at St. Louis during the same year on a river trip down the Ohio and up the Mississippi to Burlington, Iowa; his account shows an appreciation of nature and scenery. An Alabama artist, Albert S. Waugh, made a trip in 1845 from the South up the rivers to St. Louis, Lexington, Independence and Santa Fé.

Several tales describe travel in the northern Midwest in 1845. Philo M. Everett wrote two readable narratives of trips to the Upper Peninsula. The second covers the period, 1845–1857, and relates a trip from Jackson to Detroit and by steamer to Mackinaw. He mentions Copper Harbor and the Indians. Lewis Marvill records a steamer journey in 1845 from Detroit to Sandusky, Milan, and Lake Superior and a storm on the lake. Also voyaging on the Great Lakes in 1845 was Nathaniel Fish Moore, president of Columbia College, professor, and amateur mineralogist, who visited Detroit, Chicago, and the Falls of St. Anthony and returned home by way of the Ohio River. His diary, written in straightforward prose, describes lead smelting in Galena, Illinois, and Indian dances of the upper Mississippi. George W. Sears, an Easterner, in *Woodcraft* tells in an occasionally humorous style of a hike from Saginaw to Muskegon in October, 1845, and of hunting in the wilderness. George W. Thayer's tale is rather poorly written. From Buffalo he traveled by water to Detroit, took the Michigan Central Railroad to Battle Creek, and proceeded by stage and steamer to Mackinaw.

Sometime in the mid-1840's, perhaps in 1845, Calvin C. Bagley journeyed from the East to Buffalo, Cleveland, Detroit, and Milwaukee and delivered a speech, later published as a narrative, recounting his travels. He commented favorably on the soil and grass of Wisconsin; he liked Milwaukee least of the cities visited.

Cummins, Mrs. Sarah J. *Autobiography and Reminiscences* (LaGrande, Ore., LaGrande Printing Co., 1914).

Howell, John Ewing. "Diary of an Emigrant of 1845." *Wash. Hist. Quar.*, I (1907), 138–58.[51]

The Narrative of Samuel Hancock, 1845–1860 (New York, R. M. McBride and Co., 1927).[52]

"The Diary of Jacob R. Snyder." *Quarterly of the Society of California Pioneers*, VIII (1931), 224–60.[53]

Mrs. Sarah J. Cummins, John E. Howell, Samuel Hancock, and Jacob R. Snyder wrote narratives of overland trips in 1845. Mrs. Cummins' account of a journey to Oregon is part of her autobiography. Howell, a native of West Virginia, recorded a trip from Clark County, Missouri, on April 11 up the Platte and by way of the Black Hills to Oregon. His diary has brief entries mentioning the route and scenery. Samuel Hancock's journal tells of travel adventures and sufferings, escape from the Indians, and events in the Far West as late as 1860. Snyder's diary begins at Independence and relates events in a journey up the Platte, across the plains to Fort Laramie, and thence to California. The entries contain brief, routine descriptions.

Parkman, Francis. "Old Northwest Journal, 1844–1845." In *The*

Journals of Francis Parkman. Mason Wade, ed. (2 vols., New York and London, Harper and Brothers, 1947), I, 281–316.

——— "The Oregon Trail." *Knickerbocker Magazine*, XXIX (1847), 160–65. Additions made and published in book form as *The California and Oregon Trail; Being Sketches of Prairie and Rocky Mountain Life* (New York, George P. Putnam's, 1849).[54]

The Old Northwest diary-journal of Francis Parkman, the youthful New England historian whose struggles to collect material for his books are well known, tells of his quest for Pontiac material. He proceeded from Buffalo by way of the Great Lakes to Detroit, Mackinaw, and the Sault to Palmer, Michigan, where he sifted through six trunks of papers belonging to Lieutenant McDougall, Pontiac's prisoner during the siege of Detroit. On his return he crossed over to Canada to search for descendants of early French traders and then went east by way of Lake Erie.

One of the most famous of all Midwestern travel books, of course, is Parkman's *The California and Oregon Trail*, an account of his trip to the Rocky Mountains in 1846. The first few chapters are a detailed account of the journey from St. Louis up the Missouri to Westport, from there to Leavenworth and then up the Platte to Fort Laramie. The last chapters describe the return by way of the Santa Fé Trail and the Missouri River to St. Louis. Particularly interesting are the characterizations of the men who accompanied him: Quincy Adams Shaw, his friend and cousin, to whom he later dictated the manuscript of the book; Henry Chatillon, their powerful guide; and Deslauriers, a muleteer of French descent. No other book contains a more graphic presentation of the panorama of Western migration during this period: the wagon trains met along the way, the emigrant camps, the Indians, the trappers, and the buffalo hunters.

Brown, William Reynolds. *Minnesota Farmers' Diaries* (St. Paul, Publications of the Minnesota Historical Society, 1939).[55]

Dietrickson, Johannes W. C. *Reise Blandt de Norske Emigranter i "De Forende Nordamerikanske Fristater"* [*Travels among the Norwegian Emigrants in the United North American Free States*] (Stavanger, L. C. Kielland, 1846).[56]

"The Diary of Charles Peabody." William E. and Ophia D. Smith, eds. *Hist. Phil. Soc. of Ohio Bull.*, XI (1953), 274–92; XII (1954), 119–39.

Day, Rev. E. H. "Sketches of the Northwest." *Mich. Hist. Colls.*, XIV (1890), 205–56.

"The Journals of William Walker, Provisional Governor of Nebraska Territory [1845–   ]." William E. Connelley, ed. *Neb. Hist. Soc. Procs. Colls.*, 2nd Series, III (1899), 157–406.

One of the few sources for the history of Minnesota in the 1840's is the diary of William R. Brown, who was born near Urbana, Ohio, in 1816 and moved to Minnesota in 1841. His diary, which covers the period beginning on October 25, 1845, through June 14, 1846, is valuable as a record of pioneer farming, containing much information on agriculture and prices. Johannes Dietrickson, a Lutheran clergyman born in Norway, who emigrated to America, wrote about his travels in Wisconsin and Illinois in 1845–1846. He preached extensively and attempted to rule the Norwegian Church in America but left the country in 1856 when he believed his usefulness was over. The diary of the Reverend Charles Peabody, district secretary for the American Tract Society, describes a trip from Buffalo to Toledo by steamboat, by canal and river to Cincinnati, Dayton, Franklin, Oxford, Hamilton, Chillicothe, and Louisville, a return to Ohio, and a journey to Kentucky, Missouri, Iowa, and Illinois, all in 1845–1846. His observations on the customs and what he considered the depravity of the people, his appreciation of nature, and his religious sentiments make it an interesting account. Another minister who traveled west in 1845 was the Reverend E. H. Day, who went by boat to the Sault to deliver sermons to the Indians. His "Sketches" (1845–1848) describes Indian customs and dances. Early life in the Nebraska Territory is related in the diary of William Walker.

Palmer, Joel. *Journal of Travels over the Rocky Mountains, to the Mouth of the Columbia River; Made During the Years 1845 and 1846* . . . (Cincinnati, J. A. and U. P. James, 1847). Reprinted in R. G. Thwaites, ed. *Early Western Travels* . . . (32 vols., Cleveland, Arthur H. Clark Co., 1906), Vol. XXX.[57]
"Extracts from the Journal of John Steele." *Utah Hist. Quar.,* VI (1933), 3–28.[58]
"Diary of Lorenzo Dow Young." *Utah Hist. Quar.,* XIV (1946), 133–71.

Journals by Joel Palmer and John Steele record overland trips in 1845–1846. Palmer proceeded from Laurel, Indiana, to St. Louis, St. Charles, Booneville, Independence, and up the Platte. His helpful notes for emigrants made the work an important guide book for a decade. Thwaites pronounced it the best account of the Oregon Trail. The extracts from the diary of John Steele, an Irishman who became a Mormon, describe in detail his trip down the Ohio to St. Louis and Nauvoo, and the Mormon migration across Iowa to Fort Leavenworth and Salt Lake. Lorenzo D. Young, also a Mormon, records the same migration but continues to a later date, 1852. He presents Mormon life and hardships realistically.

Adams, Dennis Patterson. Journal, September, 1845–November, 1846. 47 pp., typescript. Listed in Biggert, *Guide,* No. 115.
"Atalantian Journal," 1845, 1848. MS. periodical. Indiana Historical Society Library, Indianapolis.
Francis, Samuel Dexter. Journal, describing life in Vermont, 1841–1845; travels in the Midwest and stay in Illinois, 1845–1852; and the daily record of a trip across the Plains and life in Oregon, 1852–1862. 209 pp. MS. Listed in Withington, *A Catalogue of Manuscripts in the Collection of Western Americana,* No. 203.

Dennis Patterson Adams' journal tells of a trip from Marietta, Ohio, to Boston on a sailing vessel built at Harman, Ohio, and a return overland. Unpublished manuscripts issued periodically by the Terre Haute Atalantian Literati Society contain tales of two flat-boat journeys on the Mississippi by members of the group. "The Beauties of Flat-boating" begins on July 28, 1845 (Vol. II, No. 14), and ends on September 22, 1845 (Vol. III, No. 1). "Journal of a trip to New Orleans" begins on June 26, 1848 (Vol. IV, No. 3), and ends on September 18, 1848 (Vol. IV, No. 12). The journal of Samuel Dexter Francis contains brief entries and comments on such things as crops, weather, and politics.

Chapter 14

Last of the Early Midwestern Travel Tales, Including

Walt Whitman's Notebook — 1846–1849

Decisive events in Mexico and the Far West were the reasons for numerous journeys through the Midwest during the final years of the pioneer period. The migration of the Mormons to the Salt Lake Valley, the conquest of New Mexico, the Mexican War, further settlement of Oregon and California, and the Gold Rush of 1849 were all subjects of journals. Public interest shifted to the settlement of the Far West, and the Middle West of an earlier day gradually ceased to exist. Railroads now threaded their way along the shores of Lake Erie, steamboats churned up and down the Ohio and Mississippi rivers, and towns sprang up far from the main water courses. More and more travelers thronged westward and more and more journals and tales were written. The number of well-known visitors writing accounts during these years, however, was small, the most important being Sir Charles Lyell, Horace Greeley, and Walt Whitman.

Many Midwestern travel accounts are poorly written; others, some of which are by well-known authors, rank as classics of their kind. Numerous details of history would remain unknown were it not for their existence. Indeed, as has been said, they give history a personal touch that helps make it interesting. Their contribution to other literary forms, such as narrative poetry and the novel, is also apparent. They are an important part of American literature.

Foote, Sarah. "A Pioneer Trek from Ohio to Wisconsin." *Journal of American History*, XV (1921), 25–36. Reprinted from a private edition published in 1905.[1]

"The Mexican War Journal of Henry S. Lane." Graham A Barringer, ed. *Ind. Mag. Hist.*, LIII (1957), 383–434.

Lyell, Sir Charles. *A Second Visit to the United States of North America* (2 vols., London, J. Murray, 1849).[2]

Silliman, Miss Sue I. "Overland to Michigan in 1846." *Mich. Hist.*, V (1921), 424–34.

Rauschenbusch, August. *Beschreibung einer Seereise von Bremen nach New York . . .* (2nd ed., Altona, 1847).

Ziegler, Alexander [Haas, Carl de]. *Skizzen einer Reise durch Nordamerika und Westindien, mit besonderes Berücksichtigung des deutschen Elements, der Auswanderung und der landwirtschaftlichen Verhältnisse in dem neuen Staate Wisconsin*

(2 vols., Dresden and Leipzig, Arnoldische Buchhandlung, 1848).

Révoil, Bénédict Henry. *Chasses et Pêches de l'Autre Monde* (Paris, Cadot, 1856). Translated, with revisions, as *Shooting and Fishing in the Rivers, Prairies, and Backwoods of North America* (London, Tinsley Bros., 1865).

Sarah Foote, a girl in her teens, interestingly describes her journey by ox-team and wagon from her home at Wellington, Ohio, by way of Norwalk, Perrysburg, and Edwards Prairie to Winnebago County, Wisconsin, in 1846. A brief section of Henry S. Lane's Mexican War journal mentions travel in central Indiana to Kentucky during the same year. Sir Charles Lyell, the eminent British geologist, visited the Midwest in the spring of 1846 and recorded his journey up the Mississippi to New Madrid and up the Ohio to New Harmony, where he saw Robert Owen. Later, in *A Second Visit to the United States . . .* he described Evansville, Cincinnati, and Pittsburgh. He gives details of the topography, with emphasis on geological formations. Miss Sue Silliman's story of Samuel Silliman's trek from his home in the East through Ohio to Michigan is a series of narrative letters which devotes much attention to prices.

Three foreign-language narratives were written by travelers in the Middle West in 1846. August Rauschenbusch, a German, described his trip by way of the Great Lakes to Chicago, by stage to Alton, and by steamboat to St. Louis. This appears in the second edition of his book rather than the first, which seems to have been an account of the sea voyage only. Another German, Alexander Ziegler, wrote *Skizzen einer Reise . . .*, which includes an account of travel from Buffalo to Detroit, with comments on Detroit, Mackinac, Milwaukee, and places in Wisconsin, Illinois, and farther south seen during a journey down the Mississippi. One of the sketches in Bénédict Henry Révoil's work tells of an expedition into the Midwest and describes Chicago.

Clouston, Robert. "International Buying Trip: Fort Garry to St. Louis in 1846." Extracts. Elaine A. Mitchell, ed. *Minn. Hist.*, XXXVI (1958), 37–53.

"Recollections of George Andrew Gordon." *Kans. State Hist. Soc. Colls.*, XVI (1923–1925), 497–504.

Lamare-Picquot, F. V. "A French Naturalist in Minnesota." *Minn. Hist.*, VI (1925), 270–77. Translated from *Courier des États-Unis, organ des populations Franco-Américaines*, New York, Mar. 12, 1847.

Strong, William R. "A Journey from Urbana, Illinois, to Cook County, Texas in the Spring of 1846." *Jour. Ill. State Hist. Soc.*, IX (1916), 51–60.

The extracts from the narrative by Robert Clouston, leader of the Hudson's Bay Company's purchasing expedition from Minnesota to St. Louis, are a spirited account and contain interesting descriptions of places and comments on human nature and conduct. "Recollections of George Andrew Gordon" describes in a readable style an exciting buffalo hunt in Kansas in 1846. A French naturalist, F. V. Lamare-Picquot, wrote a narrative about Indian customs and life in Minnesota in 1846. The narrative of William R. Strong records the trek of a family by wagon and ox-team. It is well-written. The hardships—improper food and weather—of crossing the hot plains are realistically presented.

Abert, James William. . . . *Notes of a Military Reconnaissance from Fort Leavenworth, in Missouri, to San Diego, in California, including Parts of the Arkansas, Del Norte, and Gila Rivers* (Washington, Wendell and Van Benthuysen, 1848).[3]

"Journal of Marcellus Bell Edwards, 1846–1847." In *Marching with the Army of the West, 1846–1848.* . . . Ralph P. Bieber, ed. (Glendale, Calif., Arthur H. Clark Co., 1936), pp. 107–280.[4]

Emory, Lieut. Col. William Hemsley. *Notes of a Military Reconnaissance from Fort Leavenworth . . . to San Diego . . . made in 1846–7 with the Advanced Guard of the "Army of the West."* Executive Document 7, 30th Congress, 1st Session (Washington, Wendell and Van Benthuysen, 1848), pp. 15–126. Reprinted as *Notes of Travel in California* . . . (New York and Philadelphia, n.p., 1849), pp. 1–275, and at Albuquerque, N. Mex. (University of New Mexico Press, 1951).[5]

Gibson, Lieut. George Rutledge. *Journal of a Soldier under Kearny and Doniphan, 1846–1847.* Ralph P. Bieber, ed. (Glendale, Calif., Arthur H. Clark Co., 1935).[6]

"Journal of Abraham Robinson Johnston, 1846." In Bieber, *Marching with the Army of the West.* Also in Emory, *Notes of a Military Reconnaissance,* pp. 565–614.[7]

Robinson, Jacob S. *Sketches of the Great West. A Journal of the Santa Fe Expedition under Colonel Doniphan* . . . (Portsmouth, N. H., William B. Loud, 1848). Reprinted in *Mag. Hist.,* Extra Number 128 (1928); reprint, Carl L. Cannon, ed. (Princeton, Princeton University Press, 1932).[8]

Edwards, Frank S. *A Campaign in New Mexico with Colonel Doniphan* . . . (Philadelphia, Carey and Hart, 1847).[9]

Journal of William H. Richardson, A Private Soldier in Col. Doniphan's Command (Baltimore, Joseph Robinson, 1847). Reprinted in *Mo. Hist. Rev.,* XXII (1928), 193–236, 331–60, 511–42.[10]

Colonel Stephen W. Kearny, whose journal of 1820 has been mentioned in Chapter 9, after organizing the Army of the West at Fort Leavenworth in June, 1846, was ordered to march to Santa Fé, capture the town, and proceed to upper California. He reached Santa Fé on August 18 and proclaimed that New Mexico had become a part of the United States.[11] Several journals of this expedition exist. The one by James W. Abert, author of an 1845 tale mentioned in Chapter 13, consists of notes taken during the march from Leavenworth to Bent's Fort. Marcellus B. Edwards was a private. His diary covers much of the same trip and mentions fighting among the soldiers, drinking, and other incidents. The entries are long and speak of Doniphan's expedition against the Indians. Emory's *Notes* do not begin until August, 1846, but the trip from Washington to Fort Leavenworth is covered by a prefatory notice. They devote much space to topography, scenery, and scientific details. Gibson's *Journal* chronicles 607 miles of the journey from Leavenworth and emphasizes army life, people, places, and customs. Similar are the journals of Captain Abraham R. Johnston and Jacob S. Robinson. Wislizenus's narrative of the Doniphan expedition has been mentioned in Chapter 12. Frank S. Edwards's tale is the most

interesting account of this expedition. He includes his enlistment at St. Louis and his departure for the West. And the journal of William H. Richardson, who started from Maryland and passed through Missouri en route to Leavenworth, gives good details.

Across the Plains by Prairie Schooner; Personal Narrative of B. F. [Benjamin Franklin] Bonney of his Trip to Sutter's Fort, California, in 1846, and of his Pioneer Experiences in Oregon . . . (Eugene, Ore., Koke-Tiffany Co., 192–?).

Bryant, Edwin. *What I Saw in California, Being the Journal of a Tour, by the Emigrant Route and South Pass of the Rocky Mountains, Across the Continent of North America, the Great Desert Basin, and through California, in the Years 1846, 1847* (Philadelphia, Appleton and Co., 1848). Reprinted at Santa Anna, Calif. (Fine Arts Press, 1936).[12]

Cone, Anson S. "Reminiscences." H. S. Lyman, ed. *Oreg. Hist. Soc. Quar.,* IV (1903), 251–59.

Dickenson, Mrs. Luella. *Reminiscences of a Trip Across the Plains in 1846, and the Early Days of California* (San Francisco, The Whitaker and Bay Co., 1904).

"Diary of Virgil K. Pringle, 1846." *Oreg. Pion. Assn. Trans.,* 48th Annual Reunion (Portland, Ore., 1920), pp. 281–300.[13]

Thornton, Jessy Quinn. *Oregon and California in 1848* . . . (2 vols., New York, Harper and Bros., 1849).[14]

The nature of Benjamin F. Bonney's trip is evident from his title. Edwin Bryant, a Kentucky journalist, left Louisville on April 18, 1846, traveled to Independence, and then went with an emigrant wagon train to Santa Fé, an account of which he preserved in his diary. Anson S. Cone's brief "Reminiscences" describes a journey up the Missouri and Platte in the same year and mentions the murder of a member of his party by the Pawnees. Luella Dickenson's *Reminiscences* . . . chronicles another trip across the plains in 1846. The "Diary of Virgil K. Pringle, 1846" tells of travel from Hickory Grove, Illinois, through Missouri, by wagon along the Kansas and Platte rivers, and finally to Oregon. It mentions seeing buffalo and pioneer parties along the way; commonplace notes. Jessy Q. Thornton's diary is descriptive of an 1846 journey from Independence to the Far West. The Donner party, later to meet its well-known tragic fate, caught up with Thornton and his group during the trip.

Gilman, William Henry. Diary on the Midwest, 1846. 11 pp. MS. New York Public Library.

Chaney, Josiah B. Diaries, 1846–1851. MSS. Listed in Grace Lee Nute and Gertrude W. Ackermann, comps. *Guide to the Personal Papers in the Manuscript Collections of the Minnesota Historical Society* (St. Paul, Minnesota Historical Society, 1935), No. 43.[15]

Moss, Cecil. Reminiscences of the Middle West, Particularly Chicago, 1846–1926. 31 pp., typescript. Chicago Historical Society.

Portions of the diary of William H. Gilman, of Exeter, New Hampshire, pertain to a boat trip on the Ohio River in June, 1846. The remainder of the manuscript records Gilman's services on board naval vessels in the Pacific from 1853 to 1858. Josiah B. Chaney's diaries contain accounts of journeys between Dover, New Hampshire, and Moline, Illinois. Almost half of the Reminiscences of Cecil Moss, written in 1926, relates to the period before 1850. The narrative begins with log cabin days in Peoria County, Illinois, and treats problems the settlers faced, their modes of travel, and routes over which they came.

"Extracts from the Journal of Henry W. Bigler." *Utah Hist. Quar.,* V (1932), 35–64, 87–102, 134–60.[16]

"The Journal of Robert S. Bliss, with the Mormon Battalion." *Utah Hist. Quar.*, IV (1931), 67–96, 110–28.[17]
"The Journal of Nathaniel V. Jones, with the Mormon Battalion." *Utah Hist. Quar.*, IV (1931), 3–23.[18]
William Clayton's Journal; a Daily Record of the Journey of the Original Company of "Mormon" Pioneers from Nauvoo, Illinois, to the Valley of the Great Salt Lake (Salt Lake City, Published by the Clayton Family, 1921).[19]

In addition to the Mormon narratives mentioned in Chapter 13, four other known Mormon journals were written during 1846 and 1847. Henry William Bigler, a native of West Virginia, took part in the march of the Mormon Battalion and wrote a diary, partially published, of the trek from Council Bluffs to Santa Fé. It gives detailed descriptions of hardships and topography. Robert S. Bliss's journal chronicles the trip across Kansas to California and return to the Missouri River and Utah, with notes on scenery, Indians, and religious and personal affairs. The diary of Nathaniel Vary Jones, only partially published, includes a brief statement about the march of the Battalion from Council Bluffs and in bold details records the continuation of the journey from the Arkansas River westward to California and the return to Missouri. *William Clayton's Journal* is the official record of the Mormon migration. Clayton became a historian and Mormon high priest. A good, simply-written narrative, it gives pictures of scenery, personalities, factions, and mob violence.

Howe, Henry. "Some Recollections of Historic Travel over New York, New Jersey, Virginia and Ohio in the Seven Years from 1840 to 1847." *Ohio Arch. Hist. Quar.*, II (1889), 419–49.[20]
Lewis, Henry. "Henry Lewis on the Upper Mississippi." Bertha L. Heilbron, ed. *Minn. Hist.*, XVII (1936), 131–49, 288–301, 421–36. Reprinted in *Making a Motion Picture in 1848 . . .* Bertha L. Heilbron, ed. (St. Paul, Minnesota Historical Society, 1936).[21]
"Autobiography of Captain John G. Parker." *Mich. Hist. Colls.*, XXX (1906), 582–85.
Bross, William. "What I Remember of Early Chicago." In *Reminiscences of Chicago During the Forties and Fifties.* Mabel McIlvaine, ed. (Chicago, R. R. Donnelley and Sons Co., 1913).[22]
Lucy Larcom; Life, Letters, and Diary. Daniel D. Addison, ed. (Boston and New York, Houghton, Mifflin Co., 1894).[23]
Ludvigh, Samuel Gottlieb. *Licht- und Schattenbilder republikanischer Zustände; Skizzirt während seiner Reise in den Vereinigten Staaten von Nord-Amerika 1846–47* (Leipzig, W. Jurany; New York, Helmich and Co., 1848).

After touring some of the Eastern and Southern states, Henry Howe, later to become a well-known historian, reached Cincinnati in January, 1846, visited Marietta and Circleville, and walked about a hundred miles over the state before buying a horse for his travels. His recollections are fluently written and conversational. Henry Lewis was a German-born artist. His travel diary (1846–1848) is a highly colored, romantic account of a canoe journey along the Mississippi from the Falls of St. Anthony to St. Louis, during which he made sketches for his enormous panorama of the upper part of the river. It includes descriptions of scenery and Indians. Captain John G. Parker's brief sketch depicts his life as a shipmate on the Great Lakes during 1846–1870. William Bross was a journalist, a leading Chicago citizen, and at one time lieutenant governor of Illinois. His reminiscences are taken from a speech delivered in 1876. He begins with his trip by steamer to Chicago in 1846 and describes a later trek to Albany and back. Lucy Larcom, a minor poet, records her travel from Massachusetts to Illinois and events as late as 1891.

The only foreign-language narrative of these years is Samuel Ludvigh's volume giving a general description and account of a trip through Chicago to St. Louis.

Down the Santa Fe Trail . . . the Diary of Susan Shelby Magoffin. . . . Stella M. Drumm, ed. (New Haven, Yale University Press; London, Oxford University Press, 1926).[24]
Kane, Paul. *Wanderings of an Artist among the Indians of North America . . .* (London, Longman, Brown, Green, and Longman, 1859). Reprinted at Toronto (Radisson Society of Canada, 1925).[25]

Susan Shelby Magoffin, a native of Kentucky, as a young woman, accompanied her husband on a trading expedition from Independence through Kansas along the Santa Fé Trail into the Southwest during 1846 and 1847 and recorded the social life, gossip, and appearance of the country in a fluent and interesting diary. Paul Kane, a Canadian artist, was born in Ireland in 1810. He made an intensive study of Indian life in America from 1846 to 1848, and his *Wanderings* reflects this interest. He journeyed first from Montreal to Mackinaw, the Sault, and Green Bay and returned and later made a trip to the Far West.

Armitage, Theodore. "Flatboating on the Wabash—a Diary of 1847." *Ind. Mag. Hist.*, IX (1913), 272–75.[26]
Barnes, George. *Field Notes.* (n. p., 1847).
Buckingham, Joseph H. "Illinois as Lincoln Knew It: A Boston Reporter's Record of a Trip in 1847." Harry E. Pratt, ed. *Ill. State Hist. Soc. Trans.*, 1937, XLIV (1938), 109–87.
Hickey, Rev. M. "A Missionary among the Indians." *Mich. Hist. Colls.*, IV (1883), 544–56.
The Diary of Philip Hone, 1828–1851. Bayard Tuckerman, ed. (2 vols., New York, Dodd, Mead and Co., 1889.) Reprint, Allan Nevins, ed. (2 vols., New York, Dodd, Mead and Co., 1927); extracts in *Old New York*, I (1890), 316–33, and "The Western Trip of Philip Hone," Paul M. Angle, ed. *Jour. Ill. State Hist. Soc.*, XXXVIII (1945), 277–94.[27]
Martin, E. C. "Leaves from an Old Time Journal. Lake Superior in 1847." *Mich. Hist. Colls.*, XXX (1906), 405–09.
"Wisconsin in 1847: Notes of John Q. Roods." Earl S. Pomeroy, ed. *Wis. Mag. Hist.*, XXXIII (1949), 216–20.[28]

Theodore Armitage's flatboating trip took him from Pittsburg, Indiana, to New Orleans in March and April 1847. George Barnes was a geologist with an eye for natural scenery who explored the Ontonagon River with J. D. Whitney in 1847. His *Field Notes* covers the trip. Joseph H. Buckingham, sent to Chicago as a delegate to the River and Harbor Convention, was fascinated by various Illinois towns during a trip by stage and steamer in the same year. His article is based on his detailed and well-written letters sent to the Boston *Courier*. The Reverend M. Hickey was a missionary among the Indians of Michigan in 1847. His article includes a very interesting Indian murder trial. Philip Hone, a wealthy man in his sixties, made a journey in 1847 down the Ohio and up the Mississippi to examine his extensive land holdings in Wisconsin and then returned by way of the Great Lakes. E. C. Martin's article, in both narrative and diary form, records an 1847 surveying trip from Detroit up Lake Huron by steamer to the Sault. John Q. Roods, a resident of Newark, Ohio, described, in picturesque language and free style, his travels during the same year to Cleveland, Sheboygan, Racine, and Chicago. He called Milwaukee, for instance, "the d--mdst place for old maids that it has ever been my lot to see before."

Pioneering the West, 1846 to 1878, Major Howard Egan's Diary . . . William M. Egan, ed. (Richmond, Utah, Howard R. Egan Estate, 1917).[29]

The Pioneer Journal of Heber C. Kimball (n. p., 1854). Reprinted in *Utah Geneal. Hist. Mag.*, XXX (1939), 9–19, 76–85, 140–49, 204–11; XXXI (1940), 18–24, 80–87, 150–58, 211–18.[30]
"Diary of Loren B. Hastings." *Oreg. Pion. Assn. Trans.*, *51st Annual Reunion* (Portland, Ore., 1923), 12–26.[31]
Geer, Mrs. Elizabeth D. S. "Diary." *Oreg. Pion. Assn. Trans.*, XXXV (1907), 153–79.
Lockley, Fred. *To Oregon by Ox-Team in '47* (Portland, Ore., the Author, n. d.).

Major Howard Egan's diary begins on April 8, 1847, and details his part in the Mormon migration of 1847. Heber Chase Kimball, a Mormon apostle, chronicles the progress and struggle of the Mormons from winter quarters on the Missouri to the Salt Lake Valley.

Loren B. Hastings was a native of Vermont. His diary describes his travels from Hancock County, Illinois, to Quincy and St. Joseph and up the North Platte to Oregon in 1847. Although parts of it are monotonous, there are some good narrative passages, particularly those about encounters with Indians. It is more important than the following two. Mrs. Elizabeth D. S. Geer's diary relates her experiences during a journey from the East to Oregon, also in 1847, and Fred Lockley's title indicates its content. His narrative is brief.

"Letters and Diary of Joh.[annes] Fr. Diederichs." Translated by Emil Baensch from the German. *Wis. Mag. Hist.*, VII (1923–24), 218–37, 350–68.[32]
Görling, Adolph. *Die Neue Welt; Skizzen, von Land und Leuten der Nordamerikanischen Freistaaten* (Leipzig, Payne, 1848).
Greening, John. "A Mazomanie Pioneer of 1847." *Wis. Mag. Hist.*, XXVI (1942), 208–18.
Lyman, H. S. "Reminiscences of Hugh Cosgrove." *Oreg. Hist. Soc. Quar.*, I (1900), 253–69.
Mackay, Alexander. *The Western World; or, Travels in the United States in 1846–47; exhibiting them in their Latest Development, Social, Political, and Industrial, and including a Chapter on California* (3 vols., London, Richard Bentley, 1849).[33]
Palliser, John. *Solitary Rambles and Adventures of a Hunter in the Prairies* (London, Murray, 1853).[34]
Point, Nicolas. "A Journey in a Barge on the Missouri from the Fort of the Blackfeet [Lewis] to that of the Assiniboines [Union]." Translated by Paul A. Barrette from the French. *Mid-Amer.*, New Series, II (1931), 238–54.[35]

Two Germans, three Englishmen, an Irishman, and a Frenchman wrote accounts of travels in the Midwest in 1847. Johannes Diederichs, who left Bremen in August, composed a diary of his trip from New York to Milwaukee and of settlement at Manitowoc. Adolph Görling's book, *Die Neue Welt*, gives details of his journey down the Ohio and up the Mississippi and contains an extensive description of Illinois.

John Greening voyaged from Liverpool to New Orleans and ascended the Mississippi to Wisconsin and wrote a narrative, partly in diary form, detailing life on the prairies. H. S. Lyman, mentioned in Chapter 13, wrote "Reminiscences of Hugh Cosgrove," an interesting tale of a trip across Missouri and Iowa and up the Platte to Oregon. He mentions pioneer hardships, the wanton slaughter of buffaloes, and cruel treatment by the Pawnees. The best known Englishman to visit the Middle West during 1847 was Alexander Mackay, a barrister of the Middle Temple, who as a boy had imagined the Mississippi a lordly stream. *The Western World* describes the life and landscape he saw during his trip up that river from New Orleans to St. Louis and up the Ohio to Pittsburgh.

Captain John Palliser, an Irish army officer, confined his 1847 travels to the United States but later explored western Canada. He descended the Ohio and Mississippi and hunted on the prairies. His book was popular in England.

Nicolas Point, a French Jesuit missionary to the Indians, in 1847 accompanied Father DeSmet from Fort Lewis as far as Fort Union at the mouth of the Yellowstone River and gave details of the trip in a diary. There are scientific notes on animals and vegetation and information about the American Fur Company.

Moore, George Turnbull. Diary, 1847. 2 vols. MS. Illinois State Historical Library, Springfield.
Wiley, Benjamin. Journal, 1847. MS. Original in private possession; microfilm copies in the Illinois State Historical Library, Springfield, and Southern Illinois University Library, Carbondale.
Mowry, Washington. Journal, April 20–[June,] 1847. MS. Illinois State Historical Library.

George Turnbull Moore, of Alton, Illinois, wrote a diary of his activities in the Mexican War. The manuscript begins on July 13 and ends on November 23, 1847. Another journal of the Mexican War is that by Benjamin L. Wiley, a member of the First Regiment of Illinois Volunteers. Wiley records the march from Fort Leavenworth to Santa Fé and events from July 6 to December 27, 1847. Washington Jefferson Mowry's journal covers a trip from Middlebury, Ohio, to LaGrange, Illinois.

Greeley, Horace. *Recollections of a Busy Life . . .* (New York, J. B. Ford and Co.; Boston, H. A. Brown and Co., 1868).[36]
Smith, Mrs. Elizabeth Dixon. Travel Diary. *Oreg. Pion. Assn. Trans.*, *35th Annual Reunion* (1907), 153–76.[37]
Playfair, Robert. *Recollections of a Visit to the United States and British Provinces of North America in the Years 1847, 1848, and 1849* (Edinburgh, Constable, 1856).
Journal of Rudolph Friederich Kurz. Extracts, Myrtle Jarrell, ed.; J. N. B. Hewitt, trans. (Washington, Government Printing Office, 1937). Extracts also in D. I. Bushnell, "Friederich Kurz, Artist-Explorer," *Smithsonian Institution Annual Report* (1927), pp. 507–27.[38]
"Diary of Philip Gooch Ferguson, 1847–1848." In Bieber, *Marching with the Army of the West.*[39]
Lester, Thomas B. Diary, 1847–1848. 50 pp., MS. photostatic copy. Listed in *Guide to the Western Historical Manuscripts Collection*, University of Missouri Bulletin, Library Series, No. 22 (Columbia, University of Missouri, 1952), No. 324.
Tower, David B. Journal, October 31, 1847–April, 1857. 26 pp. MS. Owned by Philip L. Turner, Shelbyville, Ill. Typed copy in the Illinois State Historical Library.

Horace Greeley, well-known journalist, politician, and popularizer of the phrase, "Go West, young man," took a business trip in 1847 from the East to Detroit and up Lake Huron and the St. Mary's River to visit mining property. He traveled almost the same route later in the season of the following year and visited the Rocky Mountains in 1859. His *Recollections* is well written and shows his interest in the West. Mrs. Elizabeth D. Smith was an Oregon pioneer who wrote about her trip to the Far West in 1847 and 1848. Her diary, containing brief notes and mentioning a few interesting mishaps, is of moderate value. An Englishman, Robert Playfair, visited the United States and Canada from 1847 to 1849 and in his *Recollections* included a description of Chicago and the surrounding country. Rudolph F. Kurz, a Swiss painter, wrote a journal in German which covers five years of life in America (1847–1852). From New Orleans he proceeded to St. Louis and Fort Union and underwent adventures with Indians and traders during a stay at the Western posts of fur companies on the Mississippi and upper Missouri. His diary contains valuable notes on Indian life, shows a sympathetic attitude towards the Indians, and contains comments on the Mexican War and the Gold Rush.

Private William G. Ferguson marched with the Missouri Volunteers to Santa Fé and Mexico in the Mexican War. His diary describes the trip from Jefferson Barracks up the Missouri Valley and westward. It is more personal than most Mexican War diaries and contains realistic details.

The diary of Thomas B. Lester, an acting assistant surgeon of the First Regiment of Illinois Volunteer Infantry in the Mexican War, gives accounts of trips from Fort Leavenworth to Santa Fé. Another journal of the Mexican War was written by David B. Tower, who served with the Fifth Regiment of Indiana Volunteers and later returned to his home at Darwin, Illinois.

Cabot, James Elliot. "Narrative Journal." In Louis Agassiz, *Lake Superior: its Physical Character, Vegetation, and Animals . . .* (Boston, Gould, Kendall, and Lincoln, 1850).

Goddard, Edwin. "The Upper Des Moines Valley—1848." *Ann. of Ia.*, 3rd Series, IX (1909), 94–104.

McCoy, Alexander W., John, and Samuel Finley. *Pioneering on the Plains. Journey to Mexico in 1848; the Overland Trip to California* (Kaukauma, Wis., John McCoy, 1924).

O'Donovan, Jeremiah. *A Brief Account of the Author's Interview with his Countrymen, and of the Parts of the Emerald Isle Whence They Emigrated; Together with a Direct Reference to Their Present Location in the Land of their Adoption, During his Travels, through Various States of the Union in 1854 and 1855* (Pittsburgh, the Author, 1864).

Peyton, John Lewis. *Over the Alleghanies and Across the Prairies; Personal Recollections of the Far West One and Twenty Years Ago* (London, Simpkin, etc., 1869).[40]

Root, Riley. *Journal of Travels from St. Josephs to Oregon* (Galesburg, Gazetteer and Intelligencer Prints, 1850). Described by Edward Eberstadt in "The Journal of Riley Root," *Cal. Hist. Soc. Quar.*, X (1931), 396–405.[41]

Louis Agassiz, famous naturalist, in 1848 took fourteen students and a professor into the wilds of the Lake Superior region to study geology, flora, and fauna. James Elliot Cabot, one of the students, wrote a vivid narrative of the expedition, which passed Detroit, reached the Sault and continued westward. Edwin Goddard wrote hastily a detailed diary of travel in the Des Moines Valley during June and July, 1848. Unusual because it was composed, except for an item by Samuel Finley, by three brothers—Alexander W., John, and Samuel F. McCoy—is *Pioneering on the Plains*, a collection of letters and a diary of a journey to Mexico and California in the same year. An Irishman, Jeremiah O'Donovan, in the first part of his commentary on America, tells of travel in 1848 to St. Louis and up the Mississippi to Galena, Illinois, and back. John Lewis Peyton, a minor Southern writer and later a Confederate agent, took a six-months trip to the West in the same year and devoted several chapters to Illinois and Chicago in his book. The journal of Riley Root is a detailed diary of an overland journey from Knox County, Illinois, to St. Joseph by way of the Oregon Trail and then to Oregon City and California. He describes interesting experiences with Indians.

Whitman, Walt. "Excerpts from a Traveller's Note Book—Nos. 1, 2, and 3." In Emory Holloway, ed., *The Uncollected Poetry and Prose of Walt Whitman* (2 vols., New York, Doubleday Page and Co.; London, William Heinemann, 1921), I, 181–90; II, 77–78.[42]

Walt Whitman's reading about the frontier and his actual contact with the Midwest profoundly influenced his later poetry.

Having been offered an opportunity to help start and edit the New Orleans *Daily Crescent*, he left Brooklyn on February 11, 1848, accompanied by a younger brother, and traveled across the Appalachians by stagecoach. From Wheeling he began a descent of the Ohio, explored Cincinnati, wrote some free verse about Blennerhassett Island, and gave a detailed and valuable picture of steamboat life in his notebook. After spending about three months in New Orleans, he abruptly terminated his work, probably mainly because of a disagreement with his employers, and began his return to New York. He ascended the Mississippi and Illinois rivers, stopped at St. Louis and LaSalle, Illinois, on his way to Chicago, a town then of fewer than thirty thousand. There he stayed at a hotel located at Lake Street and Wabash Avenue. While cruising up Lake Michigan, he greatly admired what he saw of Wisconsin. He visited Mackinac Island and continued his journey down the Great Lakes, stopping at Cleveland, Buffalo, and Niagara Falls. The fertility, ruggedness and promising future of the West left lasting impressions which he incorporated in his great poem, *Leaves of Grass*.

Whitman possibly made another trip to the West and South in 1849 or later, but there is insufficient evidence to prove it. Although his later visit to Kansas and Colorado in 1879 confirmed his early faith in the greatness of his country, it had little further influence on his poetry.

Parker, Isaac. Account book and diary, 1848. Leather bound MS. memo book. Indiana Historical Society Library, Indianapolis.

Pratt, Orville C. Diary of an Overland Journey from Lort Leavenworth to Los Angeles. June 9–December 25, 1848. MS. 157 pp. Listed in Mary C. Withington, comp. *A Catalogue of Manuscripts in the Collection of Western Americana Founded by William R. Coe, Yale University Library* (New Haven, 1952), No. 388.[43]

——— Diary. In Le Roy R. and Ann W. Hafen, *The Old Spanish Trail, Santa Fé to Los Angeles . . .* (Glendale, Calif., Arthur H. Clark Co., 1954).

Rollins, John. Diary, 1848. MS. Listed in Nute and Ackermann, *Guide to the Personal Papers in the Manuscript Collections of the Minnesota Historical Society*, No. 214.

Curran, Charles W. Diary, 1848–1853. 5 vols., approximately 1500 pp. MS. Held by Gordon C. Curran, Wooster, Ohio; microfilm copy in Indiana Historical Society Library, Indianapolis.

Isaac Parker's account book describes a journey on the Mississippi and Ohio rivers in 1848 and lists various expenses. Orville C. Pratt, a native of New York state who moved to Galena, Illinois, in 1843 and developed a lucrative law practice there, wrote a diary, the first volume of which is unpublished. It recorded events, including Indian encounters, during the summer of 1848 in an overland trip from Fort Leavenworth to Santa Fé. Vol. II, dealing with the Far West, has been printed. John Rollins' diary covers briefly a trip from Maine to Minnesota in 1848 by way of the Great Lakes to Milwaukee, overland to Galena, and northward along the Mississippi and St. Croix rivers. Charles W. Curran was a Methodist minister of southern Indiana.

Grace Victorious; or, the Memoir of Helen M. Cowles (Oberlin, O., n. p., 1856), 41–205 *passim*.[44]

French, A. W. "Early Reminiscences." *Ill. State Hist. Soc. Trans.*, 1901, VI (1901), 60–62.

Sherman, Simon Augustus. "Lumber Rafting on Wisconsin River." *Wis. Hist. Soc. Procs.*, LVIII (1910), 171–80.

Reminiscences of John V. Farwell. . . . Mrs. Abby Ferry, ed. (2 vols., Chicago, R. F. Seymour, 1928), I, 99–174.[45]

The Life of Elizah Coffin; with a Reminiscence, by his son Charles F. Coffin. Mary C. Johnson, ed. (Cincinnati, E. Morgan and Sons, 1863).[46]

Grace Victorious gives a rather good insight into life in a small Ohio town, Austinburg, from 1848 to 1850. It is based on the diary of a young lady, Helen M. Cowles. Teaching, weather, and visits are the main subjects discussed. A. W. French went by lake steamer from Buffalo to Sandusky, thence to Mansfield; then he took a stage to Columbus and Springfield, a train to Cincinnati, a steamboat to St. Louis, and later visited Beardstown and Pekin, Illinois. His travel tale (1848–1850) describes such events as an accident on the Mississippi River and religious services in Beardstown. Simon A. Sherman also traveled by steamer from Buffalo in 1848. He continued on to Wisconsin and in 1849 made an exciting trip by raft down the Wisconsin River to the Mississippi. This and a similar trip in 1850 are described in his narrative. John Villiers Farwell was a Chicago merchant. The *Reminiscences* publishes a part of his diary (1848–1853) and provides a valuable picture of early Chicago, including news, commercial affairs, and fire alarms, and depicts the development of a Christian businessman. Elizah Coffin, a clergyman born in North Carolina, wrote a journal of his life and religious work in Indiana and Kansas from 1848 to 1861, with occasional visits to the East. In content and style it is like the usual clerical journal.

"Early Years at St. Mary's Pottawatomie Mission. From the Diary of Father Maurice Gaillard, S. J." James M. Burke, ed. *Kans. Hist. Quar.*, XX (1953), 501–29.[47]

Dougherty, Lewis B. "Experiences of Lewis Bissell Dougherty on the Oregon Trail." Ethel M. Withers, ed. *Mo. Hist. Rev.*, XXIV (1930), 359–78, 530–67; XXV (1931), 102–15, 306–21, 474–89.

Stott, Edwin. "A Sketch of My Life." *Utah Hist. Quar.*, IX (1941), 184–89.

Emigrating from Switzerland to St. Louis and continuing westward to the mission in Linn County, Kansas, Father Maurice Gaillard began his years of missionary labors among the Indians. He contracted a fever but accompanied the Jesuits to Wakarusa. He learned the Pottawatomie language and then set out for St. Mary's, Kansas, where he dedicated himself to the spiritual welfare of the Pottawatomies. His diary covers activities at the mission (1848–1850) and was originally written in Latin. Lewis B. Dougherty's experiences on the Oregon Trail beginning in 1848 are rather interestingly told, mentioning hunts, buffaloes, and Indians and their customs. The brief "Sketch" by Edwin Stott, an Englishman, relates events on his trip up the Mississippi to St. Louis in the same year, his move to Iowa in 1849, and his trek to the West in 1852.

Baird, Robert. *Impressions and Experiences of the West Indies and North America in 1849* (2 vols., Edinburgh and London, William Blackwood and Sons, 1850).

Dixon, James. *Methodism in America; with the Personal Narrative of the Author, during a Tour Through a Part of the United States and Canada* (London, John Mason, 1849).

Waugh, William Francis. *The Houseboat Book; the Log of a Cruise from Chicago to New Orleans* (Chicago, Clinic Publishing Co., 1904).

White, Peter. "Sault Ste. Marie and the Canal Fifty Years Ago." *Mich. Hist. Colls.*, XXXV (1907), 345–58.

Books by two Englishmen who visited the Midwest give generally favorable impressions. Robert Baird ascended the Mississippi and Ohio. His book describes Cincinnati, Sandusky, and Cleveland in 1849, and comments on the country, slavery, and

British emigration. While traveling to view Methodist institutions in America, James Dixon descended the Ohio from Pittsburgh to Cincinnati, crossed the state of Ohio by way of Urbana to Sandusky, and continued on to Niagara Falls and Canada. In his *Personal Narrative* he concluded, on the basis of his observations, that America had been unfairly treated by earlier travelers.

Among Americans who recorded Middle Western travels in 1849 were William Francis Waugh and Peter White. The latter traveled by water from Buffalo to Detroit and Sault Ste. Marie and described the Soo region before the canal was built.

Anonymous. "A Dragoon on the March to Pembina in 1849." Willoughby M. Babcock, ed. *Minn. Hist.*, VIII (1927), 61–74. Reprinted from St. Paul *Minnesota Pioneer*, Mar. 6, 1850.

"Capt. L.[angdon] C. Easton's Report: Fort Laramie to Fort Leavenworth Via Republican River in 1849." Merrill J. Mattes, ed. *Kans. Hist. Quar.*, XX (1953), 392–415.

Hough, John S. "Early Western Experiences." *Colorado Magazine*, XVII (1940), 101–12.

Parry, Charles Christopher. "A Travelogue of 1849." *Miss. Val. Hist. Rev.*, XXVII (1940), 435–44.[48]

Seymour, E. Sanford. *Sketches of Minnesota, the New England of the West; with Incidents of Travel in that Territory During the Summer of 1849* . . . (New York, Harper and Brothers, 1850).[49]

Williams, Maj. William. "Journal of a Trip to Iowa in 1849." *Ann. of Ia.*, 3rd Series, XII (1920), 241–82.[50]

DeGirardin, E. Travel Journal. In *Le Tour du Monde* (Paris, 1864). Chapters I and II translated by Elizabeth Conrad in *The Palimpsest*, VIII (1927), 89–101; additional chapters translated by Mrs. S. M. Stockdale as "A Trip to the Bad Lands in 1849," *Sou. Dak. Hist. Rev.*, I (1936), 51–78.

Hospers, John. "Diary of a Journey from the Netherlands to Pella, Iowa in 1849." Translated by Jacob Van Der Zee from the Dutch. *Ia. Jour. Hist.*, X (1912), 363–82.[51]

Stuart-Wortley, Lady Emmeline Charlotte Elizabeth. *Travels in the United States, etc. During 1849 and 1850* (New York, Harper and Brothers, 1851).[52]

The anonymous "A Dragoon on the March" is a narrative of vitality with literary touches. Pembina is in North Dakota. Captain L. C. Easton was the first person to make a complete exploration of the Republican River. His report, a lengthy letter (August 2–September 18, 1849), mentions buffalo slaughter, topography of the region, and routine of the march. John S. Hough used various modes of travel when in 1849 he took a train from Baltimore to Pittsburgh, a river steamer to Independence, Missouri, and a wagon across the plains and then back to Independence. His brief but smoothly flowing narrative mentions encounters with Indians and other events. Charles C. Parry, a botanist, served on the Mexican Boundary Commission in the same year and wrote a very factual letter in diary form covering his trip from Davenport, Iowa, to Bloomington, Illinois, and Keokuk, Quincy, St. Louis, New Orleans, and up the Mississippi and Ohio rivers. E. Sanford Seymour's *Sketches of Minnesota* is also a travel account because it describes parts of Illinois and the Fever River region. It includes information about routes and expenses. Major William Williams chronicles a trip from St. Louis to Fort Snelling and back to his home in Pennsylvania. His journal, hastily written, contains comments on towns, Mormons, and scenery.

Three foreigners wrote their impressions of the Midwest in 1849. A Frenchman, E. DeGirardin, traveled by steamboat up the Missouri from St. Louis to the Bad Lands. A Dutchman, John Hospers, voyaged from Amsterdam to America in 1849 and traveled by steamer by way of the Great Lakes to Chicago, by canal boat and steamer to Peoria, and by stage to Burlington, Iowa. An English woman, a poet, Lady Emmeline Stuart-Wortley, recounts events in a trip down the Ohio to St. Louis. Two decades after Mrs. Trollope, she found Cincinnati "a very handsome city" but added that it was unkempt and uncomfortable—the Empire City of Pigs. Although St. Louis was a "large, busy noble city" and the Mississippi attracted her, she noted numerous unfavorable aspects, including cold weather and cholera. She is seemingly unbiased but outspoken in her attitude towards America.

Cross, Maj. Osborne. *A Report in the Form of a Journal . . . of the March of the Regiment of Mounted Rifleman to Oregon, from May 10 to October 5, 1849* (Philadelphia, C. Sherman, printer, 1850). Also in "Report of the Quartermaster General for 1850" in *Senate Executive Documents*, I, 31st Congress, 2nd Session, Part 2, pp. 126–244. Reprinted in R. W. Settle, ed. *The March of the Mounted Riflemen* (Glendale, Calif., Arthur H. Clark Co., 1940), pp. 33–272.[53]

Gibbs, George. Military Diary. In Settle, *The March of the Mounted Riflemen*, pp. 275–327. Reprinted from *New York Journal of Commerce*, July 25, Sept. 1, 1849.[54]

Woodhouse, Dr. Samuel Washington. Journal, 1849. MS. Listed in *Guide to the Manuscript Collections of the Historical Society of Pennsylvania* (2nd ed., Philadelphia, 1949), No. 736.[55]

Two accounts of the Cross expedition of mounted riflemen sent from Fort Leavenworth to Fort Vancouver in 1849 for the purpose of traveling the full length of the Oregon Trail are preserved. The first one, by Major Osborne Cross himself, is a full narrative report, containing information on marches, topography, scenery, and natural history. The second is an incomplete diary by George Gibbs, a civilian with Cross, which describes the country and gives some general information.

Dr. Samuel Woodhouse relates events on an expedition in 1849 under Captain L. Sitgreaves and Lieutenant I. C. Woodruff to establish a boundary between the Creek and Cherokee Indians in the Southwest.

Adam, George. *The Dreadful Sufferings and Thrilling Adventures of an Overland Party of Emigrants to California, their Terrible Conflicts with Savage Tribes of Indians!! . . .* William Beschke, comp. (St. Louis, Barclay and Co., 1850).[56]

Barnes, Laura A. and Julius. "Journals of Trek of Barnes Family." Joe H. Bailey, ed. *Ann. of Ia.*, 3rd Series, XXXII (1955), 576–99.

"E. I. Bowman Journal of events from Illinois to Ca[lifornia]." In Elizabeth Page, *Wagons West, A Story of the Oregon Trail* (New York, Farrar and Rinehart, 1930), pp. 333–35.[57]

Chamberlin, William H. "From Lewisburg (Pa.) to California in 1849." Lansing B. Bloom, ed. *New Mex. Hist. Rev.*, XX (1945), 14–57, 144–80, 239–68, 336–57.

Chapman, W. W. Travel Diary. *Wyoming History Department Quarterly Bulletin*, I (1923), No. 2, 7–9.[58]

Clark, Bennett C. "Diary of a Journey from Missouri to California in 1849." Ralph P. Bieber, ed. *Mo. Hist. Rev.*, XXIII (1928), 3–43.[59]

Clark, Sterling B. F. *How Many Miles from St. Jo?* . . . E. S. Mighels, ed. (San Francisco, Privately published, 1929), pp. 7–28.[60]

Delano, Alonzo. *Life on the Plains and among the Diggings* . . . (Auburn and Buffalo, Miller, Orton, and Milligan, 1854). Reprinted as *Across the Plains and among the Diggings* (New York, Wilson-Erickson, 1936).[61]

"Diary of the Overland Trail and Letters of Captain David Dewolf." *Ill. State Hist. Soc. Trans.*, XXXII (1925), 183–222.[62]

"From Ohio to California in 1849: The Gold Rush Journal of Elijah Bryan Farnham." Merrill J. Mattes and Esley J. Kirk, eds. *Ind. Mag. Hist.*, XLVI (1950), 297–318, 403–20.

Geiger, Vincent Eply. "Journal of the Route of the Charlestown, Va. Ming. Co. from St. Josephs, Mo. to California—Frank Smith as Guide." David M. Potter, ed. *Yale Historical Publications, Manuscripts and Edited Texts*, Vol. XX (New Haven, Yale University Press, 1945).[63]

Hackney, Joseph. "Journal." In Page, *Wagons West*, pp. 111–12, 126–30, 160–70, 174–93.[64]

Hale, Israel F. Travel Diary. *Society of California Pioneers Quarterly*, II (1925), 61–130.[65]

On January 24, 1848, James W. Marshall discovered gold at Sutter's Mill on the American branch of the Sacramento River in California. Efforts to keep the event secret were futile, and news spread to all corners of the earth and an emigration westward began such as was never seen before. The many names listed above represent only a small portion of the gold seekers, for people traveled from Europe, Asia, and around Cape Horn. In two years the population of California increased to a hundred thousand.[66] Some emigrants, of course, traveled to California and Oregon for the less glamorous purpose of finding new homes.

George Adam's account of an emigrant party's trip from New Orleans to St. Louis, Independence, Fort Leavenworth, and across the plains in the fall of 1849 is a wild, highly emotional tale. Adam was fired at by Pawnees and thought himself doomed, but finally escaped. A trek in 1849 from Boyd's Grove, Illinois, into western Iowa and Missouri and the beginning of a journey to Oregon are recorded in the journals of Laura A. and Julius Barnes. The entries are hastily written, commenting on weather, roads, and topography and giving some of the authors' interesting thoughts. Similar is E. I. Bowman's diary of a trip in the same year with a party from Jerseyville, Illinois, towards California, which ended at the Missouri River. While traveling from Pennsylvania down the Ohio and Mississippi to Memphis and Napoleon, Arkansas, and up the Arkansas River across the mountains to California, William H. Chamberlin wrote a diary, partially published, which contains good details and descriptions of the country. W. W. Chapman was a gold seeker who related incidents on a trek from Illinois to Sacramento in a brief diary of 1849. Bennett C. Clark's diary, interesting but hastily written, begins in Missouri and ends in Nevada. Sterling Clark's diary is a bare record of travel from Pennsylvania by way of St. Louis and Fort Kearny to California in the spring and summer. One of the more interesting diaries is Alonzo Delano's of an overland trip from St. Joseph, Missouri, to California. Captain David Dewolf's diary, hastily written, begins at Lexington, Kentucky, and records a trip in 1849 into Kansas, up the Platte, and on to California. His notes on Indians, Mormons, and natural phenomena add interest to his account. A gold rush journal by Elijah B. Farnham describes a journey from Ohio to California.

Journals of California expeditions beginning at St. Joseph in 1849 were written by Vincent Geiger, Joseph Hackney, and Israel F. Hale. The Geiger tale traces the route of the Charlestown, Virginia, Mining Company up the Platte and Sweetwater rivers. The "Journal" of Hackney, a member of the Jerseyville party, includes letters. Hale's diary describes difficulties with Indians and sights along the way.

Heslep, Dr. Augustus M. "The Santa Fe Trail." In R. P. Bieber, ed. *Southern Trails to California in 1849* (Glendale, Calif., Arthur H. Clark Co., 1937), pp. 353–86. Reprinted from

Daily Missouri Republican, May 24, July 4, 24, Sept. 12, 1849, and Jan. 28, 1850.[67]

Hoffman, Benjamin. Diary. In C. H. Ambler. "West Virginia Forty-Niners." *West Virginia History*, III (1941), 59–75.[68]

Johnston, William Graham. *Experiences of a Forty-Niner* . . . (Pittsburgh, n. p., 1892), pp. 23–247. Reprinted as *Overland to California* (Oakland, Calif., Biobooks, 1948).[69]

Lasselle, Stanislaus. Travel Diary. In Seymour Dunbar, *A History of Travel in America* (4 vols., Indianapolis, Bobbs-Merrill Co., 1915), IV, 1427–43, Appendix 4.[70]

McCall, Ansel J. *The Great California Trail in 1849* (Bath, N. Y., Underhill, 1882). Reprinted from the *Steuben Courier Journal*, pp. 8–85.

McIlhany, Edward Washington. *Recollections of a '49er. A Quaint and Thrilling Narrative of a Trip Across the Plains, and Life in the California Gold Fields During the Stirring Days Following the Discovery of Gold in the Far West* . . . (Kansas City, Mo., Hailman Printing Co., 1908).

"Richard J.[ames] Oglesby: Forty-Niner. His Own Narrative." Mildred Eversole, ed. *Ill. State Hist. Soc. Trans.*, XLV (1939), 158–71.[71]

Dr. Augustus M. Heslop, a Jacksonville, Illinois, physician, wrote diary notes and letters on a trip along the Santa Fé Trail from Independence to San Jose, California, from May, 1849 to January, 1850. Benjamin Hoffman's diary, a set of brief and undistinguished notes, describes scenery and events in a journey down the Ohio from Pittsburgh and up the Missouri and Platte en route to the gold fields in 1849. William G. Johnston was with the first wagon train to reach San Francisco in 1849 and in a detailed diary recorded six weeks of camping experiences on the Missouri frontier. Stanislaus Lasselle, of Logansport, Indiana, provides a diary of the Santa Fé Trail, 1849. The diary of Ansel J. McCall covers a trip from the East to Sacramento by way of St. Joseph and the South Pass in 1849. The recollections of Edward W. McIlhany comprise an unusually written story of a journey across the plains. The narrative of Richard J. Oglesby, at one time governor of Illinois, is in the form of a long letter. It devotes a small part to the Midwest and gives advice to would-be prospectors.

The Overland Diary of James A. Pritchard from Kentucky to California in 1849. Dale L. Morgan, ed. (Denver, Colo., Old West Publishing Co., 1959). Extracts in *Mo. Hist. Rev.*, XVIII (1924), 535–45.[72]

"Alexander Ramsay's Gold Rush Diary of 1849." *Pac. Hist. Rev.*, XVIII (1949), 437–68.

Shaw, R. C. *Across the Plains in Forty-Nine* (Farmland, Ind., W. C. West, 1896).

"The Journal of David Jackson Staples." Harold F. Taggart, ed. *Calif. Hist. Soc. Quar.*, XXII (1943), 119–50.

"The Jacob Y. Stover Narrative." John W. Caughey, ed. *Pac. Hist. Rev.*, VI (1937), 165–81.

Thissell, G. W. *Crossing the Plains in '49* (Oakland, Calif., n. p., 1903).[73]

"Charles Tinker's Journal. A Trip to California in 1849." Eugene H. Roseboom, ed. *Ohio Arch. Hist. Quar.*, LXI (1952), 64–85.

Watson, William J. *Journal of an Overland Trip to Oregon* (Jacksonville, Ill., 1851).[74]

Webster, Kimball. *The Gold Seekers of '49. A Personal Narrative of the Overland Trail and Adventures in California and Oregon from 1849 to 1854* (Manchester, N. H., Standard Book Co., 1917).[75]

Traveling from Kentucky to St. Louis and up the Missouri into the Indian country and on to California in 1849, Captain

J. A. Pritchard wrote a hasty but informative diary of the trip. Alexander Ramsay's Gold Rush diary is interesting and contains good descriptions of the country, buffalo, and Indians. He traveled by wagon from Park County, Indiana, with five others, all of whom protected themselves from Indians by arranging the wagons in the form of a square. R. C. Shaw went by rail, steamer, and horse and mule from Boston to Sandusky, Cincinnati, St. Louis, Independence, and across the plains. His book gives a good picture of hardships suffered, such as cholera and pursuit by Indians, and natural phenomena. Much the same route was taken by David J. Staples. He mentions such an interesting experience as taking a shower in the spray made by the wheel of a river steamer. Jacob Stover tells of a trip in 1849 across the Des Moines River by flatboat and westward by ox team along the Platte. G. W. Thissell traveled from Iowa by ox-team. Charles Tinker wrote a matter-of-fact diary about his trip from Ashtabula County, Ohio, which he left on March 20.

Two travelers to Oregon in the same year were William J. Watson and Kimball Webster, a surveyor. Watson left with a wagon train from St. Joseph and wrote notes about scenery and topography along the Oregon Trail. Webster's diary, hastily written, mentions events in his journey from the East by way of Lake Erie to Detroit, by rail and steamer to Chicago, St. Louis, and Independence, and along the Platte to Oregon and later to California.

Kelly, William. *An Excursion to California over the Prairie, Rocky Mountains, and Great Sierra Nevada* . . . (2 vols., London, Chapman and Hall, 1851).[76]

William Kelly traveled from England to America, by stage from Niagara across Canada to Detroit, by rail to Niles, Michigan, by open wagon to Chicago, by steamer to St. Louis, and along the Missouri and Platte to the Far West in 1849. He was generally unfavorably impressed by what he saw. He said, for instance, that although Detroit was beautifully situated, its progress was retarded by the obstinacy of the French, who would not sell or grant leases to induce people to invest their capital. Thus, as late as the middle of the century, the British had not discontinued the old war of words, although their attacks on the United States were milder and less numerous.

Bond, Robert. Diary, March 1–July 17, 1849. 12 pp. MS. Listed in Withington, *A Catalogue of Manuscripts in the Collection of Western Americana*, No. 38.

Gelwicks, Daniel Webster. Journal, 1849. 71 pp. MS. Copy made by John F. Snyder in the Illinois State Historical Library, Springfield.

Pease, David. Diary, April 28–September 5, 1849. 37 pp. MS. typescript copy. Nebraska State Historical Society, Lincoln.

Shombre, Henry J. Diary, March 19–June 17, 1849. MS. Kansas State Historical Society, Topeka. Photostatic copy at Yale University Library. Excerpts in K. M. Rabb's column, "Hoosier Listening Post," *Indianapolis Star*.

A larger number of unpublished accounts exist for 1849 than for any previous year. Although most of these describe trips to the California gold fields, a few are about shorter journeys. Robert Bond made an overland trek probably from Newark by way of Philadelphia, Pittsburgh, St. Louis, Independence, and Fort Laramie to Salt Lake City. His diary entries are brief and impersonal. Although Daniel W. Gelwicks set out from Belleville, Illinois, for California, his journal records the trip only as far as South Pass. The David Pease diary covers a trek from St. Joseph to Astoria, Oregon, and the diary of Henry Shombre tells of travel down the Ohio to the Platte River.

Anonymous. Diary, 1849–1850. MS. Typescript copy. Listed in Lucile M. Kane and Kathryn A. Johnson, comps. *Manuscript Collections of the Minnesota Historical Society, Guide Number 2* (St. Paul, Minnesota Historical Society, 1955), No. 489.

Armstrong, J. E. Diary, April 9–September 14, 1849. MS. Listed in Elizabeth Biggert, comp. *Guide to the Manuscript Collections in the Library of the Ohio State Archaeological and Historical Society* (Columbus, Ohio State Archaeological and Historical Society, 1953), No. 129.

Badman, Philip. Diary, April 14–October 2, 1849. 2 vols. MS. Listed in Withington, *A Catalogue of Manuscripts in the Collection of Western Americana*, No. 20.

Benson, John H. Diary, May 6–September 24, 1849. MS. Typescript copy. Nebraska State Historical Society, Lincoln.

Burbank, Augustus R. Diary, 1849. MS. Library of Congress, Washington, D. C.

Burrall, George P. A Trip across the Plains in 1849. 33 pp. Typescript from MS. in private hands. Copy listed in Ruth Lapham Butler, comp. *A Check List of Manuscripts in the Edward E. Ayer Collection of the Newberry Library* (Chicago, The Newberry Library, 1937), No. 126.

Doyle, Simon. Journal of an Overland Journey, April 2–October 4, 1849. MS. Listed in Withington, No. 144.[77]

Everts, F. D. "A Journal on & of the route to California," March 15–June 30, 1849. 31 pp. MS. Listed in Withington, No. 193.

Goulding, William R. Journal, March 10–September 18, 1849. 328 pp. MS. Listed in Withington, No. 225.

Gray, Charles G. An Overland Passage from Independence, Mo., to San Francisco by Way of Salt Lake City and Lassen's Cut-off, February 26–November 19, 1849. 2 vols. MS. Henry E. Huntington Library, San Marino, California.

Haun, Catherine Margaret. A Woman's Trip across the Plains, April 25–November 4, 1849. 45 pp. MS. Huntington Library.

Joselyn, Amos P. Journal, April 2–September 11, 1849. 24 pp. MS. California State Library. Typescript copy in the Newberry Library. Listed in Butler, *Check List of Manuscripts in the Ayer Collection*, No. 466.

Lewis, Elisha B. Diary, April–November, 1849. 74 pp. MS. typed copy. Listed in Alice E. Smith, comp. *Guide to the Manuscripts of the Wisconsin Historical Society* (Madison, State Historical Society of Wisconsin, 1944), No. 407.

Lewis, John F. Journal in the Form of a Letter, May 12–December 31, 1849. 91 pp. MS. Listed in Withington, No. 301.

Long, Charles L'hommedieu. Diary of an Overland Journey from Cincinnati, Ohio, to California, March 10–August 14, 1849. MS. 165 pp. Listed in Withington, No. 307.

Love, Alexander. Diary of an Overland Journey from Leesburg, Pennsylvania, to the California Gold Mines, March 20–August 23, 1849; Experiences in California, 1849–1852; and the Journey Home by Panama, January 15–March 5, 1852. 235 pp., 4 notebooks. MS. Listed in Withington, No. 309.

Stackhouse, Charles. "Experience of an Overland Traveler to California in 1849, in pursuit of gold." MS. 8 pp., typescript. Nebraska State Historical Society, Lincoln.

[Starr, Franklin.] Diary, March 22–August 23, 1849. MS. Illinois State Historical Library, Springfield.

Swain, William. Journal of an Overland Trip, April 11–October 31, 1849. 2 vols. MS. Listed in Withington, No. 466.

Tiffany, P. C. Diary of an Overland Journey to California, April 17–August 29, 1849; Experiences at the Mines, January 1–December 5, 1850; and the Voyage Home by the Isthmus, December 8, 1850–March 13, 1851. 3 vols. MS. Listed in Withington, No. 474.

Willis, Edward J. "Diary of Edward J. Willis, Giving account of travell [*sic*] from Independence Missouri to California in 1849 Across the Plains." May 1–September 1, 1849. 62 pp. MS. Listed in Withington, No. 527.

The unpublished Gold Rush tales listed above are often so similar that a detailed description of each is unnecessary. The anonymous diary relates events in an overland journey from Lowell, Massachusetts, to California. J. E. Armstrong made a trip from Hibbardsville, Ohio, to California. Philip Badman went from Warren, Pennsylvania, by way of St. Louis, Independence, and the Platte to California. Poorly written but has interesting descriptions. John H. Benson journeyed from St. Joseph to Sacramento, Augustus R. Burbank from Illinois to California. Simon Doyle trekked from Rushville, Illinois, across Iowa and along the Platte River Trail. F. D. Everts left LaPorte County, Indiana, for the gold fields with ten companions by way of St. Joseph, the Platte, and Fort Laramie. More detailed and interesting than the usual journal of the period is William R. Goulding's tale of the expedition of the Knickerbocker Exploring Company of New York City from Fort Smith to California by rail, wagon, and steamer.

Margaret C. Haun's tale covers her trek from Clinton, Iowa, to Sacramento. Amos P. Joselyn went from Zanesville, Ohio, to Sacramento. Elisha B. Lewis relates incidents on a journey by ox team from Turtle, Wisconsin, to California. John F. Lewis's long letter is an account of an overland trip from Randolph County, Missouri, to St. Joseph, the Platte and Sweetwater rivers, Salt Lake City, and California. Charles L'hommedieu Long seems to have been a man of some education. His diary records details of travel from Cincinnati by boat down the Ohio, overland from Independence, by the Platte to Fort Laramie and California. Alexander Love traveled by way of St. Louis, Independence, and the Platte River and back. The diary attributed to Franklin Starr describes a journey from Alton, Illinois. William Swain left Youngstown, New York, to join emigrants to California and reached the Feather River Valley but because of ill health and hardships after a few months returned to the East by way of Panama. P. C. Tiffany's diary gives vivid details of a trip from Mount Pleasant, Iowa, a boat trip from Burlington, Iowa, to St. Louis and St. Joseph, and an overland trek by way of Sublette's Cut-off to the California mines and return. Edward J. Willis traveled from Independence across the Kansas and Blue rivers to Fort Kearney, along the Platte to the South Fork Crossing, and thence westward.

Bruff, Joseph Goldsborough. . . . *The Journals, Drawings, and Other Papers. April 2, 1849–1851.* Georgia W. Read and Ruth Gaines, eds. (2 vols., New York, Columbia University Press, 1949).[78]

Journal of Samuel Rutherford Dundass (Steubenville, O., n. p., 1857).[79]

Stansbury, Capt. Howard. *Exploration and Survey of the Valley of the Great Salt Lake of Utah* (Philadelphia, Lippincott, Grambo and Co., 1852). Extracts in Lloyd McFarling, ed. *Exploring the Northern Plains* (Caldwell, Ida., The Caxton Printers, 1955), pp. 142–52.

The Santa Fe Trail to California, 1849–1852. The Journal and Drawings of H. M. T. Powell. Douglas S. Watson, ed. (San Francisco, Book Club of California, 1931).[80]

Pleasant, William James. *Twice Across the Plains, 1849 . . . 1856* (San Francisco, 1906).

Stuart, Joseph Alonzo. *My Roving Life. A Diary of Travels and Adventures by Sea and Land, during Peace and War* (2 vols., Auburn, Calif., n. p., 1895).[81]

Davis, Caleb Forbes. "The Autobiographies of an Iowa Father and Son. Part I." *Ann. of Ia.*, 3rd Series, XIX (1935), 483–538.

The authors listed above are among the last to see the Midwest before the middle of the nineteenth century. Perhaps the most significant first-hand records of the Gold Rush are the journals and diaries of Joseph G. Bruff which describe an expedition from Washington, D. C., by way of St. Joseph, Fort Kearney, and Fort Laramie to the Far West in 1849 and 1850. The *Journals* were written from diaries probably composed on the road. Samuel R. Dundass, an Ohio lawyer, wrote a full and detailed journal of a trip in 1849 and 1850 from Steubenville, Ohio, to Independence and San Francisco. Howard Stansbury was a captain in the Topographical Corps of the United States Army who was sent to Utah on an exploratory expedition in 1849, returning in 1850. His diary describes the trip from Fort Leavenworth and mentions numerous hardships. A resident of Greenville, Illinois, H. M. T. Powell, wrote a detailed diary on his journey in 1849 through St. Louis, Independence, and Santa Fé to the gold fields and return to Illinois in 1852. He described hardships of the trail, deaths along the way, and Indians. Joseph A. Stuart's roving life extended from 1849 to 1867 and covers a trip across the Midwest to California. The narrative of Caleb Davis is devoted mainly to later years but a brief part is about a trip from Clarksburg, Virginia, to Keokuk in 1849.

Casey, Charles. *Two Years on the Farm of Uncle Sam; with Sketches of his Location, Nephews and Prospects* (London, Bentley, 1852).

Houstoun, Mrs. Matilda Charlotte (Jesse) Fraser. *Hesperos; or, Travels in the West* (2 vols., London, J. W. Parker, 1850).

Marmier, Xavier. *Lettres sur L'Amérique* (Paris, E. Plon and Co., 1881).

Charles Casey came from Britain to America. His book gives an account of a trip down the Ohio in 1849 and a visit to Illinois in 1859. He describes scenery and places. A minor English novelist, Mrs. Matilda C. Houstoun, descended the Ohio in 1849 and returned up the Mississippi and Ohio the following year. Xavier Marmier, a Frenchman, also descended the Ohio and recorded his favorable impressions of Cincinnati and the Ohio Valley in a series of letters written in 1849 and 1850.

Darwin, Charles Benjamin. Journal of a Trip across the Plains . . . , May 1, 1849–August 20, 1850. 3 vols. MS. Huntington Library.

"Journal. Jos. P. Hamelin, jr. of Lexington, Missouri," April 12, 1849–February 17, 1850. 126 pp. MS. Listed in Withington, *A Catalogue of Manuscripts in the Collection of Western Americana*, No. 239.

"Reise Skitzen von Wilhelm Hoffman," March 30, 1849–October 8, 1850. 32 pp. MS. Listed in Withington, *A Catalogue of Manuscripts in the Collection of Western Americana*, No. 258.

Spooner, E. A. Diary, March 15, 1849–April 23, 1850. MS. Owned by Mrs. R. M. Smith of Kansas City, Mo. Microfilm copy in the Kansas State Historical Society, Topeka.

Parke, Charles R. Journal, 1849–1851. 149 pp. MS. Huntington Library.

Gould, Charles. Diaries, 1849, 1852. 2 vols. MS. Listed in Kane and Johnson, *Manuscript Collections of the Minnesota Historical Society, Guide Number 2*, No. 489; typed copy of Vol. I in the Nebraska State Historical Society, Lincoln.

Storer, Daniel M. Diary, 1849, 1851, 1853. MS. Listed in Kane and Johnson, *Manuscript Collections of the Minnesota Historical Society, Guide Number 2*, No. 1476.

Wood, Joseph Warren. Diary, April 9, 1849–April 4, 1853. 758 pp. MS. Photostatic copy in the Newberry Library from a copy in the Huntington Library. Listed in Butler, *Check List of Manuscripts in the Ayer Collection*, No. 1013.

Charles Benjamin Darwin chronicles a trip from Council Bluffs to San Francisco by way of Salt Lake City. Joseph P. Hamelin, Jr. gives the details of a journey from his home, on the boat *Highland Mary* to Fort Kearney, overland by the south bank of the Platte to Salt Lake, and thence to Los Angeles. The unpublished sketches of Wilhelm Hoffman tell of travel from St. Louis by wagon and oxen and then by way of St. Joseph and the Platte westward. The diary of E. A. Spooner gives information on stream crossings, water supply, and other conditions during a trip from Adrian, Michigan, to California. Charles R. Parke's journal gives an account of a trek from Illinois by way of Fort Laramie to California. One of Charles Gould's diaries is a record of his trip as a young man from Massachusetts to the gold fields in 1849 and the second describes the return journey. Daniel M. Storer's diary covers travel from Maine to Illinois in 1849 and from Illinois to Stillwater, Minnesota in 1851, and then of his move from Stillwater to Shakopee in 1853. Above average in interest, it mentions musical and theatrical companies, a steamboat excursion on the Minnesota River, real estate speculation, local politics, and economic conditions. The diary of Joseph Warren Wood tells of a trip from Walworth, Wisconsin, to California and later events from 1849 to 1853.

Notes

NOTES TO CHAPTER 1

1. William P. Trent, *et al.*, eds. *The Cambridge History of American Literature* (4 vols., New York, 1917–21), I, 185.

2. Ralph L. Rusk, *The Literature of the Middle Western Frontier* (2 vols., New York, 1925), I, 79–80.

3. Walter P. Webb, *The Great Plains* (New York, 1931), p. 454.

4. *The Cambridge History of American Literature,* I, 185.

5. William Matthews, *American Diaries; an Annotated Bibliography* . . . (Berkeley, Calif., 1945), p. ix.

6. *The Cambridge History of American Literature,* I, 190.

7. Jonathan Swift, *Gulliver's Travels* (New York, Modern Library, 1950), p. 127.

8. Robert E. Spiller, *et al.*, eds. *A Literary History of the United States,* (New York, 1948), p. 245.

9. Gilbert Chinard in *L'Amérique et le Rêve Exotique dans la Littérature Française au XVIIᵉ et au XVIIIᵉ Siècle* (Paris, 1913) has a very interesting chapter on the relations between the voyages and the utopias of French novels.

10. *The Cambridge History of American Literature,* I, 187.

11. *Ibid.*, I, 211, 212.

12. Rusk, I, 2, 90–91.

13. Ernest E. Leisy, *American Literature; an Interpretative Survey* (New York, 1929), p. 57.

14. Charles N. Coe, *Wordsworth and the Literature of Travel* (New York, 1954), p. 94.

15. *The Cambridge History of American Literature,* I, 211–13.

NOTES TO CHAPTER 2

The following lists of publications about authors and narratives are not intended to be complete bibliographies; rather, they are to serve as guides for readers desiring additional information. Those works have been listed which emphasize or at least mention the frontier element in the writers described. Unlisted are several sketches in *Lamb's Biographical Dictionary of the United States,* John H. Brown, ed. (7 vols., Boston, 1900–03) and *Appleton's Cyclopedia of American Biography,* James Grant Wilson and John Fisk, eds. (7 vols., New York, 1898–1900). The abbreviation *DAB* has been used for the many citations of *The Dictionary of American Biography,* Allan Johnson, ed. (22 vols., New York, 1928).

1. *The Pioneers of France in the New World* (Boston, 1865); *The Jesuits in North America* (Boston, 1867); and *LaSalle and the Discovery of the Great West* (Boston, 1869).

2. Not until the nineteenth century did historians realize that Nicolet was the first white man to visit the Midwest. Books and articles about him include C. W. Butterfield, *History of the Discovery of the Northwest by John Nicollet in 1634* (Cincinnati, 1881); F. H. Garneau and J. B. Ferland, "Jean Nicolet," *Wis. Hist. Soc. Colls.*, X (1888), 41–46; *DAB*, XIII, 511–12; Benjamin Sulté, "Notes on Jean Nicolet," *Wis. Hist. Soc. Colls.*, VIII (1877–79), 188–94; and Clifford P. Wilson, "Where Did Nicolet Go?" *Minn. Hist.*, XXVII (1946), 216–20.

3. Morris Bishop, *Champlain, the Life of Fortitude* (New York, 1948) and Justin Winsor, "Jacques Cartier and his Successors" and "Champlain," *Narrative and Critical History of America* (8 vols., Boston and New York, 1889), IV, 47–80, 103–34.

4. John Finley, *The French in the Heart of America* (New York, 1915), pp. 23–25.

5. H. C. Campbell, "Radisson and Groseilliers," *Parkman Club Papers*, No. 2, (1896); Donatier Frémont, *Pierre Radisson* (Montreal, 1933); Hjalmar Holand, "Radisson's Two Western Journeys," *Minn. Hist.*, XV (1934), 157–80; Agnes C. Laut, *Pathfinders of the West; Being the Thrilling Story of the Adventures of the Men Who Discovered the Great Northwest, Radisson, La Vèrendrye, Lewis and Clark* (New York, London, 1904); Edward D. Neill, "Groseilliers and Radisson, the First Explorers of Lake Superior and the State of Minnesota," *Mag. West. Hist.*, VII (1888), 412–21; *DAB*, XV, 320–21; "Radisson and Groseilliers in Wisconsin," *Wis. Hist. Soc. Colls.*, XI (1888), 64–96; Millard F. Stipes, *Radisson and Hennepin in the Mississippi Valley* (Jamesport, Mo., 1906); Benjamin Sulté, "Découverte du Mississippi en 1659," *Proceedings and Transactions of the Royal Society of Canada*, 2nd Series, IX (1903); Ronald Syme, *Bay of the North, the Story of Pierre Radisson* (New York, 1950); Warren Upham, "Groseilliers and Radisson, the First White Men in Minnesota, 1655–56, and 1659–60, and their Discovery of the Upper Mississippi River," *Colls. Minn. Hist. Soc.*, X, Part 2 (1905), 449–594 and "Founders of the Fur Trade in Northern Minnesota," *Mag. Hist.*, IV (1906), 187–97; and Stanley Vestal [Walter Stanley Campbell, pseud.], *King of the Fur Traders; the Deeds and Deviltry of Pierre Esprit Radisson* (Boston, 1940).

6. *DAB*, I, 222–23; Thomas J. Campbell, *Pioneer Priests of North America* . . . (3 vols., New York, 1908–10), Vol. III; *Among the Algonquins* (New York, 1911); J. S. LaBoule, *Claude Jean Allouez, the Apostle of the Ottawas* (Milwaukee, 1897) and Antoine I. Rezek, *History of the Diocese of Sault Ste. Marie and Marquette* . . . (2 vols., Houghton, Mich., 1906–07), II, 30-39.

7. Finley, pp. 46–54; Louise P. Kellogg, *The French Regime in Wisconsin and the Northwest* (Madison, Wis., 1925), pp. 69–71; *DAB*, XVI, 482.

8. *DAB*, V, 19–20 and Kellogg, pp. 158–63, 169, 188, 191.

9. John B. Brebner, *The Explorers of North America* (New York, 1933), pp. 243–56; John Ely Briggs, "Louis Joliet," *Illinois Catholic Historical Review*, VI (1923), 28–33; Jean Delanglez, "Louis Jolliet—the Early Years: 1645–1674; the Middle Years: 1674–1686," *Mid-Amer.*, XXVII (1945), 3–24, 67–96; Stanley Faye, "Jolliet Goes West," *Jour. Ill. State Hist. Soc.*, XXVII (1934), 5–30; John Finley, "The French in the Heart of America," *Scribner's Magazine*, LII (1912), 453; Frederick E. A. Gagnon, *Louis Joliet, Prémier Seigner de l'Île d'Anticosti: Étude Biographique et Historiographique* (Quebec, 1902); *DAB*, X, 156–57; Kellogg, pp. 191–94, 213–15, 221–57; Henry J. Morgan, *Sketches of Celebrated Canadians* (Montreal, 1865), pp. 24–25; and Francix B. Steck, *The Jolliet-Marquette Expedition* (Washington, 1927).

10. T. J. Campbell, III, 165–83; Henry H. Hurlbut, *Father Marquette at Mackinaw and Chicago*, etc. (Chicago, 1878); "Joliet and Marquette Discover the Upper Mississippi," *Wis. Hist. Soc. Colls.*, XVI (1902), 89–92; Kellogg, 221–57, 260–80; "Marquette," *Mich. Hist. Colls.*, VI (1884), 352–54; Ruth Middaugh, "Father Marquette," *The Palimpsest*, IV (1923), 229–39 and "Father Marquette," *Cath. Hist. Rev.*, VI (1923), 22–27; Morgan, pp. 25–27; Henry L. Nelson, "The Pleasant Life of Père Marquette," *Harper's*, CXI (1905), 74–82; Agnes Repplier, *Père Marquette, Priest, Pioneer and Adventurer* (Garden City, New York, 1929); John D. G. Shea, *Discovery and Exploration of the Mississippi Valley* (New York, 1952), pp. xli–lxxviii, and "Marquette's Journal at Chicago," *Historical Magazine*, V, 99; Steck; Joseph J. Thompson, "Father Marquette's Second Journey to Illinois," *Cath. Hist. Rev.*, VII (1924), 144–54; R. G. Thwaites, *Father Marquette* (New York, 1902); Thomas A. E. Weadock, "Père Marquette, the Missionary Explorer," *Mich. Hist. Colls.*, XXI (1894), 447–66; L. G. Weld, "Joliet and Marquette in Iowa," *Ia. Jour. Hist.*, I (1903), 3–16; and Edwin O. Wood, "Father Marquette at Michilimackinac," *Mich. Hist.*, II (1918), 125–42; and *DAB*, XII, 294–95.

11. Jean Delanglez, "The Voyages of Tonti in North America," *Mid.-Amer.*, XXVI (1944), 255–300; Kellogg, pp. 281–322; H. E. Legler, "Chevalier Henry de Tonty," *Parkman Club Publications*, I, No. 3 (1890); Ethel Owen Merrill, "Henri de Tonty," *Mid-Amer.*, XV (1932), 80–101; Edmund R. Murphy, *Henry de Tonty, Fur Trader of the Mississippi* (Baltimore, 1941); John Carl Parish, *The Man with the Iron Hand* (Boston and New York, 1913); Francis Parkman, *LaSalle and the Discovery of the Great West . . .* (Boston, 1915), pp. 115–41 *passim;* Benjamin Sulté, "Les Tonty," *Proceedings and Transactions of the Royal Society of Canada*, XI, Sec. 1 (1894), 1–31; *DAB*, XVIII, 587–88; and R. C. Werner, "The French Foundation, 1680–1693," *Ill. Hist. Colls.*, XXIII (1904).

12. Samuel M. Davis, "Hennepin as Discoverer and Author," *Colls. Minn. Hist. Soc.*, IX (1901), 223–40; Jean Delanglez, "Hennepin's Description of Louisiana," *Mid-Amer.*, XXIII (1941), 3–44, 99–137 and "Hennepin's Voyage to the Gulf of Mexico, 1680," *Mid-Amer.*, XXI (1939), 32–81; Prince Albert deLigne, "Father Louis Hennepin, Belgian," *Minn. Hist.*, XI (1930), 343–52; Edward C. Gale, "On the Hennepin Trail," *Minn. Hist.*, XI (1930), 3–10; *DAB*, VIII, 540; "Louis Hennepin, the Franciscan," *Colls. Minn. Hist. Soc.*, I (1872), 302–13; Morgan, pp. 27–28; Grace Lee Nute, "Father Hennepin's Later Years," *Minn. Hist.*, XIX (1938), 393–98; Victor H. Paltsits, *Bibliography of the Works of Father Louis Hennepin* (Chicago, 1903); Millard F. Stipes, *Radisson and Hennepin in the Mississippi Valley* (Jamesport, Mo., 1906); and Justin Winsor, "Father Louis Hennepin and his Real or Disputed Discoveries," *Narrative and Critical History of America* (8 vols., Boston and New York, 1884–89), IV, 247–56.

13. *DAB*, VIII, 540.

14. L. P. Kellogg, ed. *Early Narratives of the Old Northwest, 1634–1699* (New York, 1917), pp. 292–96 and "A Wisconsin Anabasis," *Wis. Mag. Hist.* (1924); *DAB*, XII, 526–27; and Shea, "Notice on Father Zenobius Membré," in Shea, *Discovery and Exploration*, pp. 147–48.

15. *DAB*, X, 224–25, and Baron Marc de Villiers, *L'Expédition de Cavelier de la Salle dans le Golfe du Mexique* (Paris, 1931).

16. John B. Brebner, *The Explorers of North America* (New York, 1933); Jean Delanglez, "A Calendar of LaSalle's Travels, 1643–1683," *Mid-Amer.*, XXII (1940), 278–305; "LaSalle, 1669–1673," *Mid-Amer.*, XIX (1937), 197–216, 237–53; and "La-

Salle's Expedition of 1682," *Mid-Amer.*, XXII (1940), 3–35; William W. Folwell, *A History of Minnesota* (4 vols., St. Paul, 1921), I, 25–40; Frances Ormond Gaither, *The Fatal River, the Life and Death of LaSalle* (New York, 1931); Gabriel Gravier, *Découvertes et Établissements de Cavelier de LaSalle de Rouen dans l'Amérique du Nord* (Paris, 1870) and "Robert Cavelier de la Salle of Rouen," *Mag. of Amer. Hist.*, VIII (1882), 305–14; Marion A. Habig, "Eyewitness Accounts of LaSalle's Expedition down the Mississippi River in 1682," *Mid-Amer.*, XVI (1934), 165–84; Louise S. Hasbrouck, *LaSalle* (New York, 1916); Henry H. Hurlbut, "The LaSalle 'Memoir,'" *Mag. of Amer. Hist.*, VIII (1882), 620–22; Leo V. Jacks, *LaSalle* (New York, London, 1931); "LaSalle and the Mississippi, 1682–1882," *Mag. of Amer. Hist.*, VIII (1882), 182–86; Pierre Margry, "LaSalle's Account of the American Indian," *Mag. of Amer. Hist.*, II (1878), 238–47 and "Rivers and Peoples Discovered by LaSalle," *Mag. of Amer. Hist.*, II (1878), 619–23; Jeannette C. Nolan, *LaSalle and the Grand Enterprise* (New York, 1951); Parkman, *passim;* Clifford H. Prator, "LaSalle's Trip across Southern Michigan in 1680," *Mich. Hist.*, XXV (1941), 188–98; Clifford Smyth, *LaSalle and the Pioneers of New France* (New York and London, 1931); Ronald Syme, *LaSalle of the Mississippi* (New York, 1953); and *DAB*, XI, 10–13.

17. Ralph L. Rusk, *The Literature of the Middle Western Frontier* (2 vols., New York, 1925), I, 83.

18. F. C. B. Crompton, *Glimpses of Early Canadians: Lahonton* (Toronto, 1925); Kellogg, pp. 238–40; *DAB*, X, 548; Stephen Leacock, "Lahonton in Minnesota," *Minn. Hist.*, XIV (1933), 367–77; *Proceedings and Transactions of the Royal Society of Canada*, XII (1895); and Rusk, I, 82–83.

19. See Chapter 1, p. 2.

20. William Matthews, *American Diaries . . .* (Berkeley, Calif., 1945), p. 15.

21. *Ibid.*, p. 23.

22. *DAB*, IV, 23–24; J. Edmond Roy, "Essai sur Charlevoix," *Proceedings and Transactions of the Royal Society of Canada*, 3rd Series, I, Sec. 1 (1907), 3–25; Rusk, I, 84, 95; Robert E. Spiller, *et al.*, eds. *Literary History of the United States* (New York, 1948), p. 260; and Colton Storm, "They Called It the West," *Hist. Phil. Soc. of Ohio Bull.*, XIV (1956), 3–20.

23. Matthews, pp. 25–26.

24. LaPerrière (also called Pierre Boucher, Sieur de Boucherville) wrote a narrative of Indian captivity which is discussed in Chapter 3.

25. Lawrence J. Burpee, *Pathfinders of the Great Plains; a Chronicle of LaVèrendrye and his Sons* (Toronto, 1921); Agnes C. Laut, *Pathfinders of the West;* Francis Parkman, *Half Century of Conflict* (2 vols., Boston, 1903), II, 29ff; L. A. Prud'Homme, "Pierre Gaultier de Varennes, Sieur de la Vèrendrye," *Proceedings and Transactions of the Royal Society of Canada*, 2nd Series, IX (1903); and Warren Upham, "The Explorations of Vèrendrye and his Sons," *Miss. Val. Hist. Assn. Procs.*, I (1907–1908), 43–55.

26. See Joseph Tassé, "Memoir of Charles de Langlade," *Wis. Hist. Soc. Colls.*, VII (1876), 123–85.

27. Mr. William Kaye Lamb, Dominion Archivist, Ottawa, has supplied bibliographical information about these journals.

28. *DAB*, III, 581–82; O. H. Marshall, "DeCéloron's Expedition to the Ohio in 1749," *Amer. Mag. of Hist.*, II (1878), 129–50, reprinted from *The Historical Writings of O. H. Marshall* (Albany, 1887); and Matthews, p. 51.

29. The author of a memoir of about 1759, the manuscript of which is at Paris, concluded that the Ohio River was a tributary to the Wabash and had information on the voyages of Joliet, Marquette, Hennepin, LaSalle, and Tonty.

30. Auguste Chouteau's journal of 1762–1764, while not, strictly speaking, a travel narrative, is the only surviving account of the founding of St. Louis and relates a few of the travels of M. LaClede Ligueste, founder of the city; see "Diary, 1762–1764," *St. Louis Mercantile Library Association, 12th Annual Report* (St. Louis, 1858), Appendix; reprinted (French and English texts) as "Chouteau's Journal of the Founding of St. Louis," *Mo. Hist. Soc. Colls.*, IV (1911), 335–66. Matthews, p. 87. Fragments of the manuscript of the Chouteau narrative are at the Bibliothèque Nationale, Paris.

NOTES TO CHAPTER 3

1. Howard H. Peckham, *Captured by Indians, True Tales of Pioneer Survivors* (New Brunswick, N. J., 1954).

2. The tales told in Logan Esarey's "Indian Captivities in Early Indiana," *Ind. Mag. Hist.*, IX (1913), 95–112 were originally in the form of letters and, hence, are excluded from this study.

3. A biographical sketch of Smith written by Robert Clarke appears in the 1870 edition of *An Account of the Remarkable Occurrences . . .* (Cincinnati, 1870). See also Lewis and R. H. Collins, *History of Kentucky* (2 vols., 1874); Henry Howe, *Historical Collections of Ohio* (3 vols., Columbus, 1891); Ralph L. Rusk, *The Literature of the Middle Western Frontier* (2 vols., New York, 1925), I, 92; *DAB*, XVII, 284–85; and P. G. Thomson, *A Bibliography of the State of Ohio* (Cincinnati, 1880).

4. 22nd ed. revised by C. D. Vail (1925). See *DAB*, X, 39–40; *Red Man* (Carlisle, Pa., 1913); *Rochester Historical Society Publications Fund Series*, III (1924); *American Scenic and Historic Preservation Society*, Twelfth (1907) and Sixteenth (1911) Annual Report; E. W. Vanderhoof, *Historical Sketches of Western New York . . .* (Buffalo, 1907). Even a poem was based upon Mary Jemison's adventures, John M. Fisk's *Story of the Female Captive . . .* (Palmer, Mass., 1844).

5. Willard R. Jibson, *A Bibliography of the Life and Writings of Col. James Smith of Bourbon County, Kentucky, 1737–1812* (Frankfort, Ky., 1948).

6. Rusk, I, 92–93.

7. Addington Bruce, *Daniel Boone and the Wilderness Road* (New York, 1930); *DAB*, II, 441–43; Rusk, I, 2, 13, 22n., 94, 122, 243, 251, 274, 278, 347; II, 14; Reuben G. Thwaites, *Daniel Boone* (New York, 1902); and Stewart Edward White, *Daniel Boone, Wilderness Scout* (Garden City, New York, 1922).

8. Rusk, I, 121–23 and 251. Significant information about Filson is contained in R. T. Durret, *John Filson, the First Historian of Kentucky . . .* Filson Club Publications, No. 1 (Louisville, Ky., 1884).

9. Rusk, I, 93.

10. Martha B. Phelps, *Frances Slocum* (New York, 1905) and *DAB*, XVII, 215–16.

11. Claude M. Nowlin, "Hugh Henry Brackenridge, Writer," *Western Pennsylvania History Magazine*, X (1927), 224–56, is a study of Brackenridge's literary work. See *DAB*, II, 544–45. See *Mag. West. Hist.* (1885) for additional information on the Crawford expedition.

12. William Matthews, *American Diaries . . .* (Berkeley, Calif., 1945), p. 162.

13. Rusk, I, 93.

14. *DAB*, IX, 577; Rusk, I, 94; and Henry R. Wagner and Charles L. Camp, *The Plains and the Rockies . . .* (Columbus, 1953), p. 68.

15. A reprint from Keating's *Narrative . . .* is entitled "John Tanner, Indian Captive among the Ojibways," *Nor. Dak. Hist. Soc. Colls.*, III (1910), 491–97.

16. Rusk, I, 92.

17. Quaife's introduction contains information about Spencer.

18. Rusk, I, 92, 308.

19. Much has been written about the veracity of Hunter's book. An account of the discovery of its fictitious character and a summary of the controversy down to 1827 is given in "Tanner's Indian Narrative," *The American Quarterly Review*, VIII (1830), 113–15. See also "Hunter's Narrative," *Nor. Amer. Rev.*, XXII (1826), 94–108; Detroit *Gazette*, Jan. 31, 1826; and Elias Norgate, *Mr. John Dunn Hunter Defended; or, Some Remarks on an Article in the North American Review, in Which that Gentleman Is Branded as an Imposter* (London, 1826); Rusk, I, 94; and Wagner and Camp, pp. 46–47.

20. American concern over the cruel treatment of prisoners by Indians during the War of 1812 is shown by the appearance of the following report: *U. S. Congress. House Committee to Inquire into the Manner in Which the War Has Been Waged by the Enemy. Barbarities of the Enemy, Exposed in a Report of the Committee of the House of Representatives of the United States, Appointed to Enquire into the Spirit and Manner in Which the War Has Been Waged by the Enemy. And the Documents, Accompanying Said Reports* (Worcester, 1814). This gives accounts of soldiers and inhabitants taken by the Indians on the River Raisin and at Princeton, Illinois.

21. Wagner and Camp, pp. 26–28.

22. See the account by her husband described in Chapter 8. See also *DAB*, X, 422.

23. Matthews, p. 219.

24. Rusk, I, 92–93.

25. *Ibid.*, I, 92. An anecdote told by Antoine St. Maur in the manuscript journal of Captain John R. Bell of Major Stephen Long's expedition deals with the rescue of a female captive in 1821 by a Pawnee brave. See Wagner and Camp, p. 104.

26. Rusk, I, 94.

27. Cf. Elmer Baldwin, *History of LaSalle County, Illinois* (Chicago, 1877), pp. 98–104, for their own statement, written Sept. 7, 1867. Charles M. Scanlan retold the story in *Indian Creek Massacre . . .* (2nd ed., Milwaukee, 1915).

NOTES TO CHAPTER 4

1. E. Douglas Branch, *Westward, the Romance of the American Frontier* (New York and London, 1930), pp. 4–5.

2. *Ibid.*, pp. 52–57 and William Matthews, *American Diaries . . .* (Berkeley, Calif., 1945), p. 37.

3. A folk-recollection of Salley's journey is contained in A. J. Withers, *Chronicles of Border Warfare* (Clarksburg, Va., 1831). R. G. Thwaites's edition of the *Chronicles* (Cincinnati, 1895) adds variants.

4. Matthews, pp. 19–20; *DAB*, XIX, 614–15; and C. Z. Weiser, *The Life of Conrad Weiser* (Reading, Pa., 1878). A photostatic copy is in the Conrad Weiser Papers in the Historical Society of Pennsylvania, Philadelphia; see *Guide to the Manuscript Collections of the Historical Society of Pennsylvania* (2nd ed., Philadelphia, 1949), No. 700.

5. Kenneth P. Bailey, "Christopher Gist and the Trans-Allegheny Frontier: A Phase of the Westward Movement," *Pac. Hist. Rev.*, XIV (1945), 45–56; Branch, pp. 64–66; *DAB*, VII, 323–24; Matthews, p. 52; and Ralph L. Rusk, *The Literature of the Middle Western Frontier* (2 vols., New York, 1925), I, 85.

6. Part of the manuscript is in the custody of the Pennsylvania Historical Society. See David W. Bowman, *Pathway of Progress* (New York, 1943), pp. 43, 67; *DAB*, IV, 557; C. A. Hanna, *The Wilderness Trail* (New York, 1911), p. 56; "Life of Col.

Croghan," by a contemporary in the *Port Folio* (Philadelphia, Mar., 1815), pp. 212–20; Matthews, pp. 53–54; A. C. Quisenberry, "Colonel George Croghan 'The Hero of Fort Stephenson [Ohio],'" *Ky. Hist. Soc. Reg.*, X (1912), 23–29; Rusk, I, 85; Albert T. Volwiler, *George Croghan and the Westward Movement, 1741–1782* (Cleveland, 1926), in part in *Penna. Mag. Hist. Biog.*, XLVI (1922), 273–311; XLVII (1923), 28–57, 115–42; and Charles R. Williams, "George Croghan," *Ohio Arch. Hist. Quar.*, XII (1903), 375–409.

7. Branch, p. 69; Charles I. Landis, *Captain William Trent . . .* (Lancaster, Pa., 1919); Matthews, pp. 55–56; *DAB*, XVIII, 638–39; and Volwiler.

8. G. C. Davidson, *The North West Company* (Berkeley, Calif., 1918); Richard H. Dillon, "Peter Pond and the Overland Route to Cook's Inlet," *Pac. Northw. Quar.*, XLII (1951), 324–29; Harold Adams Innis, *Peter Pond, Fur Trader and Adventurer* (Toronto, 1930); Matthews, p. 67; and *DAB*, XV, 61.

9. The manuscript of the 1758 journal is in the custody of the Pennsylvania Historical Society. Writings about Post include H. H. Humrichouse, *Rev. Christian Frederick Post and Peter Humrichouse . . .* (Hagerstown?, Md., 1913); Matthews, pp. 75–76; *DAB*, XV, 113–14; and Rusk, I, 40.

10. The Rogers journal manuscript is in the Canadian Archives, Ottawa. See Matthews, pp. 63–64; John R. Cuneo, *Robert Rogers of the Rangers* (New York, 1959); Allan Nevins, *Ponteach* (Chicago, 1914); V. H. Paltaitz, "Journal of Robert Rogers . . .," *Bulletin of the New York Public Library*, XXXVII (1933), 261–76; Arthur Pount, *Native Stock . . .* (New York, 1931), pp. 109–48; M. M. Quaife, "Robert Rogers," *Burton Hist. Coll. Leaflet*, Sept., 1928; *DAB*, XVI, 108–9; Rusk, I, 85; and Caleb Stark, *Memoir of John Stark* (Concord, N. H., 1860).

11. *DAB*, IX, 433–56; Matthews, p. 84; and Rusk, I, 97.

12. See *The Papers of Col. Henry Bouquet* (3 vols., Harrisburg, Pa., 1940–1941). See also *DAB*, II, 480–81; Douglas Brymmer, *Report on Canadian Archives* (1889); Mary C. Darlington, ed. *History of Col. Henry Bouquet and the Western Frontiers of Pennsylvania, 1747–1768* (n. p., privately printed, 1920); *Mich. Hist. Colls.*, XIX (1891), 27–295; Francis Parkman, *The Conspiracy of Pontiac* (6th ed., rev. Boston, 1851); J. C. Reeve, "Henry Bouquet," *Ohio Arch. Hist. Soc. Pubs.*, XXVI (1916), 489–568; and Charles Whittlesey, "Colonel Bouquet's Expedition," *Cleveland Herald*, Dec., 1846, reprinted in *Fugitive Essays* (Hudson, O., 1852), pp. 264–81.

13. Beginning during the same year and continuing into 1795 is W. F. Horn's *The Horn Papers: Early Westward Movement on the Monongahela and Upper Ohio, 1765–1795* (3 vols., Waynesburg, Pa., 1946); the Papers are demonstrated to be forgeries. See *William and Mary Quarterly*, 3rd Series, IV (1947), 409–44.

14. *DAB*, II, 100; Rusk, I, 97; and William B. Sprague, *Annals of the American Pulpit . . .* (9 vols., New York, 1858), III, 119.

15. Matthews, p. 93.

16. John Hall, *Memoirs of Matthew Clarkson of Philadelphia, 1735–1800 by his Great-grandson, John Hall, and of his Brother, Gerardus Clarkson, 1737–1790, by his Great-grandson, Samuel Clarkson* (Philadelphia, 1890) and Matthews, p. 93.

17. *Ill. Hist. Colls.*, I (1903); Matthews, p. 94; *DAB*, XIII, 169–70; and Max Savelle, *George Morgan* (New York, 1932).

18. The original Carver manuscript is in the British Museum. See C. V. Alvord, "Jonathan Carver Vindicated," *Mag. Hist.*, XVI (1913), 196–99; "The Authenticity of Carver's 'Travels,'" *Mag. Hist.*, I (1905), 105–6; Edward G. Bourne, "The Travels of Jonathan Carver," *Amer. Hist. Rev.*, XI (1906), 287–302; William Browning, "The Early History of Jonathan Carver," *Wis. Mag. Hist.*, III (1920), 291–305; "Captain Jonathan Carver

and his Explorations," *Colls. Minn. Hist. Soc.*, I (1872), 349–67; *DAB*, III, 552; D. S. Durrie, "Captain Jonathan Carver and 'Carver's Grant,'" *Wis. Hist. Soc. Colls.*, VI (1872), 220–70; Russell W. Fridley, "The Writings of Jonathan Carver," *Minn. Hist.*, XXXIV (1954), 154–59; John G. Gregory, *Jonathan Carver, His Travels in the Northwest, 1766–1768* (Milwaukee, 1896); Louise P. Kellogg, "The Mission of Jonathan Carver," *Wis. Mag. Hist.*, XII (1928), 127–45; John T. Lee, "A Bibliography of Carver's Travels," *Wis. Hist. Soc., Procs.*, LVII (1909), 143–83 and "Captain Jonathan Carver: Additional Data," *Wis. Hist. Soc. Procs.*, LX (1912), 87–123; Milo M. Quaife, "Jonathan Carver and the Carver Land Grant," *Miss. Val. Hist. Rev.*, VII (1920), 3–25, and "More Light on Carver," *Wis. Mag. Hist.*, IV (1920–1921), 345–47; and Rusk, I, 86. A summary of Carver's journey appears in *Wis. Hist. Soc. Colls.*, XVIII (1908), 280–85. A facsimile reprint of the 1781 edition was published at Minneapolis in 1956.

19. *DAB*, X, 56–57 and Matthews, pp. 93–94.

20. Matthews, p. 95.

21. Rusk, I, 86.

22. Most of the Washington manuscripts are in the Library of Congress. See Jared Sparks, ed. *George Washington's Writings* (12 vols., Boston, 1834–1837). The following articles and books on Washington most adequately emphasize the Western element in his life: Charles H. Ambler, *George Washington and the West* (Chapel Hill, N. C., 1936); George B. Catlin, "George Washington Looks Westward," *Mich. Hist.*, XVI (1932), 127–42; Hugh Cleland, *George Washington in the Ohio Valley* (Pittsburgh, 1955); Roy Bird Cook, *Washington's Western Lands* (Strasburg, Va., 1931); Theodore F. Dwight, "The Journals of Washington," *Mag. of Amer. Hist.*, VI (1881), 81–88; John C. Fitzpatrick, *George Washington Himself* (Indianapolis, 1933); C. B. Galbreath, "Bicentennial Celebration—George Washington's Voyage on the Ohio River in 1770," *Ohio Arch. Hist. Quar.*, XLII (1933), 3–56 and "George Washington's Interest in the Ohio Country," *Ohio Arch. Hist. Quar.*, XLI (1932), 20–27; Ada H. Hixon, "George Washington, Land Speculator," *Jour. Ill. State Hist. Soc.*, XI (1919), 566–75; Rupert Hughes, *George Washington* (New York, 1930); Archer B. Hulbert, "The Debt of the West to Washington," *Ohio Arch. Hist. Quar.*, IX (1900), 205–13 and *Washington's Road . . . the First Chapter of the Old French War* (Cleveland, 1903); Louis K. Koontz, "Washington on the Frontier," *Va. Mag. Hist. Biog.*, XXXVI (1928), 305–27; Frederic L. Paxson, "Washington and the Western Fronts, 1753–1795," *Jour. Ill. State Hist. Soc.*, XXIV (1932), 589–605; Emilius Oviatt Randall, "Washington and Ohio," *Ohio Arch. Hist. Quar.*, XVI (1907), 471–501; W. J. Showalter, "The Travels of George Washington," *National Geographic Magazine*, XX (1932), 274–83; Guy-Harold Smith, "George Washington at the Great Bend of the Ohio River," *Ohio Arch. Hist. Quar.*, XLI (1932), 655–67; and John Tebbel, *George Washington's America* (New York, 1954), pp. 47–50.

23. Only two copies of the first edition (Williamsburg, Va., 1754) are known to exist. It was reprinted in Worthington C. Ford, ed. *Writings of George Washington* (14 vols., New York and London, 1889–93), I, 11–40 and in John G. Fitzpatrick, ed. *The Diaries of George Washington, 1748–1799* (4 vols., Boston and New York, 1925), I, 37–67.

24. *DAB*, X, 165–66; J. B. Linn and W. H. Egle, *Pennsylvania in the War of the Revolution* (2 vols., Harrisburg, 1860); Matthews, pp. 101–2; Rusk, I, 97; W. B. Sprague, VI (1860); C. J. Stillé, *Major General Anthony Wayne and the Pennsylvania Line in the Continental Army* (Philadelphia, 1893).

25. Matthews, p. 104.

26. *Ibid.* Lacey's memoirs have been published in *Penna. Mag. Hist. Biog.*, XXV (1901), 1–13, 191–207, 341–54, 498–515; XXVI (1902), 101–11, 265–70.

27. Rusk, I, 97.

28. Matthews, p. 105.

29. Additional information on Heckewelder in *DAB*, VIII, 495–97; Matthews, p. 181; William H. Rice, "The Rev. John Heckewelder . . . ," *Ohio Arch. Hist. Quar.*, VII (1899), 314–48; Edward Rondthaler, *Life of John Heckewelder* (Philadelphia, 1847); and Rusk, I, 40. The manuscript of "Notes of Travel . . ." is in the Historical Society of Pennsylvania, Philadelphia.

30. "Heckewelder's Narrative," *Ohio Arch. Hist. Quar.*, XVIII (1909), 258–61 and Rusk, I, 96; II, 34.

31. Matthews, p. 106.

NOTES TO CHAPTER 5

1. A travel narrative whose title reflects the existence of the Revolution was written by a man probably named George Walker, *A View of North America, in its Former Happy, and its Present Belligerent State, with Travels and Adventures of the Author, through Great Part of that Continent, in the Years 1774, 75, 76 and 78 . . .* (Glasgow, 1781).

2. William Matthews, *American Diaries . . .* (Berkeley, Calif., 1945), p. 145.

3. Asa Earl Martin, *History of the United States, 1492–1865* (2 vols., Boston, etc., 1928), I, 171–73.

4. John Bakeless, *Background to Glory, the Life of George Rogers Clark* (New York, 1957); C. C. Baldwin, "Francis Vigo and General George Rogers Clark," *Mag. West. Hist.*, I (1885), 230–36; Temple Bodley, *George Rogers Clark; his Life and Public Service* (Boston and New York, 1926); C. W. Butterfield, *History of George Rogers Clark's Conquest of the Illinois and the Wabash Towns . . .* (Columbus, O., 1904); *DAB*, IV, 127–30; Mary Cone, "The Expedition and Conquests of General George Rogers Clark, in 1778–79, *Mag. West. Hist.*, II (1885), 133–55; Minnie G. Cook, "The History of George Rogers Clark's 'Memoir.' Documents and Comments," *Va. Mag. Hist. Biog.*, XV (1907), 205–11; George Creer, *Sons of the Eagle* (Indianapolis, 1896); J. Dalton, "George Rogers Clark: Conqueror of an Empire," *Current History*, XXX (1929), 74–79; W. H. English, *Conquest of the Country Northwest of the River Ohio, 1778–1783; and Life of George Rogers Clark . . .* (Indianapolis and Kansas City, Mo., 1896); "George Rogers Clark—A Soldier of the Early West," *Mag. West. Hist.*, XIV (1891), 561–72; Walter Havighurst, *George Rogers Clark, Soldier in the West* (New York, 1952); Archer B. Hulbert, *Conquest of the Old Northwest* (Cleveland, 1904); James A. James, *The Life of George Rogers Clark* (Chicago, 1928); Laurence J. Kenny, "George Rogers Clark in Ohio," *Catholic Historical Review*, X (1928), 248–60; Ross F. Lockridge, *Pioneer Hero of the Old Northwest* (Chicago, 1927); Edward G. Mason, *Chapters from Illinois History* (Chicago, 1901); Matthews, p. 125; John Moses, "The Expedition of General George Rogers Clark," *Mag. West. Hist.*, III (1886), 267–70; Frederick Palmer, *Clark of the Ohio; a Life of George Rogers Clark* (New York, 1929); T. C. Pease, *Revolution in Illinois . . .* (Springfield, 1929); M. M. Quaife, *The Conquest of the Illinois* (Chicago, 1920) and *The Captive of Old Vincennes* (Indianapolis, 1927); Theodore Roosevelt, *The Winning of the West* (4 vols., New York and London, 1889–96), Vols. I, II, *passim*; Z. F. Smith, "Gen. George Rogers Clark," *Ky. Hist. Soc. Reg.*, IV (1906), 31–37; Hambleton Tapp, "George Rogers Clark . . . ," *Filson Club History Quarterly*, XV (1941), 133–58; R. G. Thwaites, *How George Rogers Clark Won the Northwest*

. . . (Chicago, 1903); F. J. Turner, "George Rogers Clark and the Kaskaskia Campaign, 1777–1778," *Amer. Hist. Rev.*, VIII (1903), 491–506; Claude H. VanTyne, *The American Revolution . . .* (New York, 1905); and W. E. Wilson, *The Big Knife* (New York, 1940).

5. See *Col. George Rogers Clark's Sketch of His Campaign in the Illinois* (Cincinnati, 1907), pp. 82–94, and Matthews, p. 148.

6. *DAB*, XI, 538.

7. See Chapter 3, n. 8.

8. Matthews, p. 160.

9. *Ibid.*, p. 159.

10. *Ibid.*, p. 50; Ralph L. Rusk, *The Literature of the Middle Western Frontier* (2 vols., New York, 1925), I, 271n.

11. Matthews, p. 164.

12. Joseph Tassé, *Les Canadiens de l'Ouest* (2 vols., Montreal, 1878).

13. Rusk, I, 102.

14. Matthews, p. 166.

15. O. F. Emerson, "Notes on Gilbert Imlay . . . ," *P. M. L. A.* XXXIX (1924), 406–39; *DAB*, IX, 461–62; Rusk, I, 122, 128, and "The Adventures of Gilbert Imlay," *Indiana University Studies*, Vol. X, No. 57 (Bloomington, 1923).

16. See Chapter 3, n. 8. John Walton, *John Filson of Kentucky* (Lexington, 1956), pp. 73–83, does not doubt Filson's authorship of this journal.

17. Matthews, p. 168.

18. *Ibid.*, p. 164.

19. *Ibid.*, pp. 166–67; Benjamin H. Pershing, "Winthrop Sargent," *Ohio Arch. Hist. Quar.*, XXXV (1926), 583–692 and *Winthrop Sargent: A Builder of the Old Northwest* (Dissertation, University of Chicago, 1927); *DAB*, XVI, 368–69.

20. John B. Linn, "Erkuries Beatty, Paymaster in the Western Army, 1786–1787," *Amer. Mag. Hist.*, I (1877), 372ff. and Matthews, pp. 147–48. The manuscript, consisting of 49 leaves, is in the New-York Historical Society.

21. Rusk, *The Literature of the Middle Western Frontier*, I, 93–94.

22. Matthews, p. 170. The manuscript is at Marietta College, Ohio.

23. *Ibid.*, p. 171. The 38-page manuscript is in the Durrett Collection, University of Chicago.

24. Aubrey Diller, "James Mackay's Journey in Nebraska in 1796," *Neb. Hist.*, XXXVI (1955), 123–28; Louis Houck, *A History of Missouri . . .* (3 vols., Chicago, 1908), Vols. II, III; *DAB*, XII, 74–75; "Mackay's Table of Distances," *Miss. Val. Hist. Rev.*, X (1924), 428–46; Matthews, p. 191; *Wis. Hist. Soc. Colls.*, IV (1912), 20–21; and *St. Louis Enquirer*, Mar. 23, 1822.

25. *DAB*, I, 304, and Mrs. Louise L. Lovell, *Israel Angell, Colonel of the Second Rhode Island Regiment* (New York, 1920). Angell's published diary does not cover this trip. The Midwestern manuscript was originally under the care of Mr. Harris W. Brown.

26. *DAB*, V, 12–14; Martin, I, 295; Matthews, p. 91; and John C. Ridpath, *The New Complete History of the United States of America* (12 vols., Washington and Cincinnati, 1904–1907), VII, 3520–21. The manuscripts were owned by Mr. Charles Dawes, Chicago.

27. The title was *An Explanation of the Map which Delineates that Part of the Federal Lands, Comprehended between Pennsylvania West Line, the Rivers Ohio and Scioto, and Lake Erie . . .* (Salem, Mass., 1787). A French translation appeared in 1789.

28. H. M. Brackenridge, *Recollections of Persons and Places*

in the West (rev. ed., Philadelphia, 1868); William V. Byars, *A Memoir of the Life and Work of Dr. Antoine François Saugrain, the First Scientist of the Mississippi Valley* (n. p., n. d.); N. P. Dandridge, "Antoine François Saugrain (de Vigne) . . . ," *Ohio Arch. Hist. Quar.*, XV (1906), 192–206; Matthews, p. 173; Rusk, I, 90; and *DAB*, XVI, 377–78.

29. Matthews, p. 155.

30. *Ibid.*, p. 173.

31. *Ibid.*, p. 172 and Mrs. Josephine E. Phillips, "James Backus, Citizen of Marietta, 1788–91," *Ohio Arch. Hist. Quar.*, XLV (1936), 161–72.

32. Rowena Buell's *The Memoirs of Rufus Putnam* (Boston and New York, 1903) contains much official correspondence. See *DAB*, XV, 284–85 and Israel Putnam, *The Two Putnams, Israel and Rufus* (Hartford, 1931), pp. 143–262. The manuscript of Rufus Putnam's autobiography, written in 1812, is in the Marietta College Library.

33. J. M. Buckley, . . . *A History of Methodism in the United States* (2 vols., New York, 1896); *DAB*, VI, 389–90; Rusk, I, 47, 48, 97; William B. Sprague, *Annals of the American Pulpit* . . . (9 vols., New York, 1857–[69]), VII, 531; and Abel Stevens, *The History of the Religious Movement of the Eighteenth Century, Called Methodism* . . . (4 vols., New York and London, 1867), Vol. IV. Manuscripts covering the years 1810–1840, including a diary, are in the Rutherford B. Hayes Library, Fremont, O.

NOTES TO CHAPTER 6

1. William Matthews, *American Diaries* . . . (Berkeley, Calif., 1945), p. 175. The manuscript is in the New-York Historical Society.

2. *Ibid.*, p. 174.

3. See Chapter 5, n. 19.

4. *DAB*, XXI, 36.

5. George Bryce, *Mackenzie, Selkirk, Simpson* (Toronto, 1905); George B. Grinnell, *Trails of the Pathfinders* (New York, 1911); Agnes C. Laut, *Pathfinders of the West* . . . (New York, London, 1904); Leslie Stephens and Sidney Lee, eds. *Dictionary of National Biography* (22 vols., New York and London, 1921–22), XII, 578–79, (hereafter abbreviated *DNB*); Matthews, p. 174; Jeannette Mirsky, *The Westward Crossings* . . . (New York, 1946); Mark S. Wade, *Mackenzie of Canada* . . . (Edinburgh and London, 1927); Henry R. Wagner and Charles L. Camp, *The Plains and the Rockies* (Columbus, O., 1953), pp. 1–3; and Humphrey H. Wrong, *Sir Alexander Mackenzie, Explorer and Fur-Trader* (Toronto, 1927).

6. Matthews, p. 176.

7. *Ibid.*, p. 177. The original manuscript is in the Burton Historical Collection, Detroit.

8. Ellis Beals, "Arthur St. Clair, Western Pennsylvania's Leading Citizen," *West. Penn. Hist. Mag.*, XII (1929), 75–96, 175–96; Albert Douglas, "Major General Arthur St. Clair," *Ohio. Arch. Hist. Quar.*, XVI (1907), 455–76; R. C. Downes, "The Statehood Contest in Ohio," *Miss. Val. Hist. Rev.*, XVIII (1931), 155–71; Asa Earl Martin, *History of the United States, 1492–1865* (2 vols., Boston, etc., 1928), I, 296; Ralph L. Rusk, *The Literature of the Middle Western Frontier* (2 vols., New York, 1925), I, 54n., 308; and *DAB*, XVI, 293–95.

9. Matthews, p. 178 and Wagner and Camp, pp. 4–7.

10. Matthews, p. 177.

11. *Ibid.*, p. 178.

12. Selections from the journal appear in E. S. Tipple, ed. *The Heart of Asbury's Journal* (New York, 1904). See *DAB*, I, 379–83; Herbert Asbury, *A Methodist Saint* . . . (New York, 1927);

Ezekiel Cooper, *The Substance of a Funeral Discourse* . . . *on the Death of the Rev. Francis Asbury* . . . (Philadelphia, 1819); William L. Duren, *Francis Asbury, Founder of American Methodism* . . . (New York, 1928); Matthews, p. 99; Rusk, I, 19n., 50–51, 98; W. P. Strickland, *The Pioneer Bishop* . . . (New York, 1858); and E. S. Tipple, *Francis Asbury, the Prophet of the Long Road* (New York and Cincinnati, 1916).

13. Matthews, p. 169.

14. One of his books, translated as *Recollections of Italy, England, and America, with Essays on Various Subjects* . . . (London, 1812), relates travels no farther west than Niagara. See Joseph Bedier, *Études Critiques* (1903); Gilbert Chinard, *Notes sur le Voyage de Chateaubriand en Amérique* (*Juillet–Décembre, 1791*) (Berkeley, Calif., 1915); and Rusk, I, 2, 90–91.

15. Matthews, p. 180.

16. *Ibid.*, p. 178.

17. See the account of Lincoln by Francis Bowin in Jared Sparks, ed. *The Library of American Biography*, 2nd Series (25 vols., Boston and London, 1847), Vol. XIII; *DAB*, XI, 259–61; and Matthews, p. 183.

18. *DAB*, XI, 275–76; Matthews, p. 183; and Charles M. Walker, *History of Athens County, Ohio* (Cincinnati, 1869).

19. See Chapter 5, n. 19, and n. 3 above.

20. *DAB*, II, 543–44; William F. Keller, "A Glimpse of the Life and Letters of Henry Marie Brackenridge," *West. Penn. Hist. Mag.*, XXXVII (1954), 1–17; J. F. McDermott, "Henry Marie Brackenridge and his Writings," *West. Penn. Hist. Mag.*, XX (1937), 181–96; and Rusk, I, 90, 124, 304. A good list of Brackenridge's writings appears in Joseph Sabin, *A Dictionary of Books Relating to America* . . . (29 vols., New York, 1869), Vol. II.

21. The manuscript is in the Indiana State Historical Society, Indianapolis.

22. Many Clark manuscripts are in the Wisconsin State Historical Library, Madison; the Missouri Historical Society of St. Louis; and the Kansas State Historical Society, Topeka. See *DAB*, IV, 141–44; Harlow Lindley, "William Clark—the Indian Agent," *Miss. Val. Hist. Assn. Procs.*, 1908–09 (1910), II, 63–75; Matthews, p. 186; R. G. Thwaites, "William Clark: Soldier, Explorer, Statesman," *Mo. Hist. Soc. Colls.*, II (1906), 1–24; and Wagner and Camp, pp. 7–8.

23. Rusk, I, 11n., mentions a note by Witherell in the Burton Historical Collection, Detroit.

24. Matthews, p. 187.

25. *Ibid.*, p. 188.

26. The Truteau letters are in the Missouri Historical Society. See Matthews, p. 188; *DAB*, XIX, 20–21; and "Trudeau's Description of the Upper Missouri," *Miss. Val. Hist. Rev.*, VIII (1921), 149–79.

27. Jefferson's letter is printed in R. G. Thwaites, ed. *Original Journals of the Lewis and Clark Expedition, 1804–1806* (8 vols., New York, 1905), VII, 292–93.

28. Matthews, p. 189.

29. J. P. F. Deleuze, "Notice Historique sur André Michaux," *Annales du Museum National d'Histoire Naturelle*, III (1804); Matthews, p. 184; *DAB*, XII, 591–92; and Rusk, I, 8n., 99, 256.

30. Large portions of Cleaveland's journal and other papers have been lost. See Elbert J. Benton, *The Connecticut Land Company and Accompanying Papers* (1916); *DAB*, IV, 188–89; Martin, I, 295n; Matthews, p. 190; Samuel P. Orth, *A History of Cleveland, Ohio* (Cleveland, 1910), pp. 793, 801; and Harvey Rice, *The Founder of the City of Cleveland* . . . (Boston, 1892).

31. Matthews, p. 191.

32. *Ibid.*, p. 190.

33. Farmer wrote *The History of Detroit and Michigan* (Detroit, 1884). See Rusk, I, 11n. and 361n.

34. The manuscript is in the Burton Historical Collection, Detroit. See *DAB*, X, 165–66.

35. Rusk, I, 8n., 100–1. Both editions of this work were probably printed before the author's death in 1805 but were not published until 1826.

36. *Ibid.*, I, 7–8.

37. *DAB*, I, 435–36. "The Austin Papers," *Amer. Hist. Assn. Ann. Rep.*, I (1919) and II (1924); Eugene C. Barker, *The Life of Stephen F. Austin* (Nashville, Dallas, 1925); Matthews, p. 190; and James A. Gardner, "The Business Career of Moses Austin in Missouri," *Mo. Hist. Rev.*, L (1956), 237–47.

38. Matthews, p. 190.

39. Mrs. Sally Alexander, "A Sketch of the Life of Major Andrew Ellicott," *Col. Hist. Soc. Recs.*, II (1899), 158–202; *DAB*, VI, 89–90; Charles W. Evans, *Biographical and Historical Account of the Fox, Ellicott, and Evans Families* (Buffalo, 1882); Catherine V. C. Mathews, *Andrew Ellicott, His Life and Letters* (New York, 1908); and Matthews, p. 191.

40. Matthews, p. 190.

41. Frank T. Cole, "Thomas Worthington," *Ohio Arch. Hist. Quar.*, XII (1903), 339–74, and *Thomas Worthington of Ohio, Founder, Senator, Governor and First Citizen* (Columbus, 1903); Sarah W. K. Peter, *Private Memoir of Thomas Worthington* (n. p., 1882); Alfred B. Sears, *Thomas Worthington, Father of Ohio Statehood* (Columbus, 1958), pp. 13–20; and *DAB*, XX, 540–41.

42. *DAB*, III, 294–95; Charles T. Greve, *Centennial History of Cincinnati and Representative Cities* (Chicago, 1904), vol. I *passim;* Rusk, I, 238; and Graham A. Worth, *Recollections of Cincinnati, 1817–21* (Albany, N. Y., 1851), p. 61.

43. Matthews, p. 194.

44. Samuel F. Bemis, "David Thompson, Explorer," *Sunset*, L (1923), 28–29; C. N. Cochrane, *David Thompson, the Explorer* (Toronto, 1924); Matthews, p. 216; and *DAB*, XVIII, 455.

45. Letters and photostats are in the Library of Congress. See (Hartford) *Connecticut Courant*, July 29, 1807; F. B. Dexter, *Biographical Sketches of the Graduates of Yale College . . .* (4 vols., New York, 1901), Vol. IV; Payne K. Kilbourne, *Sketches and Chronicles of the Town of Litchfield, Conn. . . .* (Hartford, 1859); and *DAB*, XVIII, 624–25.

46. Matthews, p. 198.

47. *Ibid.*

48. Rusk, I, 117–18.

49. *American Quarterly Register*, XIII (1841), 317–28 contains Badger's autobiography. See also *DAB*, I, 487–88; H. N. Day, ed. *Memoir of Joseph Badger* (Hudson, O., 1851); Byron B. Long, "Joseph Badger, the First Missionary to the Western Reserve," *Ohio Arch. Hist. Quar.*, XXVI (1917), 1–42; Matthews, p. 199; and William B. Sprague, *Annals of the American Pulpit . . .* (9 vols., New York, 1857–[69]), III, 473–79.

50. Lawrence J. Burpee, *The Search for the Western Sea; the Story of the Exploration of North-Western America* (London, 1908) and Matthews, p. 197.

51. *The John Askin Papers* (2 vols., Detroit, 1928–31); "Biographical Sketch of the Late Alexander Henry, Esq.," *Canadian Magazine and Literary Repository*, II (1824), 289–304, 385–97; *DAB*, XXI, 393–94; Matthews, pp. 197–98; W. E. Stevens, *The Northwest Fur Trade, 1763–1800* (Urbana, Ill., 1928); *David Thompson's Narrative . . .* (Toronto, 1916); and Wagner and Camp, pp. 14–16.

52. This was taken from a manuscript journal in the Minnesota Historical Society Library, St. Paul.

53. Thomas Ford, *A History of Illinois . . .* (Chicago and New York, 1854); Josephine L. Harper, "John Reynolds, 'The Old Ranger' of Illinois, 1788–1865" (thesis, University of Illinois, 1949); Randall Parrish, *Historic Illinois . . .* (Chicago, 1905); *DAB*, XV, 519–20; and John P. Snyder, *Adam W. Snyder . . .* (Springfield, Ill., 1903).

54. Christian Bay, "Dr. Daniel Drake, 1785–1852," *Filson Club History Quarterly*, VII (1933), 1–17; R. C. Buley, *The Old Northwest . . .* (2 vols., Indianapolis, 1950), II, 543–45; *DAB*, V, 426–27; J. T. Flexner, "Western Doctor," *Literary Digest*, CXXIV (Oct. 23, 1937), 28; E. F. Horine, ed. *Pioneer Life in Kentucky, 1785–1800* (New York, 1941), pp. xvi–36 *passim;* O. Justiner, *Daniel Drake and his Followers . . .* (Cincinnati, 1909); E. D. Mansfield, *Memoirs of the Life and Services of Daniel Drake, M.D. . . .* (Cincinnati, 1855); George Rosen and G. R. Beste, eds. *400 Years of a Doctor's Life* (New York, 1947), pp. 6–11, 33–34, 63–66; Alice M. Ruggles, "Unpublished Letters of Dr. Daniel Drake," *Ohio Arch. Hist., Quar.*, XLIX (1940), 191–211; Rusk, I, 59, 123, 135n., 136n., 195, 196, 206–7, 234, 235, 272, 356; II, 34; George X. Schwemlein, "Daniel Drake, M.D., 1785–1852," *Hist. Phil. Soc. of Ohio Bull.*, IX (1951), 238–40; and David A. Tucker, Jr., "Daniel Drake and the Origin of Medicine in the Ohio Valley," *Ohio Arch. Hist. Quar.*, XLIV (1935), 451–68.

55. Matthews, p. 225.

56. The manuscript is in the Lane County Pioneer Museum, Eugene, Oregon.

NOTES TO CHAPTER 7

1. See Chapter 6, n. 37.

2. William Matthews, *American Diaries . . .* (Berkeley, Calif., 1945), p. 199.

3. *Ibid.*, p. 198.

4. *DAB*, I, 474–75; T. W. Baldwin, *Michael Bacon of Dedham, 1640, and His Descendants* (Cambridge, 1915) and biographical sketch by E. N. Sill and address by Bacon's son, Leonard Bacon, both in *Proceedings in Commemoration of the Fiftieth Anniversary of the Settlement of Tallmadge* (1857).

5. Matthews, p. 201. The original 129-page manuscript is in the William L. Clements Library, University of Michigan, Ann Arbor.

6. Elias Darnell, "Biographical Memoir of the Late François André Michaux," *American Philosophical Society Tracts*, XI (1800); *DAB*, XII, 592–93; and Ralph L. Rusk, *The Literature of the Middle Western Frontier* (2 vols., New York, 1925), I, 46, 99.

7. See A. H. Abel, "Trudeau's Description of the Upper Missouri," *Miss. Val. Hist. Rev.*, VIII (1921), 153–57.

8. Nathaniel L. Frothingham, "Memoir of Rev. Thaddeus Mason Harris," *Mass. Hist. Soc. Colls.*, 4th Series (Cambridge, 1855), Vol. II; *DAB*, VIII, 320–21; Rusk, I, 120; and W. B. Sprague, *Annals of the American Unitarian Pulpit . . .* (9 vols., New York, 1857–[69]).

9. Matthews, p. 206. See n. 23 of this chapter for information about the 1804–1806 Expedition. On Ordway see Matthews, p. 207; *DAB*, XIV, 51; and "Some New-Found Records of the Lewis and Clark Expedition," *Miss. Val. Hist. Rev.*, II (1915), 109.

10. Matthews, p. 204.

11. *Ibid.*, p. 202. The manuscript is in the Masson papers in the Canadian Archives, Ottawa.

12. The original manuscript is in the Archives of the Archbishop's Palace, Montreal. A manuscript was made by Jacques Viger and is now at the Archives of the Quebec Seminary in *la*

Saberdache (rouge), C, 1–139. Another manuscript copy is at Washington, D. C.

13. Elliot Coues, ed. *The Journal of Jacob Fowler* (New York, 1898) and *DAB*, IX, 587–88.

14. Matthews, p. 206.

15. *Ibid.*, p. 207.

16. Louis Houck, *A History of Missouri* . . . (3 vols., Chicago, 1908), vol. II; John T. Scharf, *History of St. Louis City and County* . . . (2 vols., Philadelphia, 1883), Vol. I; E. W. Stoddard, *Anthony Stoddard, of Boston, Mass.* . . . (New York, 1865); and *DAB*, XVIII, 51–52.

17. Herbert Asbury, *A Methodist Saint* . . . (New York, 1927); *DAB*, V, 410; *The Eccentric Preacher; A Sketch of the Life of the Celebrated Lorenzo Dow* (Lowell, Mass., 1841); Matthews, p. 186; Rusk, I, 49–50, 226–27; Charles C. Sellers, *Lorenzo Dow, the Bearer of the Word* (New York, 1928); and W. J. Townsend, H. B. Workman, and G. Eayrs, *A New History of Methodism* (London, 1909).

18. Matthews, p. 205.

19. *Ibid.*, p. 206.

20. *DAB*, VII, 178–79; John G. Jacob, *The Life and Times of Patrick Gass* . . . (Wellsburg, Va., 1859); Matthews, p. 206; and Henry R. Wagner and Charles L. Camp, *The Plains and the Rockies* . . . (Columbus, 1953), pp. 12–13.

21. Matthews, p. 205.

22. *Ibid.*, pp. 207–8.

23. See Chapter 6, n. 22. A letter by William Clark to his brother, George Rogers Clark, dated at St. Louis, Sept. 23, 1806, printed at Philadelphia in 1806, summarizes the expedition. See John E. Bakeless, *Lewis and Clark, Partners in Discovery* (New York, 1947); "Big American Find," *Newsweek*, XLI (Apr. 6, 1953), 94, 96, 98; John B. Brebner, *The Explorers of North America, 1492–1806* (New York, 1953); Noah Brooks, *First across the Continent* . . . (New York, 1902); "By Land from the United States in 1804 and 1806," *Time Magazine*, LXIV (Oct. 10, 1955), 21, 64, 73; *The Cambridge History of American Literature*, William P. Trent *et al.*, eds. (4 vols., New York, 1917–21), I, 204–5; David H. Coyner, *The Lost Trappers; a Collection of Interesting Scenes and Events* . . . (Chicago, 1855); Bernard De Voto, "The Turning Point for Lewis and Clark," *Harper's*, CCV (1952), 36–43; A. R. Fulton, "Lewis and Clark's Expedition," *Ann. of Ia.*, 2nd Series, II (1883), 17–19; Charles G. Gray, "Lewis and Clark at the Mouth of Wood River," *Jour. Ill. State Hist. Soc.*, XIII (1920), 180–91; Ralph B. Guinness, "The Purpose of the Lewis and Clark Expedition," *Miss. Val. Hist. Rev.*, XX (1933), 90–100; Hildegarde Hawthorne, *Westward the Course* . . . (New York, 1946); Louis Houck, *A History of Missouri* (3 vols., Chicago, 1908), III, 408; Emerson Hough, *The Magnificent Adventure* . . . (New York, 1916); Thomas Jefferson's Biography of Lewis in *History of the Expedition under the Command of Captains Lewis and Clark* (2 vols., Philadelphia, 1812); Agnes Laut, *Pathfinders of the West* (New York, 1904); Andrew T. Lewis, "Meriwether Lewis," *Oreg. Hist. Soc. Quar.*, VI (1905), 391–402; *Lewis and Clark Anniversary Number, Washington Academy of Sciences Journal*, XLIV (1954), 333–73; "The Lewis and Clark Expedition in its Relation to Iowa History and Geography," *Ann. of Ia.*, 3rd Series, XIII (1921), 99–125, (1922), 163–92; William R. Lighton, *Lewis and Clark* (Boston and New York, 1901); Matthews, p. 206; Lee Meriwether, "Meriwether Lewis. His Work, and his Place in American History," *Va. Mag. Hist. Biog.*, XLV (1937), 329–45; Milo M. Quaife, "Some New-Found Records of the Lewis and Clark Expedition," *Miss Val. Hist. Rev.*, II (1915), 106–18; Doane Robinson, "Medical Adventures of Lewis and Clark," *Sou. Dak.*

Hist. Colls., XII (1924), 53–66; Rusk, I, 87–88; Albert P. Salisbury, *Two Captains West* . . . (Seattle, 1950); R. G. Thwaites, "The Story of Lewis and Clark's Journals," *Oreg. Hist. Soc. Quar.*, VI (1905), 26–53; Olin D. Wheeler, *The Trail of Lewis and Clark, 1804–1904* . . . (New York and London, 1904); Charles M. Wilson, *Meriwether Lewis of Lewis and Clark* (New York, 1934); and Marcus J. Wright, "Governor Meriwether Lewis, 1774–1809," *Mag. of Amer. Hist.*, XXVI (1891), 135–42. See also Grace R. Hebard, *Sagajawea, A Guide and Interpreter of the Lewis and Clark Expedition, with an Account of the Travels of Toussaint Charbonneau, and of Jean Baptiste, the Expedition Papoose* (Glendale, Cal., 1957); *DAB*, XI, 219–22.

24. Matthews, p. 208.

25. *Ibid.*, p. 209.

26. LeRoy R. Hafen, "Zebulon Montgomery Pike," *Colorado Magazine*, VIII (1931), 132–42; W. Eugene Hollon, *The Lost Pathfinder, Zebulon Montgomery Pike* (Norman, Okla., 1949), "Zebulon Montgomery Pike's Lost Papers," *Miss. Val. Hist. Rev.*, XXXIV (1947), 264–73 and "Zebulon Montgomery Pike's Mississippi Voyage," *Wis. Mag. Hist.*, XXXII (1949), 445–55; Ethyl E. Martin, "The Expedition of Zebulon Montgomery Pike to the Sources of the Mississippi," *Iowa Jour. Hist.*, IX (1911), 335–58; Matthews, p. 210; "Papers of Zebulon M. Pike, 1806–1807 . . . ," *Amer. Hist. Rev.*, XIII (1908), 798–827; *DAB*, XIV, 599–600; "Pike's Explorations," *Ann. of Ia.*, 3rd Series, I (1894), 531–36; N. L. Prentis, "Pike of Pike's Peak," *Kans. State Hist. Soc. Trans.*, VI (1897–1900), 325–36; Rusk, I, 87, 89; Wagner and Camp, pp. 19–26; R. M. Warner, "The Death of Zebulon M. Pike," *Ann. of Ia.*, 3rd Series, XXXIII (1955), 44–46; and Henry Whiting, "Life of Zebulon Montgomery Pike," in Jared Sparks, *The Library of American Biography*, 2nd Series (25 vols., Boston, 1834–48), Vol. V.

27. *Handbook of Manuscripts in the Library of Congress* (Washington, 1918), pp. 365–66.

28. Matthews, p. 210.

29. *DNB*, I, 641; Walter L. Fleming "Thomas Ashe's Travels," *Miss. Val. Hist. Rev.*, I (1915), 574–76; Francis H. Herrick, "Thomas Ashe and the Authenticity of his Travels in America," *Miss. Val. Hist. Rev.*, XIII (1926), 50–57; Matthews, p. 211; Rusk, I, 75n., 102–4, 105, 106, 114; and William H. Venable, *Beginnings of Literary Culture in the Ohio Valley* . . . (New York, 1891).

30. Matthews, p. 211.

31. W. J. Finck, "Paul Henkel, the Lutheran Pioneer," *Lutheran Quarterly*, LVI (1926), 307–34; *DAB*, VIII, 538–39; Matthews, p. 211; John G. Morris, *Fifty Years in the Lutheran Ministry* (Baltimore, 1878).

32. *DAB*, IX, 21–22 and Rusk, I, 238. Hildreth became interested in history and published *Contributions to the Early History of the Northwest, including the Moravian Missions in Ohio* . . . (Cincinnati and New York, c. 1864), which contains an account of the capture of Joseph Kelly.

33. Matthews, p. 215.

34. *Ibid.*, p. 211.

35. Rusk, I, 118.

36. *Ibid.*, I, 74; *DAB*, IV, 592; "Retrospective Review," *Western Monthly Magazine*, III (1833), 314–16.

37. Matthews, p. 202.

38. See Chapter 6, n. 22.

39. *DAB*, II, 526–27; J. P. Boyd, *Documents and Facts Relative to Military Events* . . . (n. p., 1816); Herbert Compton, *A Particular Account of the European Military Adventures of Hindustan* . . . (London, 1893); Edward A. Powell, *Gentlemen Rovers* (New York, 1913); Francis B. Heitman, *Historical Reg-*

ister and Dictionary of the United States Army . . . (Washington, 1890).

40. James F. Leishman, *A Son of Knox and Other Studies Antiquarian and Biographical* (Glasgow, 1909) and Rusk, I, 121.

41. John Scott Gilmour, *British Botanists* (London, 1944); "John Bradbury, the Earliest St. Louisan of Botanical Note," *Mo. Hist. Rev.*, XXIV (1930), 414–19; Matthews, p. 215; Rusk, I, 99, 256, 304; "Travellers in America," *Edin. Rev.*, XXXI (1818), 132–50; R. H. True, "A Sketch of the Life of John Bradbury . . . ," *American Philosophical Society Proceedings*, LXVIII (1929), 133–50; and Wagner and Camp, pp. 33–34.

42. Matthews, p. 215, and Rusk, I, 49.

43. Constance Rourke's *Audubon* (New York, 1936) emphasizes Audubon's frontier life. See also *DAB*, I, 423–27; John J. Audubon, *Audubon's America: the Narratives and Experiences of John James Audubon*, Donald C. Peattie, ed. (Boston, 1940); George C. Fisher, *The Life of Audubon* (New York, 1949); Clyde R. Henson, "A Note on the Early Travels of John James Audubon in Southern Illinois," *Jour. Ill. State Hist. Soc.*, XL (1947), 336–39; F. H. Herrick, *Audubon the Naturalist* . . . (2 vols., New York and London, 1917); *The Life and Adventures of John James Audubon* . . . Robert Buchanan, ed. (London, 1869); Matthews, p. 238; David C. Mott, "John J. Audubon and his Visit to Iowa," *Ann. of Ia.*, 3rd Series, XVI (1928), 403–19; Edward A. Muschamp, *Audacious Audubon* (New York, 1929); E. M. Roberts, "Life of Audubon," *New Republic* (Nov. 4, 1936), p. 24; Rusk, I, 99–100; and O. A. Stevens, "Audubon's Journey up the Missouri River, 1843," *Nor. Dak. Hist. Quar.*, X (1943), 63–82. For the last trip, see Edward Harris, *Up the Missouri with Audubon* . . . (Norman, Okla., 1951).

44. Matthews, p. 217.

45. *DAB*, II, 222–23 and *DNB*, II, 382–83.

46. George D. Brewerton, *Overland with Kit Carson* . . . (New York, 1930); *DAB*, III, 530–32; DeWitt C. Peters, *The Life and Adventures of Kit Carson, the Nestor of the Rocky Mountains* . . . (New York, 1858); Edwin L. Sabin, *Kit Carson Days* . . . (rev. ed., New York, 1935); and Stanley Vestal, *Kit Carson* . . . (Boston and New York, 1928). Sabin's *With Carson and Frémont* is a work of fiction based upon Carson's adventures with Frémont in 1842–1844.

47. *DAB*, II, 543–44; John F. McDermott, "Henry Marie Brackenridge and His Writings," *West. Penn. Hist. Mag.*, XX (1937), 181–96; Matthews, p. 217; *Pittsburgh Daily Gazette*, Jan. 19, 1871; Rusk, I, 8, 9, 90, 95, 99, 124, 304; and Wagner and Camp, pp. 29–30.

48. *DAB*, XII, 513–14; and Rusk, I, 28n., 74n., 114, 128.

49. The Sibley Papers are in the Missouri Historical Society and at Lindenwood College, St. Charles, Mo. See Louis Houck, *A History of Missouri* . . . (3 vols., Chicago, 1908), Vols. I, III; J. C. Luttig, *Journal of a Fur-Trading Expedition on the Upper Missouri, 1812–1813*. Stella M. Drumm, ed. (St. Louis, 1920); *DAB*, XVII, 144; and Lucinda de Leftwich Templin, *Two Illustrious Pioneers in the Education of Women in Missouri* . . . (St. Charles, Mo., 1926).

50. Matthews, p. 218.

51. The Indiana State Library, Indianapolis, has over 5,000 original Tipton documents and photostats. See Matthews, p. 218; M. W. Pershing, *Life of General John Tipton and Early Indiana History* (Tipton, Ind., [1905?]); N. K. Reid, "Sketches of Early Indiana Senators—(IV) John Tipton," *Ind. Mag. Hist.*, IX (1913), 247–68; and *DAB*, XVIII, 563–64.

52. The 78-page manuscript is in the New-York Historical Society.

53. F. L. Billion, *Annals of St. Louis in its Territorial Days* (St. Louis, 1888); *DAB*, IX, 398–99; Matthews, p. 217; Rusk, I, 95, 99, 304; and Wagner and Camp, pp. 40–41.

54. Matthews, p. 218 and Rusk, I, 92.

NOTES TO CHAPTER 8

1. William Matthews, *American Diaries* . . . (Berkeley, Calif., 1945), p. 219.

2. Benjamin F. Shambaugh, "Documents Relating to Governor Lucas," *Ia. Hist. Rec.*, XVI (1900), 56–72, 95–96; Nelson W. Evans, *A History of Scioto County* (Portsmouth, O., 1903); Frederick Lloyd; "Robert Lucas," *Ann. of Ia.*, 1st Series, VIII (1870), 50, 155–69, 283–90; *DAB*, XI, 487–88; Matthews, p. 220; and John Carl Parish, *Robert Lucas*, Iowa State Historical Society Biographical Series, No. 1 (Iowa City, 1907).

3. Matthews, p. 226 and Jedediah P. Merritt, *Biography of the Hon. W. H. Merritt* . . . (St. Catharines, 1875).

4. Matthews, pp. 220–21.

5. "Eleanor Little, Pioneer," *Burton Hist. Coll. Leaflets* (Jan., 1930); Mrs. E. L. K. Gordon, *John Kinzie* . . . (Savannah, Ga., 1910); *DAB*, X, 422; Milo M. Quaife, *Chicago and the Old Northwest* (Chicago, 1913) and Milo M. Quaife, ed. *The John Askin Papers* (2 vols., Detroit, 1928–), I, 305–6, 309.

6. Matthews, p. 220.

7. *Ibid.*

8. Calvin Durfee, *Williams Biographical Annals* (New York, 1871); Matthews, p. 228; *DAB*, XIII, 15–16; T. C. Richards, *Samuel J. Mills, Missionary, Pathfinder, Pioneer, and Promotor* (Boston, New York, etc., 1906); Ralph L. Rusk, *The Literature of the Middle Western Frontier* (2 vols., New York, 1925), I, 98; W. B. Sprague, *Annals of the American Pulpit,* . . . (9 vols., New York, 1857–[69]), Vol. II; Gardiner Spring, *Memoirs of the Rev. Samuel J. Mills* . . . (New York, 1820); and E. G. Stryker, *Missionary Annals; A Story of One Short Life* (1888).

9. The manuscript of the diary is in the New York Public Library. See Matthews, p. 221; Friend Palmer, *Early Days in Detroit* . . . (Detroit, 1906); Kenneth W. Porter, *John Jacob Astor, Business Man* (2 vols., Cambridge, 1931); "Sketch of the Life of Hon. Robert Stuart," *Mich. Hist. Colls.*, III (1881), 52–56; and *DAB*, XVIII, 175–76.

10. Rusk, I, 121.

11. *DAB*, IV, 234, and Matthews, p. 296.

12. Matthews, p. 273, and J. C. Bay, *Going West* . . . (Cedar Rapids, Ia., 1951).

13. The manuscript is in the New York Public Library. See *DAB*, VII, 227, and Matthews, p. 223.

14. Matthews, p. 222.

15. *Ibid.*, p. 225.

16. *DAB*, IX, 6–7; S. M. Janney, *History of the Religious Society of Friends* . . . (4 vols., Philadelphia, 1859–1867); Matthews, p. 223; and Henry W. Wilbur, *The Life and Labors of Elias Hicks* (Philadelphia, 1910). See also Bliss Forbush, "The Newly Discovered Manuscript Journal of Elias Hicks . . . ," *Bull. Fr. Hist. Assn.*, XXXIX (1950), 16–26.

17. *DAB*, IX, 306.

18. The Minnesota Historical Society has a large collection of Taliaferro's diaries and papers. See W. M. Babcock, Jr., "Major Lawrence Taliaferro, Indian Agent," *Miss. Val. Hist. Rev.*, XI (1924), 358–75; *Minn. Hist.*, III (1919), 93, 369; and *DAB*, XVIII, 283.

19. Rusk, I, 12n., 28n., 36n., 129.

20. Matthews, p. 225.

21. Rusk, I, 98.

22. Matthews, p. 227.

23. *Biographical Dictionary of American Congressmen* (1928); Jacob P. Dunn, *Indiana and Indianans* . . . (5 vols., Chicago and New York, 1919), Vol. I; Logan Esarey, *A History of Indiana* . . . (2 vols., Indianapolis, 1918), Vol. II; *DAB*, IX, 270–71; Charles J. Hovey, "Alvin Peterson Hovey," *Ind. Hist. Bull.* (Extra number) (Dec., 1925), 29–33; Daniel Hovey Association, comp. *The Hovey Book* (Haverhill, Mass., 1913); and C. M. Walker, *Hovey and Chase* (Indianapolis, 1888).

24. Matthews, p. 227, and H. M. Chittenden, *The American Fur Trade of the Far West* . . . (3 vols., New York, 1902), II, 497–99, 545–47.

25. Eileen Bigland, *The Indomitable Mrs. Trollope* (Philadelphia, 1954), p. 115; R. C. Buley, *The Old Northwest* . . . (2 vols., Indianapolis, 1950), I, 49–50, 440–41, 475–76; II, 539–43; *Cambridge History of American Literature*, William P. Trent *et al.*, eds. (4 vols., New York, 1917–21), I, 211; *DAB*, VI, 474–75; John E. Kirkpatrick, *Timothy Flint, Pioneer, Missionary, Author, Editor, 1780–1840* . . . (Cleveland, 1911); Rusk, I, 14n., 16n., 28n., 36, 48n., 72n., 95, 126–27, 168–71, 173, 176, 205–6, 246, 251, 253n., 261, 266, 275, 282, 283, 287–96, 300, 316, 332; II, 7n., 10, 17, 18, 27n., 35; Robert E. Spiller, *et al.*, *Literary History of the United States* (New York, 1948), p. 263; and Mrs. Frances Trollope, *Domestic Manners of the Americans*, Donald Smalley, ed. (New York, 1949), pp. xxxviiiff, 90–91. See Flint's *A Condensed Geography and History of the Western States* . . . (2 vols., Cincinnati, 1828) for a detailed picture of Indiana and the Midwest.

26. *DAB*, VI, 478; Edgar L. Dukes, "George Flower of Albion Seeks a Loan," *Jour. Ill. State Hist. Soc.*, XLIX (1956), 221–27; Matthews, p. 229; and Frederic L. Paxson, *History of the American Frontier* (Boston and New York, 1924), pp. 269, 290.

27. Matthews, pp. 229–30. The continuation of the diary has been published in "From Louisville to New Orleans in 1816," E. A. Davis and J. C. L. Andreassen, eds., *Jour. Sou. Hist.*, II (1936), 390–402.

28. Matthews, p. 230.

29. *Ibid.* and Rusk, I, 103n., 121.

30. Rusk, I, 7n.

31. Matthews, p. 229.

32. Daniel Berry, "Morris Birkbeck and his Friends," *Ill. State Hist. Soc. Trans.*, IX (1904), 259–73; *DAB*, II, 289–90; Robert Birkbeck, *The Birkbecks of Westmorland and Their Descendants* (London, 1900) and "Morris Birkbeck: Eminent Englishman," *Ind. Mag. Hist.*, XXXI (1935), 222–25; Solon J. Buck, *Illinois in 1818*, "Illinois Centennial Publications" (Springfield, Ill., 1917) and *Travel and Description, 1765–1865* (Springfield, Ill., 1914); Review of *Notes on a Journey in America* . . . , *Edin. Rev.*, XXX (1818), 120–40; Lucius Embree, "Morris Birkbeck's Estimate of the People of Princeton [Ill.] in 1817," *Ind. Mag. Hist.*, XXI (1925), 289–99; *The English Settlement in the Illinois; Reprints of Three Rare Tracts on the Illinois Country* . . . E. E. Sparks, ed. (London, 1907); William Faux, *Memorable Days in America* . . . (London, 1823); Henry B. Fearon, *Sketches of America* . . . (London, 1818); George Flower, *History of the English Settlements in Edwards Co., Illinois* . . . (Glasgow, 1882); Elias P. Fordham, *Personal Narrative of Travels* . . . (Cleveland, 1906); Matthews, p. 231; T. C. Pease, *The Frontier State, 1818–48*, "Illinois Centennial Publications" (Springfield, Ill., 1918); Jane Rodman, "The English Settlement in Southern Illinois," *Ind. Mag. Hist.*, XLIII (1947), 329–62; Rusk, I, 31, 105, 106, 113, 124–25, 216, 279, 290, 303; Charles W. Smith, "A Contribution towards a Bibliography of Morris Birkbeck," *Ill. State Hist. Soc. Trans.*, X (1905), 167–77; and John Woods, *Two Years' Residence* . . . *in the Illinois Country* (London, 1822).

33. Matthews, p. 231.

34. *Ibid.*

35. Rusk, I, 105–6; II, 2, 3.

36. Matthews, p. 231.

37. The manuscript is in the Minnesota Historical Society, St. Paul. See Constantino Beltrami's attack on Long in *A Pilgrimage in Europe and America* . . . (London, 1828). Beltrami joined Long's expedition of 1823 at Fort St. Peter but suffered harsh treatment from Long and left. See G. T. Chapman, *Sketches of the Alumni of Dartmouth College* (Cambridge, 1867); Chittenden, II, 567–87; T. Christianson, "The Long and Beltrami Explorations in Minnesota One Hundred Years Ago," *Minn. Hist.*, V (1923), 249–64; F. B. Heitman, *Historical Register and Dictionary of the U. S. Army* . . . (Washington, 1890); Edward Hungerford, *The Story of the Baltimore and Ohio Railroad* . . . (2 vols., New York, 1928), Vol. I; *DAB*, XI, 380; Matthews, p. 232; W. T. Norton, *Centennial History of Madison County, Illinois and Its People* (2 vols., Chicago and New York, 1912), Vol. I; Rusk, I, 87–89; and R. G. Thwaites, ed. *Early Western Travels* . . . 32 vols., Cleveland, 1905), Preface to Vol. XIV. See also the journals of Edwin James and Titian Ramsay Peale (1819–1820) described later in this chapter.

38. Matthews, p. 232.

39. The following title is also given: *Narrative of a Tour of Observation, Made during the Summer of 1817, by James Monroe, President of the United States, through the North-eastern and North-western Departments of the Union* . . . (Philadelphia, 1818).

40. Matthews, p. 231.

41. *Ibid.*, pp. 231–32.

42. *Ibid.*, p. 232.

43. The Schoolcraft manuscripts are in the Library of Congress. See James H. Baker, "The Sources of the Mississippi," *Colls. Minn. Hist. Soc.*, VI (1894), 3–26; "Henry Rowe Schoolcraft . . . ," *Colls. Minn. Hist. Soc.*, VII (1893), 142–51; "Henry Rowe Schoolcraft," *Ann. of Ia.*, 1st Series, III (1865), 498–505; Matthews, p. 236; G. Harrison Orians, "The Souvenir of the Lakes," *Northw. Ohio Quar.*, XL (1939), 1–24; Chase S. Osborn, *Schoolcraft, Longfellow, Hiawatha* (Lancaster, Pa., 1942); Rusk, I, 86n., 88–89, 94, 95, 128, 237, 240–41; G. W. Samson, *Henry R. Schoolcraft* (Washington, 1864); *DAB*, XVI, 456–57; Schoolcraft's sketch of his own life in *Personal Memoirs* . . . (Philadelphia, 1851); and Henry R. Wagner and Charles L. Camp, *The Plains and the Rockies* . . . (Columbus, 1953), pp. 42–43.

44. Rusk, I, 323, 327; II, 19, 32, 33.

45. Matthews, p. 233.

46. Robert S. Bailey, *The Church in the Wilderness* . . . (Charleston, 1839); *DAB*, IV, 26–27; *Journal Annual Convention of the Protestant Episcopal Church in Ohio to 1831*; *Journal Annual Convention of the Protestant Episcopal Church in Illinois, 1835–1852*; G. M. Royce, "Kenyon College," *The Churchman*, No. 14, 1896; Rusk, I, 45–46n., 62, 229, 235; Mrs. Laura Smith, *The Life of Philander Chase, First Bishop of Ohio and Illinois, Founder of Kenyon and Jubilee College* (New York, 1903); George F. Smythe, *Kenyon College, Its First Century* (New Haven, 1924); and William B. Sprague, *Annals of the American Pulpit* (New York, 1859), V, 453–62.

47. Matthews, p. 233.

48. Austen K. deBlois, *The Pioneer School; A History of Shurtleff College* (Chicago, New York, etc., 1900); Coe S. Hayne, *Vanguard of the Caravans* . . . (Philadelphia, etc., 1931); Matthews, p. 224; *DAB*, XIV, 381–82; Merton L. Dillon, "John Mason Peck . . . ," *Jour. Ill. State Hist. Soc.*, L (1957), 385–90; I. B. Peck, *A Genealogical History of the Descendants of Joseph*

Peck . . . (Boston, 1868); Matthews, p. 224; and Rusk, I, 39, 50–51, 129, 163, 244.

49. *DAB*, V, 73.

50. Rusk, I, 8, 74, 118, 362, 433.

51. *Ibid.*, I, 32n., 41, 114.

52. *Ibid.*, I, 32, 114; *The Cambridge History of American Literature*, I, 210–11; and Matthews, p. 235.

53. Rusk, I, 46n., 48n., 74n.; II, 3n., 13.

54. Samuel A. Allibone, *A Critical Dictionary of English Literature* . . . (3 vols., Philadelphia, etc., 1908), II, 1445; H. M. Brackenridge, *Views of Louisiana* . . . (Pittsburgh, 1814), pp. 239–40; Elias Durand, "Biographical Notice of the Late Thomas Nuttall," *Procs. Amer. Phil. Soc.*, VII (1861); J. W. Harshberger, *The Botanists of Philadelphia and Their Work* (Philadelphia, 1890); C. R. Keyes, *Pop. Sci.*, Mar., 1895; Jan., 1909; Feb., 1914; Matthews, p. 235; "Nuttall's Journal," *Nor. Amer. Rev.*, XVI (1823), 59–75; *DAB*, XIII, 596–97; *DNB*, XIV, 721–22; Thomas Nuttall, *The North American Sylva* (3 vols., Philadelphia, 1853), I, v–xii; George E. Osterhout, "Nuttall and Pursh . . . ," *Plant World*, X (1907), 80–84; Rusk, I, 99; F. O. Vaille, comp. *The Harvard Book* . . . (2 vols., Cambridge, Mass., 1875), II, 314; and Wagner and Camp, p. 41.

55. R. E. Call, *The Life and Writings of Rafinesque. Filson Club Publications*, No. 10 (Louisville, 1895); T. J. Fitzpatrick, "Constantine Samuel Rafinesque–a Sketch," *Ann. of Ia.*, 3rd Series, VII (1905), 196–224 and *Rafinesque, a Sketch of his Life* . . . (Des Moines, 1911); *DAB*, XV, 322–24; and Rusk, I, 59, 66–67, 160, 167–68, 243, 256–57, 325, 326.

56. A manuscript, "Reminiscences of Vermilion County," in the form of an address delivered before the Old Settlers' Society at Danville, describes Chicago and Hubbard's life as a trader with the Pottawatomie Indians in 1832. See H. W. Beckwith, *History of Vermilion County* . . . (Chicago, 1879), p. 334; *Chicago Historical Society Collections*, IV (1890); (Chicago) *Daily Inter Ocean*, Sept. 15, 1886; Edward W. Day, *One Thousand Years of Hubbard History* . . . (New York, 1895); *DAB*, IX, 326–27; and Mary Ann Hubbard, *Family Memories* (Chicago, 1912).

57. Wagner and Camp, p. 40.

58. Rusk, I, 129.

59. Matthews, p. 236.

60. Forsyth's manuscripts are in the Missouri Historical Society and the Wisconsin Historical Society. See *DAB*, VI, 536; Matthews, p. 237; John Reynolds, *The Pioneer History of Illinois* . . . (Chicago, 1887); and Elihu B. Washburne, . . . *The Edwards Papers* . . . (Chicago, 1884).

61. Matthews, p. 237.

62. The chief source is J. F. H. Claiborne, *Life and Correspondence of John A. Quitman* . . . (2 vols., New York, 1860). See *DAB*, XV, 315–16.

63. Matthews, pp. 237–38.

64. *DAB*, I, 410; Chittenden, I, 278; II, 567, 608–16; F. B. Heitman, *Historical Register of the U. S. Army* . . . (Washington, 1903); "Journal of S. W. Kearny, 1820," *Mo. Hist. Soc. Colls.*, III (1908), 1–2; and Bruce E. Mahan, *Old Fort Crawford and the Frontier* (Iowa City, 1926).

65. Matthews, p. 234; Rusk, I, 32, 75, 107. Faux's book was made the basis of a famous review in the *Quar. Rev.*, XXIX (1823), 338–70, which was answered by Edward Everett in the *Nor. Amer. Rev.*, XIX (1824), 92–125.

66. "Views, Visits, and Tours in North America," *Quar. Rev.*, XXVII (1822), 71 and Rusk, I, 32, 106–7.

67. E. Douglas Branch, *Westward* . . . (New York and London, 1930); Burlington (Ia.) *Daily Hawkeye*, Oct. 27, 1861; Chittenden, II, 563–87 *passim*; "Episodes in the Early History

of the Western Iowa Country," *Iowa Jour. Hist.*, XI (1913), 335, 342–44; "A Forgotten Iowa Author," *Ann. of Ia.*, 3rd Series, IV (1899), 233–34; Edmund W. Gilbert, *The Exploration of Western America* (Cambridge, Eng., 1933); F. B. Heitman, *Historical Register of the U. S. Army* (Washington, 1890); *DAB*, IX, 576; William H. Keating, *Narrative of an Expedition* . . . (2 vols., Philadelphia, 1824), I, 12; "Major Long's Account of the Republican Pawnee and the Kansas Villages," *Neb. Hist.*, X (1927), 204–16; L. H. Pammel, "Dr. Edwin James," *Ann. of Ia.*, 3rd Series, VIII (1907), 161–85, (1908), 277–95; Rusk, I, 87, 94; F. A. Sampson, "Books of Early Travel in Missouri," *Mo. Hist. Rev.*, IX (1915), 94–101; R. G. Thwaites, *Early Western Travels*, Preface to vol. XIV; Wagner and Camp, pp. 49–50; and Richard G. Wood, "Dr. Edwin James: A Disappointed Explorer," *Minn. Hist.*, XXXIV (1955), 284–86.

68. The manuscript is in the Library of Congress. See Edwin James's narrative; "Titian Ramsey [*sic*] Peale," *Entomot News*, Jan., 1913; *DAB*, XIV, 351–52; and Charles Wilkes, *Narrative of the U. S. Exploring Expedition* . . . (Philadelphia, 1845).

69. The author of "Views, Visits, and Tours in North America," *Quar. Rev.*, XXVII (1822), 71, purposely selected certain passages from Flower's, Welby's, and Fanny Wright's books to make America appear in a very unfavorable light. See Benjamin Flower, *Statement of Facts Relating to the Conduct, etc.* (Harlow, Eng., 1808) and *DNB*, VII, 339. George Flower's *History of the English Settlement in Edwards County, Ill.*, E. B. Washburne, ed. (Chicago, 1882) is the ultimate source of most information about him. See also *DAB*, VI, 479 and Rusk, I, 125.

70. Matthews, p. 238.

71. *Ibid.*, p. 241 and Rusk, I, 74n.

NOTES TO CHAPTER 9

1. Fuller, the co-editor, discovered the manuscript.

2. William Matthews, *American Diaries* . . . (Berkeley, Calif., 1945), p. 239.

3. The manuscript is in the Wisconsin State Historical Library, Madison. See *DAB*, V, 390–91; Albert G. Ellis, "Life and Public Service of J. D. Doty," *Wis. Hist. Soc. Colls.*, V (1868), 369–77; and Matthews, p. 239.

4. Ralph L. Rusk, *The Literature of the Middle Western Frontier* (2 vols., New York, 1925), I, 361–62.

5. F. B. Heitman, *Historical Register and Dictionary of the United States Army* . . . (Washington, 1903); *DAB*, X, 272–74; Matthews, p. 240; "The First Fort Kearny," *Neb. Hist. Soc. Pubs.*, XX (1922), 150–54; and William J. Peterson, "Kearny in Iowa," *The Palimpsest*, XII (1931), 289–334.

6. Matthews, p. 232.

7. *DAB*, XIII, 245–46; Rusk, I, 128, 263; and W. B. Sprague, *Annals of the American Pulpit* . . . (9 vols., New York, 1857–[69]), Vol. II.

8. The Tipton Collection (1806–1858) is in the Indiana State Library, Indianapolis. See C. B. Heinemann, "Tipton Family," typescript (1934), Library of Congress; Matthews, p. 218; M. W. Pershing, *Life of Gen. John Tipton and Early Indiana History* (Tipton, Ind., [1905?]); N. K. Reid, "Sketches of Early Indiana Senators–(IV) John Tipton," *Ind. Mag. Hist.*, IX (1913), 247–68; and *DAB*, XVIII, 563–64.

9. Dorothy Dondore. *The Prairie and the Making of Middle America* (Cedar Rapids, Ia., 1926), p. 443; Matthews, p. 240; and Rusk, I, 76, 120.

10. Matthews, p. 240.

11. Part of Hall's *Letters from the West* appeared in Dennie's *Portfolio* during 1821–1825. See R. C. Buley, *The Old North-*

west . . . (2 vols., Indianapolis, 1950), II, 376, 493, 527–30, 535–39, 560; *Cambridge History of American Literature,* William P. Trent *et al.,* eds. (4 vols., New York, 1917–21), I, 211: R. P. Eckert, Jr., "The Path of the Pioneer," *Colophon,* New Series, III (1936), 404–21; John T. Flanagan, *James Hall, Literary Pioneer* . . . (Minneapolis, 1941) and "James Hall, Pioneer Vandalia Editor and Publicist," *Jour. Ill. State Hist. Soc.,* XLVIII (1955), 119–36; *DAB,* VIII, 134–35; R. R. Hubach, "Illinois, Host to Well-Known Nineteenth Century Authors," *Jour. Ill. State Hist. Soc.,* XXXVIII (1945), 447–48; David L. James, "Judge James Hall," *Ohio Arch. Hist. Quar.,* XVIII (1909), 468–83; Rusk, I, 22n., 72, 77, 94n., 95, 104n., 126–28, 171–77, 179, 237, 246, 250, 253, 261n., 265, 266, 272, 274–84, 287, 293, 295–96, 300, 304–5, 310, 311, 343; II, 17, 18, 20, 27; Esther Schultz, "James Hall in Shawneetown," *Jour. Ill. State Hist. Soc.,* XXII (1929), 388–400 and "James Hall in Vandalia," *Jour. Ill. State Hist. Soc.,* XXIII (1930), 92–112; and W. H. Venable, *Beginnings of Literary Culture in the Ohio Valley* (Cincinnati, 1891), pp. 31, 70, 71, 250, 361–85.

12. James M. Buckley, *A History of Methodism in the United States* (2 vols. New York, 1897); *DAB,* VI, 389–90; J. B. Finley, *History of the Wyandott Mission* . . . (Cincinnati, 1840); Rusk, I, 47–48, 97, 229n.; W. B. Sprague, *Annals of the American Pulpit,* VII, 531; and Abel Stevens, *History of the Methodist Episcopal Church in the U. S. A.* (4 vols., New York, 1867), Vol. IV.

13. J. H. Hanson, *The Lost Prince* . . . (New York, 1854); D. B. Martin, *Eleazar Williams, 1821–1921* (n. p., 1921); William W. Wight, *Eleazar Williams—his Forerunners, Himself* (Milwaukee, 1896); and *DAB,* XX, 255–56.

14. *DAB,* VI, 496–97.

15. *Ibid.,* II, 122.

16. Henry R. Wagner and Charles L. Camp, *The Plains and the Rockies* . . . (Columbus, 1953), p. 56.

17. Matthews, p. 242.

18. *Ibid.,* p. 241.

19. *Ibid.,* p. 239; *DNB,* VII, 464–65.

20. Rusk, I, 121.

21. Matthews, p. 243.

22. Charles Francis Adams, ed. *Memoirs of John Quincy Adams* . . . (12 vols., Philadelphia, 1875), Vols. IV and V· *American State Papers, Foreign Relations,* IV, 412–18; *DAB,* V, 196–97; J. W. DeForest, *The DeForests of Ave-nes* . . . (New Haven, 1900); and Henry Hill, *Recollections of an Octogenarian* (Boston, 1884).

23. Milo M. Quaife, *Pictures of Illinois One Hundred Years Ago* (Chicago, 1918) and Rusk, I, 32, 103n., 114–15; II, 13n.

24. Also translated into English by Sister Dolorita Marie Dougherty (M. A. Thesis, St. Louis University, 1948). See Wagner and Camp, pp. 88–90.

25. C. W. Butterfield, *History of LaFayette County, Wis.* (Chicago, 1881); *DAB,* XII, 496–97; Joseph Schafer, *The Wisconsin Lead Region* (Madison, 1932); H. A. Tenney and David Atwood, *Memorial Record of the Fathers of Wisconsin* . . . (Madison, 1880); and *The U. S. Biographical Dictionary and Portrait Gallery of Eminent and Self-Made Men:* Wisconsin Volume (Chicago, New York, etc., 1877).

26. Theodore Christianson, "The Long and Beltrami Expedition in Minnesota One Hundred Years Ago," *Minn. Hist.,* V (1923), 249–64; "Constantine Beltrami," *Colls. Minn. Hist. Soc.,* II (1867), 13–20; Edward C. Gale, "A Newly Discovered Work of Beltrami," *Minn. Hist.,* X (1929), 261–71; Alfred J. Hill, "Constantine Beltrami," *Colls. Minn. Hist. Soc.,* III (1867), 13–20 and 1889 reprint, Vol. II; Rusk, I, 89; and Robert E. Spiller *et al.,* *A Literary History of the United States* (New York, 1948), p. 269.

27. C. H. Hart, "Kentucky's Master-Painter . . . ," *Harper's Mag.,* XCVII (1899), 914–21; *DAB,* X, 222–23; *Kentucky Reporter* (Lexington), Aug. 15, 1827; and Samuel W. Price, *The Old Masters of the Bluegrass* . . . (Louisville, 1902).

28. Winfield S. Downs, ed., *Encyclopedia of Pennsylvania Biography* (20 vols., New York, 1924), Vol. XV; *DAB,* X, 276–77; Wyndham D. Miles, "A Versatile Explorer . . . ," *Minn. Hist.,* XXXVI (1959), 294–99; Rusk, I, 86n., 87–88; and Mentor L. Williams, "Men with Hammers," *Michigan Alumnus,* LII (1946), 241.

29. Matthews, p. 245.

30. *Allgemeine Deutsche Biographie,* R. v. Williencron, ed. (56 vols., Leipzig, 1875–91), Vol. XXXIII; Albert B. Faust, *Charles Sealsfield . . . Materials for a Biography* . . . (Baltimore, 1891); Otto Heller, "Charles Sealsfield, A Forgotten Discoverer of the Valley of the Mississippi," *Mo. Hist. Rev.,* XXXI (1937), 283–401; London *Times,* June 6, 1864; D. Milosch, *Charles Sealsfield's Auffassung des Amerikanertums und seine Literarhistorische Stellung* (Weimar, 1931); *DAB,* XVI, 532–33; Rusk, I, 64, 74n., 102; Leo Smolle, *Charles Sealsfield* . . . (Vienna, 1875); Emil Soffé, *Charles Sealsfield* (Brünn, 1922); and Spiller *et al.,* *A Literary History of the United States,* p. 269.

31. D. D. Banta, "Early Sketches of Indiana University," MS. Indiana University Library, Bloomington; Buley, II, 372, 388–89; J. P. Dunn, ed., *Indiana and Indianans* . . . (5 vols., Chicago and New York, 1919), II, 873–74; E. A. and G. L. Duyckinck, *Cyclopedia of American Literature* . . . (2 vols., Philadelphia, New York, and London, 1875), Vol. II; *DAB,* VIII, 118–19; Agnes M. Murray, "Early Literary Developments in Indiana," *Ind. Mag. Hist.,* XXXVI (1940), 327–33; *New York Times,* Jan. 27, 1863; Meredith Nicholson, *The Hoosiers* (New York and London, 1900); and Rusk, I, 55n.

32. Heber Blankenhorn, "The Grandma of the Muckrackers," *American Mercury,* XII (1927), 87–93; Sarah H. Porter, "The Life and Times of Anne Royall . . . ," *Col. Hist. Soc. Recs.,* X (1907), 1–37; *DAB,* XVI, 204–5; *Washington Evening Star,* Oct. 2, 1854; and R. L. Wright, *Forgotten Ladies* . . . (Philadelphia and London, 1928).

33. *DAB,* III, 546–48; M. H. Chamberlin, "Rev. Peter Cartwright, D.D.," *Ill. State Hist. Soc. Trans.,* VII (1902), 47–56; Sydney Greenbie, *Hoof Beats to Heaven* . . . (Penobscot, Me., 1955); *Minutes of the Annual Conferences of the M. E. Church for the Year 1873,* pp. 113–17; Harvey L. Ross, *The Early Pioneers* . . . (Chicago, 1899); Rusk, I, 50, 226, 227–28; Abel Stevens, *A Compendious History of American Methodism* (New York, 1868), pp. 482–86; and William W. Sweet, "Peter Cartwright in Illinois History," *Ill. State Hist. Soc. Trans.,* XXVIII (1921), 116–23.

34. R. B. Coffin, "The Coffin Family," *Amer. Hist. Recs.,* II (1873), 14–19; *Cincinnati Daily Gazette,* Sept. 17, 20, 1877; *Cincinnati Enquirer,* Sept. 18, 1877; *DAB,* IV, 268–69; and *New Eng. Hist. Geneal. Reg.,* Oct., 1848.

35. Matthews, p. 248.

36. *Ibid.*

37. *Ibid.* and Rusk, I, 159–60.

38. Jessie J. Kile, "Duden and his Critics," *Ill. State Hist. Soc. Trans.,* XXI (1915), 63–70 and Rusk, I, 3n., 20n.

39. *DNB,* V, 196; Matthews, p. 248.

40. *DAB,* XIV, 310–11; Rusk, I, 94–95; Wagner and Camp, pp. 73–76; and William Waldo, "Recollections of a Septuagenarian," *Mo. Hist. Soc. Colls.,* I, No. 2 (1880), 1–20.

41. W. J. Beal, *History of the Michigan Agricultural College and Biographical Sketches* . . . (East Lansing, Mich., 1915); *Detroit Free Press,* Nov. 8, 1902; *DAB,* X, 277; H. A. Kelly and

W. L. Burrage, *American Medical Biographies* (Baltimore, 1920); and L. S. Munson, "A Memoir of the Late R. C. Kedzie," *U. S. Department of Agriculture, Bureau of Chemistry Bulletin No. 73* (1903).

42. Matthews, p. 249.

43. *DAB*, I, 391–92; Donald M. Frost, "Notes on General Ashley, the Overland Trail, and South Pass," *Amer. Ant. Soc. Procs.*, LIV (1943), 161–312; Matthews, p. 247; J. T. Scharf, *History of St. Louis City and County . . .* (Philadelphia, 1883), pp. 196–97; and William F. Switzler, "Gen. William Henry Ashley," *American Monthly Magazine*, XXXII (1908), 318–30.

44. Rusk, I, 6n., 8n., 52n., 101.

45. Matthews, p. 250; Rusk, I, 55n., 98.

46. Rusk, I, 33n., 41, 102, 240.

47. A. H. Estabrook, "The Family History of Robert Owen," *Ind. Mag. Hist.*, XIX (1923), 63–101; *Indianapolis Journal*, June 27, 1877; *Indianapolis Sentinel*, June 26, 1877; George B. Lockwood, *The New Harmony Movement* (New York, 1905); *DAB*, XIV, 118–20; "Robert Dale Owen and Indiana's Common School Fund," Harlow Lindley, ed. *Ind. Mag. Hist.*, XXV (1929), 52–60; Frank Podmore, *Robert Owen; A Biography* (2 vols., London, 1906); Rusk, I, 159, 425; Louis M. Sears, "Robert Dale Owen as a Mystic," *Ind. Mag. Hist.*, XXIV (1928), 15–25.

48. See John D. Lee, *Mormonism Unveiled . . .* (St. Louis, 1877); *DAB*, XI, 114–15; W. A. Linn, *The Story of the Mormons . . .* (New York and London, 1902); and Matthews, p. 303.

49. Rusk, I, 8.

NOTES TO CHAPTER 10

1. John B. McMaster, *A History of the People of the United States . . .* (8 vols., New York and London, 1927), V, 132–50.

2. A. H. Abel, "The History of Events Resulting in Indian Consolidation West of the Mississippi," *Amer. Hist. Assn. Ann. Rep. . . . 1906* (Washington, 1908), I, 259, 303, 356, 362, 375, 377, 405, 406; Charles F. Adams, ed. *Memoirs of John Quincy Adams* (12 vols., Philadelphia, 1875), Vols. VI–VIII; *DAB*, XII, 89–90; and Ralph L. Rusk, *The Literature of the Middle Western Frontier* (2 vols., New York, 1925), I, 95, 250.

3. *DNB*, III, 256; Rusk, I, 125; and Mrs. Frances Trollope, *Domestic Manners of the Americans*, Donald Smalley, ed. (New York, 1949), pp. 50–51, 61, 67.

4. William Matthews, *American Diaries . . .* (Berkeley, Calif., 1945), p. 253.

5. Barbara A. S. Adams, "Early Days at Red River Settlement and Fort Snelling," *Colls. Minn. Hist. Soc.*, VI (1894); Edward D. Neill, *Fort Snelling, Minn. . . .* (New York, 1888); *DAB*, XVII, 381–82; Allen E. Woodall, *William Joseph Snelling* (Pittsburgh, 1933), abstract of Ph.D. dissertation, University of Pittsburgh, 1932, reprinted from *University of Pittsburgh Bulletin*, XXIX (1933).

6. Rusk, I, 363n., 392, 393, 446.

7. Lieut. Col. W. H. Emory's *Notes of a Military Reconnaissance . . .*, described in Chapter 14, relates events in an expedition from Leavenworth to California in 1846–1847 headed by Cooke. See also *Bulletin of the Association of Graduates of the U. S. Military Academy* (n. p., 1895), pp. 79–86; *DAB*, IV, 389; G. W. Cullum, *Biographical Register of the Officers and Graduates of the U. S. Military Academy at West Point . . .* (3rd ed., Boston and New York, 1891); Carolyn T. Foreman, "General Philip St. George Cooke," *Chrons. of Okla.*, XXXII (1954), 195–213; Hamilton Gardner, "Captain Philip St. George Cooke and the March of the 1st Dragoons to the Rocky Mountains in 1845," *Colorado Magazine*, XXX (1953), 246–67; Frank A. Golder, *The March of the Mormon Battalion . . .* (New York and

London, 1928); Matthews, p. 293; "A Journal of the Santa Fé Trail," W. E. Connelley, ed., *Miss. Val. Hist. Rev.*, XII (1925), 73n.; *Official Records of the U. S. Army*, 1st Series, Vol. XI, Parts 1, 2, 3; Vol. XXVI, Part 1; Vol. XXXIV, Parts 2, 3; Vol. LI, Part 1; and Otis E. Young, *The West of Philip St. George Cooke, 1809–1895* (Glendale, Calif., 1955). The manuscript of the 1843 journal is in the archives of the State Department, Washington.

8. R. G. Thwaites, "Sketch of Morgan L. Martin," *Wis. Hist. Soc. Colls.*, XI (1888), 380–84.

9. Pitcher has a chapter on Indian medicine in Schoolcraft's *Information Respecting the History, Condition, and Prospects of the Indian Tribes of the United States* (6 vols., Philadelphia, 1854), Vol. IV. He helped establish the medical school of the University of Michigan. See *Detroit Free Press*, Apr. 6, 1872; *Detroit Medical Journal*, July, 1909; Burke A. Hinsdale, *History of the University of Michigan* (Ann Arbor, 1906); *Michigan University Medical Journal*, Mar., 1872; F. G. Novy, biography of Pitcher in *Physician and Surgeon*, Feb., 1908; *DAB*, XIV, 636–37; and *Transactions of the State Medical Society of Michigan*, 2nd Series, VI (1874).

10. Matthews, p. 252.

11. *Ibid.*, p. 254.

12. *The Cambridge History of American Literature*, William P. Trent *et al.*, eds. (4 vols., New York, 1917–21), I, 207; *DNB*, VIII, 942–43; "Obituary," *Journal of the Royal Geographical Society*, XV (1845), xlii; Allan Nevins, *American Social History as Recorded by British Travellers* (New York, 1923), p. 118; Rusk, I, 108; Smalley, p. lvii; and Mark Twain, *Life on the Mississippi* (New York, 1950), p. 226.

13. See, for example, Richard Biddle, *Captain Hall in America, By an American* (Philadelphia, 1830). Mrs. Trollope in *Domestic Manners . . .* (p. 354, Smalley edition) said the appearance of Hall's book produced "a sort of moral earthquake." It was highly successful, running through three English editions. A French translation was published in 1829.

14. A. H. Abel, "The History of Events Resulting in Indian Consolidation West of the Mississippi," *Amer. Hist. Assoc. Ann. Rep. . . . 1906*, I (Washington, 1908), 250, 367, 368, 377, 412; Luther B. Hill, *A History of the State of Oklahoma* (2 vols., Chicago and New York, 1908), Vol. I; *Kans. State Hist. Soc. Colls.*, Vols. II, IV, IX, X, XII, XVI (1881–1925); *DAB*, XI, 617–18; Matthews, p. 256; Joseph B. Thoburn, *A Standard History of Oklahoma . . .* (5 vols., Chicago and New York, 1916), Vol. I; Henry R. Wagner and Charles L. Camp, *The Plains and the Rockies . . .* (Columbus, O., 1953), pp. 66–67; and Walter N. Wyeth, *Isaac McCoy . . .* (Philadelphia, 1895).

15. Matthews, pp. 251–52; and *DNB*, XVIII, 108.

16. Matthews, p. 256 and Rusk, I, 111n., 129, 163, 283, 421.

17. See also A. S. Allibone, *A Critical Dictionary of English Literature* (Philadelphia, etc., 1908); S. C. Chew, "Family Named Trollope," *Monthly Magazine* (Nov. 24, 1945), p. 14; Janet E. Courtney, *The Adventurous Thirties . . .* (London, 1933), pp. 127–37; C. Gaul, "Anthony Trollope's Mother," *Christian Century*, LXIII (June 5, 1946), 720–21; Russell A. Griffin, "Mrs. Trollope and the Queen City," *Miss. Val. Hist. Rev.*, XXXVII (1950), 289–302; William H. Hildreth, "Mrs. Trollope in Parkopolis," *Ohio Arch. Hist. Quar.*, LVIII (1949), 35–51; D. L. Hobman, "Mrs. Trollope—the Novelist's Mother," *Contemporary Review*, CLXVIII (1945), 304–8; John C. Jeaffreson, *Novels and Novelists . . .* (2 vols., London, 1858), II, 396; John F. McDermott, "A Note on Mrs. Trollope," *Ohio Arch. Hist. Quar.*, LXV (1936), 369–70; Nevins, p. 117; Una Pope-Hennessy, *Three English Women in America* (London, 1929); Rusk, I, 29, 37–38, 108–13, 115, 117, 119, 125n., 131, 285, 293,

329, 357, 433–34; II, 7n., 10; Michael Sadleir, *Anthony Trollope* . . . (New York, 1927); Lucy P. and Richard P. Stebbins, *The Trollopes* . . . (New York, 1945); Eleanor Ternan, *Frances Trollope, her Life and Literary Work* . . . (London, 1895); *DNB*, XIX, 1170–73; Twain, *Life on the Mississippi*, p. xi; and Stanley T. Williams, "Founders of Main Street," *Nor. Amer. Rev.*, CCXV (1922), 775–84.

18. Eileen Bigland, *The Indomitable Mrs. Trollope* (Philadelphia, 1954), p. 75.

19. Edition of New York, 1916, pp. 20–21.

20. *Domestic Manners of the Americans*, Donald Smalley, ed., pp. lviii, lxi.

21. LV, 479, 526.

22. XXXI (1832), 829–47.

23. XII (1832), 109–33.

24. Rusk, I, 109–10.

25. *Ibid.*, pp. 110–11.

26. Rusk, I, 108.

27. *Ibid.*, I, 16n., 28n., 45n., 64, 125–26.

28. The Chicago Historical Society also owns two letters written by Mrs. Letts to the Society.

29. Mazzuchelli's letters and documents are in the St. Louis Archdiocesan Archives, St. Clara Convent, Sinsinawa, Wis. See James D. Butler, "Father Samuel Mazzuchelli," *Wis. Hist. Soc. Colls.*, XIV (1898), 155–61; Rosemary Crepean, *Le Père . . . Mazzuchelli* (Paris, 1932); Albert Hyanson, *A Dictionary of Universal Biography* (2nd ed., London, 1951), p. 409; *DAB*, XII, 470–71; E. E. Reed, "Mazzuchelli . . . ," *Measure*, II (1951), 241–53; and "Who Designed Iowa's Old Capitol?," *The Witness* (Dubuque), June 21, 1928.

30. Caleb Atwater, *The Writings of Caleb Atwater* (Columbus, 1833) contains the account of the Prairie du Chien trip. See Atwater, "A Country Fit for Princes," *Palimpsest*, XII (1931), 144–59; *DAB*, I, 415–16; Francis Atwater, *Atwater History and Genealogy* (2 vols., Meriden, Conn., 1907), Vol. II; Clement L. Martzolff, "Caleb Atwater," *Ohio Arch. Hist. Quar.*, XIV (1905), 247–71; Rusk, I, 53n., 123–24, 128, 166, 168, 236, 240, 245; Henry C. Shetrone, "Caleb Atwater: Versatile Pioneer," *Ohio Arch. Hist. Quar.*, LIV (1945), 79–103; and Francis P. Weisenburger, "Caleb Atwater: Pioneer Politician and Historian," *Ohio Hist. Quar.*, LXVIII (1959), 18–37.

31. Matthews, p. 259, and *DAB*, XV, 608–9.

32. Elizabeth D. Putnam's *The Life and Services of Joseph Duncan, Governor of Illinois, 1834–1838* (Springfield, Ill., 1922) contains as an appendix a diary covering part of Duncan's congressional career. See also *DAB*, V, 510–11; *Illinoisan* (Jacksonville), Jan. 19, 1844; Julia D. Kirby, "Biographical Sketch of Joseph Duncan," *Fergus Historical Series* No. 29 (Chicago, 1888); and Matthews, pp. 257–58.

33. Brownell's autobiography is printed in E. E. Beardsley, *History of the Episcopal Church in Connecticut* (2 vols., Cambridge, Mass., 1868), Vol. II. See *DAB*, III, 171–72, and Matthews, p. 257.

34. *Daily Inter Ocean* (Chicago), Feb. 12, 1886; G. F. Magoun, *Asa Turner, a Home Missionary Patriarch* . . . (Boston and Chicago, 1889); Charles H. Rammelkamp, *Illinois College: A Centennial History* . . . (New Haven, 1928); and *DAB*, XVIII, 186.

35. The Brown Papers are at the University of Michigan; see *Guide to Manuscript Collections in Michigan*, Vol. I, No. 64 (Detroit, 1941).

36. Extracts from the journal for the year 1832 have been reprinted in H. H. Chittenden, *The American Fur Trade of the Far West* . . . (2 vols., Stanford, Calif., 1954), II, 975–83.

37. *DAB*, I, 511–12 and Henry M. Baird, *The Life of the Rev. Robert Baird* . . . (New York, 1866).

38. *American Christian Review*, X (1857–1858), 309–10; *DAB*, IV, 320–21; George W. Colton, *Quartermaster George Colton and His Descendants* . . . (Lancaster, Pa., 1912); F. B. Dexter, *Biographical Sketches of the Graduates of Yale College* (6 vols., New York, 1912), Vol. VI; "Rev. Calvin Colton," *International Monthly Magazine*, IV (1851), 1–3; and Rusk, I, 8, 96–97, 109, 129, 261.

39. Matthews, p. 261.

40. *Ibid.*

41. *Ibid.*, p. 262.

42. *Ibid.*, p. 261.

43. *Ibid.*

44. *Ibid.*

45. *DAB*, VI, 424, and biographical sketch by C. V. Riley in *American Entomologist*, III (May, 1880).

46. Thomas C. Belden, *So Fell the Angels* (New York, 1956); *DAB*, IV, 27–34; A. B. Hart, . . . *Salmon Portland Chase* (Boston and New York, 1899); Hugh McCulloch, *Men and Measures of Half a Century* . . . (New York, 1880); Rusk, I, 245; Arthur M. Schlesinger, "Salmon Portland Chase, Undergraduate and Pedagogue," *Ohio Arch. Hist. Quar.*, XXVIII (1910), 119–61; Norton S. Townshend, "Salmon P. Chase," *Ohio Arch. Hist. Quar.*, I (1887), 109–24; and John T. Trowbridge, *The Ferry Boy and the Financier* (Boston, 1864).

47. In Robert B. Warden, *An Account of the Private Life and Public Services of Salmon Portland Chase* (Cincinnati, 1874); J. W. Schuckers, *The Life and Public Services of Salmon Portland Chase* . . . (New York, 1874); and "Diary and Correspondence of Salmon P. Chase," S. H. Dodson, comp. *Amer. Hist. Assn. Ann. Rep.* (Washington, 1902), vol. II.

48. The manuscript is in the New York Public Library. Hamilton became a valued contributor to *Blackwood's Magazine*; *DNB*, VIII, 1097; and Rusk, I, 74n.–75n., 113.

49. The manuscript is in the New York Public Library.

50. W. H. G. Armytage, "James Stuart's Journey up the River Mississippi in 1830," *Mid-Amer.*, XXXI (1949), 92–100; Rusk, I, 115, 405, 432n.; *DNB*, XIX, 90–91; and James Stuart, *Refutation of Aspersions on Stuart's "Three Years in North America,"* (London, 1834).

51. Matthews, p. 259.

52. *Ibid.*, p. 260.

53. *Ibid.*, p. 265; John E. Chapin, "Sketch of Cutting Marsh," *Wis. Hist. Soc. Colls.*, XV (1900), 25–38.

54. Matthews, p. 259.

55. *Ibid.*

56. Rusk, I, 33n., 48n., 74, 408.

57. W. R. Johnson, *A Memoir of the Late Lewis David von Schweinitz* . . . (Philadelphia, 1835); "Memoirs of Brother Louis David De Schweinitz," *United Brethren's Missionary Intelligencer* (3rd quarter, 1834); "Sketch of L. D. von Schweinitz," *Pop. Sci.*, XLIV (1894), 833–40; *Poulson's American Daily Advertiser*, LXIII (Feb. 13, 1834); Rusk, I, 88; *DAB*, XVI, 483–84.

58. *DNB*, XX, 309.

59. Jacob P. Mayer, *Alexis de Tocqueville; a Biographical Essay in Political Science* (New York, 1940); George W. Pierson, *Tocqueville and Beaumont in America* (New York, 1938); Rusk, I, 3, 7n., 22n., 43n., 90, 101, 119, 204; II, 6n.; and *Memoirs, Letters and Remains of Alexis de Tocqueville* (London, 1861).

60. Rusk I, 115.

61. L. H. C., "Rev. Sherman Hall," *Home Missionary*, LII (1879), 174; *DAB*, VIII, 144; Matthews, p. 262; Grace L. Nute,

"The Letters of Sherman Hall, Missionary to the Chippewa Indians," *Minn. Hist.*, VII (1926), 62–65; S. R. Riggs, "Protestant Missions in the Northwest," *Colls. Minn. Hist. Soc.*, VI (1894), 117–87; and *St. Paul Daily Globe*, Sept. 2, 1879.

62. The original manuscript is in the Wisconsin State Historical Society, Madison.

63. Matthews, p. 263 and *DNB*, XIV, 784–85.

64. *DAB*, XI, 180 and W. F. Wagner, ed. *Adventures of Zenas Leonard, Fur Trader and Trapper, 1831–1836* (Cleveland, 1904).

65. William E. Connelley, "Dr. Josiah Gregg, Historian of the Old Santa Fé Trail," *Miss. Val. Hist. Assn. Procs.*, X (1919–1920), 334–48; Howard T. Demick, "Visits of Josiah Gregg to Louisiana . . . ," *La. Hist. Rev.*, XXIX (1946), 5–13; *DAB*, VII, 597–98; J. T. Lee, "The Authorship of Gregg's Commerce of the Prairies," *Miss. Val. Hist. Rev.*, XVI (1930), 451–66; Matthews, p. 287; and R. E. Twitchell, "Dr. Josiah Gregg," *New Mex. Hist. Soc. Pubs.*, No. 26 (1924).

66. Pond also wrote "The Dakotas or Sioux in Minnesota as They Were in 1834," *Colls. Minn. Hist. Soc.*, XII (1908), 319–501. The Pond Family papers are in the Minnesota Historical Society. See E. D. Neill, "A Memorial of the Brothers Pond . . . ," *Macalester College Contributions*, 2nd Series, No. 8 (St. Paul, 1892); D. S. Pond, *A Genealogical Record of Samuel Pond . . .* (New London, O., 1875); *DAB*, XV, 61–62; and S. W. Pond, Jr., *Two Volunteer Missionaries among the Dakotas, or, The Story of the Labors of Samuel W. and Gideon H. Pond* (Boston and Chicago, 1893).

67. *The Biographical Encyclopedia of Illinois* (Philadelphia, 1875); *Illinois State Register* (Springfield), Sept. 26, 1900; and *DAB*, XIV, 187–88.

NOTES TO CHAPTER 11

1. John B. McMaster, *A History of the People of the United States . . .* (8 vols., New York and London, 1927–29), VI, 69.

2. "The Prairie States," I, 1.

3. William Matthews, *American Diaries . . .* (Berkeley, Calif., 1945), p. 264.

4. *Ibid.*, p. 265.

5. *Ibid.*, pp. 327–29. Black Hawk's own narrative is called *Life of Ma-ka-tai-me-she-kia-kiak; or, Black Hawk, Embracing the Tradition of his Nation. . . . Encroachments by the Whites, Contrary to Treaty—Removal from His Villages in 1831. With an Account of the Cause and General History of the Late War, his Surrender and Confinement at Jefferson Barracks, and Travels through the United States, Dictated by Himself . . .* (Boston, 1834). Other editions (the latest published at Urbana, Ill., in 1955) have appeared. See also *An Account of the Indian Chief Black Hawk, and his Tribes, the Sac and Fox Indians, with the Affecting Narrative of a Lady Who Was Taken Prisoner by the Indians . . .* (Philadelphia, 1834); Perry A. Armstrong, *The Sauks and the Black Hawk War . . .* (Springfield, Ill., 1887); *DAB*, II, 313–14; Benjamin Drake, *Life and Adventures of Black Hawk with Sketches of Keokuk . . .* (Cincinnati, 1839); J. MacIvor, "So We Commemorate a Good and Dead Indian," *Saturday Evening Post*, CCXVI (March 13, 1945), 96; Frank E. Stevens, *The Black Hawk War* (Chicago, 1903); and Jacob Van der Zee, "The Black Hawk War and the Treaty of 1832," *Ia. Jour. Hist.*, XIII (1915), 418–28.

6. Matthews, p. 264. See Edward D. Neill, "Memoir of William T. Boutwell . . . ," *Macalaster College Contributions*, 2nd Series, No. 1 (1892), pp. 1–59.

7. Ralph L. Rusk, *The Literature of the Middle Western Frontier* (2 vols., New York, 1925), I, 121.

8. An important collection of Irving manuscripts is in the New York Public Library and another is at Yale University. "A Tour on the Prairies" was reviewed in the *Nor. Amer. Rev.*, XLI (1835), 1–28. See also H. W. Boynton, *Washington Irving* (Boston and New York, 1901); R. R. Hubach, "Nineteenth Century Literary Visitors to the Hoosier State . . . ," *Ind. Mag. Hist.*, XLV (1949), 43; Pierre M. Irving, *The Life and Letters of Washington Irving* (4 vols., New York, 1862–1864); *DAB*, IX, 505–11; Albert Keiser, *The Indian in American Literature* (New York, 1933); Matthews, pp. 203–4; Rusk, I, 115, 119, 291, 418; II, 31, 33, 37; A. J. Russell, "Irving: Recorder of Indian Life," *Jour. Amer. Hist.*, XLV (1931), 185–95; F. B. Streeter, "Knickerbocker on the Prairie," *Aerend*, III (1932), 229–30; Henry R. Wagner and Charles L. Camp, *The Plains and the Rockies . . .* (Columbus, O., 1953), pp. 87, 100–1; C. D. Warner, *Washington Irving* (Boston, 1881); and Stanley T. Williams, *The Life of Washington Irving* (2 vols., New York and London, 1935). Henry Leavitt Ellsworth's *Washington Irving on the Prairies . . .* (New York, 1937) is actually a long letter describing the trip.

9. Rusk, II, 33.

10. *The Cambridge History of American Literature*, William P. Trent et al., eds. (4 vols., New York, 1917–21), I, 209.

11. Matthews, p. 266.

12. *DAB*, XX, 577.

13. Charles H. Carey, *History of Oregon* (Chicago, 1922); Matthews, p. 267; and *DAB*, XX, 576–77.

14. Matthews, p. 264.

15. *Ibid.*

16. Rusk, I, 109n., 433.

17. Wagner and Camp, pp. 112–13.

18. Matthews, p. 265.

19. The chief collection of Purcell's letters is in the archives of Notre Dame University, South Bend, Ind. See Sister Mary A. McCann, "The Most Reverend John Baptist Purcell," *Cath. Hist. Rev.*, VI (1920), 172–99; *Cincinnati Inquirer*, July 4, 1883; Richard H. Clarke, *Lives of the Deceased Bishops of the Catholic Church in the United States* (2 vols., New York, 1888), Vol. II; Mary A. McCann, *Archbishop Purcell and the Archdiocese of Cincinnati* (Washington, 1918); Matthews, p. 269; *DAB*, XV, 266–68; and Rusk, I, 233, 239.

20. *DAB*, III, 574–75; Harold McCracken, *George Catlin and the Old Frontier* (New York, 1959); *Sou. Dak. Hist. Colls.*, I (1902), 344–48; and Wagner and Camp, pp. 123–25.

21. Matthews, p. 268.

22. For a description of the Nicollet manuscripts, see *Report of the Librarian of Congress . . . for the Fiscal Year Ending June 30, 1921* (Washington, 1921), pp. 40–41. See also J. C. Frémont, *Memoirs of My Life* (Chicago, 1887); *Colls. Minn. Hist. Soc.*, I (1872), VI (1894), and VII (1893); *DAB*, XIII, 514; C. A. Stevens, "Nicollet's Expedition of 1839," *Nor. Dak. Hist.*, XXI (1954), 75–82; Wagner and Camp, pp. 139–40; and *Washington Globe*, Sept. 11, 1843.

23. John Bigelow, *William Cullen Bryant* (Boston and New York, 1890); William A. Bradley, *William Cullen Bryant* (New York and London, 1905); *DAB*, III, 200–5; E. W. Gage, "William Cullen Bryant," *Jour. Amer. Hist.*, XIX (1925), 279–86; Parke Godwin, *A Biography of William Cullen Bryant . . .* (2 vols., New York, 1883); Keith Huntress and F. W. Lorch, "Bryant and Illinois," *New England Quarterly*, XVI (1943), 634–47; E. E. Leisy, "Bryant and Illinois," *Saturday Review of Literature*, III (Dec. 4, 1926), 407; Harry H. Peckham, *Gotham Yankee; a Biography of William Cullen Bryant* (New York, 1950); Donald A. Ringer, "William Cullen Bryant's Account of Michigan in 1846," *Mich. Hist.*, XL (1956), 317–27; Rusk, I,

14–15n.; II, 31, 35; Arthur J. Symington, *William Cullen Bryant . . .* (New York, 1880); and James G. Wilson, *Bryant and his Friends . . .* (New York, 1886).

24. His writing had become known on the frontier by about 1825 but had received no wide acclaim. See Rusk, II, 35.

25. She wrote a diary of her trip from Cummington, Mass., to Illinois, retold by Amanda Mathews in "The Diary of a Poet's Mother," *Mag. Hist.,* II (1905), 206–9; see also George V. Bohman, "A Poet's Mother: Sarah Snell Bryant in Illinois," *Jour. Ill. State Hist. Soc.,* XXXIII (1940), 166–89.

26. Rusk, II, 35.

27. Matthews, p. 248.

28. The journal is in the Kansas State Historical Society, Topeka. See Matthews, pp. 265–66; *DAB,* XII, 496; and *Missionary Magazine* (Boston), XXXV (Apr., July, 1855).

29. Matthews, p. 276.

30. *Ann Arbor Argus,* June 19, 1896; *Ann Arbor Courier,* June 17, 1896; *Ann Arbor Register,* June 18, 1896; *DAB,* VI, 313–14; and C. B. Grant, "Life and Character of Alpheus Felch," *Mich. Hist. Colls.,* XXVIII (1900), 94–104.

31. Matthews, p. 267.

32. *Ibid.*

33. *Columbia University Quarterly,* June, 1906; *DAB,* IX, 503; P. M. Irving, *The Life and Letters of Washington Irving* (4 vols., New York, 1862–1864), III, 69, 73; *New York Times,* Feb. 28, 1906; and Wagner and Camp, pp. 86–87, 100.

34. Rusk, I, 98.

35. *DNB,* XI, 623–24; Rusk, I, 15n., 35, 111n., 115; and Wagner and Camp, pp. 87–88.

36. Rusk, I, 74–75, 113.

37. *DAB,* III, 575–76; Robert Fergus, *Biographical Sketch of John Dean Caton . . .* (Chicago, 1882); and M. M. Folansbee in William D. Lewis, ed. *Great American Lawyers* (8 vols., Philadelphia, 1909), VI, 307.

38. Homer F. Barnes, *Charles Fenno Hoffman* (New York, 1930); *DAB,* IX, 110–11; R. R. Hubach, "Nineteenth-Century Literary Visitors to the Hoosier State . . . ," *Ind. Mag. Hist.,* XLV (1949), 43; D. G. Mitchell, *American Lands and Letters* (2 vols., New York, 1899), Vol. II; *New York Herald,* June 9, 1884; and Rusk, I, 10n., 18n., 35n., 36n., 73, 119.

39. *National Cyclopedia of American Biography* (42 vols., New York, 1921), II, 465.

40. *Chicago Tribune,* Jan. 12, 1899; J. W. Cook, *Educational History of Illinois . . .* (Chicago, 1912); C. H. Rammelkamp, *Illinois College, a Centennial History, 1829–1929* (New Haven, 1928); and *DAB,* XIX, 68.

41. Cornelius J. Bronson, *James Lee, Prophet of the New Oregon* (New York, 1932); *DAB,* XI, 111–12; Leonard and S. F. Lee, *John Lee of Farmington . . . Conn. . . .* (Meriden, Conn., 1897); McMaster, VI, 446–47; and Matthews, p. 268.

42. *New York Tribune,* Oct. 28, 1898; *DAB,* XVI, 130–31; and Theophilus Packard, *The Genealogies of Samuel Packard of Bridgewater, Mass. . . .* (New York, 1871).

43. Cyrus Bussey, "The Battle of Athens, Missouri," *Ann. of Ia.,* 3rd Series, V (1901), 81–92, and XII (1915), 153–54; *DAB,* III, 354–55 F. B. Heitman, *Historical Register of the U. S. Army* (2 vols., Washington, 1903), I, 268; and *Who's Who in America 1914–1915* (Chicago, 1914–1915).

44. A. L. Larpenteur, "Recollections of the City and People of St. Paul, 1843–98," *Colls., Minn. Hist. Soc.,* IX (1901), 365–94; and *DAB,* XI, 4–5.

45. "Körner," *DAB,* X, 496–97; John M. Palmer, *The Bench and Bar of Illinois* (2 vols., Chicago, 1899), Vol. I; H. A. Rattermann, *Gustav Körner . . .* (Cincinnati, 1902); Rusk, I, 15n.,

19n., 20n., 21n., 28n., 209; and *St. Louis Globe-Democrat,* Apr. 10, 1896.

46. *DNB,* I, 30–31; Matthews, p. 267; and Rusk, I, 171n.

47. Matthews, p. 271.

48. Rusk, I, 102.

49. Matthews, p. 269.

50. *Ibid.,* p. 270.

51. The diaries and letters are in the Wisconsin State Historical Society, Madison. See *DAB,* X, 321–22; M. T. Gardner, *Conqueror of the Continent . . .* (New York, 1911); Matthews, p. 272; Grace L. Nute, "Minnesota as Seen by Travelers," *Minn. Hist.,* VII (1926), 264–73; W. S. Perry, *The Bishops of the American Church . . .* (New York, 1897); Greenough White, *An Apostle of the Western Church . . .* (New York, 1900); and *Wisconsin State Journal* (Madison), May 25, 1870.

52. Matthews, p. 272.

53. Lucius E. Smith, *Heroes and Martyrs of the Modern Missionary Enterprise; a Record of their Lives and Labors . . .* (Chicago, 1853).

54. Matthews, p. 270, and Wagner and Camp, pp. 98–99.

55. Matthews, p. 271.

56. Rusk, I, 121.

57. F. H. Herrick, *Audubon the Naturalist . . .* (2 vols., New York, London, 1917); Matthews, pp. 272–73; Rusk, I, 121; and *DAB,* XVII, 617–18.

58. Rusk, I, 78, 101–2.

59. Matthews, p. 270.

60. Wagner and Camp, pp. 85–86.

61. Matthews, p. 271.

62. *Ibid.,* p. 268.

63. Rusk, I, 36, 115–16.

64. *Life on the Mississippi* (New York, 1950), p. 227.

65. Matthews, p. 273.

66. *Ibid.*

67. Rusk, I, 17n., 18n., 95, 119. Gilman also wrote *Legends of a Log Cabin* (1835), the setting of which is a hut in the wilderness of the Wabash country.

68. Rusk, I, 98.

69. Matthews, p. 274.

70. *Ibid.,* and Wagner and Camp, pp. 96–98.

71. The manuscript is in the Oregon Historical Society, Portland, and is listed in *Guide to the Manuscript Collections of the Oregon Historical Society* (Portland, 1940), No. 362. See Myron Eells, *Marcus Whitman, Pathfinder and Patriot* (Seattle, 1909); A. B. and D. P. Hulbert, eds. *Marcus Whitman, Crusader* (Denver, 1926), Part I, pp. 98–135; A. B. Hulbert, "Underdeveloped Factors in the Life of Marcus Whitman," in J. F. Willard and C. B. Goodykoontz, eds. *The Trans-Mississippi West* (Boulder, Colo., 1930); McMaster, VI, 449–50; Matthews, p. 275; H. W. Parker, "Rev. Samuel Parker, Missionary to Oregon," *The Church at Home and Abroad,* Mar., 1895; and Wagner and Camp, pp. 104–5.

72. E. G. Bourne, "The Legend of Marcus Whitman," *Amer. Hist. Rev.,* VI (1901), 276–300; James G. Craighead, *The Story of Marcus Whitman; Early Protestant Minister in the Northwest* (Philadelphia, 1895); Eells; Charles H. Farnam, *History of the Descendants of John Whitman of Weymouth, Mass.* (New Haven, 1889); A. B. and D. P. Hulbert, pp. 146–65; A. B. Hulbert; Matthews, p. 275; *Missionary Herald,* XXXI–XLIII (1835–1847), *passim;* and *DAB,* XX, 141–43.

73. *DNB,* XVI, 831–32, and Rusk, I, 98.

74. The manuscript is owned by the Historical Society of Pennsylvania, Philadelphia, and is listed in *Guide to the Manuscript Collections in the Historical Society of Pennsylvania* (Phila-

delphia, 1949), No. 476. See M. V. Agnew, *The Book of Agnews . . .* (Philadelphia, 1926); F. B. Heitman, *Historical Register and Directory of the U. S. Army* (1905); Matthews, p. 275; *DAB*, XIV, 306–7; and *Philadelphia Inquirer*, Aug. 8–12, 1881.

75. IV (1835), 276–81.

76. Matthews, p. 274.

77. Theodore Bosanquet, *Harriet Martineau . . .* (London, 1927); Mrs. Janet E. H. Courtney, *Free Thinkers of the Nineteenth Century* (London, 1920); *DNB*, XII, 1194–99; F. S. Martin, "Harriet Martineau: Triumph and Tragedy," *Hibbert Journal*, XXV (1928), 631–40; Mrs. Fenwick Miller, *Harriet Martineau* (London, 1884); J. C. Nevill, *Harriet Martineau* (London, 1944); Rusk, I, 35n., 38n., 76n., 116, 210n., 272; William R. Seat, "A Rebuttal to Mrs. Trollope . . . ," *Ohio Hist. Quar.*, LXVIII (1959), 276–89; and Vera Wheatley, *The Life and Work of Harriet Martineau* (London, 1957).

78. Rusk, I, 116.

79. II, 39–56.

80. *Society in America . . .* (2nd ed., London, 1837), I, 349–64.

81. Bessie L. Pierce, ed. *As Others See Chicago* (New York, 1935), p. 30, and Max Berger, *The British Traveller in America, 1836–1860* (New York, 1945), pp. 51–52.

82. Rusk, I, 117.

83. Matthews, p. 279.

84. Featherstonhaugh edited the monthly *American Journal of Geology and Natural Science*, Vol. I, No. 6 (1831); see Rusk, I, 85n. He traveled in the Midwest in 1834, as evidenced by his *Geological Report of an Examination Made in 1834, of the Elevated Country between the Missouri and Red Rivers* (Washington, 1835), and he issued a report of the 1835 trip, *Report of a Geological Reconnaissance Made in 1835, from the Seat of Government, by the Way of Green Bay and the Wisconsin Territory, to the Coteau de Prairie . . .* (Washington, 1836).

85. *DNB*, XI, 1038.

86. *DAB*, VI, 282.

NOTES TO CHAPTER 12

1. John B. McMaster, *A History of the People of the United States . . .* (8 vols., New York and London, 1927–29), VI, 366–460 passim, 468–81.

2. Bridge's home was in Augusta, Maine.

3. William Matthews, *American Diaries . . .* (Berkeley, Calif., 1945), p. 277; *DAB*, XIII, 27; Alfred J. Morrison, ed. *Six Addresses on the State of Letters and Science in Virginia . . .* (Roanoke, 1917); and "The Late Lucian Minor," *Southern Literary Messenger*, XXVII (1858), 225–27.

4. The manuscript is in the McCormick Historical Society, Chicago. See Matthews, p. 276.

5. *Ibid.*, p. 277.

6. *Ibid.*, p. 275.

7. William T. Coggeshall, *Poets and Poetry of the West* (Columbus, 1860); *DAB*, VI, 447–48; G. B. Griffith, *The Poets of Maine* (Portland, Me., 1888); S. H. Lancey, *The Native Poets of Maine* (Bangor, 1854); Ralph L. Rusk, *The Literature of the Middle Western Frontier* (2 vols., New York, 1925), I, 7n., 8n., 9n., 17n., 20n., 39, 62, 124, 163, 237n., 316; II, 17, 37; and Henry R. Wagner and Charles L. Camp, *The Plains and the Rockies . . .* (Columbus, O., 1953), pp. 52–53, 99.

8. Wagner and Camp, p. 97.

9. Rusk, I, 35n.

10. Howard L. Conard, ed. *Encyclopedia of the History of Missouri* (New York, etc., 1901); North T. Gentry, "William F. Switzler," *Mo. Hist. Rev.*, XXIV (1930), 161–76; *Kansas City Star*, Feb. 4, 1900; *St. Louis Post-Dispatch*, May 24, 1906; and *DAB*, XVIII, 254–55.

11. Walter Geer, *The Geer Genealogy . . .* (New York, 1923); *DAB*, XII, 357–58; and J. C. Parish, *Robert Lucas* (Iowa City, 1907).

12. J. W. Flucke, *Evangelical Pioneers* (St. Louis and Chicago, 1931); Edward Huber, "Pastor Joseph Rieger . . . ," *Eighth Annual Report of the . . . Society for the History of the Germans in Maryland* (1894); Matthews, p. 277; *DAB*, XV, 599–600; and Joseph Rieger, *Ein Lebensbild . . .* (1871).

13. The manuscript of the first journal is in the Oregon Historical Society, Portland, and is listed in *Guide to the Manuscript Collections of the Oregon Historical Society* (Portland, 1940), No. 218. See Matthews, p. 276, and Wagner and Camp, pp. 102, 159.

14. John King, "John Plumbe, Originator of the Pacific Railroad," *Ann. of Ia.*, 3rd Series, VI (1904), 289–96; *DAB*, XV, 11–12; and Rusk, I, 37, 143.

15. *DAB*, XII, 133–34; Matthews, p. 227; Grace L. Nute, "James Dickson; a Filibuster in Minnesota in 1836," *Miss. Val. Hist. Rev.*, X (1923), 127–40; C. J. Ritchey, "Martin McLeod and the Minnesota Valley," *Minn. Hist.*, X (1929), 387–402; and Wagner and Camp, p. 287.

16. Rusk, I, 26n.

17. Matthews, p. 280.

18. *Ibid.*, p. 282. The manuscript is in the Wisconsin Historical Society, Madison.

19. "Mrs. Jameson," *Athenaeum*, no. 1691 (Mar. 24, 1860), 108–09; "Memoirs of Mrs. Jameson," *Edin. Rev.*, CXLIX (1879), 84–104; *DNB*, X, 667–69; Geraldine Macpherson, *Memoirs of the Life of Anna Jameson* (London, 1878); and Rusk, I, 7n.

20. Matthews, p. 281.

21. *Ibid.*, p. 279.

22. *Ibid.*, p. 281.

23. *Ibid.*

24. R. B. Anderson, *The First Chapter of Norwegian Immigration, 1821–1840 . . .* (Madison, 1895); T. C. Blegen, *Norwegian Migration to America* (Northfield, Minn., 1931); Ole K. Nattestad, *Beschrivetze over en Reise til Nordamerka* (Drammer, 1839), translated by R. B. Anderson in *Wis. Mag. Hist.*, I (1917), 167–86; and *DAB*, XVI, 273–74.

25. The North Dakota State Historical Society, Bismarck, has a typed copy of a portion of the journal written during 1843–1847.

26. Matthews, p. 280.

27. *Ibid.*, pp. 278–79.

28. The manuscript is in the Francis Family Papers, Item XXVI, Connecticut State Library.

29. A. L. Bader, "Captain Marryat in Michigan," *Mich. Hist.*, XX (1936), 163–75 and "The Gallant Captain and Brother Jonathan," *Colophon*, II (1936), 114–29; John T. Flanagan, "Captain Marryat at Old St. Peters," *Minn. Hist.*, XVIII (1937), 152–64; "Naval Novelists," *Fraser's Magazine*, XVII (1838), 571–75; David Hannay, *Life of Frederick Marryat* (London, etc., 1889); Florence Marryat, *Life and Letters of Captain Marryat* (2 vols., London, 1872); *DNB*, XII, 1086–88; Rusk, I, 14n., 22, 117, 163; II, 14, 15, 30; Wagner and Camp pp. 138–39, 155; and Oliver Warner, *Captain Marryat, a Rediscovery* (London, 1953).

30. Matthews, pp. 281–82; *DNB*, XVIII, 502–3.

31. Matthews, p. 282.

32. Dorothy Dondore, *The Prairie and the Making of Middle America* (Cedar Rapids, Ia., 1926); J. S. Hart, *The Female Prose Writers of America* (Philadelphia, 1852); Langley C.

Keyes, *Caroline M. Kirkland. A Pioneer in American Realism* (Doctoral dissertation, Harvard University, 1935); *DAB*, X, 430–31; Louise N. Knudson, *Caroline Kirkland, Pioneer* (M. A. thesis, Michigan State University, 1934), "Death of Mrs. Kirkland," *Littell's Living Age*, 3rd Series, XXV (Apr. 30, 1864), 237; *New York Evening Post*, Apr., 6, 7, 11, 1864; Rusk, I, 66n,. 284–86; V. C. Sanborn, *The Kirkland or Kirtland Family* (Boston, 1894); and Edna M. Twamley, "The Westward Sketches of Caroline M . . . Kirkland," *Mich. Hist. Colls.*, XXXIX (1915), 89–124.

33. In his *Literati of New York*. Quoted in Nerber's edition of *A New Home* . . . , p. 4,

34. The Keyes manuscripts are in the Wisconsin State Historical Society Library, Madison. See *DAB*, X, 365; Elisha W. Keyes, *History of Dane County* (Madison, 1906); *Madison* (Wis.) *Democrat*, Nov. 29, 30, 1910; Ellis B. Usher, *Wisconsin* . . . (8 vols., Chicago and New York, 1914), Vol. IV; and "Death of Curators Keyes and Backford," *Wis. Hist. Soc. Procs.* . . . *1911* (Madison, 1912), pp. 20–21.

35. Matthews, p. 340; *DAB*, XVIII, 168–69; and Wagner and Camp, pp. 553–55, 557.

36. The Stephen R. Riggs papers are in the Minnesota Historical Society, St. Paul. See *Colls. Minn. Hist. Soc.*, I (1872), *passim*; III (1880), 107–28, 358–85, and *passim*; and VI (1894), 117–88; *DAB*, XV, 605–6; Wagner and Camp, p. 148; and J. H. Wallace, *Genealogy of the Riggs Family* . . . (New York, 1901).

37. G. W. Cullum, *Biographical Register of the Officers and Graduates of the U. S. Military Academy* . . . (3rd ed., Boston and New York, 1891); *DAB*, IX, 73–74; and Matthews, p. 235.

38. See Chapter 11, n. 51.

39. Mrs. Mary Bird, *Life of Robert Montgomery Bird* . . . (Philadelphia, 1945); *DAB*, II, 286–88; Clement E. Foust, *Life and Dramatic Works of Robert Montgomery Bird* (New York, 1919); Rusk, I, 73, 421; and C. B. Williams, "R. M. Bird's Plans for Novels of the Frontier," *American Literature*, XXI (1949), 321–24.

40. Matthews, p. 285.

41. *Ibid.* and Rusk, I, 233.

42. Matthews, p. 286.

43. Rusk, I, 120.

44. "Accessions," *Minn. Hist.*, V (1923), 64, and VIII (1927), 98.

45. Ruth Craker, *First Protestant Mission in the Grand Traverse Region* (Leland, Mich., 1935).

46. Matthews, p. 284.

47. *Ibid.*, p. 285.

48. *Ibid.*, p. 286.

49. Eugene P. Jefferson, *Intimate Recollections of Joseph Jefferson* (New York, 1909); *DAB*, X, 15–17; *New York Times*, Apr. 24, 1905; Rusk, I, 396n., 397n.; Francis Wilson, *Joseph Jefferson* . . . (New York, 1906); and William Winter, *The Life and Art of Joseph Jefferson* (New York and London, 1894).

50. Matthews, p. 283.

51. Milburn's work, *The Lance, Cross and Canoe; the Flatboat, Rifle and Plough in the Valley of the Mississippi* . . . (New York and St. Louis, 1892), contains much of the same information in its last chapter. See *Christian Advocate* (New York), LXXVIII (Apr. 16, 23, 1903), 611–13, 653–56; John McClintock, Introduction to *The Rifle, Axe, and Saddle-Bags and Other Lectures* (New York, 1857); *DAB*, XII, 610–11; *Washington Evening Star*, Apr. 11, 1903; and *Who's Who in America*, 1901–1902 (Chicago, 1901).

52. Frémont's surviving papers are in the Bancroft Library, University of California, Berkeley. See Herbert Bashford and Harr Wagner, *A Man Unafraid; the Story of John Charles Frémont* (San Francisco, 1927); *The Cambridge History of American Literature*, William P. Trent *et al.*, eds. (4 vols., New York, 1917–21), I, 212; Mrs. Jessie (Benton) Frémont, *Souvenirs of My Time* (Boston, 1887); *DAB*, VII, 19–23; John R. Howard, *Remembrance of Things Past* (New York, 1925); Matthews, p. 292; Allan Nevins, *Frémont, the West's Greatest Adventurer* (2 vols., New York and London, 1928); *New York Tribune*, July 14, 1890; Samuel M. Smucker, *The Life of Col. John Charles Frémont, and his Narrative of Explorations and Adventures* . . . (New York, 1881); and Wagner and Camp, pp. 137, 140, 160–62, 210–11, 306, 360–538 *passim*.

53. Matthews, p. 287.

54. Susan S. Magoffin, *Down the Santa Fe Trail* . . . (New Haven, 1926); Rusk, I, 21; *St. Louis Republican*, Sept. 24, 25, 1889; *DAB*, XX, 430–31; and Wagner and Camp, pp. 122, 220, 333, 390.

55. *Californian* (San Francisco), Sept. 16, 1848; *DAB*, VI, 283–84; and Wagner and Camp, pp. 122, 125–27, 150–51.

56. Matthews, p. 287.

57. *Ibid.*

58. C. B. Galbreath, "Ezra Meeker; Ohio's Illustrious Pioneer," *Ohio Arch. Hist. Quar.*, XXXVI (1927), 3–47; *DAB*, XII, 495–96; *Seattle Post-Intelligencer*, Dec. 3–4, 1928; and *Who's Who in America*, 1926–27 (Chicago, 1926).

59. Matthews, p. 288.

60. *Ibid.*

61. Robert F. Seybolt, "Rabb: Tour Through Indiana," *Miss. Val. Hist. Rev.*, VIII (1921), 283–84 and Rusk, I, 363n., 396n., 425n.

62. Matthews, p. 287.

63. *Ibid.*, p. 283.

64. The Haraszthy documents are in the Wisconsin State Historical Society, Madison. See H. E. Cole, *A Standard History of Sauk County, Wis.* (2 vols., Chicago and New York, 1892); *DAB*, VIII, 236–37; and V. S. Pease, "Agoston Haraszthy," *Wis. Hist. Soc. Procs.*, 1906 (Madison, 1907), pp. 224–45.

65. The Lanman papers are in the Library of Congress. See *DAB*, X, 606–7; Matthews, p. 303; *New York Tribune*, Mar. 6, 1895; *Washington Evening Star*, Mar. 5, 1895; and *Washington Post*, Mar. 5, 6, 1895.

66. Matthews, p. 289.

67. *Ibid.*, pp. 199–200; *DAB*, V, 255–56; W. Patrick Donnelly, *Father Pierre-Jean de Smet; United States Ambassador to the Indians* (M. A. thesis, St. Louis University, 1934); E. Laveille, *Life of Father DeSmet* (New York, 1915); Thomas F. O'Connor, "Pierre DeSmet: Frontier Missionary," *Mid-Amer.*, XVII (1935), 191–96; L. B. Palladino, *Indian and White in the Northwest* . . . (Lancaster, Pa., 1922); J. D. Shea, *History of the Catholic Missions among the Indian Tribes of the United States* . . . (New York, 1855); and Wagner and Camp, pp. 127, 129, 142–44, 148, 195–96, 296–97, 400–1, 519–20. Extracts from various letters appear in W. L. Davis, "Peter John DeSmet, the Journey of 1840," *Pac. Northw. Quar.*, XXXV (1944), 29–43.

NOTES TO CHAPTER 13

1. *Chicago Weekly Chronicle*, Nov. 21, 1835.

2. John B. McMaster, *A History of the United States* . . . (8 vols., New York and London, 1927–29), VII, 10–11, 18, 23–25, 28, 29, 190–207.

3. *DNB*, XVIII, 269–70; and Henry R. Wagner and Charles L. Camp, *The Plains and the Rockies* . . . (Columbus, O., 1953), pp. 193–94, 347, 394, 429.

4. William Matthews, *American Diaries* . . . (Berkeley, Calif., 1945), pp. 290–91.

5. Marcus Benjamin, *John Bidwell, Pioneer* . . . (Washington, 1907); John Bidwell, "The First Emigrant Train to California," *Century Magazine*, XLI (1890), 106–30; *DAB*, II, 247–48; Matthews, p. 289; C. C. Royce, *John Bidwell* . . . (Chico, Calif., 1906); *San Francisco Chronicle*, Apr. 5, 1900; and Wagner and Camp, pp. 130–32.

6. The manuscript is in the Bancroft Collection, University of California Library, Berkeley. See Matthews, p. 291, and Wagner and Camp, pp. 131–32, 147–48.

7. Unonius also wrote *New Upsala, the First Swedish Settlement in Wisconsin* (Milwaukee, 1936), most of which appeared serially in "New Upsala," F. A. Forsbeck, trans. *Wis. Mag. Hist.*, XIX (1935–1936), 3–31, 161–81, 294–318.

8. H. J. Eckenrode, *Rutherford B. Hayes, Statesman of Reunion* (New York, 1930); *DAB*, VIII, 446–51; Matthews, p. 290; and Charles R. Williams, *The Life of Rutherford Birchard Hayes* . . . (2 vols., Boston and New York, 1914).

9. "Charles Dickens Unimpressed by St. Louisans," *Mo. Hist. Rev.*, XXXVI (1942), 474–76; *DNB*, V, 925–37; Alfred R. Ferguson, "Charles Dickens in Ohio," *Ohio Arch. Hist. Quar.*, LIX (1950), 14–25; Roy F. Fleming, "Charles Dickens Visits the Great Lakes," *Inland Seas*, XII (1956), 301–03; John Forster, *The Life of Charles Dickens* (3 vols., Boston, 1872–74); "Four Months with Charles Dickens, During his First Visit to America (in 1842). By his Secretary," *Atlantic Monthly*, XXVI (1870), 475–82, 581–99; Eleanor Graham, *The Story of Charles Dickens* (New York, 1954); Edgar Johnson, *Charles Dickens, his Tragedy and Triumph* (2 vols., New York, 1952), I, 443–46; S. B. Leacock, *Charles Dickens, his Life and Work* (New York, 1934); H. K. Lunn, *The Sentimental Journey; a Life of Charles Dickens* (London, 1934); "In Memoriam," *Macmillan's Magazine*, XXII (1870), 236–40; André Maurois, *Dickens* (New York and London, 1935); H. L. Peeke, "Charles Dickens in Ohio in 1842," *Ohio Arch. Hist. Quar.*, XXVIII (1919), 72, 81; Una Pope-Hennessy, *Charles Dickens* (New York, 1946); Robert Price, "Boz Reports on Ohio," *Ohio Arch. Hist. Quar.*, LI (1942), 195–202; Ralph L. Rusk, *The Literature of the Middle Western Frontier* (2 vols., New York, 1925), I, 298; II, 30; Samuel H. Stille, "Charles Dickens in Ohio," in *Ohio Builds a Nation* (Chicago, etc., 1939); Ralph Straus, *Charles Dickens* . . . (New York, 1928); Julian Symons, *Charles Dickens* (New York, 1951); Edward Wagenknecht, *The Man Charles Dickens* (Boston and New York, 1929); and William C. Wilkins, *Charles Dickens in America* (London, 1911).

10. Robert R. Hubach, "Illinois, Host to Well-Known Nineteenth Century Authors," *Jour. Ill. State Hist. Soc.*, XXXVIII (1945), 451.

11. J. F. Snyder, "Charles Dickens in Illinois," *Jour. Ill. State Hist. Soc.*, III (1910), 20–22.

12. William Kinney, a Baptist minister, wrote an "Answer to Dickens' American Notes" serially in the *Belleville Advocate* in the fall of 1842. This was republished by Robert K. Fleming and an abstract from it appeared in *Ill. State Hist. Soc. Trans.* . . . *1904*, pp. 441–44.

13. See *The Dismissal of Major Granville O. Haller, of the Regular Army of the United States by Order of the Secretary of War in Special Orders, No. 331, of July 25th, 1863. Also a Brief Memoir of his Military Services* . . . (Patterson, N. J., 1863) and Wagner and Camp, p. 512.

14. Matthews, p. 291 and Wagner and Camp, pp. 163, 200, 506, 508, 511, 513.

15. Wagner and Camp, pp. 162–64, 200, 225.

16. *Ibid.*, p. 138.

17. E. A. and G. L. Duyckinck, *Cylopedia of American Literature* (2 vols., New York, 1856), Vol. II; Amos L. Harold, *James Kirke Paulding, Versatile American* (New York, 1926); P. M. Irving, *The Life and Letters of Washington Irving* (4 vols., London, 1862–1864), *passim*; Vernon L. Parrington, *Main Currents in American Thought* (3 vols., New York, 1927–1930), Vol. II; *DAB*, XIV, 321–23; Rusk, I, 22n., 113, 272, 420; II, 1; and Arlin Turner, "James K. Paulding and Timothy Flint," *Miss. Val. Hist. Rev.*, XXXIV (1947), 105–11.

18. Matthews, p. 292.

19. Listed in Wright Howe, *U. S.-iana (1700–1950), a Descriptive Check-list of 11,450 Printed Sources* (New York, 1954).

20. Hubert H. Bancroft, *History of California* . . . (7 vols., San Francisco, 1884–90), Vol. VI; *DAB*, III, 300–1; Theodore H. Hittell, *History of California* (4 vols., San Francisco, 1885–97); San Francisco, 1884–90), Vol. VI; *DAB*, III, 300–1; Theodore H. Camp, p. 170.

21. Matthews, p. 311.

22. *Colls. Minn. Hist. Soc.*, Vols. IV (St. Paul, 1876), *passim*; IX (St. Paul, 1898–1900), 149, 171, 172, 320, 654–58; XII (St. Paul, 1905–1908), *passim*; *Daily Pioneer Press* (St. Paul), Jan. 10, 1896; *DAB*, XII, 333.

23. Matthews, p. 292, and Wagner and Camp, p. 170.

24. See *The Memoirs of Margaret Fuller Ossoli* (2 vols., Boston, 1852). See also David D. Anderson, "Margaret Fuller's Great Lakes Tour," *Inland Seas*, XV (1959), 22–28; Katharine S. Anthony, *Margaret Fuller; a Psychological Biography* (New York, 1920); Margaret Bell, *Margaret Fuller* . . . (New York, 1930); Richard V. Carpenter, "Margaret Fuller's Visit to Northern Illinois," *Jour. Ill. State Hist. Soc.*, II (1910), 7–22; *DAB*, VII, 63–66; Thomas W. Higginson, *Margaret Fuller Ossoli* (New York, 1884); Julia Ward Howe, *Margaret Fuller* (Boston, 1883); R. R. Hubach, "Illinois, Host to Well-Known Nineteenth Century Authors," *Jour. Ill. State Hist. Soc.*, XXXVIII (1945), 452–54; Rusk, I, 181–82; Madeline B. Stern, *The Life of Margaret Fuller* (New York, 1942) and "Margaret Fuller's Summer in the West . . . ," *Mich. Hist.*, XXV (1941), 300–30; and Mason Wade, *Margaret Fuller, Whetstone of Genius* (New York, 1940).

25. Wagner and Camp, p. 135.

26. *Ibid.*, pp. 174–75, 225, and Matthews, p. 294.

27. Wagner and Camp, p. 147.

28. *Ibid.*, p. 169; Matthews, p. 294; James W. Nesmith and Joseph Lane, "The Council of Table Rock," *Oreg. Hist. Soc. Quar.*, VII (1906), 211–21; J. W. Nesmith, "The Occasional Address," *Oreg. Pion. Assn. Trans.* (1876), pp. 42–62; *DAB*, XIII, 430–31; G. H. Williams, "Political History of Oregon . . . ," *Oreg. Hist. Soc. Quar.*, II (1901), 25; W. D. Fenton, "Political History of Oregon . . . ," *Oreg. Hist. Soc. Quar.*, II (1901), 325–26; W. C. Woodward, "Political Parties in Oregon," *Oreg. Hist. Soc. Quar.*, XIII (1912), 33, 35, 49–50, 57–59.

29. Matthews, p. 294, and Wagner and Camp, p. 170.

30. The journal is from p. 63 to p. 113 of the book. See C. B. Bagley, "George Wilkes," *Wash. Hist. Quar.*, V (1914), 3–11; Wagner and Camp, pp. 168–70; and *DAB*, XX, 218.

31. See Chapter 11, n. 51 and Kemper's journals of 1834 and 1838.

32. *DAB*, X, 611–12; Matthews, p. 263; and Rusk, I, 258.

33. The manuscript is in the Indiana University Library, Bloomington.

34. The manuscript is in the Illinois State Historical Library, Springfield.

35. Matthews, p. 294 and Wagner and Camp, p. 170.

36. The Subtlette manuscripts are in the Missouri Historical

Society. See H. M. Chittenden, *The American Fur Trade of the Far West* (2nd ed., 2 vols., New York, 1935); *Daily Missouri Republican*, Aug. 1, 1845; Matthews, p. 295; *Missouri Republican* (St. Louis), Oct. 19, 1830; Oct. 16, 1832; June 16, 1837; *DAB*, XVIII, 189; and Wagner and Camp, pp. 72, 76, 80, 85, 99, 122, 147, 194, 219.

37. *Encyclopedia Britannica* (14th ed., Chicago, etc., 1950), X, 315.

38. The Whipple diaries are in the possession of the Minnesota Historical Society, the Protestant Episcopal Diocese of Minnesota, and descendants. See Matthews, p. 295; *Minneapolis Journal*, Sept. 16, 1901; Warren Upham and R. B. Dunlap, "Minnesota Biographies," *Colls. Minn. Hist. Soc.*, XIV (1912), 846; *DAB*, XX, 68–69; and *Who's Who in America, 1901–1902* (Chicago, 1901).

39. Matthews, p. 294 and Wagner and Camp, p. 201.

40. Ephraim Adams, *The Iowa Band* (n. p., 1870); *Des Moines Register and Leader*, Aug. 16, 1910; James L. Hill, *Rev. William Salter* . . . (Des Moines, 1911), reprinted (with bibliography added) from *Ann. of Ia.*, 3rd Series, IX (1911), 561–644; Matthews, p. 294; *DAB*, XVI, 314–15; and *Who's Who in America, 1908–1909* (Chicago, 1908). See also *Ann. of Ia.*, 3rd Series, XXIV (1943), 106–85.

41. The manuscript is in the Library of Congress. See Matthews, p. 295 and Wagner and Camp, pp. 162, 209.

42. Matthews, p. 296.

43. *Ibid.*

44. *Ibid.* and Wagner and Camp, pp. 153–54.

45. Matthews, p. 297.

46. In the second edition (1867), the name "Henry Thacker" and the title *Muskrat Hunting* appear before Newhouse's name.

47. Matthews, p. 297.

48. *Ibid.* and Wagner and Camp, p. 165.

49. Matthews, p. 297.

50. *DAB*, XIII, 134–35.

51. Matthews, p. 298 and Wagner and Camp, p. 202.

52. The manuscript is in the Yale University Library.

53. Matthews, p. 299, and Wagner and Camp, p. 170.

54. Parkman related the story of the LaVérendryes in his *Half Century of Conflict* (2 vols., Boston, 1903), II, 29ff., reprinted in *Sou. Dak. Hist. Quar.*, VII (1914), 380–402. See also C. W. Alvard, "Francis Parkman," *The Nation*, CXVII (Oct. 10, 1923), 394–96; *Boston Transcript*, Nov. 9, 1893; "Epic Labors," *Time*, LII (Dec. 13, 1948), 110, 112; Charles H. Farnham, *A Life of Francis Parkman* (Boston, 1901) contains extracts from Parkman's autobiography; L. Feller, "Heroic Historian," *The Nation*, CLVI (Feb. 6, 1943), 211–12; Arthur L. Ford, "A Study of Francis Parkman's Reworking of his *Oregon Trail* Notes" (M. A. thesis, Bowling Green State University, 1960); *DAB*, XIV, 247–50; "Parkman's Wanderings," *Newsweek*, XXX (Dec. 1, 1947), 94; Edgar Pelham, *The Struggle for a Continent* (Boston, 1909); Doane Robinson, "Parkman Not in Dakota," *Sou. Dak. Hist. Colls.*, XII (1924), 102–7; Joseph Schafer, "Francis Parkman," *Wis. Mag. Hist.*, VII (1924), 265–80, and "Francis Parkman, 1823–1923," *Miss. Val. Hist. Rev.*, X (1924), 351–64; W. L. Schramm, "A New Englander on the Road to Oregon," *New England Quarterly*, XIII (1940), 49–64; H. D. Sedgwick, *Francis Parkman* (Boston and New York, 1904); "Strenuous Historian," *Time*, L (Dec. 29, 1947), 66; Mason Wade, *Francis Parkman, Heroic Historian* (New York, 1942); Wagner and Camp, pp. 232–33; Edward Wheelwright, "Memoir of Francis Parkman," *Colonial Society of Massachusetts Publications*, I (1895); and Edith F. Wyatt, "Francis Parkman: 1823–1893," *Nor. Amer. Rev.*, CCXVIII (1923), 484–96.

55. Matthews, p. 297.

56. *DAB*, V, 307–8; J. M. Rohne, *Norwegian American Lutheranism Up to 1872* (New York, 1926); and *Who's Who Among Pastors in All the Norwegian Lutheran Synods of America* . . . (Minneapolis, 1928).

57. For information on Palmer's return trip, see *St. Louis Republican*, July 18, 1846, and *Niles (Michigan) Register*, Aug. 1, 1846. See also Matthews, p. 298; *DAB*, XIV, 186–87; Stanley J. Spaid "The Later Life and Activities of General Joel Palmer," *Oreg. Hist. Soc. Quar.*, LV (1954), 311–32; and Wagner and Camp, pp. 188–91.

58. Matthews, p. 299, and Wagner and Camp, p. 227.

NOTES TO CHAPTER 14

1. William Matthews, *American Diaries* . . . (Berkeley, Calif., 1945), p. 301.

2. *Ibid.*, p. 290; *Life, Letters, and Journals of Sir Charles Lyell*, edited by his sister-in-law, Mrs. Lyell (2 vols., London, 1881); *DNB*, XII, 319–24.

3. Henry R. Wagner and Charles L. Camp, *The Plains and the Rockies* . . . (Columbus, O., 1953), pp. 171–172, 192, 198–99, 206, 409; Matthews, p. 297.

4. Matthews, p. 301.

5. *Ibid.*; *Annual Reunion of Graduates of the United States Military Academy* (Saginaw, Mich., 1888); *DAB*, VI, 153–54; and Wagner and Camp, pp. 206–9, 301, 375–77, 409.

6. Matthews, p. 302 and Wagner and Camp, p. 185.

7. Wagner and Camp, pp. 184, 207.

8. *Ibid.*, p. 213 and Matthews, p. 305.

9. Wagner and Camp, pp. 184–85.

10. *Ibid.*, p. 191 and Matthews, p. 305.

11. John T. Hughes, *Doniphan's Expedition. Account of the Conquest of New Mexico, General Kearny's Expedition to California* . . . (Washington, 1914); and John B. McMaster, *A History of the People of the United States* . . . (8 vols., New York and London, 1927), VI, 462–63.

12. The work has been frequently reprinted. See Matthews, p. 300; *San Francisco Californian*, June 5, 1847; and Wagner and Camp, pp. 203–4.

13. Wagner and Camp, p. 202 and Matthews, p. 304.

14. H. H. Bancroft, *History of Oregon* (2 vols., San Francisco, 1886–88), Vol. I; Matthews, p. 312; *Portland Morning Oregonian*, Feb. 7, 1888; and *DAB*, XVIII, 502–3.

15. *Minn. Hist.*, I (1915), 230.

16. Matthews, p. 300 and Wagner and Camp, p. 227.

17. Wagner and Camp, p. 227 and Matthews, p. 300.

18. Matthews, p. 302 and Wagner and Camp, p. 227.

19. Wagner and Camp, pp. 204–5 and Matthews, p. 301. Much of this journal was combined with Orson Pratt's account in a serial article, "The Pioneers of 1847," in *Historical Record* (Salt Lake City), IX (1890), 1–23, 33–60, 65–121.

20. The manuscript is in the Library of the Ohio Historical Society, Columbus. See *Cincinnati Enquirer*, Oct. 15, 1893; F. A. Howe, "Ohio's Historian," *The Honey Jar*, Apr., 1906; *DAB*, IX, 288–89; Henry Howe, "Reminiscences" in his *Historical Collections of Ohio* . . . (Columbus, 1890–91); Ralph L. Rusk, *The Literature of the Middle Western Frontier* (2 vols., New York, 1925), I, 30, 304; and Joseph P. Smith, "Henry Howe, the Historian," *Ohio Arch. Hist. Quar.*, IV (1895), 311–37.

21. Matthews, p. 312.

22. *Biographical Sketches of the Leading Men of Chicago* (Chicago, 1868); *DAB*, III, 93–44; *Chicago Herald*, Mar. 20, 1890; *Chicago Tribune*, Jan. 28–31, 1890; and Charles A. Yount, *William Bross, 1813–1890* (Lake Forest, Ill., 1940).

23. Mary L. Dow, *Old Days at Beverly Farms* (Beverly, Mass., 1921); Frances Harp, *Women of the Day* . . . (London, 1883); *DAB*, X, 614; Matthews, p. 303; and *New York Tribune*, Apr. 19, 1893.

24. *DAB*, XII, 201; Matthews, p. 304; and Wagner and Camp, p. 213.

25. Wagner and Camp, pp. 428–29 and Matthews, p. 302–3.

26. Matthews, p. 306.

27. Hone's twenty-eight volumes of manuscripts are in the New-York Historical Society. See *DAB*, IX, 192; Matthews, p. 255; *New York Daily Tribune*, May 6, 1851; and Mentor Williams, "Philip Hone, Wisconsin Land Speculator," *Jour. Ill. State Hist. Soc.*, XLIII (1950), 479–84.

28. The manuscript is in the New York Public Library.

29. The manuscript is in the Yale University Library. See Matthews, p. 307.

30. Ruth and Reginald W. Kauffman, *The Latter-Day Saints* (London, 1912); *DAB*, X, 377–78; Andrew Jenson, ed., *Latter-Day Saint Biographical Encyclopedia* (4 vols., Salt Lake City, 1901), I, 34–37; Matthews, p. 308; Frederick Piercy, *Route from Liverpool to Great Salt Lake Valley* . . . (Liverpool, 1855); Wagner and Camp, pp. 241, 242, 326; and Orson F. Whitney, *Life of Heber C. Kimball* . . . (Salt Lake City, 1888).

31. The manuscript is in the Coe Collection at Yale University Library. See Matthews, p. 308.

32. Matthews, p. 307.

33. *DNB*, XII, 561–62; and Mark Twain, *Life on the Mississippi* (New York, 1950), p. 229.

34. George B. Grinnell, *Beyond the Old Frontier* . . . (New York, 1913); Matthews, p. 346; *DNB*, XV, 116–17; and Wagner and Camp, pp. 293–94, 307, 411, 437–39.

35. Sister Agnes M. Baer, *Diary of Reverend Nicholas Point* . . . (M. A. thesis, St. Louis University, 1952); Matthews, p. 309; and Wagner and Camp, p. 401.

36. *DAB*, VII, 528–34; William H. Hale, *Horace Greeley* . . . (New York, 1950); H. H. Horner, *Lincoln and Greeley* (Urbana, Ill., 1953); L. D. Ingersoll, *The Life of Horace Greeley* . . . (Chicago, 1873); James Parton, *The Life of Horace Greeley* (Boston, 1885); E. D. Ross, "Horace Greeley and the West," *Miss. Val. Hist. Rev.*, XX (1933), 63–74; H. L. Stoddard, *Horace Greeley* . . . (New York, 1946); G. Van Deusen, *Horace Greeley* . . . *Crusader* (Philadelphia, 1953); and Wagner and Camp, pp. 470–71, 480, 490, 536.

37. Wagner and Camp, p. 211, and Matthews, p. 310.

38. Matthews, pp. 308–9, and Wagner and Camp, p. 294.

39. Matthews, pp. 307–8.

40. Thompson Cooper, *Men of the Time* (9th ed., 1875, and 10th ed., 1895); H. E. Hayden, *Virginia Genealogies* . . . (Wilkes-Barre, Pa., 1891); and *DAB*, XIV, 520.

41. Matthews, p. 312 and Wagner and Camp, pp. 253–54.

42. See the bibliography in Robert R. Hubach, *Walt Whitman and the West* (Ph. D. dissertation, Indiana University, 1943) for a lengthy list of books and articles. See also Gay W. Allen, *The Solitary Singer* (New York, 1955), pp. 92–94, 99–100; Emory Holloway, *Whitman, an Interpretation in Narrative* (New York, 1926), pp. 39–44, 75–76; and *DAB*, XX, 143–52.

43. Wagner and Camp, p. 289.

44. Matthews, p. 311.

45. The diaries are in the Chicago Historical Society. See *Chicago Daily News*, Aug. 21, 1908; *Chicago Tribune*, Aug. 21, 1908; *DAB*, VI, 295–96; John V. Farwell, Jr., *Some Recollections of John V. Farwell* . . . (Chicago, 1911); Matthews, p. 311; and George W. Smith, *History of Illinois and her People* (6 vols., Chicago and New York, 1927), IV, 355.

46. Matthews, p. 311.

47. James M. Burke, *Diary of the Pottawatomie Mission of St. Mary's on the Lake* . . . (M. A. thesis, St. Louis University, 1951).

48. *Iowa State Register* (Des Moines), Feb. 21, 1890; Matthews, p. 321; *DAB*, XIV, 261–62; C. C. Parry, autobiographical letter in *Proceedings of the Davenport* (Ia.) *Academy of Natural Sciences*, II, Part 2 (1880), 279–82; and C. H. Preston, *Proceedings of the Davenport Academy*, VI (1899).

49. Wagner and Camp, pp. 236–37.

50. Matthews, p. 323.

51. *Ibid.*, p. 318.

52. Austin Allibone, *A Critical Dictionary of English Literature* . . . (3 vols., Philadelphia, 1908), III, 2853; and *DNB*, XIX, 109–10.

53. Matthews, pp. 314–15 and Wagner and Camp, pp. 245–47.

54. *DAB*, VII, 245–46; Matthews, p. 316; *New Haven Morning Journal and Courier*, Apr. 11, 1873; John A. Stevens, *A Memorial of George Gibbs* (Washington, 1874); and Wagner and Camp, p. 247.

55. Wagner and Camp, p. 296.

56. Wagner and Camp, p. 244.

57. Matthews, p. 313.

58. *Ibid.*

59. *Ibid.*, p. 314.

60. *Ibid.*, p. 315 and Wagner and Camp, pp. 240, 304–5.

61. Matthews, p. 315.

62. The manuscript is in the Yale University Library.

63. Matthews, p. 317.

64. *Ibid.*

65. *Ibid.*, p. 318.

66. Joseph H. Jackson, *Gold Rush Album* (New York, 1949) is a modern, well written and pictorial record of the Gold Rush.

67. Matthews, p. 318.

68. *Ibid.*

69. *Ibid.*, p. 319.

70. *Ibid.*, p. 319.

71. *The Biographical Encyclopedia of Illinois* . . . (Philadelphia, 1875); *Illinois State Register* (Springfield), Apr. 25, 1899; J. M. Johns, *Personal Recollections of Early Decatur* . . . (Decatur, Ill., 1912); *DAB*, XIII, 648–49.

72. Matthews, p. 321. The manuscript is in the Western Historical Manuscripts Collection, University of Missouri, Columbia.

73. Matthews, p. 328.

74. *Ibid.*, p. 323.

75. *Ibid.*

76. Wagner and Camp, pp. 266–67. Reprints of the book appeared in 1852.

77. Wagner and Camp, p. 261.

78. *Ibid.*, pp. 232, 237, 262, 267. The manuscript is in the Coe Collection, Yale University Library.

79. Wagner and Camp, pp. 374–75.

80. Matthews, p. 321.

81. *Ibid.*, p. 322.

Index

Names of travel narrators are in capital letters, and are followed in parentheses by dates which in nearly all cases represent the years the writers spent in the Midwest as described in their works, rather than longer periods. Accounts by anonymous authors are not indexed. Names of foreign countries, except for Canada and Mexico, are omitted, as are specific sections of America, such as New England. Since Indians are mentioned on nearly every page, this word has been omitted, but names of specific Indian tribes are included. Important topics of a general nature, such as travel narratives, are also given. Titles are omitted.

Manuscript edited by Elizabeth Sapere
Design and hand lettering by William A. Bostick
Set in Linotype Caledonia
Printed on Warren's Silkote
Bound in Jersey Antique Cover
Manufactured in the United States of America